MIDNIGHTER

ANTHEM

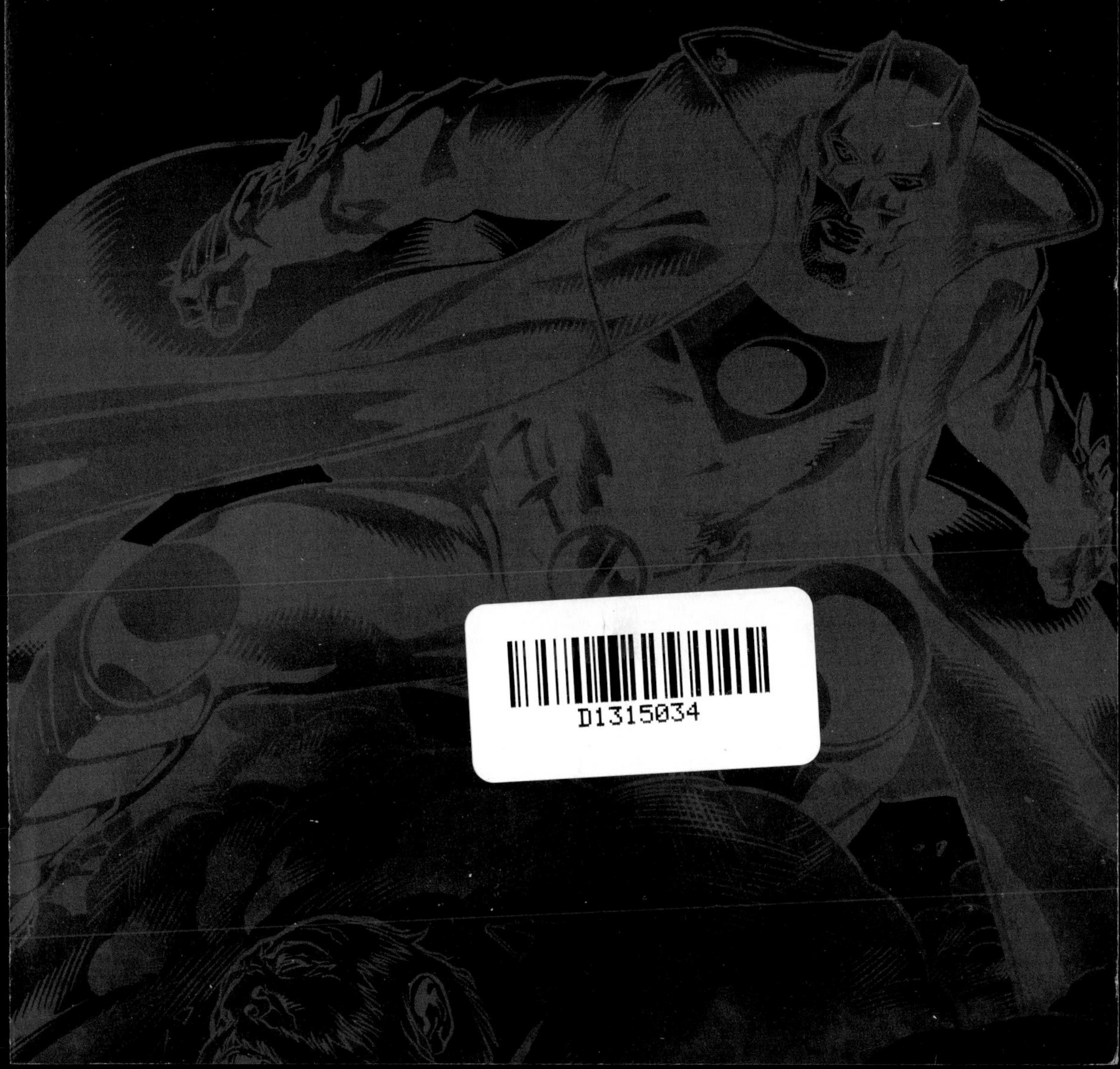

FAIT ACCOMPLI
Writer: Brian K. Vaughan
Penciller: Darick Robertson
Inker: Karl Story

Colorists: Randy Mayor and Jonny Rench
Letterer: Phil Balsman

ANTHEM
Writer: Keith Giffen
Pencillers: Chris Sprouse (#10)
Chriscross (#11) Rafael Sandoval (#12)
Jon Buran (#13-15)
Inkers: Karl Story (#10, 12)
Troy Hubbs with Chriscross (#11)
Rick Burchett (#13-15)

Colorists: Randy Mayor (#10-11)
with Darlene Royer (#12, 14) Darlene Royer (#13)
Pete Pantazis (#15)

Letterers: Travis Lanham (#10, 14),
Pat Brosseau (#11), Steve Wands (#12-13, 15)

Collected Edition Cover and Original Series Covers (#7, 10-12, 14-15) by Chris
Sprouse and Karl Story with Randy Mayor
Cover #13 Chris Sprouse and Brian Stelfreeze

Jim Lee, Editorial Director
John Nee, Senior VP—Business Development
Scott Dunbier and Scott Peterson, Editors—Original Series
Scott Peterson, Editor—Collected Edition
Kristy Quinn, Assistant Editor
Ed Roeder, Art Director
Paul Levitz, President & Publisher
Georg Brewer, VP—Design & DC Direct Creative
Richard Bruning, Senior VP—Creative Director
Patrick Caldon, Executive VP—Finance & Operations
Chris Caramalis, VP—Finance
John Cunningham, VP—Marketing
Terri Cunningham, VP—Managing Editor
Alison Gill, VP—Manufacturing
David Hyde, VP—Publicity
Hank Kanalz, VP—General Manager, WildStorm
Paula Lowitt, Senior VP—Business & Legal Affairs
MaryEllen McLaughlin, VP—Advertising & Custom Publishing
Gregory Noveck, Senior VP—Creative Affairs
Sue Pohja, VP—Book Trade Sales
Steve Rotterdam, Senior VP—Sales & Marketing
Cheryl Rubin, Senior VP—Brand Management
Jeff Trojan, VP—Business Development, DC Direct
Bob Wayne, VP—Sales

MIDNIGHTER: ANTHEM published by WildStorm Productions. 888 Prospect St. #240, La Jolla, CA 92037. Compilation Copyright © 2008 WildStorm Productions, an imprint of DC Comics. All Rights
Reserved. Originally published in single magazine form as THE MIDNIGHTER #7, 10-15 © 2007, 2008 WildStorm Productions, an imprint of DC Comics.
WildStorm and logo, The Midnighter, all characters, the distinctive likenesses thereof and all related elements are trademarks of DC Comics. The stories, characters, and incidents mentioned in this
magazine are entirely fictional. Printed on recyclable paper. WildStorm does not read or accept unsolicited submissions of ideas, stories or artwork. Printed in Canada.

DC Comics, a Warner Bros. Entertainment Company.

ISBN: 978-1-4012-1670-2

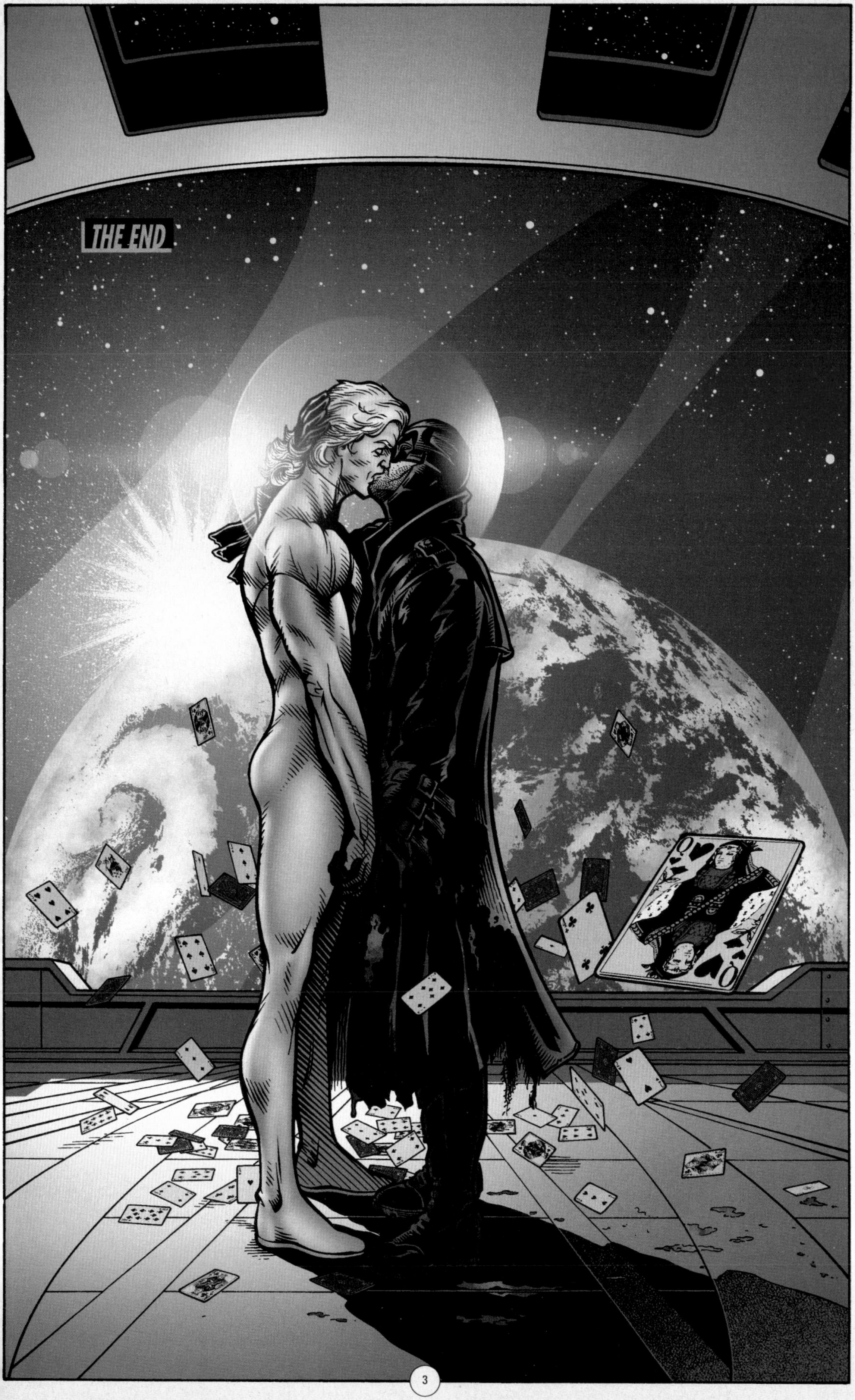
THE END

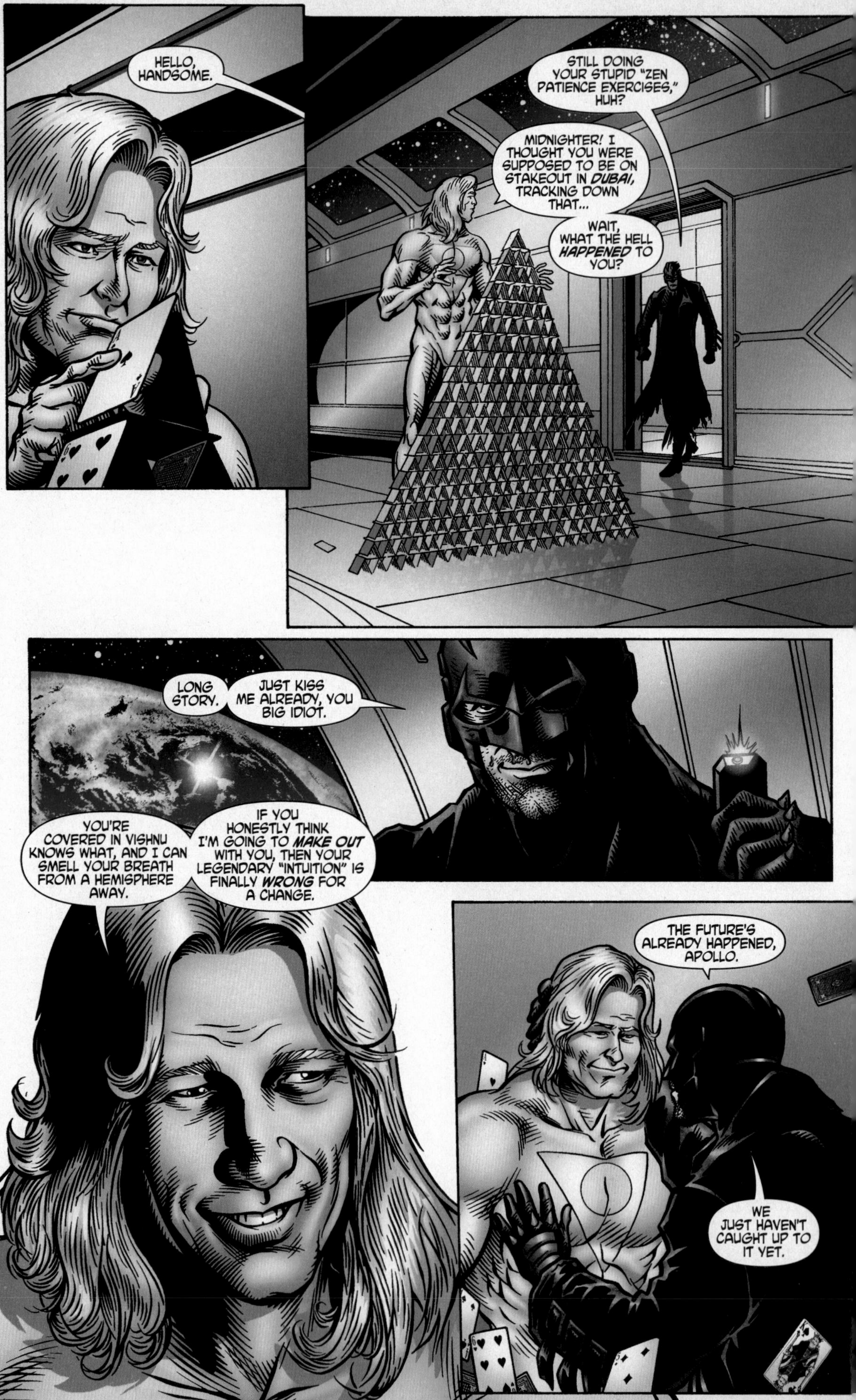
HELLO, HANDSOME.
STILL DOING YOUR STUPID "ZEN PATIENCE EXERCISES," HUH?
MIDNIGHTER! I THOUGHT YOU WERE SUPPOSED TO BE ON STAKEOUT IN DUBAI, TRACKING DOWN THAT...
WAIT, WHAT THE HELL HAPPENED TO YOU?
LONG STORY.
JUST KISS ME ALREADY, YOU BIG IDIOT.
YOU'RE COVERED IN VISHNU KNOWS WHAT, AND I CAN SMELL YOUR BREATH FROM A HEMISPHERE AWAY.
IF YOU HONESTLY THINK I'M GOING TO MAKE OUT WITH YOU, THEN YOUR LEGENDARY "INTUITION" IS FINALLY WRONG FOR A CHANGE.
THE FUTURE'S ALREADY HAPPENED, APOLLO.
WE JUST HAVEN'T CAUGHT UP TO IT YET.

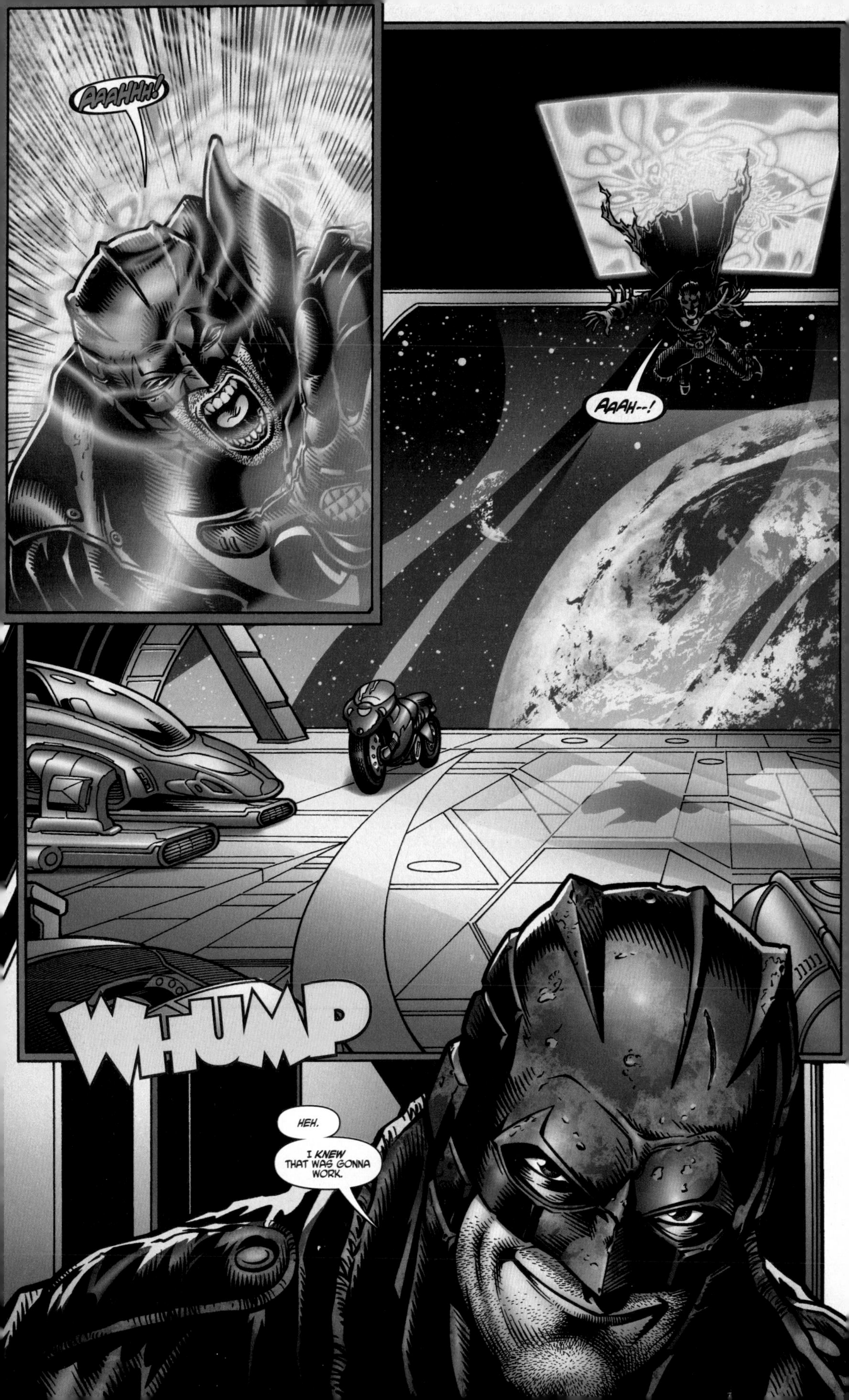
AAAHHH!
AAAH--!
WHUMP
HEH.
I KNEW THAT WAS GONNA WORK.

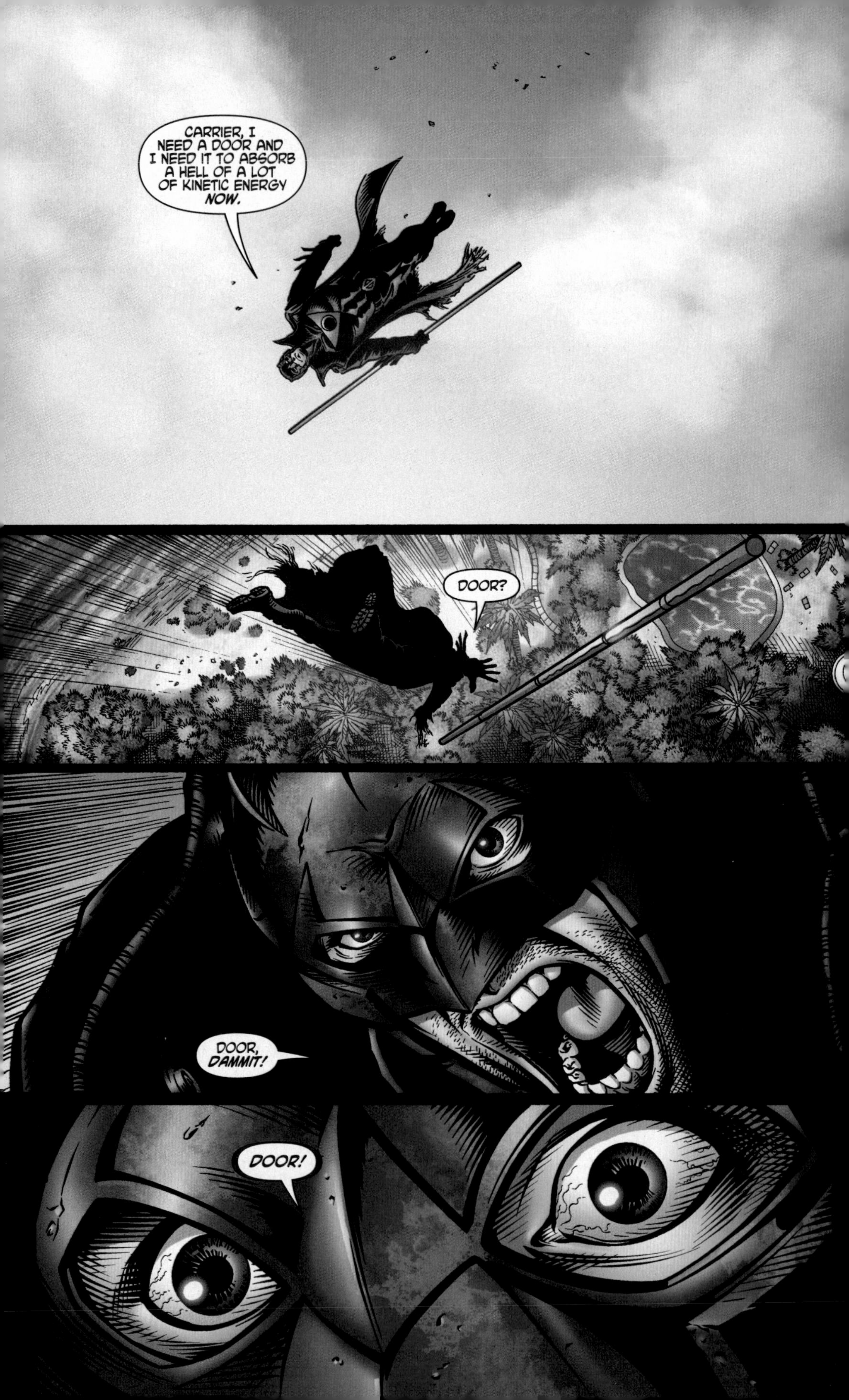
CARRIER, I NEED A DOOR AND I NEED IT TO ABSORB A HELL OF A LOT OF KINETIC ENERGY *NOW.*
DOOR?
DOOR, *DAMMIT!*
DOOR!

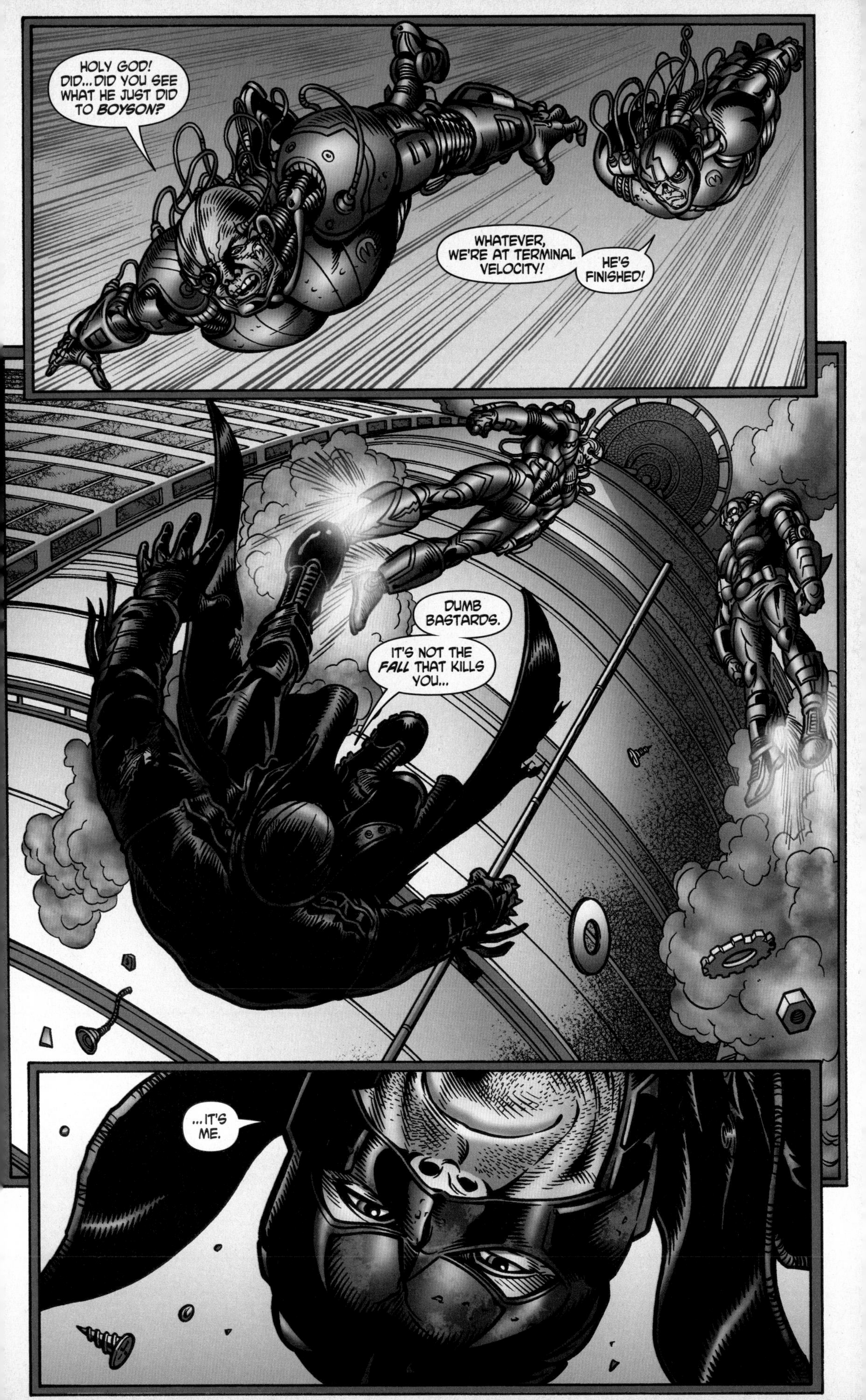
HOLY GOD! DID...DID YOU SEE WHAT HE JUST DID TO BOYSON?
WHATEVER, WE'RE AT TERMINAL VELOCITY!
HE'S FINISHED!
DUMB BASTARDS.
IT'S NOT THE FALL THAT KILLS YOU...
...IT'S ME.

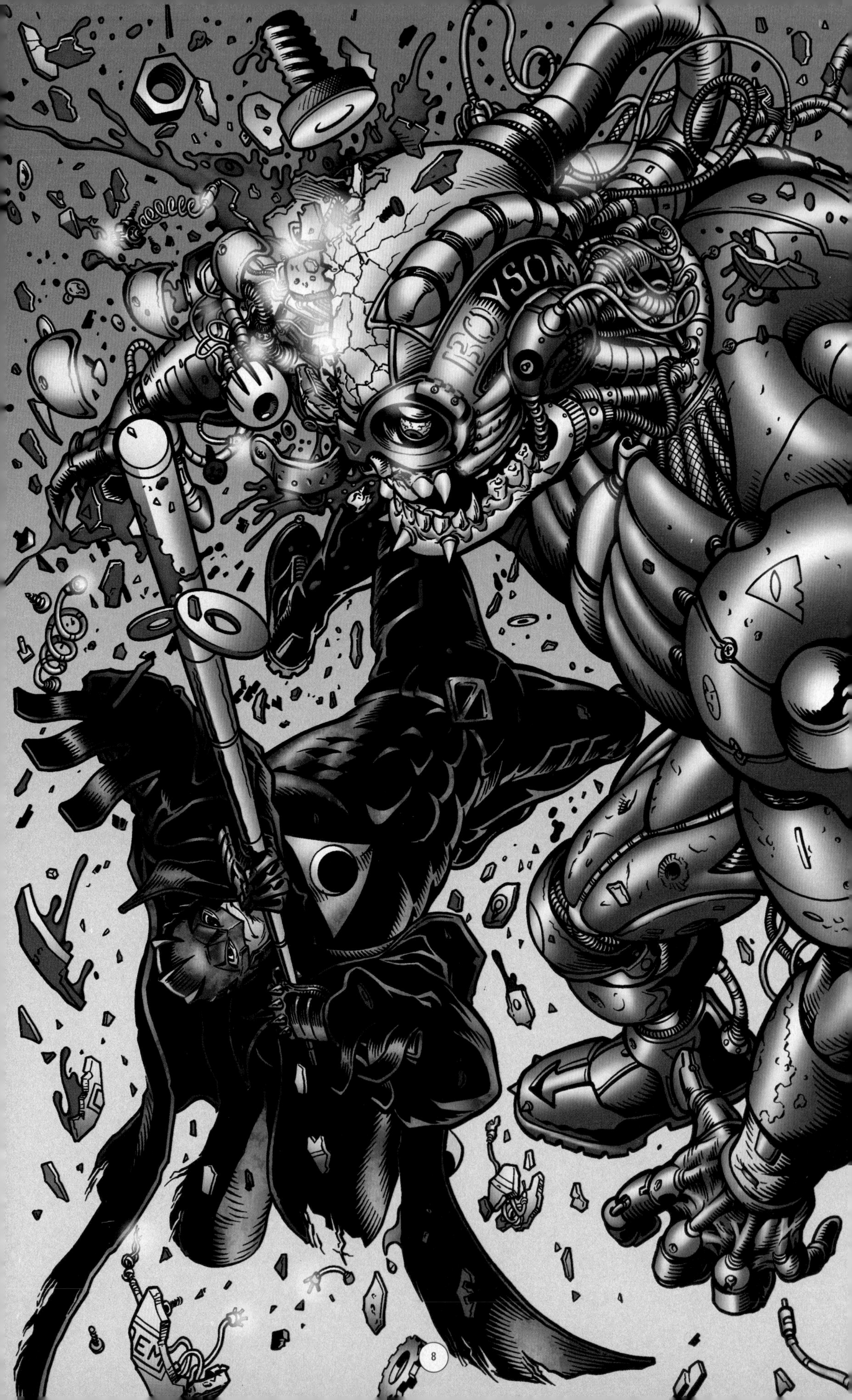

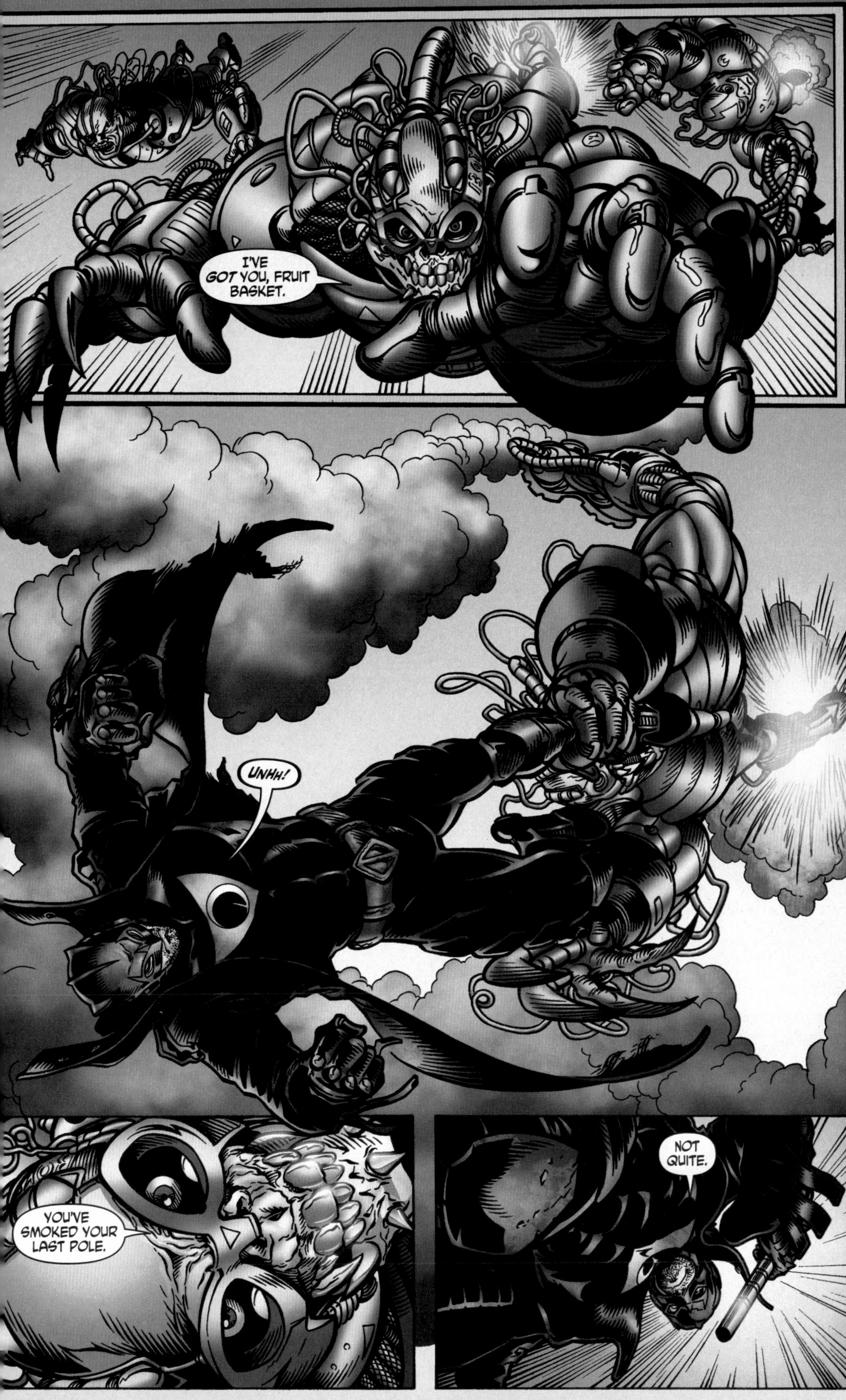
I'VE GOT YOU, FRUIT BASKET.
UNHH!
YOU'VE SMOKED YOUR LAST POLE.
NOT QUITE.

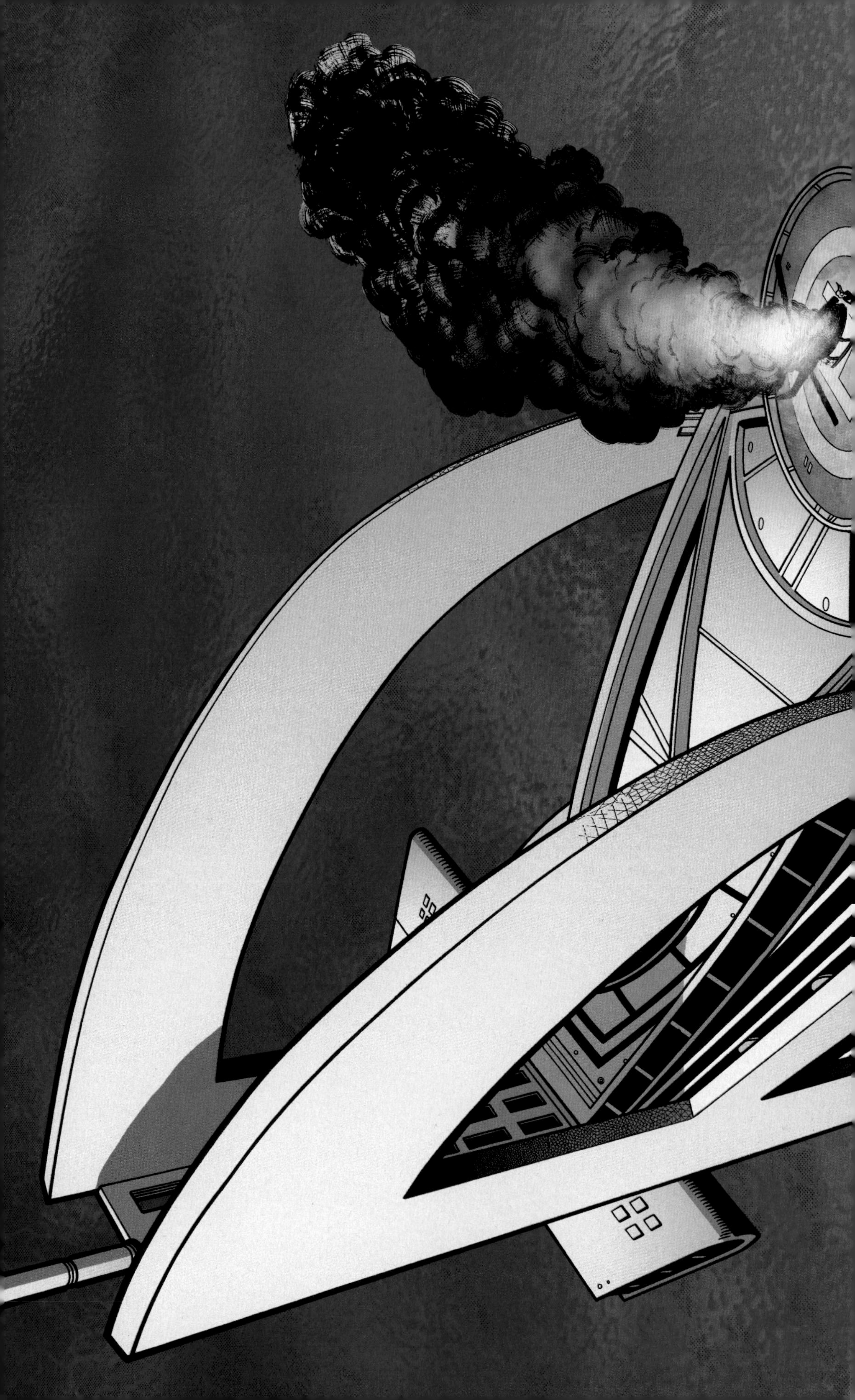

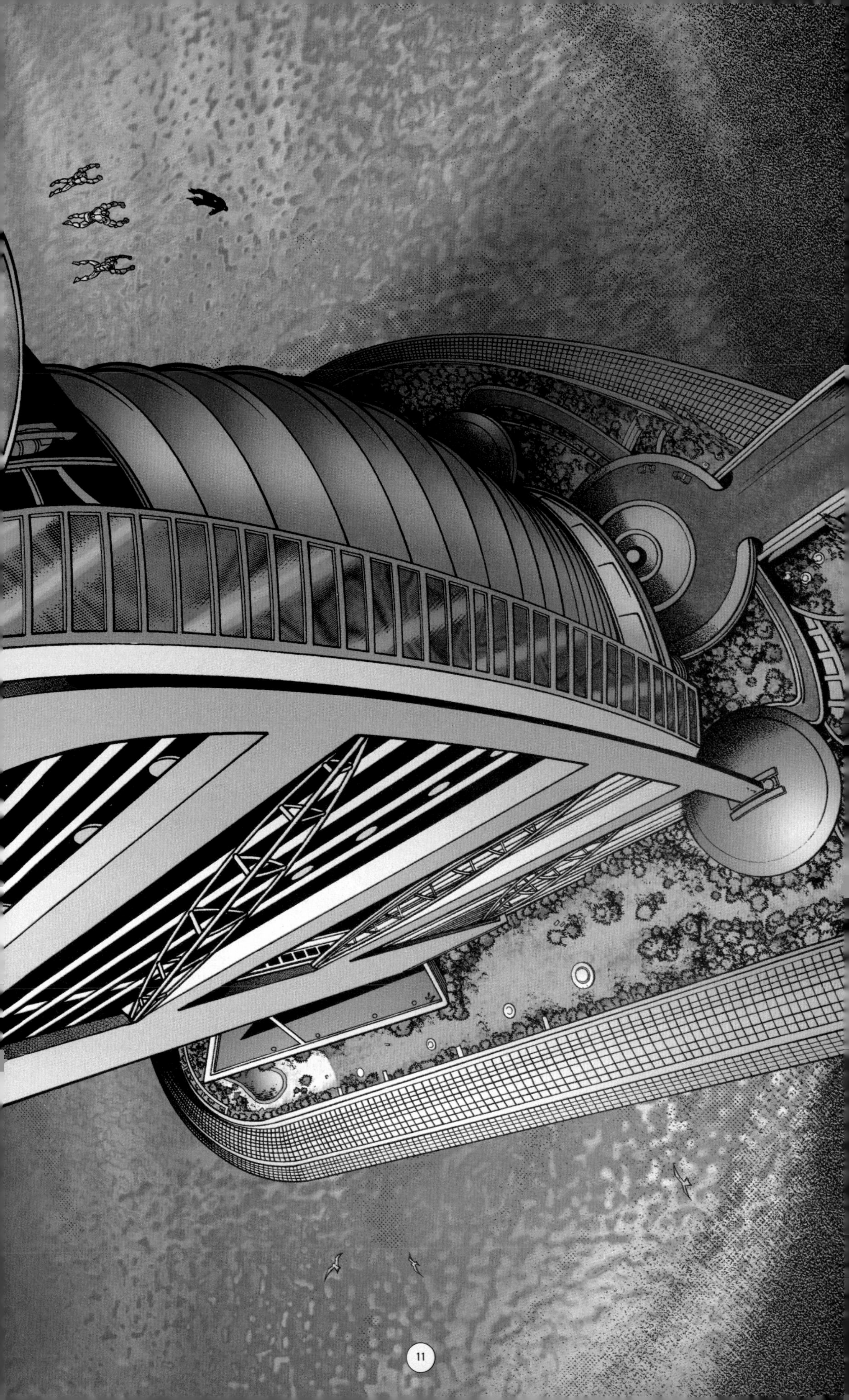

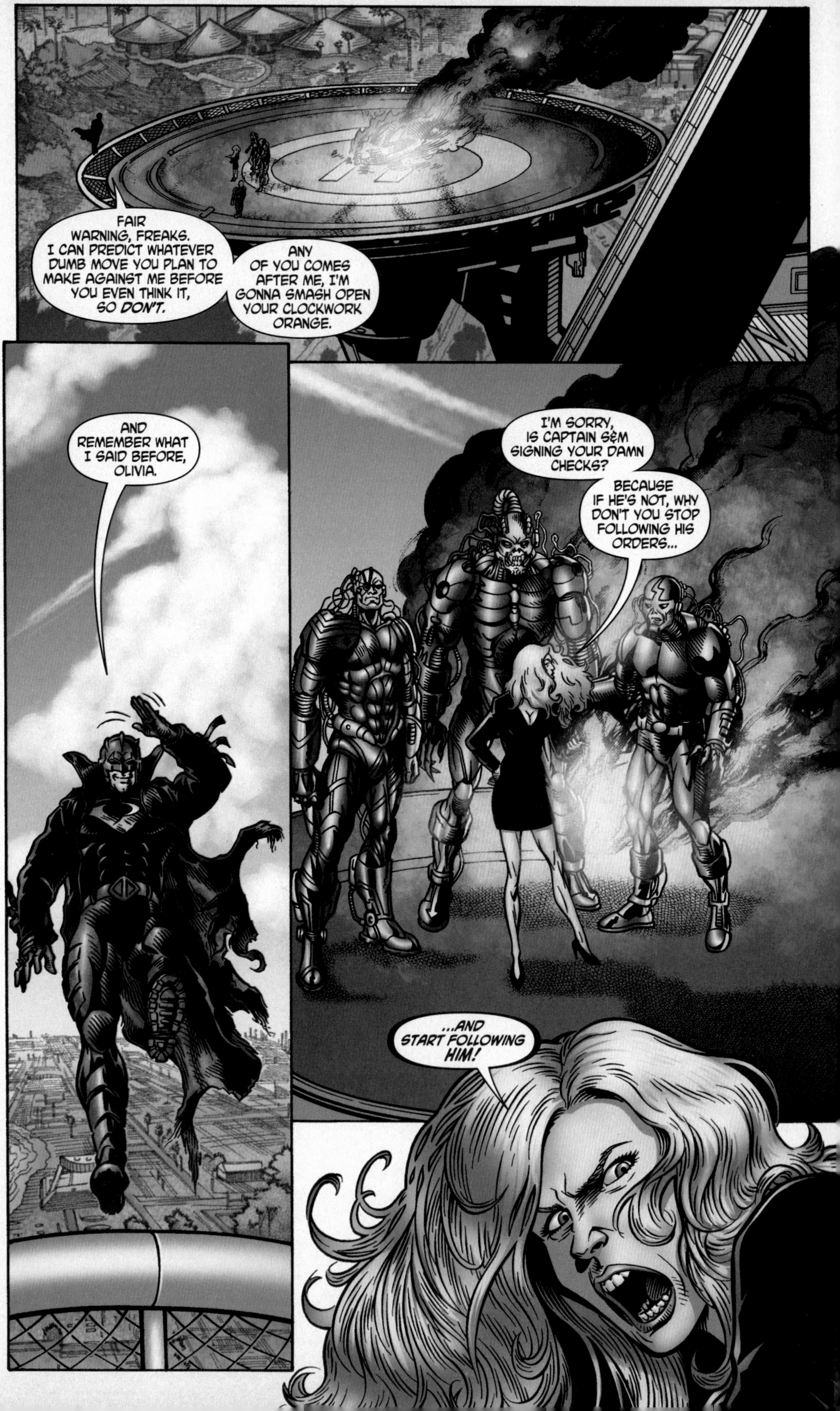
FAIR WARNING, FREAKS. I CAN PREDICT WHATEVER DUMB MOVE YOU PLAN TO MAKE AGAINST ME BEFORE YOU EVEN THINK IT, SO DON'T.
ANY OF YOU COMES AFTER ME, I'M GONNA SMASH OPEN YOUR CLOCKWORK ORANGE.
AND REMEMBER WHAT I SAID BEFORE, OLIVIA.
I'M SORRY, IS CAPTAIN S&M SIGNING YOUR DAMN CHECKS?
BECAUSE IF HE'S NOT, WHY DON'T YOU STOP FOLLOWING HIS ORDERS...
...AND START FOLLOWING HIM!

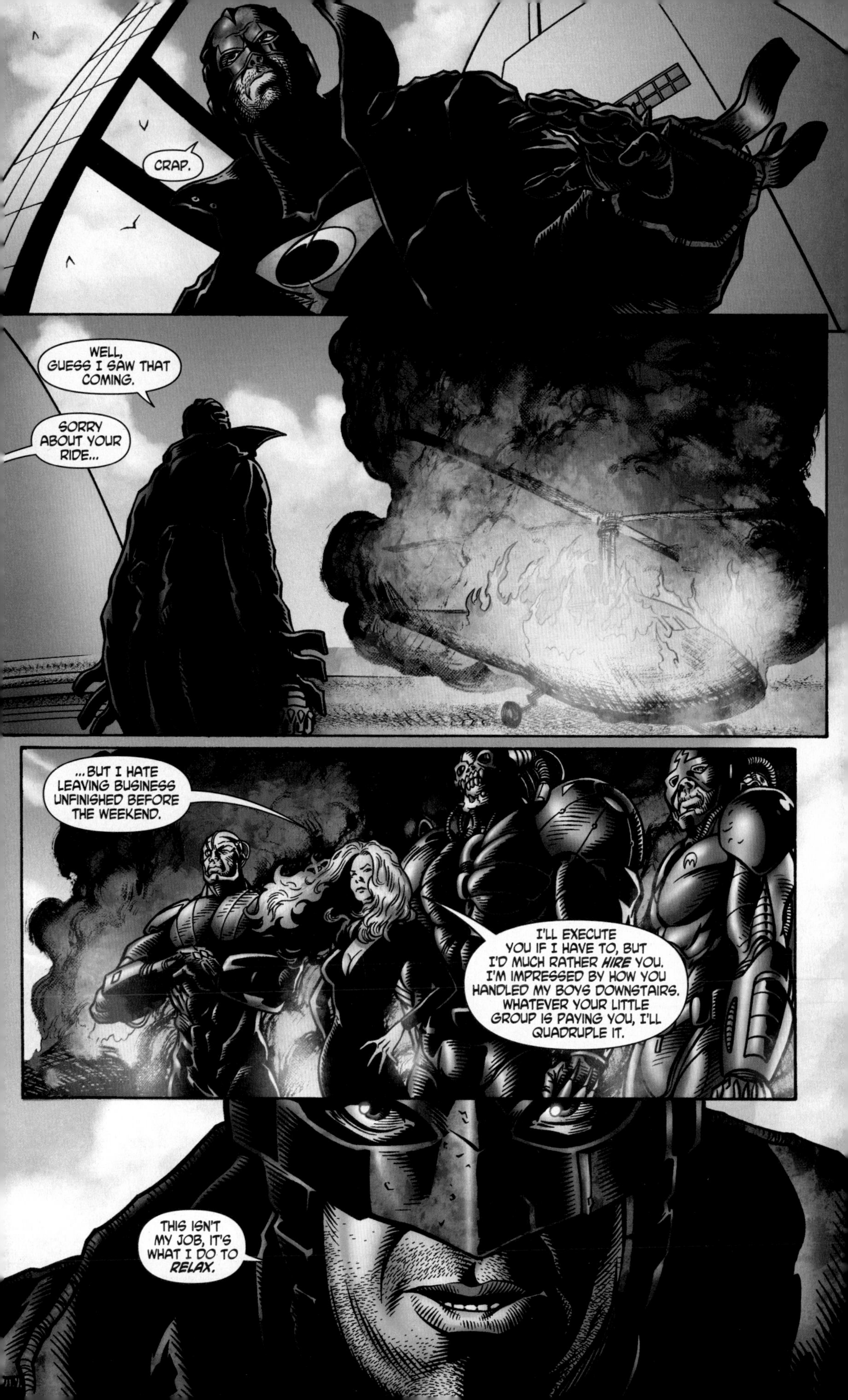
CRAP.
WELL, GUESS I SAW THAT COMING.
SORRY ABOUT YOUR RIDE...
...BUT I HATE LEAVING BUSINESS UNFINISHED BEFORE THE WEEKEND.
I'LL EXECUTE YOU IF I HAVE TO, BUT I'D MUCH RATHER *HIRE* YOU. I'M IMPRESSED BY HOW YOU HANDLED MY BOYS DOWNSTAIRS. WHATEVER YOUR LITTLE GROUP IS PAYING YOU, I'LL QUADRUPLE IT.
THIS ISN'T MY JOB, IT'S WHAT I DO TO *RELAX.*

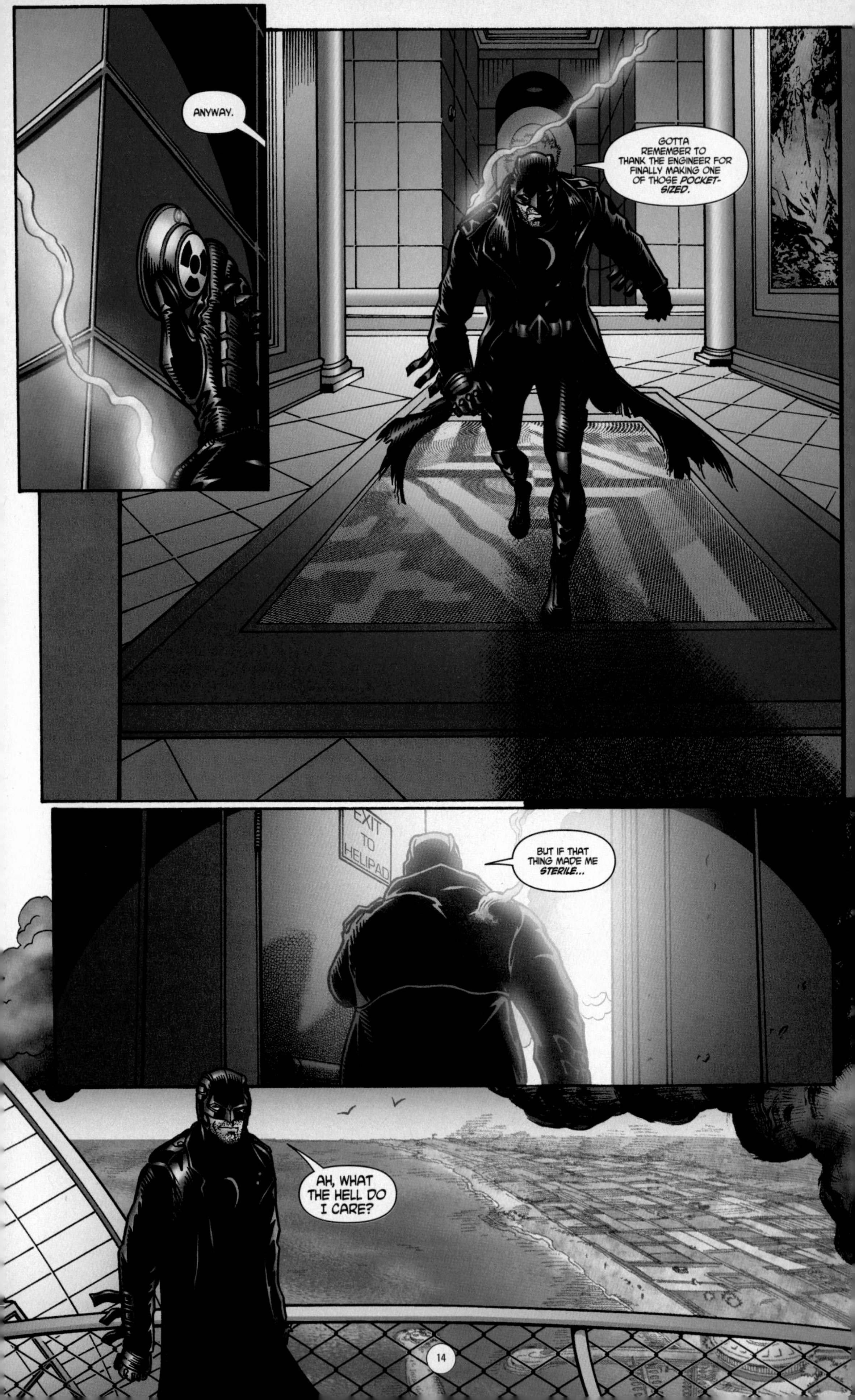
ANYWAY.
GOTTA REMEMBER TO THANK THE ENGINEER FOR FINALLY MAKING ONE OF THOSE POCKET-SIZED.
BUT IF THAT THING MADE ME STERILE...
AH, WHAT THE HELL DO I CARE?

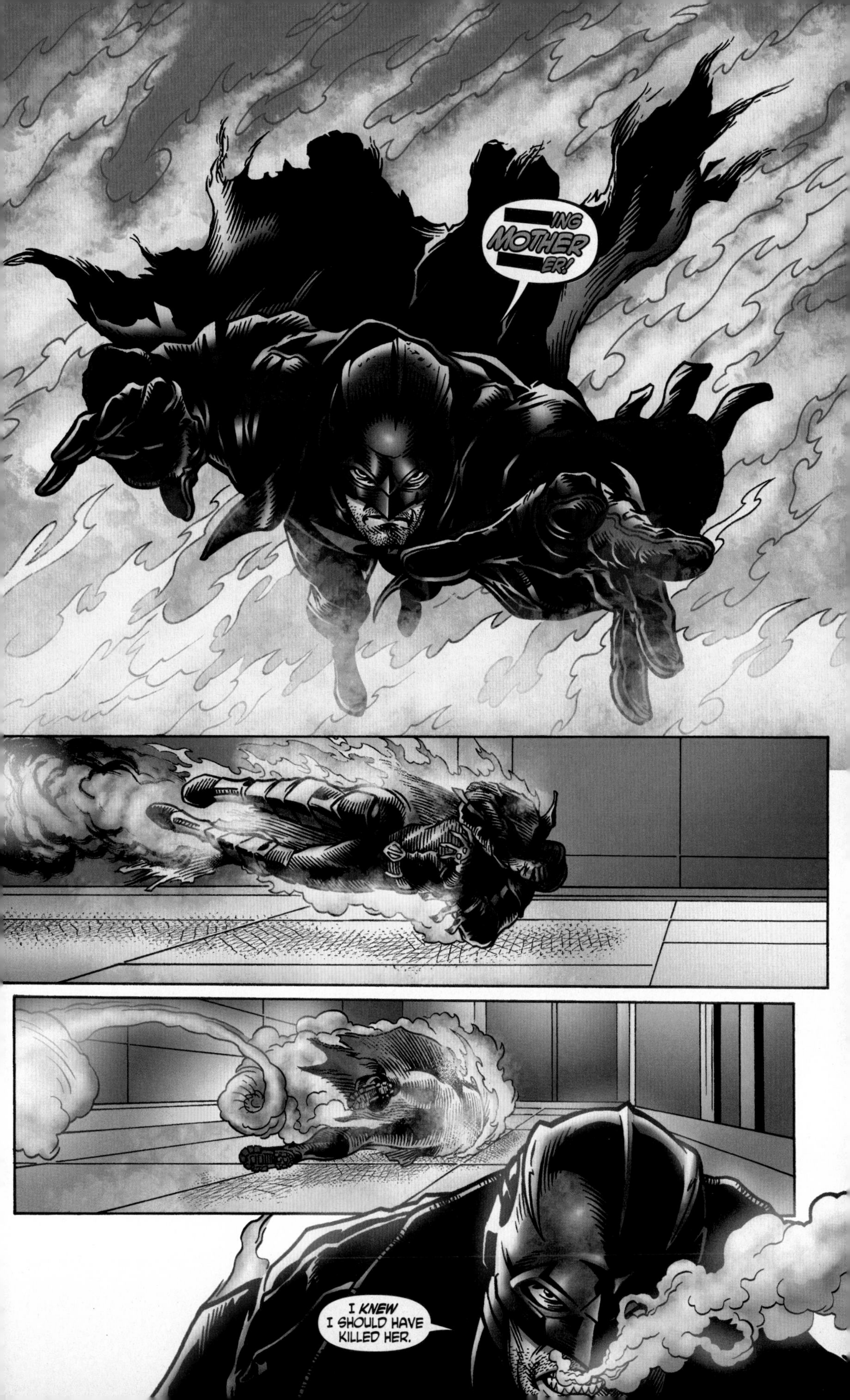
[redacted]ING MOTHER[redacted]ER!
I KNEW I SHOULD HAVE KILLED HER.

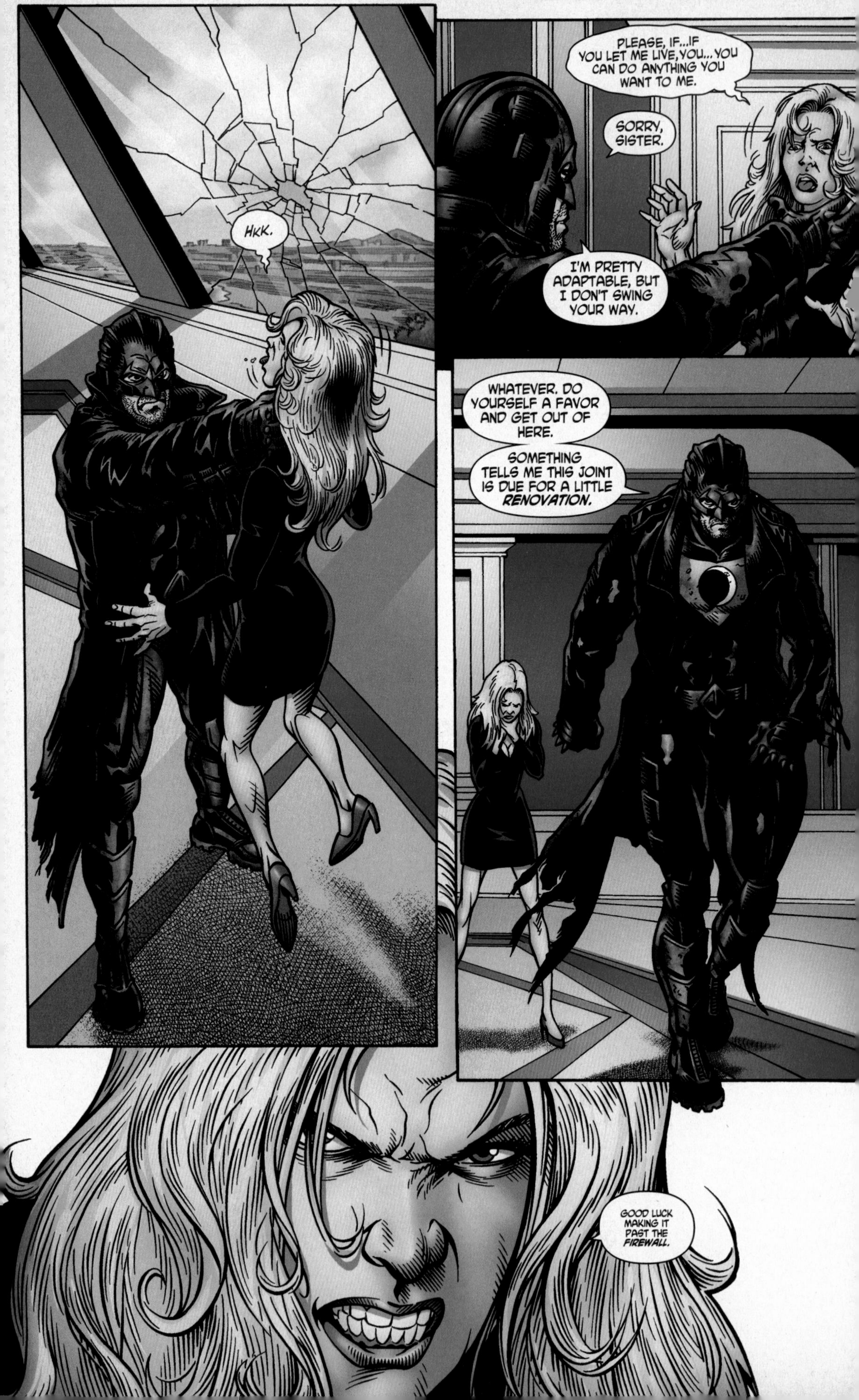
HKK.
PLEASE, IF...IF YOU LET ME LIVE, YOU... YOU CAN DO ANYTHING YOU WANT TO ME.
SORRY, SISTER.
I'M PRETTY ADAPTABLE, BUT I DON'T SWING YOUR WAY.
WHATEVER. DO YOURSELF A FAVOR AND GET OUT OF HERE.
SOMETHING TELLS ME THIS JOINT IS DUE FOR A LITTLE RENOVATION.
GOOD LUCK MAKING IT PAST THE FIREWALL.

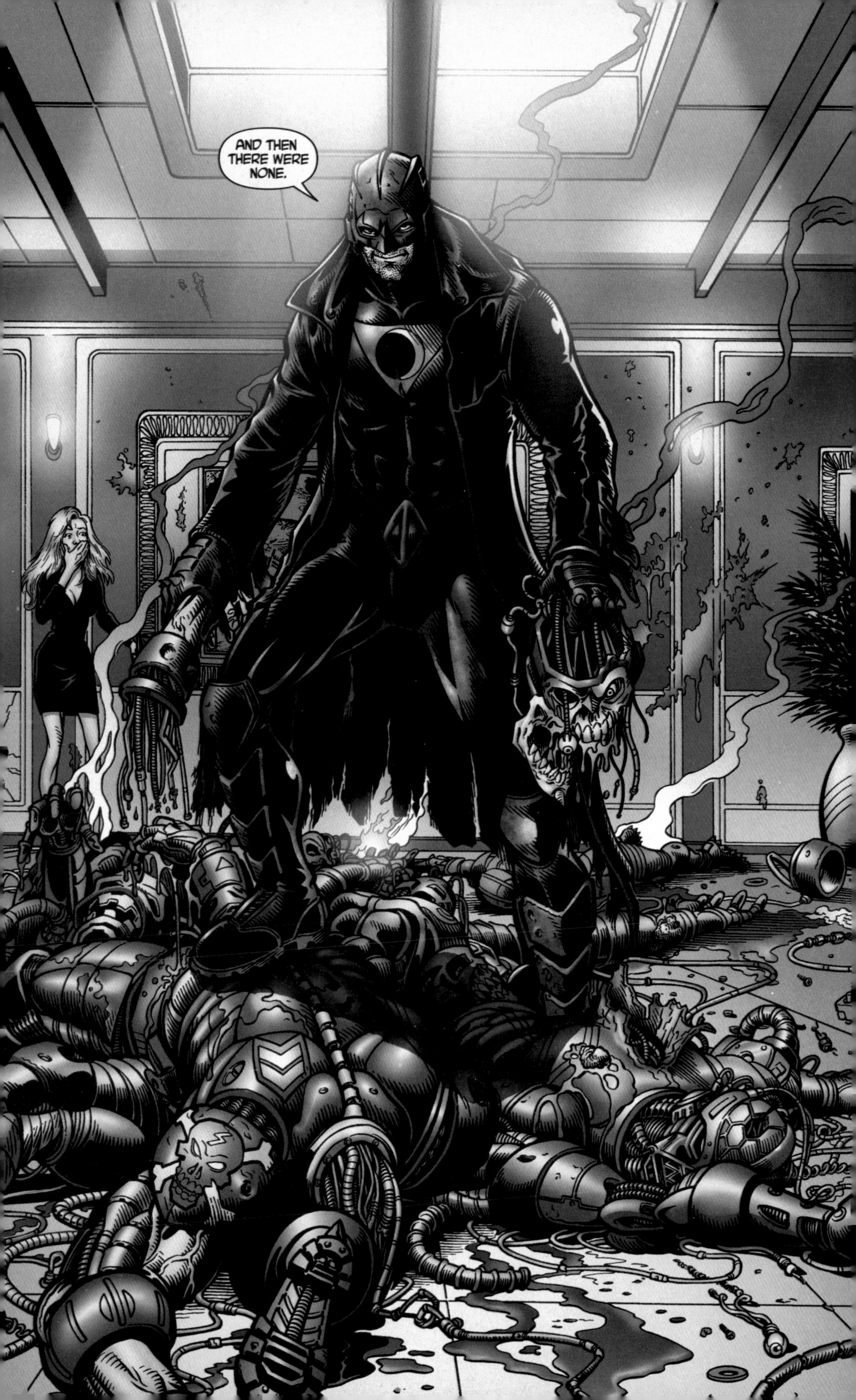
AND THEN THERE WERE NONE.

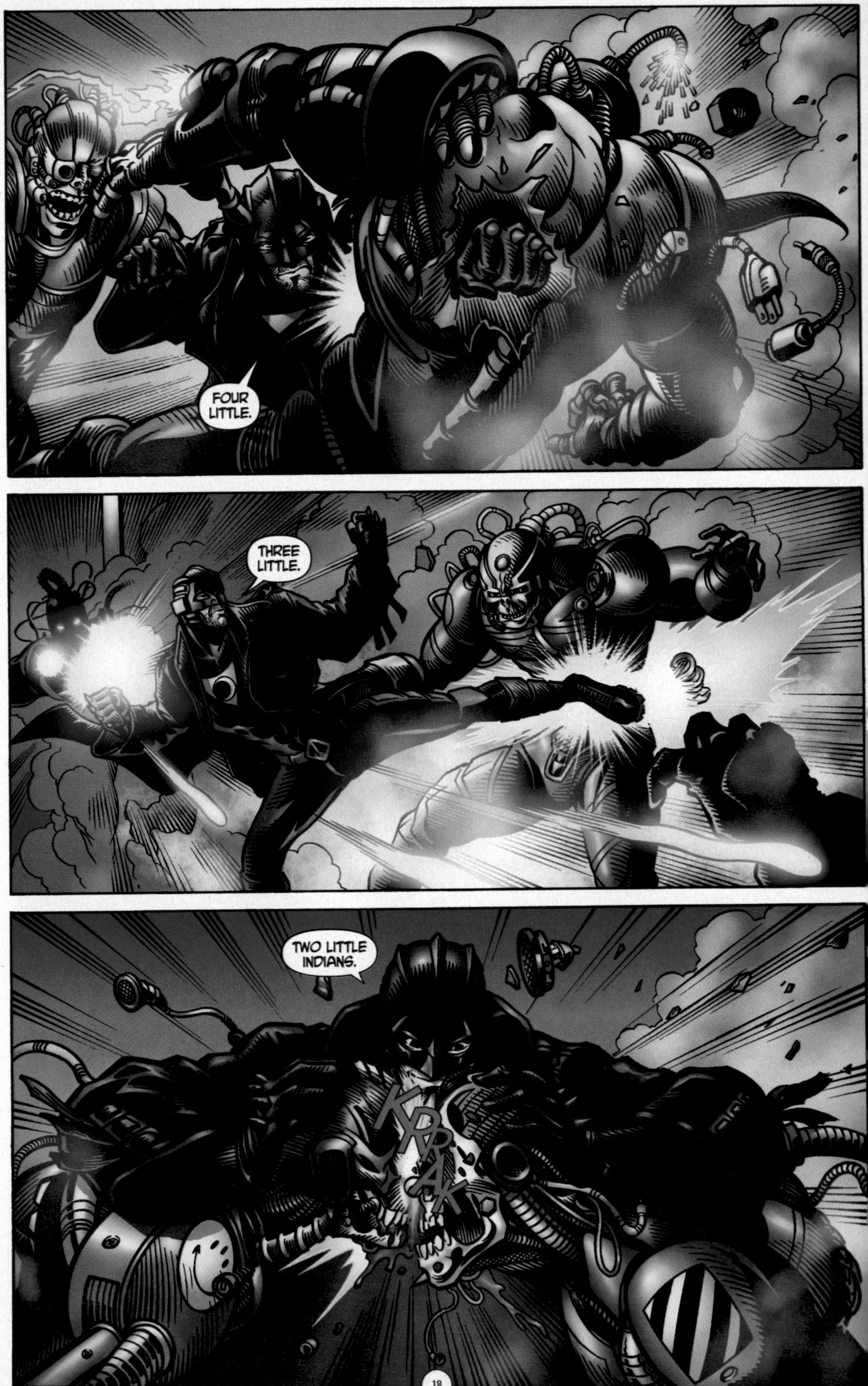
FOUR LITTLE.
THREE LITTLE.
TWO LITTLE INDIANS.
KRRAK

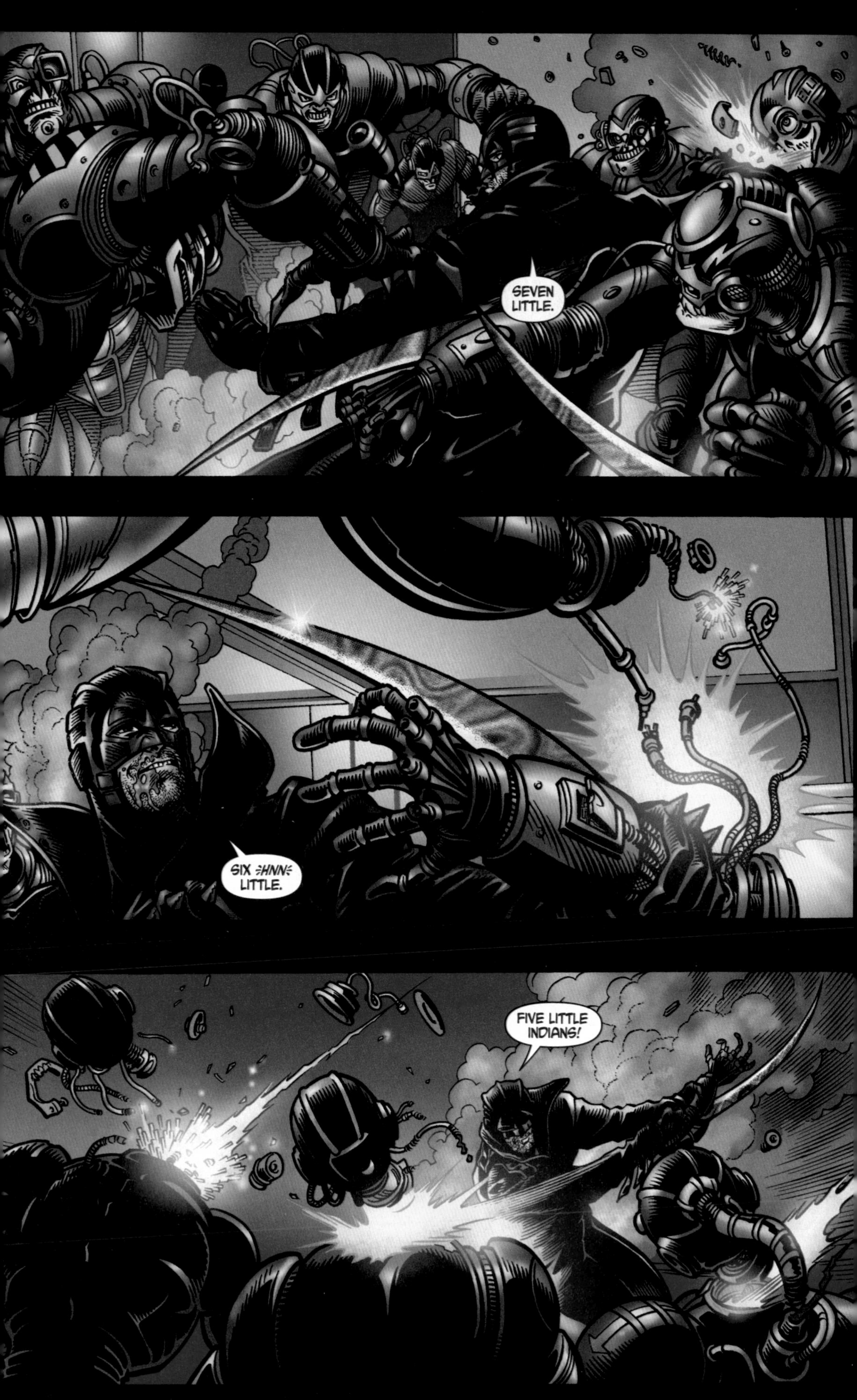

SEVEN LITTLE.
SIX =HNN= LITTLE.
FIVE LITTLE INDIANS!

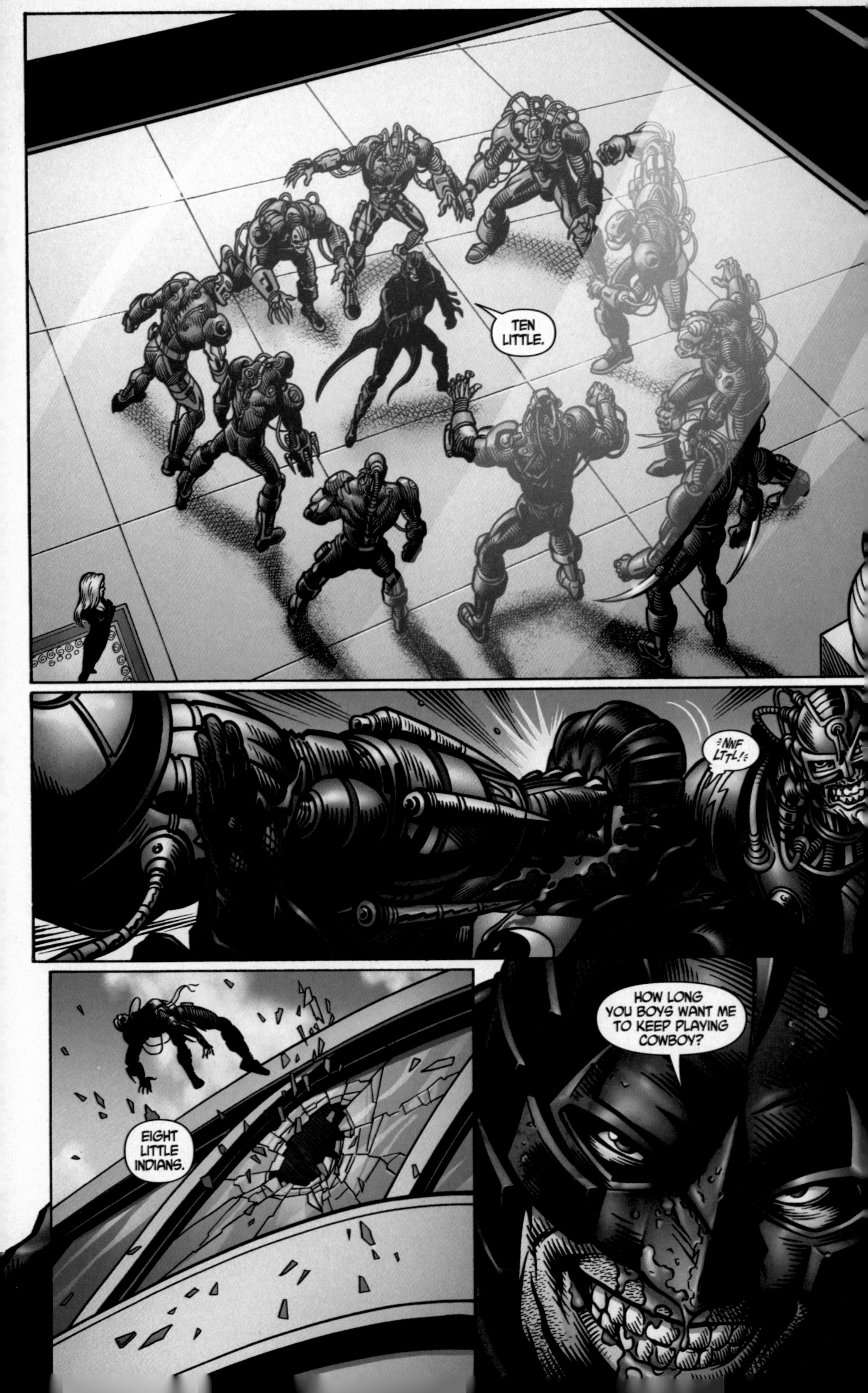
TEN LITTLE.
NNF LTTL!
EIGHT LITTLE INDIANS.
HOW LONG YOU BOYS WANT ME TO KEEP PLAYING COWBOY?

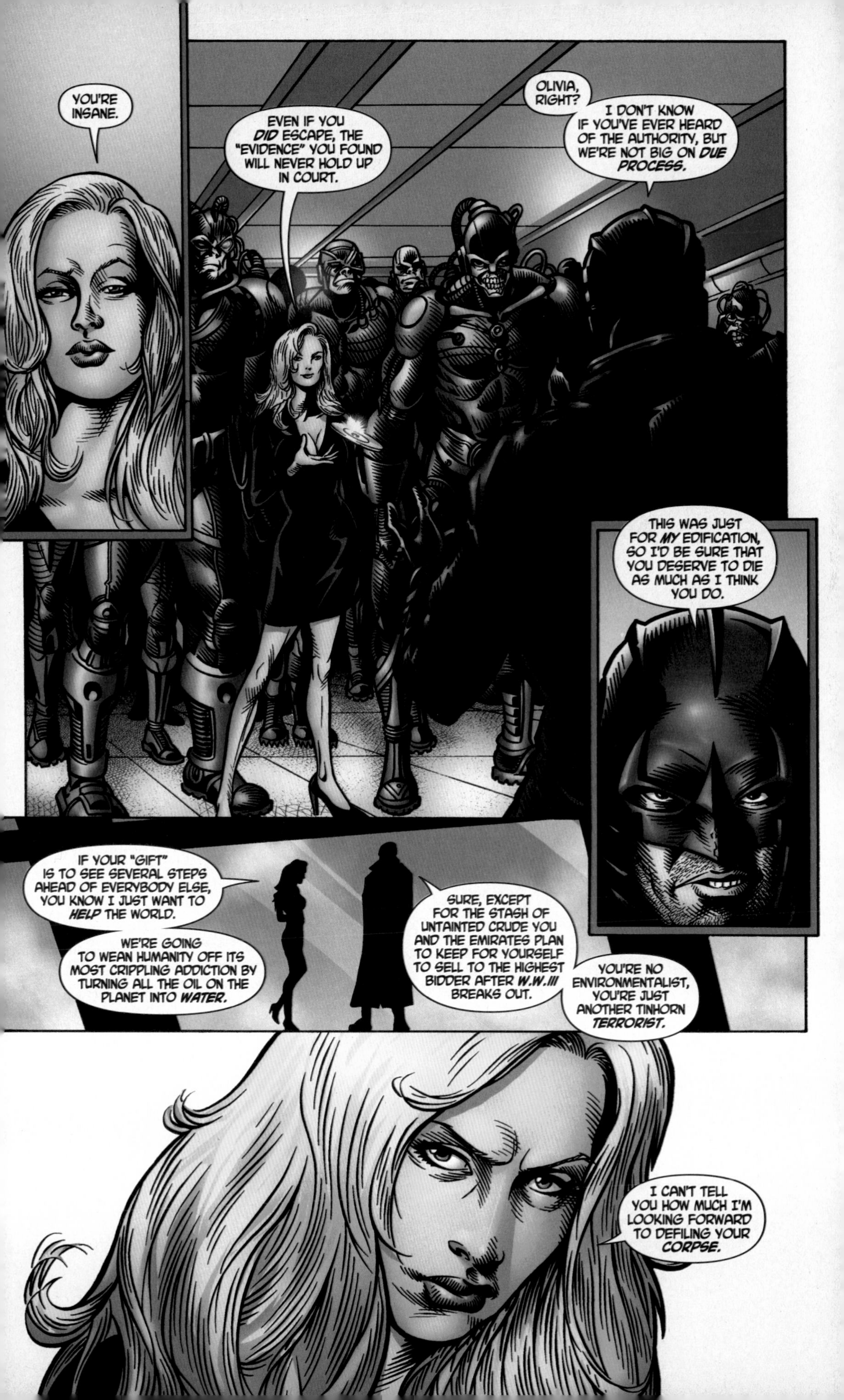
YOU'RE INSANE.
EVEN IF YOU DID ESCAPE, THE "EVIDENCE" YOU FOUND WILL NEVER HOLD UP IN COURT.
OLIVIA, RIGHT?
I DON'T KNOW IF YOU'VE EVER HEARD OF THE AUTHORITY, BUT WE'RE NOT BIG ON DUE PROCESS.
THIS WAS JUST FOR MY EDIFICATION, SO I'D BE SURE THAT YOU DESERVE TO DIE AS MUCH AS I THINK YOU DO.
IF YOUR "GIFT" IS TO SEE SEVERAL STEPS AHEAD OF EVERYBODY ELSE, YOU KNOW I JUST WANT TO HELP THE WORLD.
WE'RE GOING TO WEAN HUMANITY OFF ITS MOST CRIPPLING ADDICTION BY TURNING ALL THE OIL ON THE PLANET INTO WATER.
SURE, EXCEPT FOR THE STASH OF UNTAINTED CRUDE YOU AND THE EMIRATES PLAN TO KEEP FOR YOURSELF TO SELL TO THE HIGHEST BIDDER AFTER W.W.III BREAKS OUT.
YOU'RE NO ENVIRONMENTALIST, YOU'RE JUST ANOTHER TINHORN TERRORIST.
I CAN'T TELL YOU HOW MUCH I'M LOOKING FORWARD TO DEFILING YOUR CORPSE.

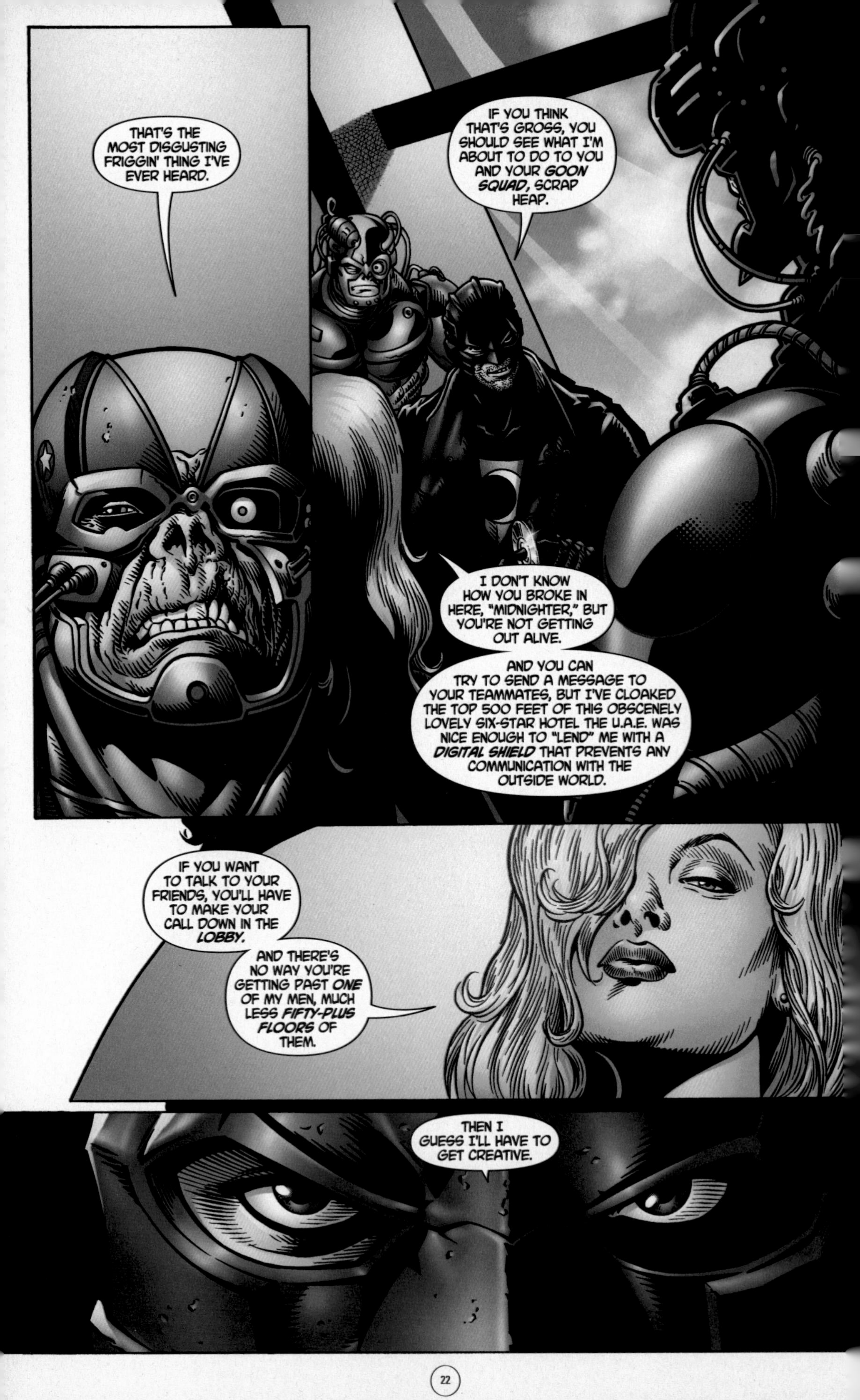
THAT'S THE MOST DISGUSTING FRIGGIN' THING I'VE EVER HEARD.
IF YOU THINK THAT'S GROSS, YOU SHOULD SEE WHAT I'M ABOUT TO DO TO YOU AND YOUR GOON SQUAD, SCRAP HEAP.
I DON'T KNOW HOW YOU BROKE IN HERE, "MIDNIGHTER," BUT YOU'RE NOT GETTING OUT ALIVE.
AND YOU CAN TRY TO SEND A MESSAGE TO YOUR TEAMMATES, BUT I'VE CLOAKED THE TOP 500 FEET OF THIS OBSCENELY LOVELY SIX-STAR HOTEL THE U.A.E. WAS NICE ENOUGH TO "LEND" ME WITH A DIGITAL SHIELD THAT PREVENTS ANY COMMUNICATION WITH THE OUTSIDE WORLD.
IF YOU WANT TO TALK TO YOUR FRIENDS, YOU'LL HAVE TO MAKE YOUR CALL DOWN IN THE LOBBY.
AND THERE'S NO WAY YOU'RE GETTING PAST ONE OF MY MEN, MUCH LESS FIFTY-PLUS FLOORS OF THEM.
THEN I GUESS I'LL HAVE TO GET CREATIVE.

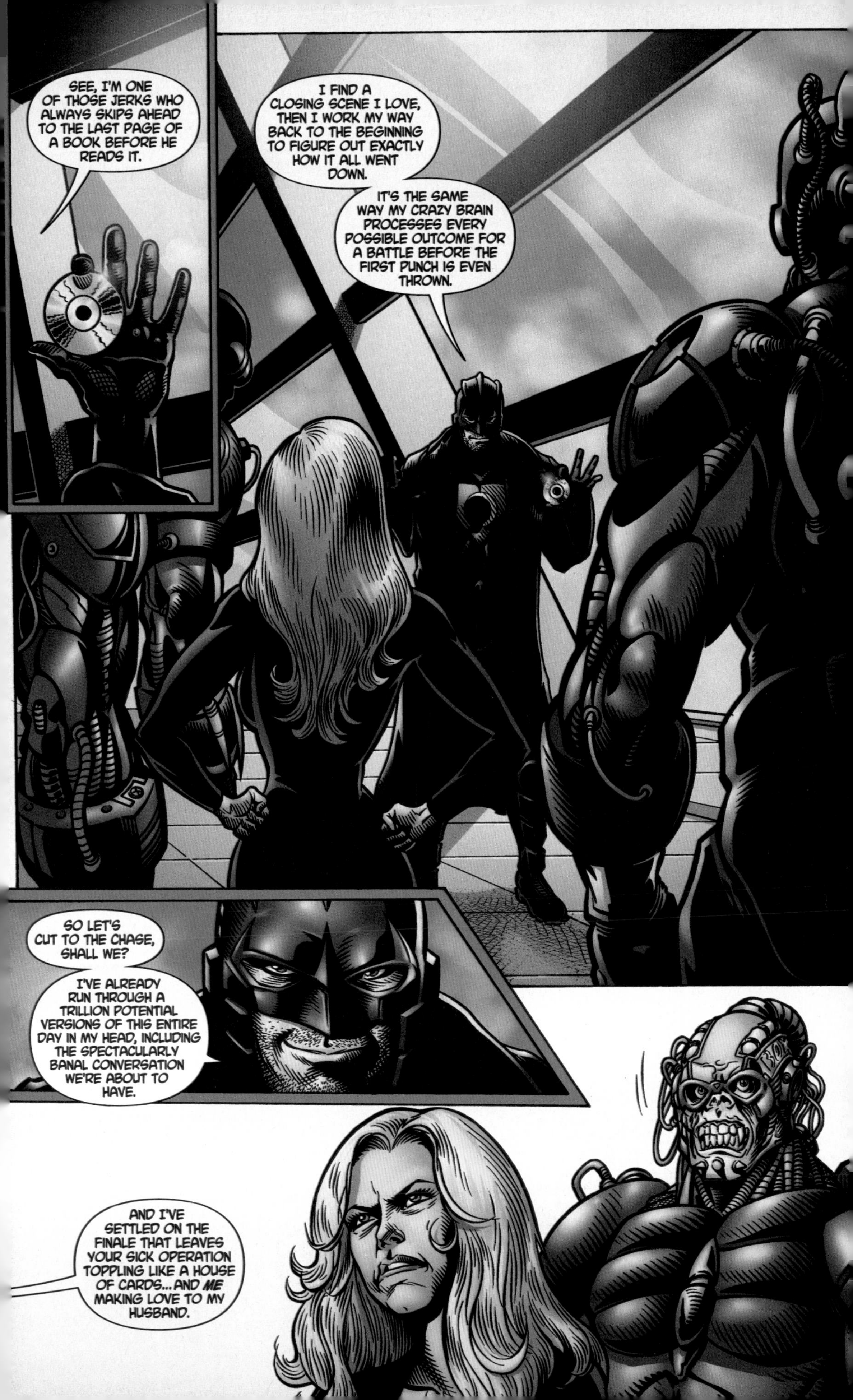
SEE, I'M ONE OF THOSE JERKS WHO ALWAYS SKIPS AHEAD TO THE LAST PAGE OF A BOOK BEFORE HE READS IT.
I FIND A CLOSING SCENE I LOVE, THEN I WORK MY WAY BACK TO THE BEGINNING TO FIGURE OUT EXACTLY HOW IT ALL WENT DOWN.
IT'S THE SAME WAY MY CRAZY BRAIN PROCESSES EVERY POSSIBLE OUTCOME FOR A BATTLE BEFORE THE FIRST PUNCH IS EVEN THROWN.
SO LET'S CUT TO THE CHASE, SHALL WE?
I'VE ALREADY RUN THROUGH A TRILLION POTENTIAL VERSIONS OF THIS ENTIRE DAY IN MY HEAD, INCLUDING THE SPECTACULARLY BANAL CONVERSATION WE'RE ABOUT TO HAVE.
AND I'VE SETTLED ON THE FINALE THAT LEAVES YOUR SICK OPERATION TOPPLING LIKE A HOUSE OF CARDS... AND *ME* MAKING LOVE TO MY HUSBAND.

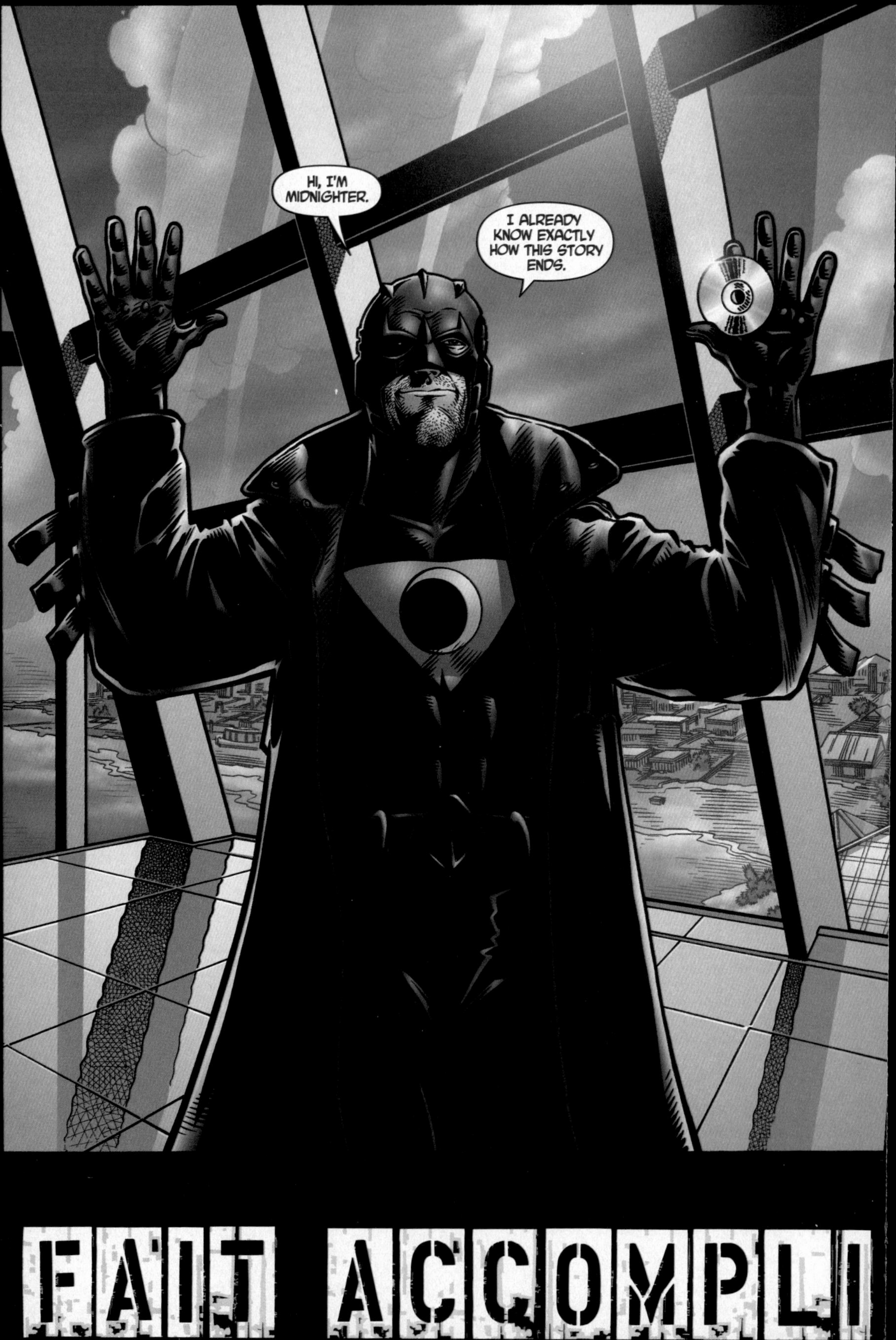
HI, I'M MIDNIGHTER.
I ALREADY KNOW EXACTLY HOW THIS STORY ENDS.
FAIT ACCOMPLI

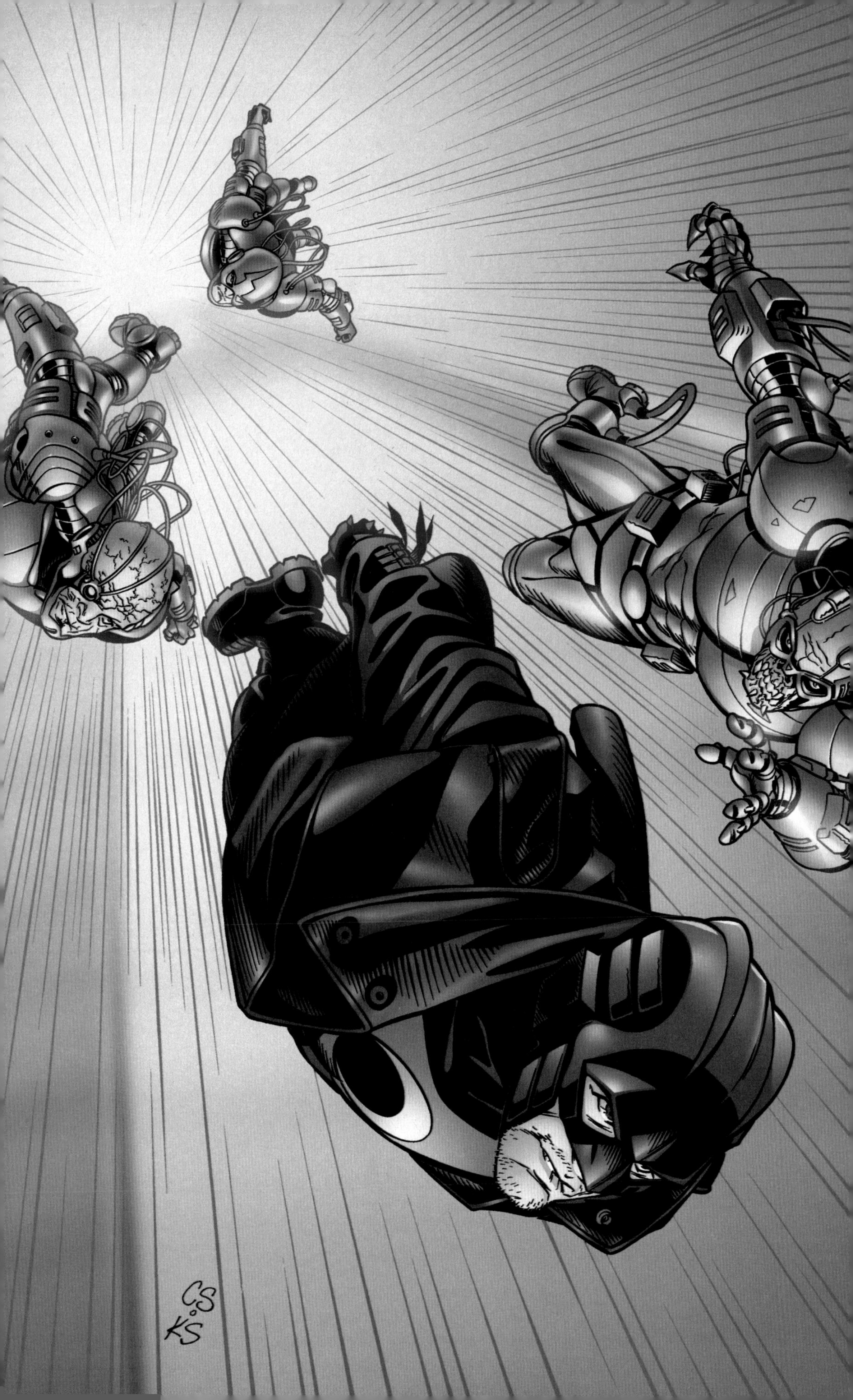

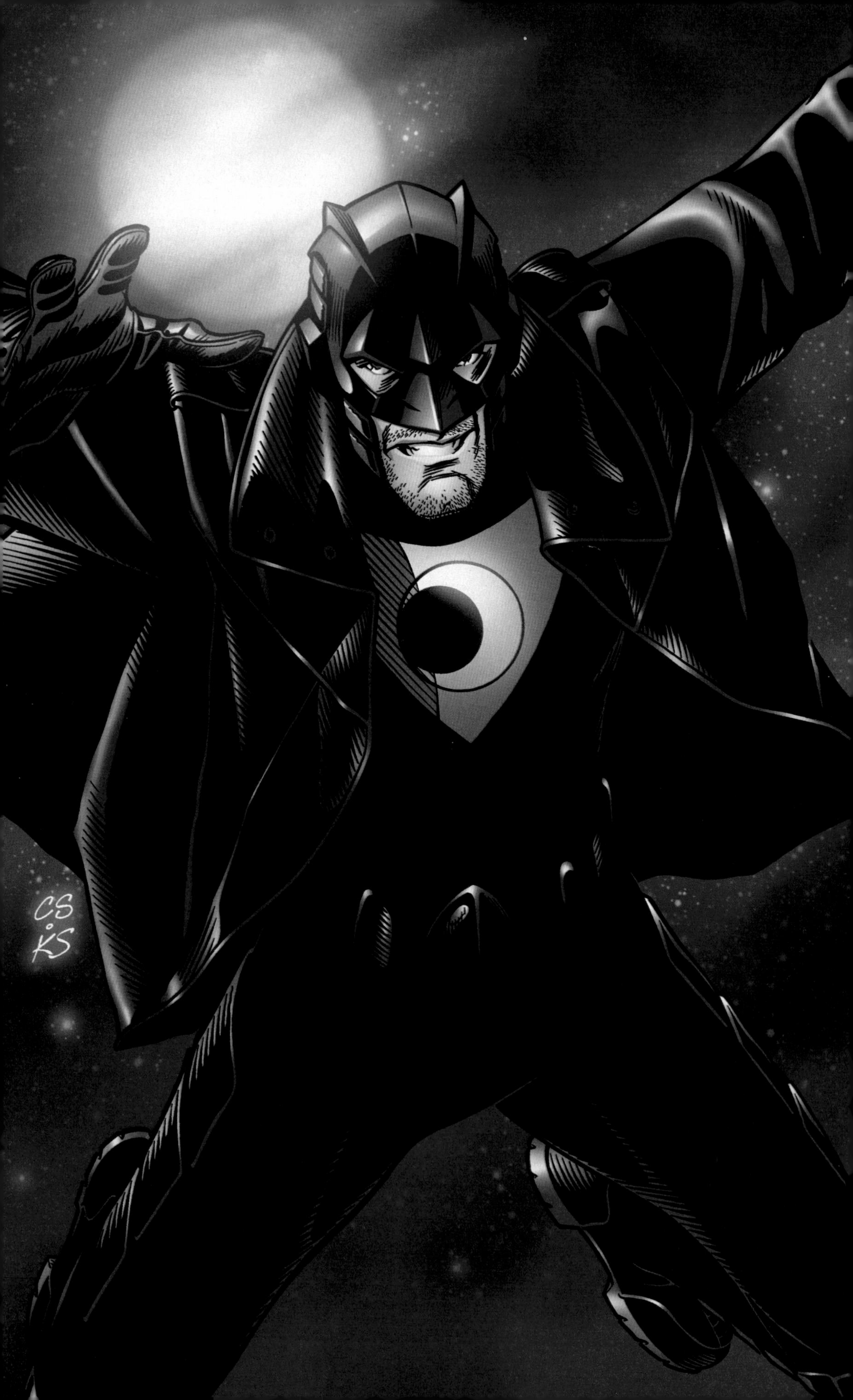

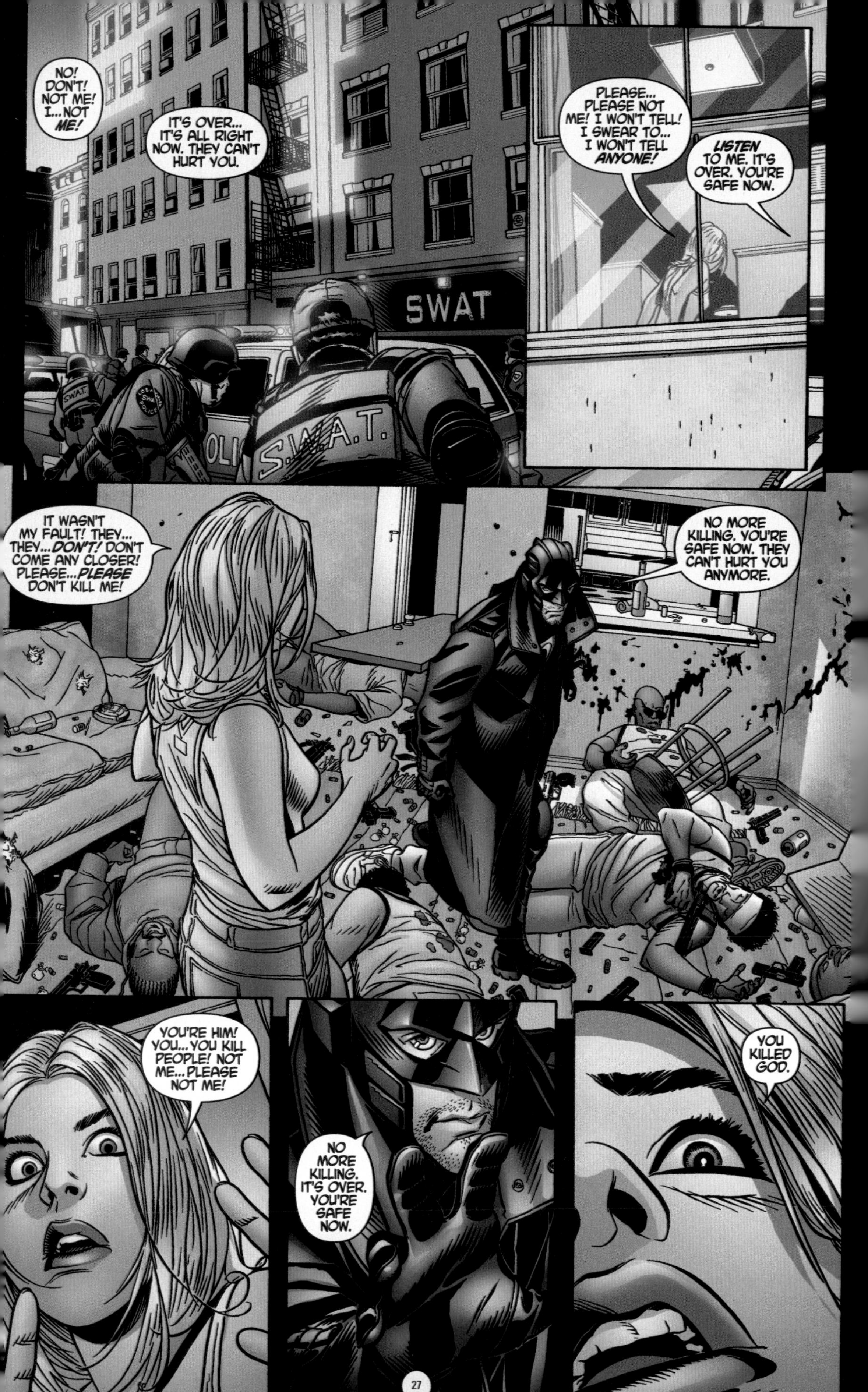

NO! DON'T! NOT ME! I...NOT *ME!*
IT'S OVER... IT'S ALL RIGHT NOW. THEY CAN'T HURT YOU.
SWAT
S.W.A.T.
S.W.A.T.
PLEASE... PLEASE NOT ME! I WON'T TELL! I SWEAR TO... I WON'T TELL *ANYONE!*
LISTEN TO ME. IT'S OVER. YOU'RE SAFE NOW.
IT WASN'T MY FAULT! THEY... THEY...*DON'T!* DON'T COME ANY CLOSER! PLEASE...*PLEASE* DON'T KILL ME!
NO MORE KILLING. YOU'RE SAFE NOW. THEY CAN'T HURT YOU ANYMORE.
YOU'RE HIM! YOU...YOU KILL PEOPLE! NOT ME...PLEASE NOT ME!
NO MORE KILLING. IT'S OVER. YOU'RE SAFE NOW.
YOU KILLED GOD.

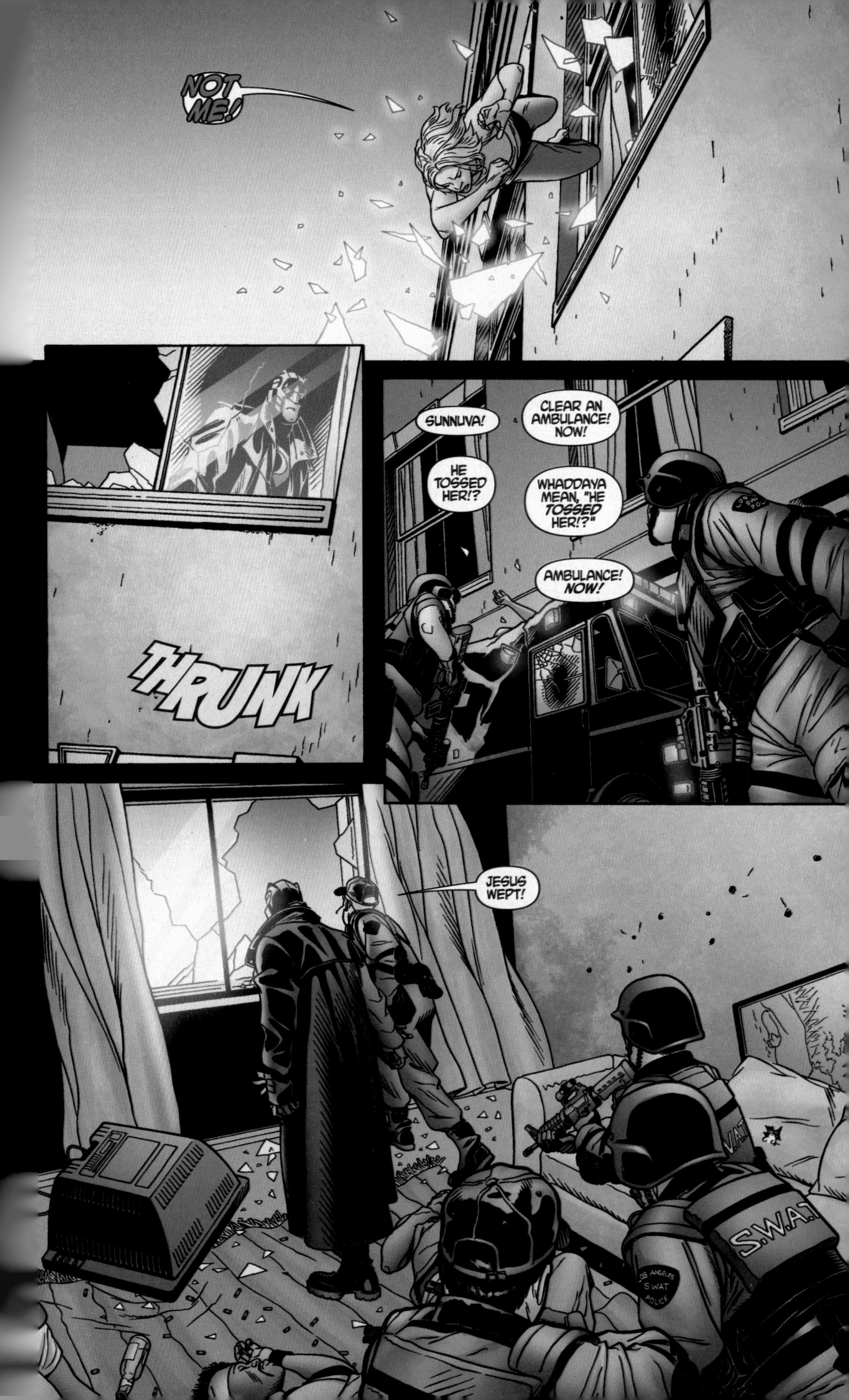
NOT ME!
THRUNK
SUNNUVA!
HE TOSSED HER!?
CLEAR AN AMBULANCE! NOW!
WHADDAYA MEAN, "HE TOSSED HER!?"
AMBULANCE! NOW!
JESUS WEPT!
S.W.A.T.
LOS ANGELES S.W.A.T. POLICE

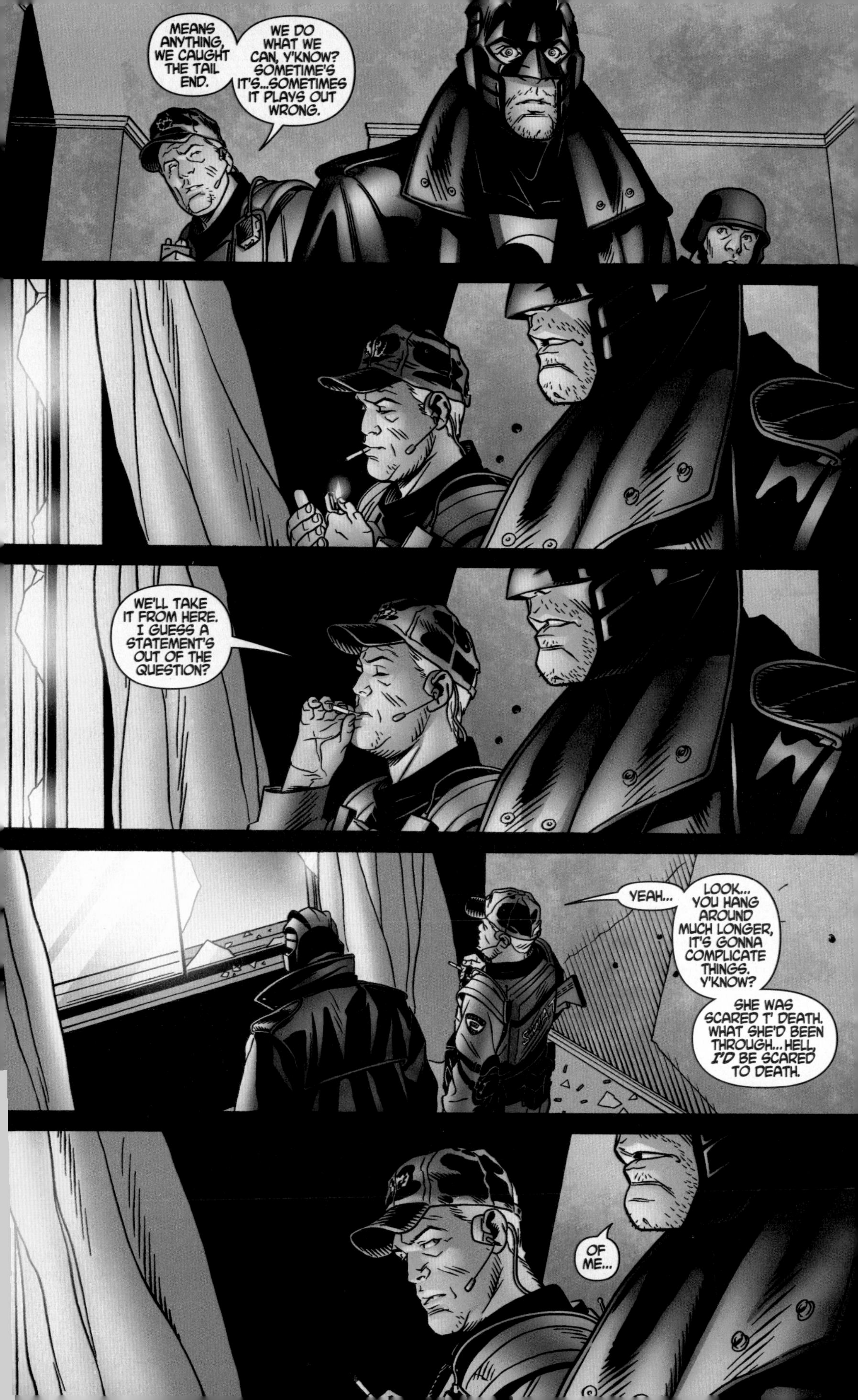
MEANS ANYTHING, WE CAUGHT THE TAIL END.
WE DO WHAT WE CAN, Y'KNOW? SOMETIME'S IT'S...SOMETIMES IT PLAYS OUT WRONG.
WE'LL TAKE IT FROM HERE. I GUESS A STATEMENT'S OUT OF THE QUESTION?
YEAH...
LOOK... YOU HANG AROUND MUCH LONGER, IT'S GONNA COMPLICATE THINGS. Y'KNOW?
SHE WAS SCARED T' DEATH. WHAT SHE'D BEEN THROUGH... HELL, I'D BE SCARED TO DEATH.
OF ME...

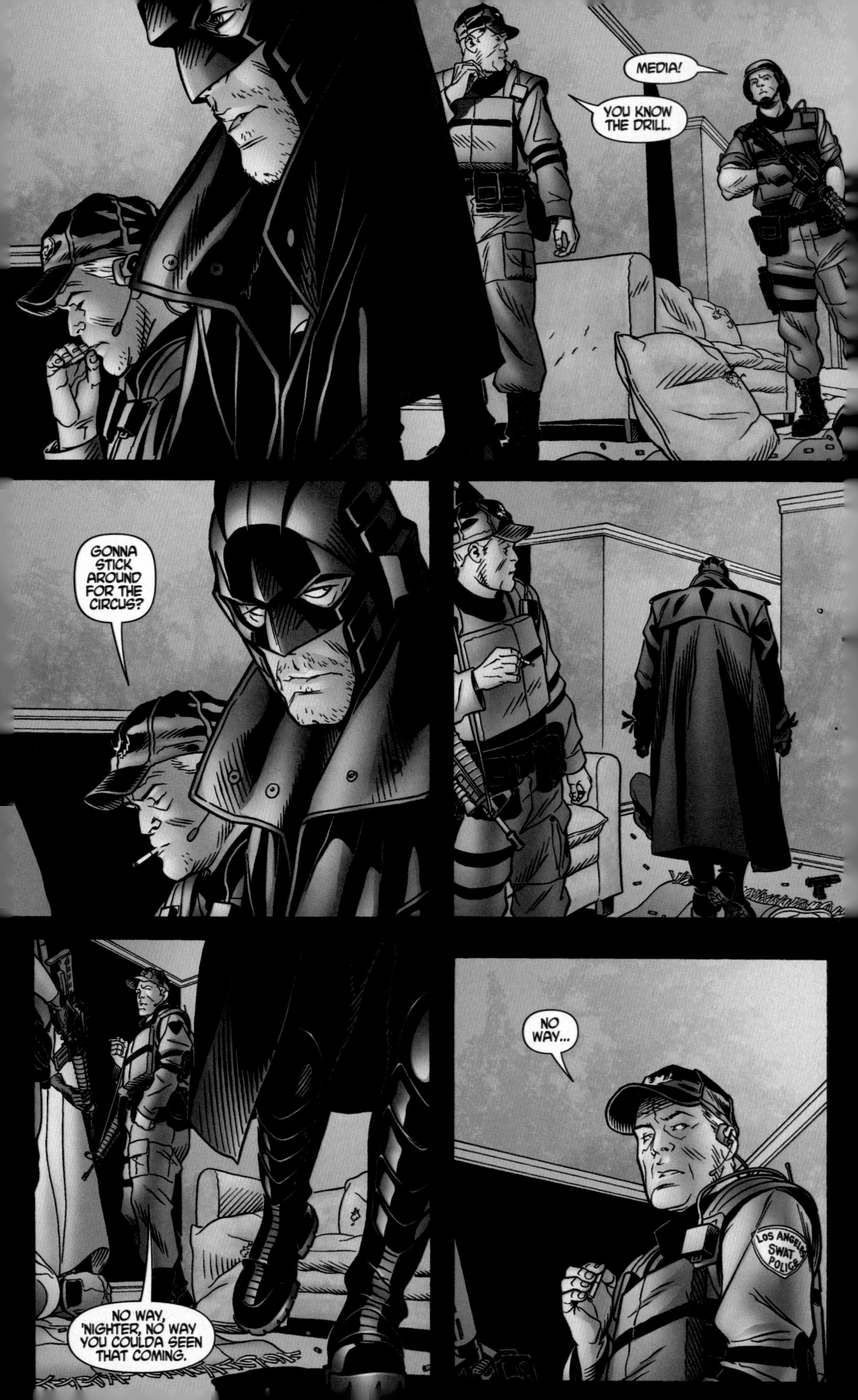
MEDIA!
YOU KNOW THE DRILL.
GONNA STICK AROUND FOR THE CIRCUS?
NO WAY, 'NIGHTER, NO WAY YOU COULDA SEEN THAT COMING.
NO WAY...
LOS ANGELES SWAT POLICE

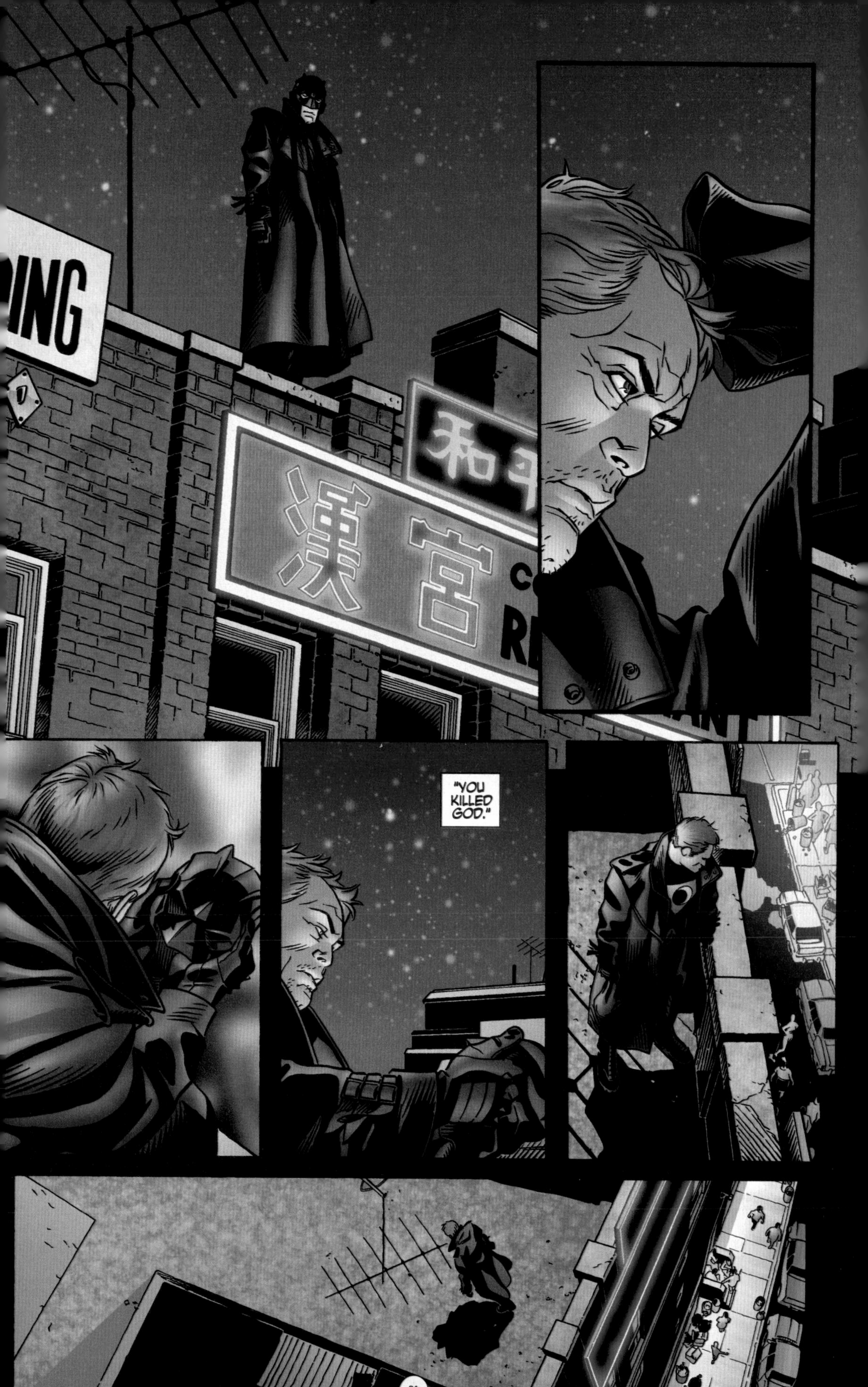
漢宮
"YOU KILLED GOD."

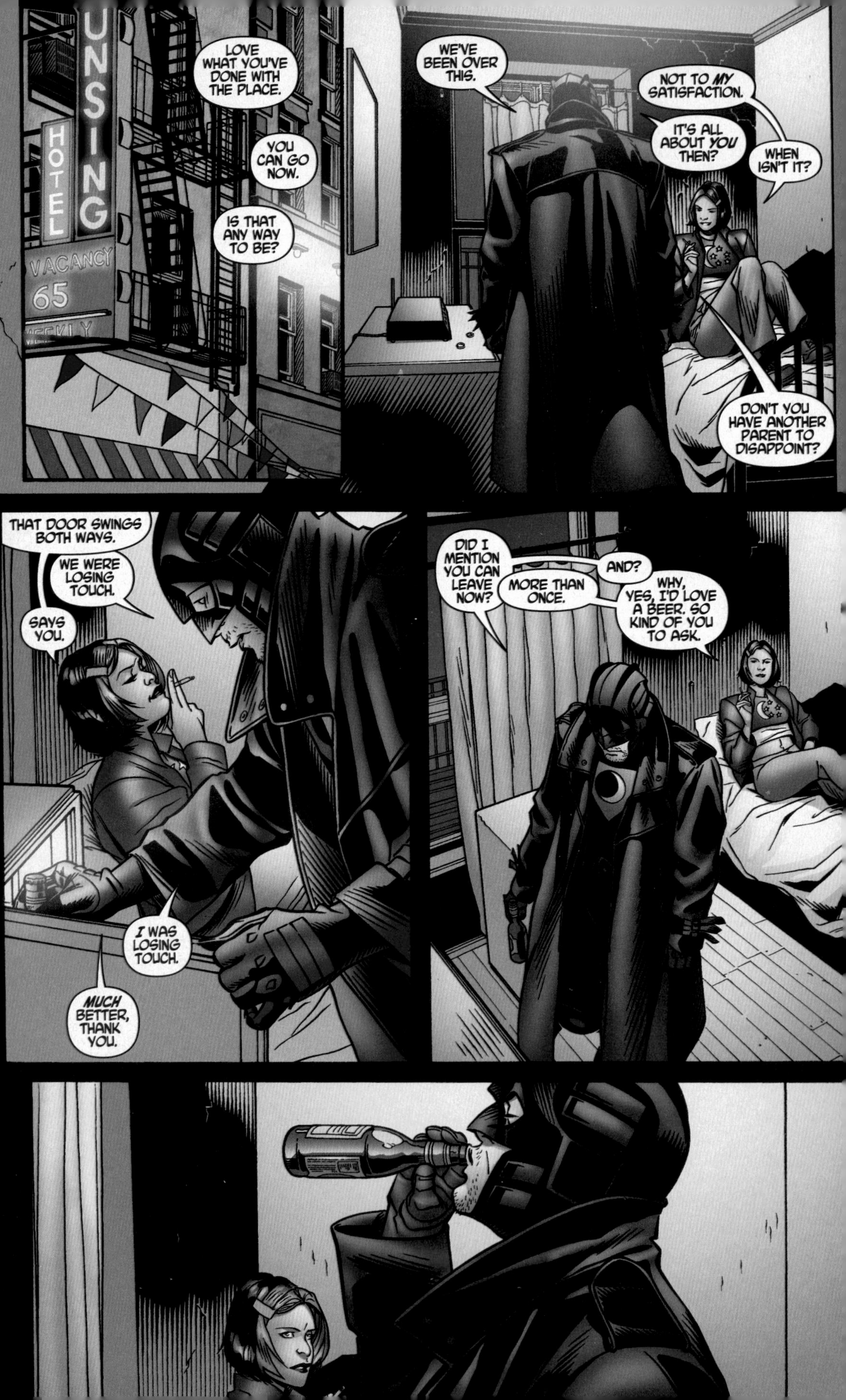
UNSING
HOTEL
VACANCY
65
LOVE WHAT YOU'VE DONE WITH THE PLACE.
YOU CAN GO NOW.
IS THAT ANY WAY TO BE?
WE'VE BEEN OVER THIS.
NOT TO MY SATISFACTION.
IT'S ALL ABOUT YOU THEN?
WHEN ISN'T IT?
DON'T YOU HAVE ANOTHER PARENT TO DISAPPOINT?
THAT DOOR SWINGS BOTH WAYS.
WE WERE LOSING TOUCH.
SAYS YOU.
I WAS LOSING TOUCH.
MUCH BETTER, THANK YOU.
DID I MENTION YOU CAN LEAVE NOW?
MORE THAN ONCE.
AND?
WHY, YES, I'D LOVE A BEER. SO KIND OF YOU TO ASK.

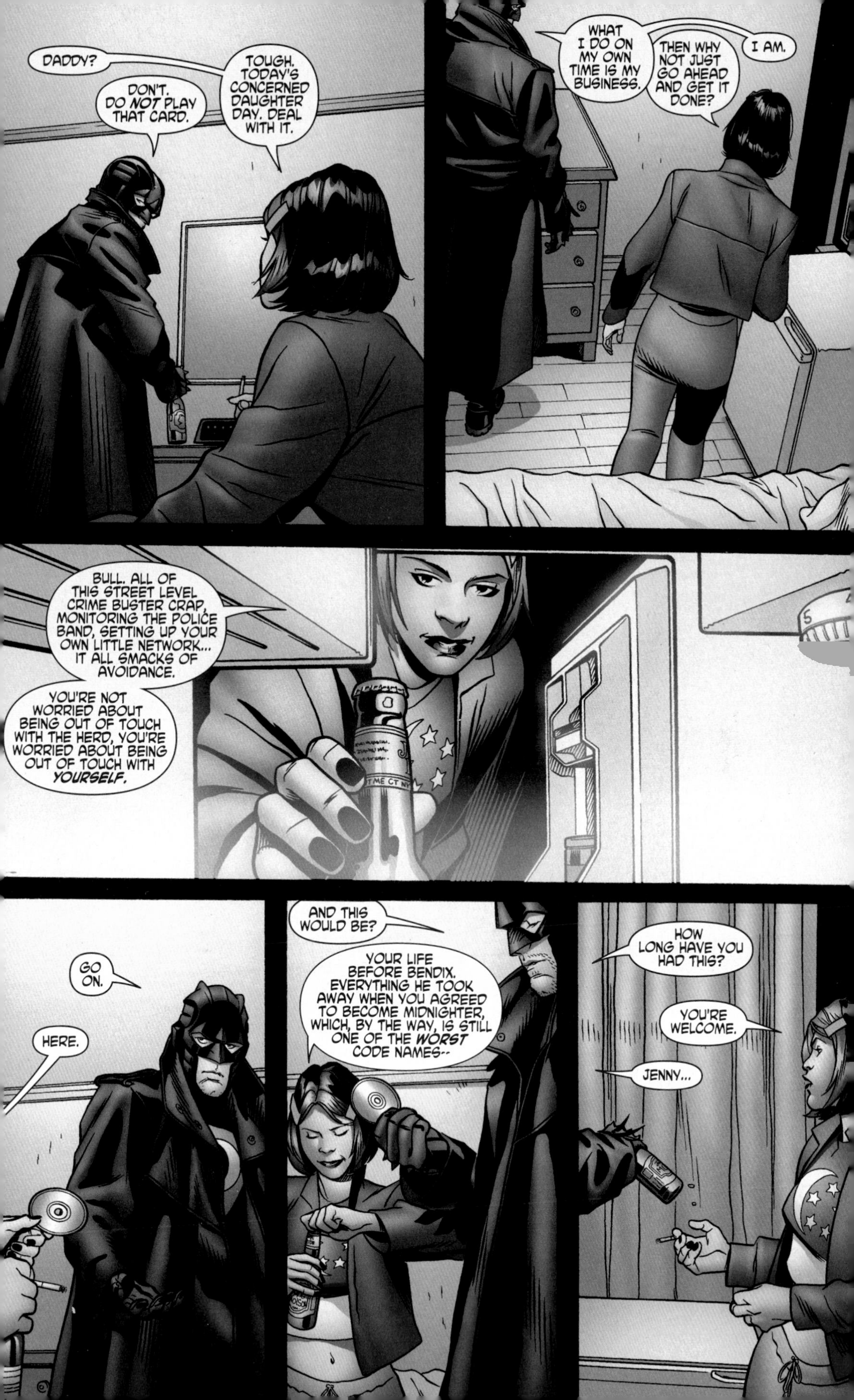
DADDY?
DON'T. DO NOT PLAY THAT CARD.
TOUGH. TODAY'S CONCERNED DAUGHTER DAY. DEAL WITH IT.
WHAT I DO ON MY OWN TIME IS MY BUSINESS.
I AM.
THEN WHY NOT JUST GO AHEAD AND GET IT DONE?
BULL. ALL OF THIS STREET LEVEL CRIME BUSTER CRAP, MONITORING THE POLICE BAND, SETTING UP YOUR OWN LITTLE NETWORK... IT ALL SMACKS OF AVOIDANCE.
YOU'RE NOT WORRIED ABOUT BEING OUT OF TOUCH WITH THE HERD, YOU'RE WORRIED ABOUT BEING OUT OF TOUCH WITH YOURSELF.
GO ON.
HERE.
AND THIS WOULD BE?
YOUR LIFE BEFORE BENDIX. EVERYTHING HE TOOK AWAY WHEN YOU AGREED TO BECOME MIDNIGHTER, WHICH, BY THE WAY, IS STILL ONE OF THE WORST CODE NAMES--
HOW LONG HAVE YOU HAD THIS?
YOU'RE WELCOME.
JENNY...

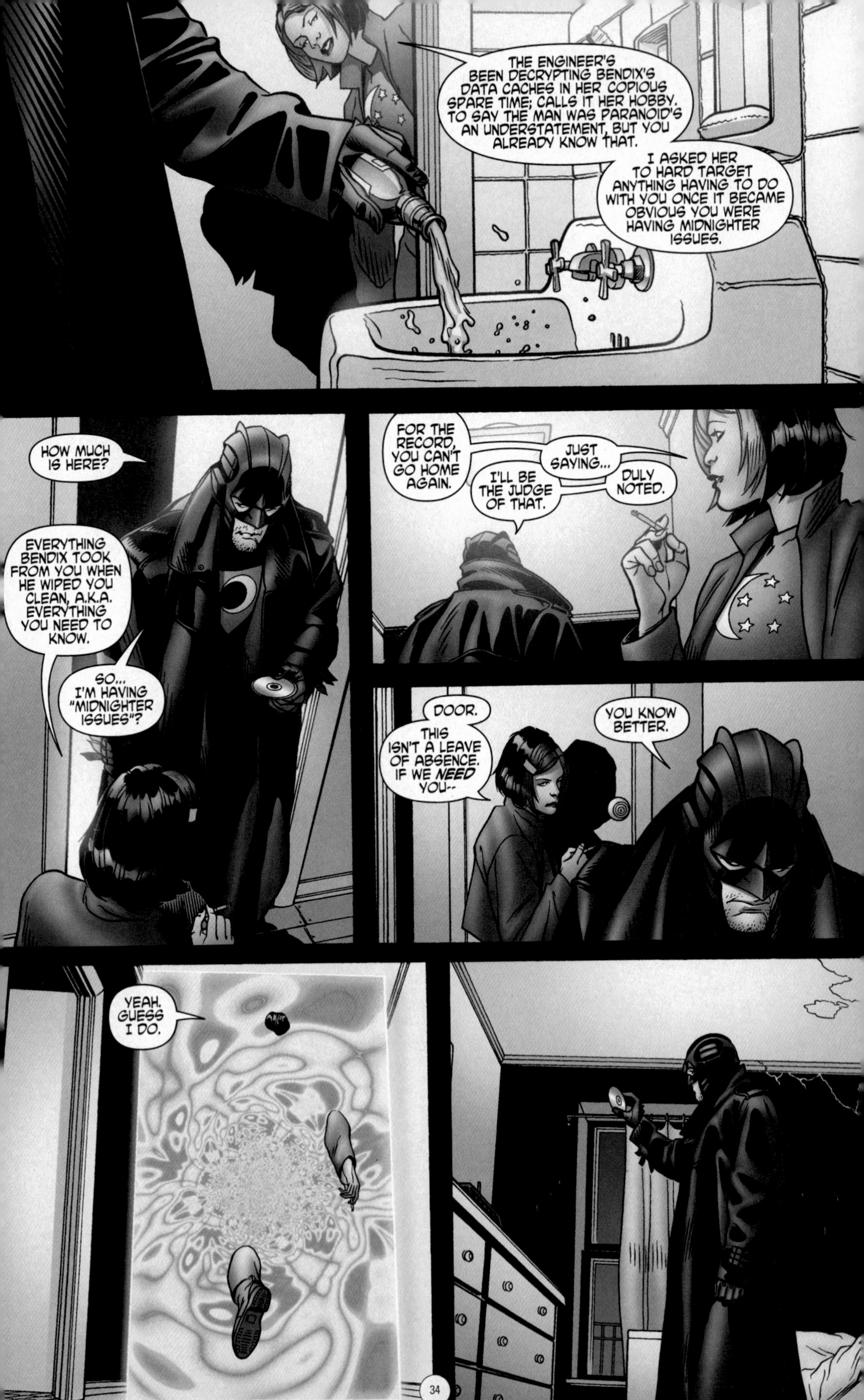
THE ENGINEER'S BEEN DECRYPTING BENDIX'S DATA CACHES IN HER COPIOUS SPARE TIME; CALLS IT HER HOBBY. TO SAY THE MAN WAS PARANOID'S AN UNDERSTATEMENT, BUT YOU ALREADY KNOW THAT.
I ASKED HER TO HARD TARGET ANYTHING HAVING TO DO WITH YOU ONCE IT BECAME OBVIOUS YOU WERE HAVING MIDNIGHTER ISSUES.
HOW MUCH IS HERE?
EVERYTHING BENDIX TOOK FROM YOU WHEN HE WIPED YOU CLEAN, A.K.A. EVERYTHING YOU NEED TO KNOW.
SO... I'M HAVING "MIDNIGHTER ISSUES"?
FOR THE RECORD, YOU CAN'T GO HOME AGAIN.
I'LL BE THE JUDGE OF THAT.
JUST SAYING...
DULY NOTED.
DOOR.
THIS ISN'T A LEAVE OF ABSENCE. IF WE *NEED* YOU--
YOU KNOW BETTER.
YEAH. GUESS I DO.

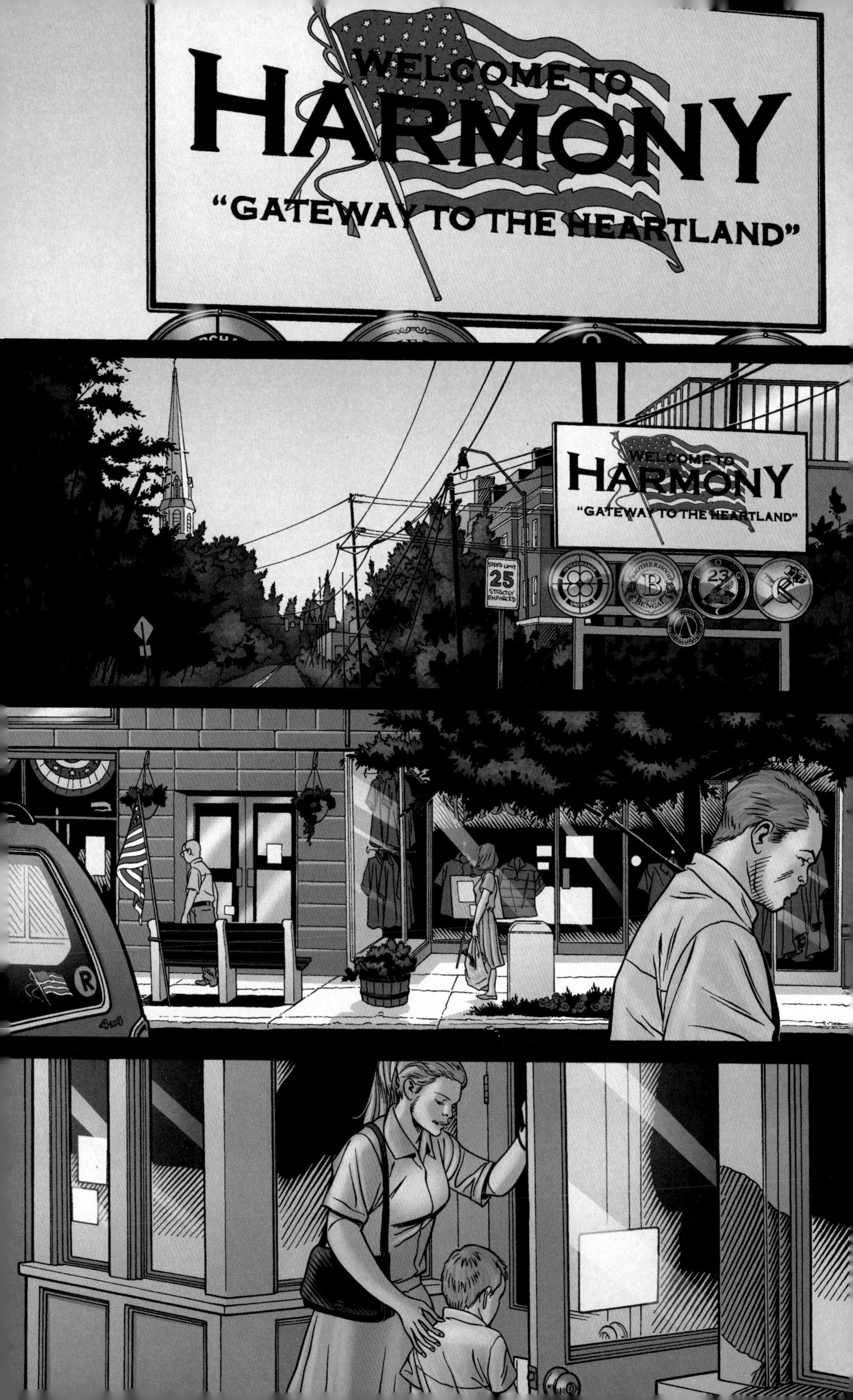
WELCOME TO
HARMONY
"GATEWAY TO THE HEARTLAND"
SPEED LIMIT
25
STRICTLY ENFORCED
WELCOME TO
HARMONY
"GATEWAY TO THE HEARTLAND"
INTERCHANGE
UNITED
BROTHERHOOD
BENGAL
23
R
4x4

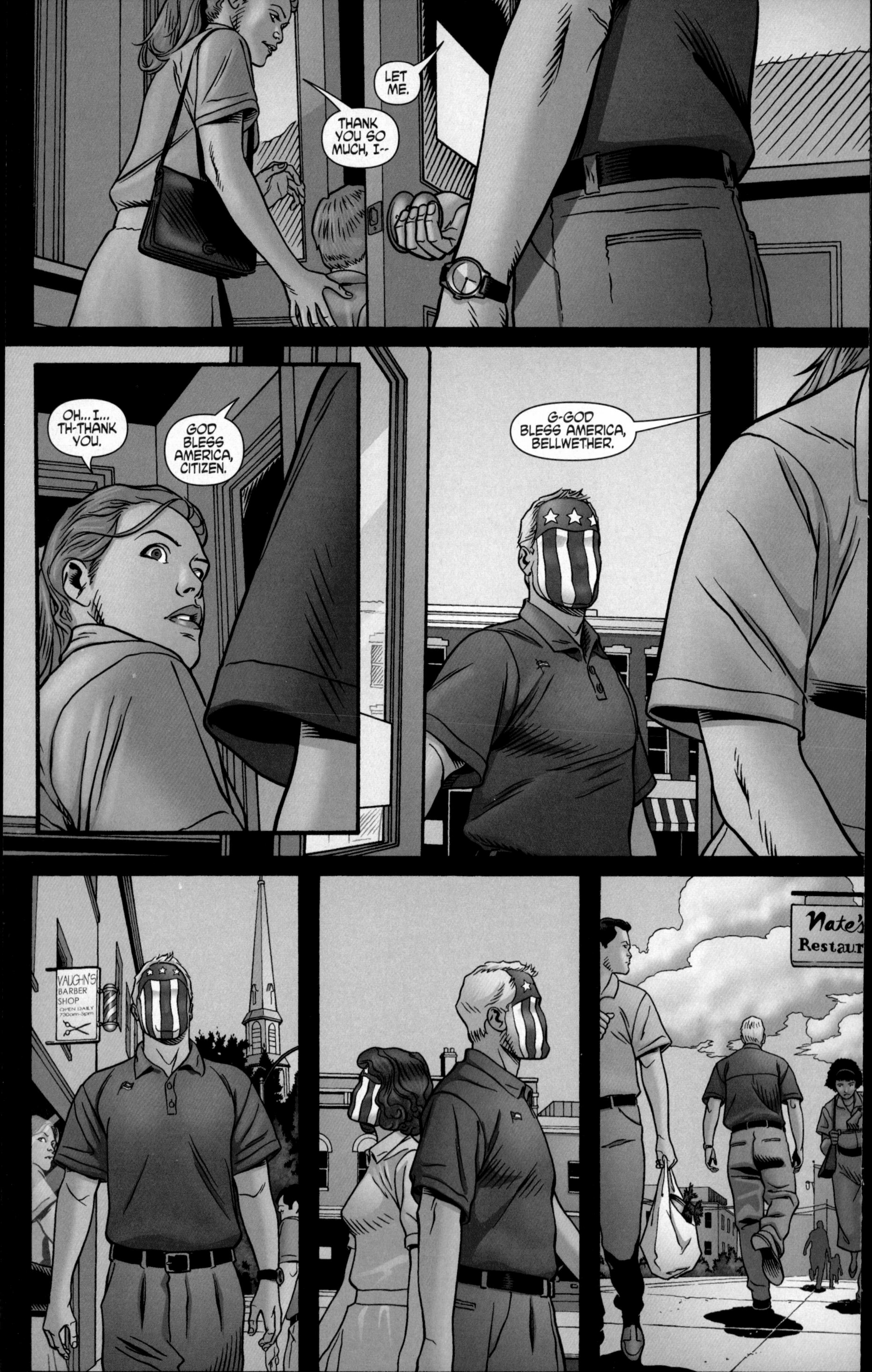

LET ME.
THANK YOU SO MUCH, I--
OH... I... TH-THANK YOU.
GOD BLESS AMERICA, CITIZEN.
G-GOD BLESS AMERICA, BELLWETHER.
VAUGHN'S BARBER SHOP OPEN DAILY 730am-5pm
Nate's Restaur

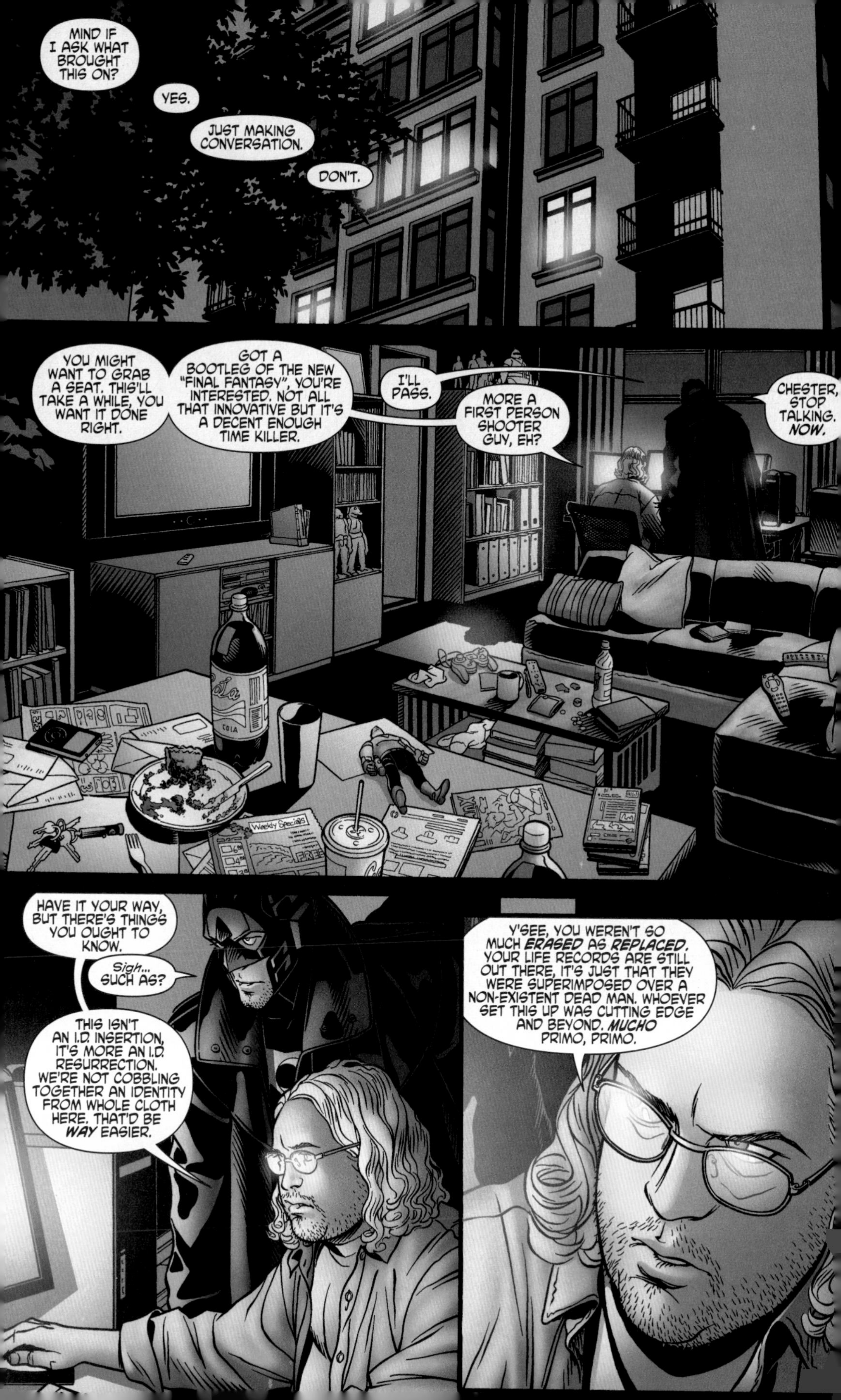
MIND IF I ASK WHAT BROUGHT THIS ON?
YES.
JUST MAKING CONVERSATION.
DON'T.
YOU MIGHT WANT TO GRAB A SEAT. THIS'LL TAKE A WHILE, YOU WANT IT DONE RIGHT.
GOT A BOOTLEG OF THE NEW "FINAL FANTASY", YOU'RE INTERESTED. NOT ALL THAT INNOVATIVE BUT IT'S A DECENT ENOUGH TIME KILLER.
I'LL PASS.
MORE A FIRST PERSON SHOOTER GUY, EH?
CHESTER, STOP TALKING. NOW.
HAVE IT YOUR WAY, BUT THERE'S THINGS YOU OUGHT TO KNOW.
Sigh... SUCH AS?
THIS ISN'T AN I.D. INSERTION, IT'S MORE AN I.D. RESURRECTION. WE'RE NOT COBBLING TOGETHER AN IDENTITY FROM WHOLE CLOTH HERE. THAT'D BE WAY EASIER.
Y'SEE, YOU WEREN'T SO MUCH ERASED AS REPLACED. YOUR LIFE RECORDS ARE STILL OUT THERE, IT'S JUST THAT THEY WERE SUPERIMPOSED OVER A NON-EXISTENT DEAD MAN. WHOEVER SET THIS UP WAS CUTTING EDGE AND BEYOND. MUCHO PRIMO, PRIMO.

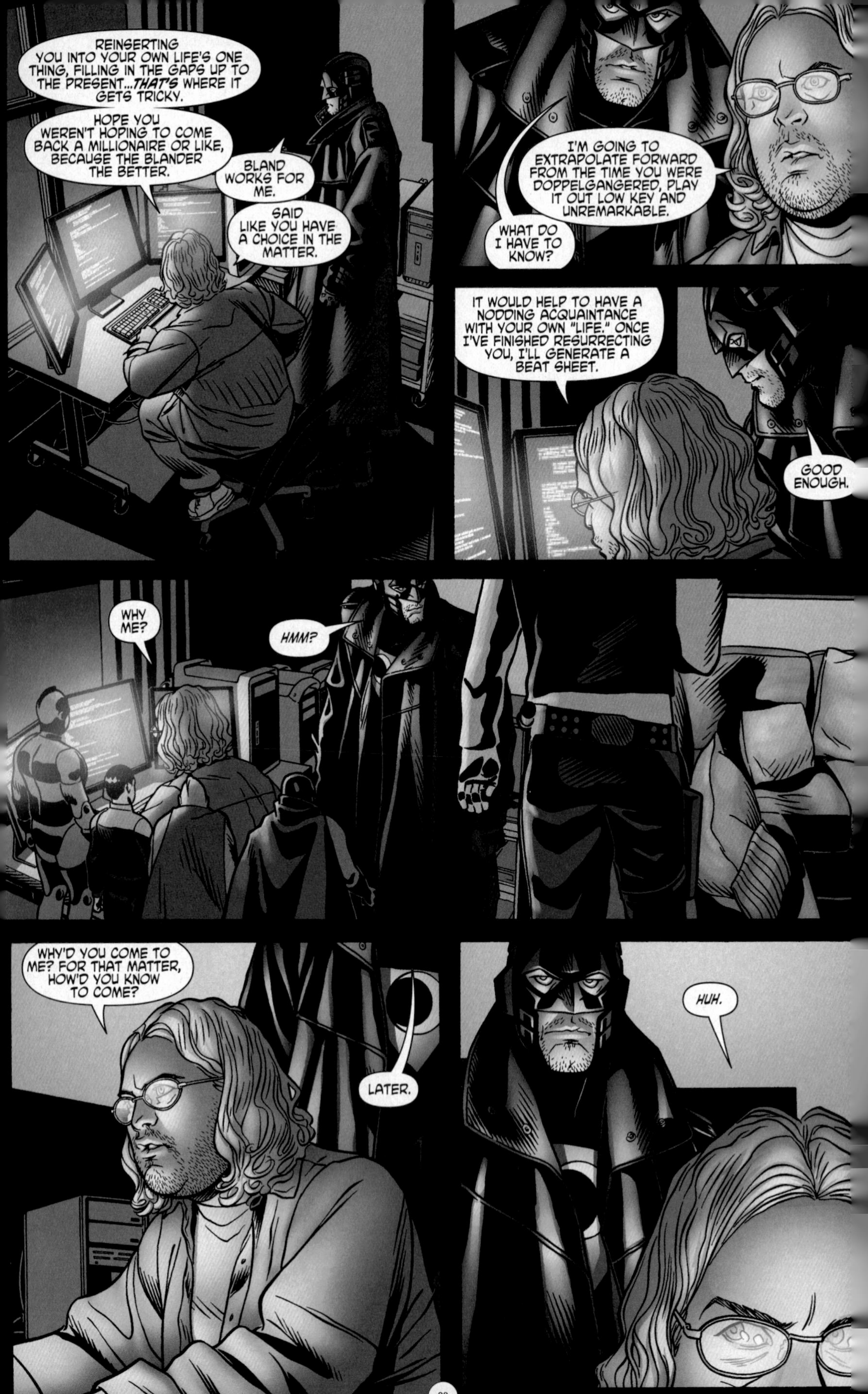
REINSERTING YOU INTO YOUR OWN LIFE'S ONE THING, FILLING IN THE GAPS UP TO THE PRESENT...THAT'S WHERE IT GETS TRICKY.
HOPE YOU WEREN'T HOPING TO COME BACK A MILLIONAIRE OR LIKE, BECAUSE THE BLANDER THE BETTER.
BLAND WORKS FOR ME.
SAID LIKE YOU HAVE A CHOICE IN THE MATTER.
I'M GOING TO EXTRAPOLATE FORWARD FROM THE TIME YOU WERE DOPPELGANGERED, PLAY IT OUT LOW KEY AND UNREMARKABLE.
WHAT DO I HAVE TO KNOW?
IT WOULD HELP TO HAVE A NODDING ACQUAINTANCE WITH YOUR OWN "LIFE." ONCE I'VE FINISHED RESURRECTING YOU, I'LL GENERATE A BEAT SHEET.
GOOD ENOUGH.
WHY ME?
HMM?
WHY'D YOU COME TO ME? FOR THAT MATTER, HOW'D YOU KNOW TO COME?
LATER.
HUH.

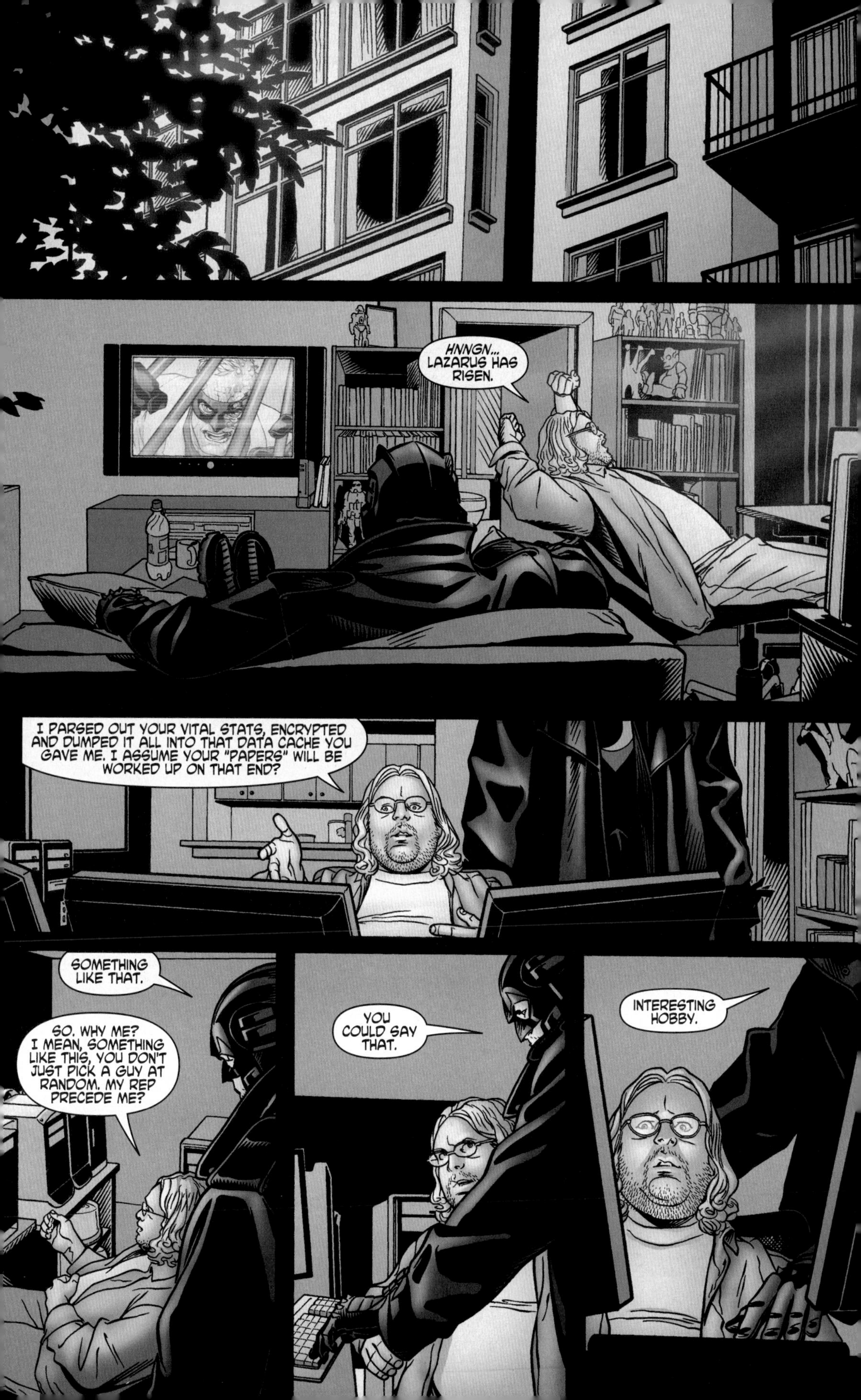
HNNGN... LAZARUS HAS RISEN.
I PARSED OUT YOUR VITAL STATS, ENCRYPTED AND DUMPED IT ALL INTO THAT DATA CACHE YOU GAVE ME. I ASSUME YOUR "PAPERS" WILL BE WORKED UP ON THAT END?
SOMETHING LIKE THAT.
SO. WHY ME? I MEAN, SOMETHING LIKE THIS, YOU DON'T JUST PICK A GUY AT RANDOM. MY REP PRECEDE ME?
YOU COULD SAY THAT.
INTERESTING HOBBY.

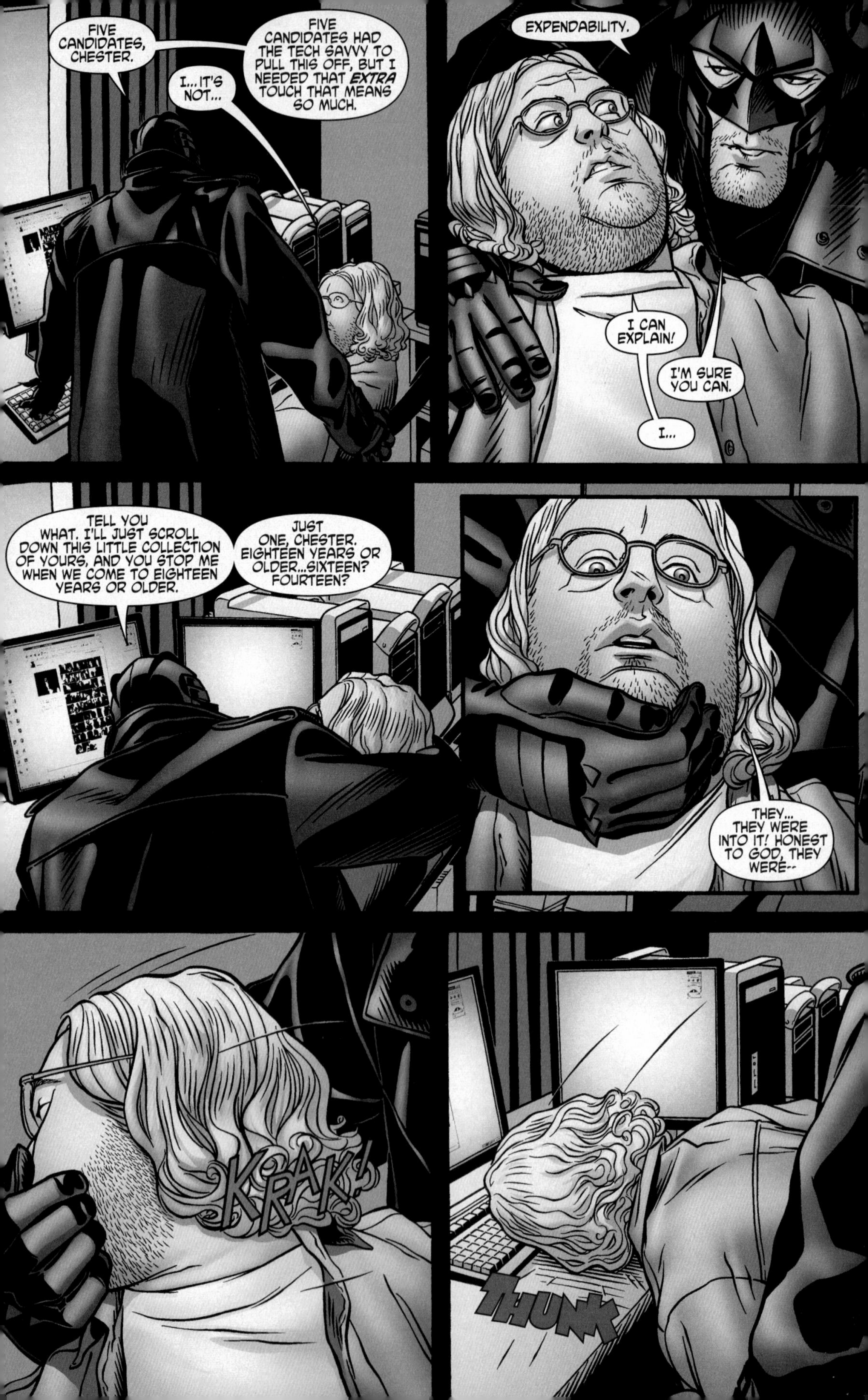
FIVE CANDIDATES, CHESTER.
FIVE CANDIDATES HAD THE TECH SAVVY TO PULL THIS OFF, BUT I NEEDED THAT EXTRA TOUCH THAT MEANS SO MUCH.
I...IT'S NOT...
EXPENDABILITY.
I CAN EXPLAIN!
I'M SURE YOU CAN.
I...
TELL YOU WHAT. I'LL JUST SCROLL DOWN THIS LITTLE COLLECTION OF YOURS, AND YOU STOP ME WHEN WE COME TO EIGHTEEN YEARS OR OLDER.
JUST ONE, CHESTER. EIGHTEEN YEARS OR OLDER...SIXTEEN? FOURTEEN?
THEY... THEY WERE INTO IT! HONEST TO GOD, THEY WERE--
KRAK!
THUNK

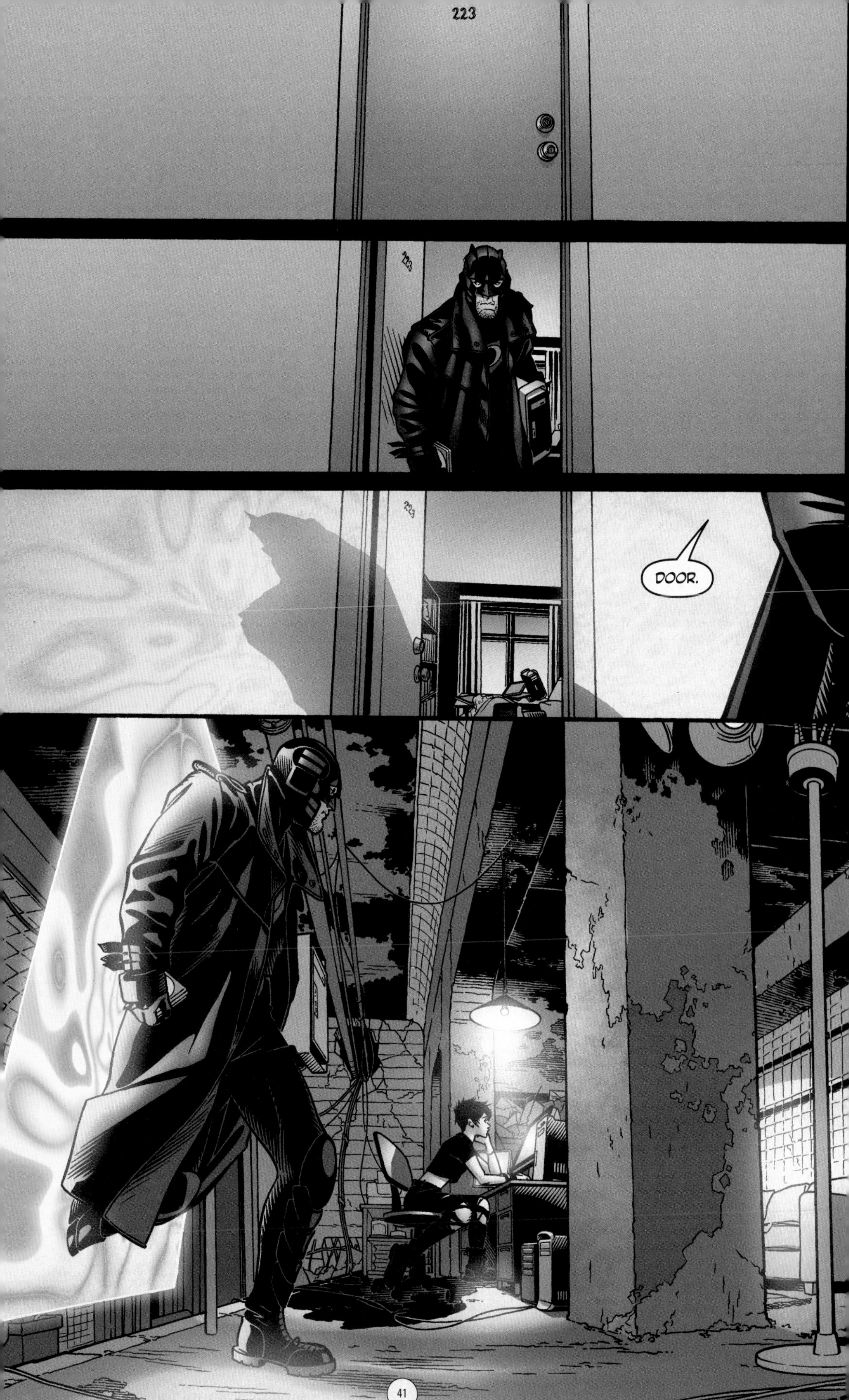
223
DOOR.

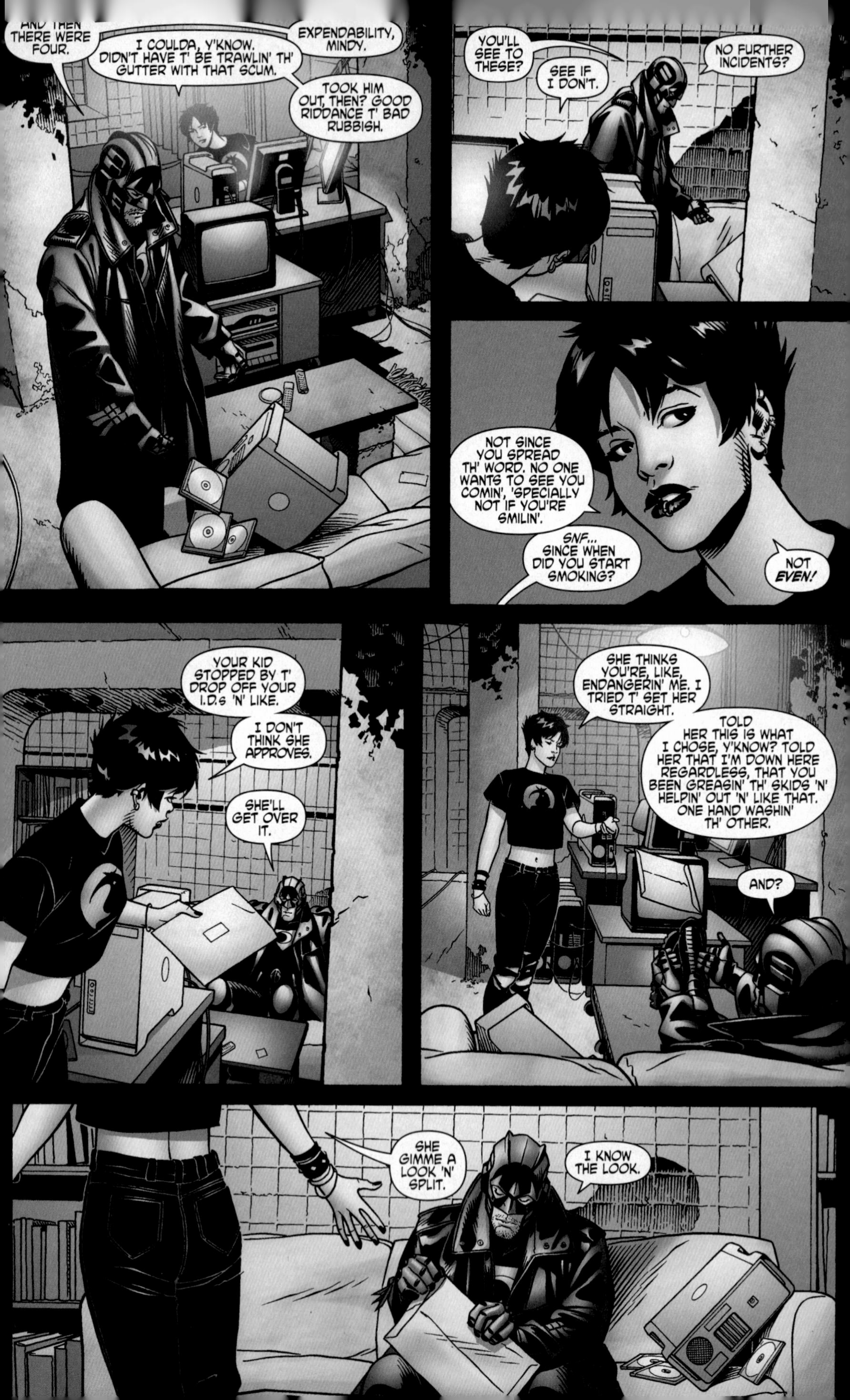
AND THEN THERE WERE FOUR.
I COULDA, Y'KNOW. DIDN'T HAVE T' BE TRAWLIN' TH' GUTTER WITH THAT SCUM.
EXPENDABILITY, MINDY.
TOOK HIM OUT, THEN? GOOD RIDDANCE T' BAD RUBBISH.
YOU'LL SEE TO THESE?
SEE IF I DON'T.
NO FURTHER INCIDENTS?
NOT SINCE YOU SPREAD TH' WORD. NO ONE WANTS TO SEE YOU COMIN', 'SPECIALLY NOT IF YOU'RE SMILIN'.
SNF... SINCE WHEN DID YOU START SMOKING?
NOT EVEN!
YOUR KID STOPPED BY T' DROP OFF YOUR I.D.s 'N' LIKE.
I DON'T THINK SHE APPROVES.
SHE'LL GET OVER IT.
SHE THINKS YOU'RE, LIKE, ENDANGERIN' ME. I TRIED T' SET HER STRAIGHT.
TOLD HER THIS IS WHAT I CHOSE, Y'KNOW? TOLD HER THAT I'M DOWN HERE REGARDLESS, THAT YOU BEEN GREASIN' TH' SKIDS 'N' HELPIN' OUT 'N' LIKE THAT. ONE HAND WASHIN' TH' OTHER.
AND?
SHE GIMME A LOOK 'N' SPLIT.
I KNOW THE LOOK.

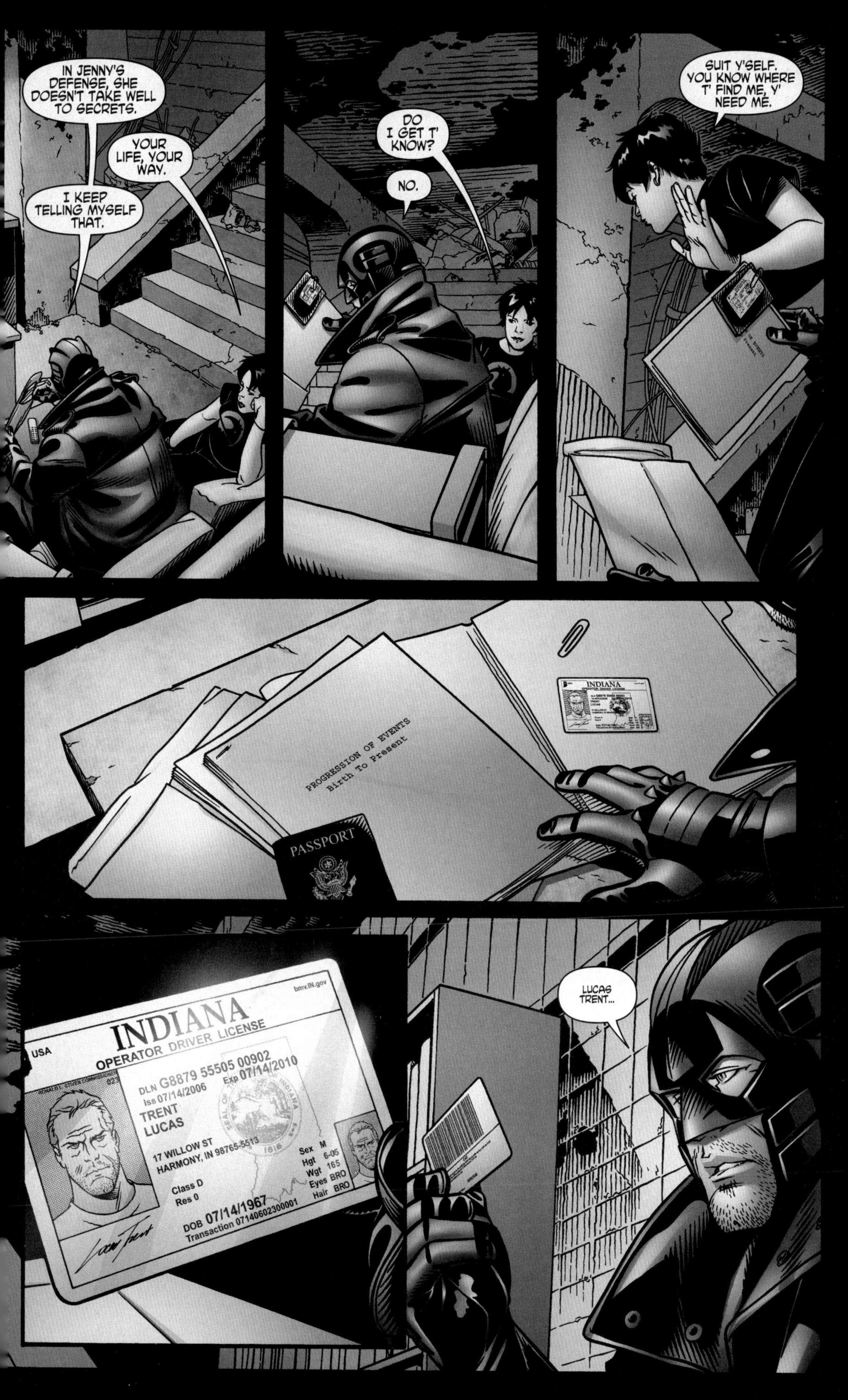
IN JENNY'S DEFENSE, SHE DOESN'T TAKE WELL TO SECRETS.
YOUR LIFE, YOUR WAY.
I KEEP TELLING MYSELF THAT.
DO I GET T' KNOW?
NO.
SUIT Y'SELF. YOU KNOW WHERE T' FIND ME, Y' NEED ME.
PROGRESSION OF EVENTS
Birth To Present
PASSPORT
bmv.IN.gov
INDIANA
OPERATOR DRIVER LICENSE
USA
DLN G8879 55505 00902
Iss 07/14/2006
Exp 07/14/2010
TRENT
LUCAS
17 WILLOW ST
HARMONY, IN 98765-5513
Sex M
Hgt 6-05
Wgt 165
Eyes BRO
Hair BRO
Class D
Res 0
DOB 07/14/1967
Transaction 07140602300001
LUCAS TRENT...

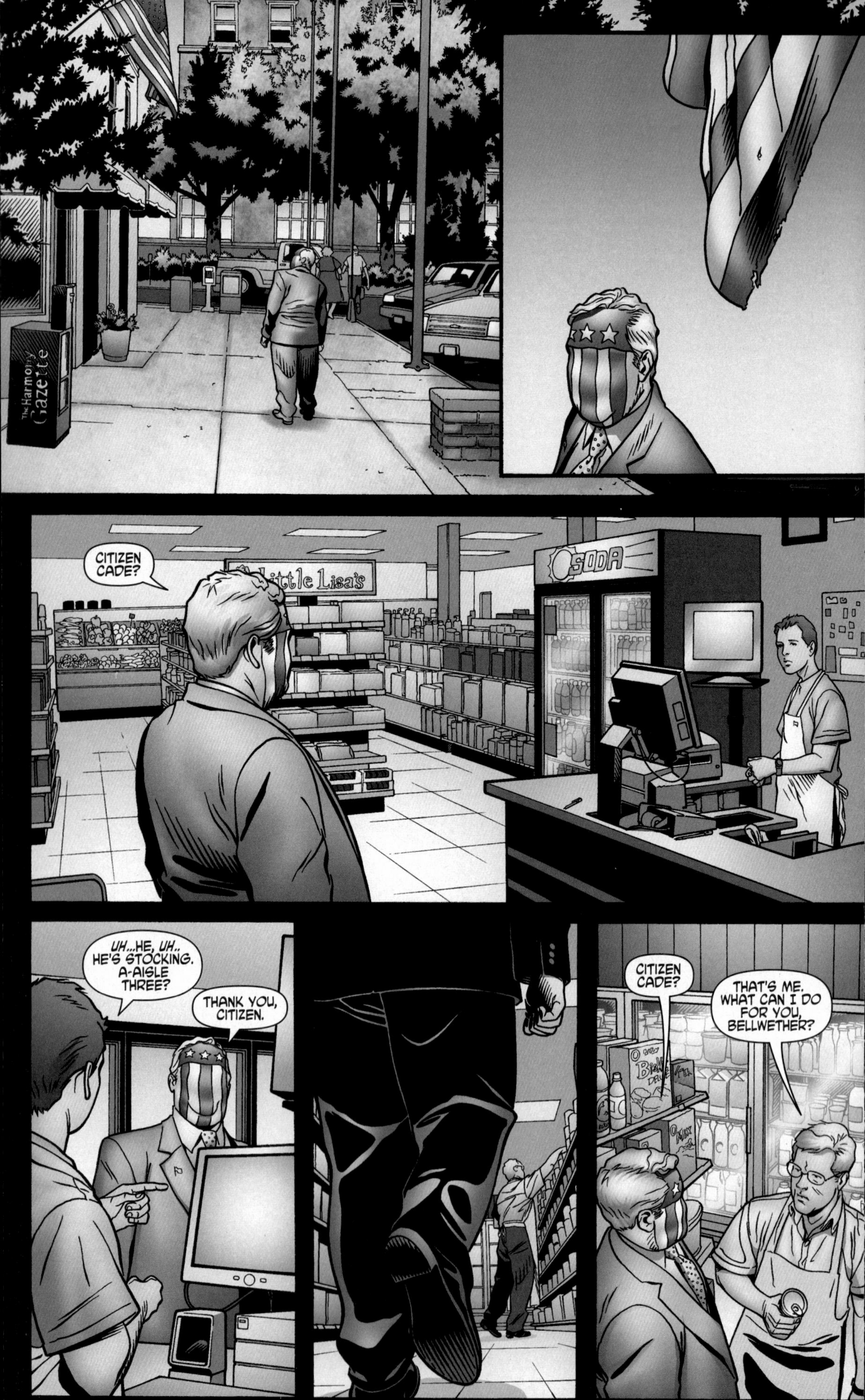
The Harmony Gazette
CITIZEN CADE?
Little Lisa's
SODA
UH...HE, UH.. HE'S STOCKING. A-AISLE THREE?
THANK YOU, CITIZEN.
CITIZEN CADE?
THAT'S ME. WHAT CAN I DO FOR YOU, BELLWETHER?

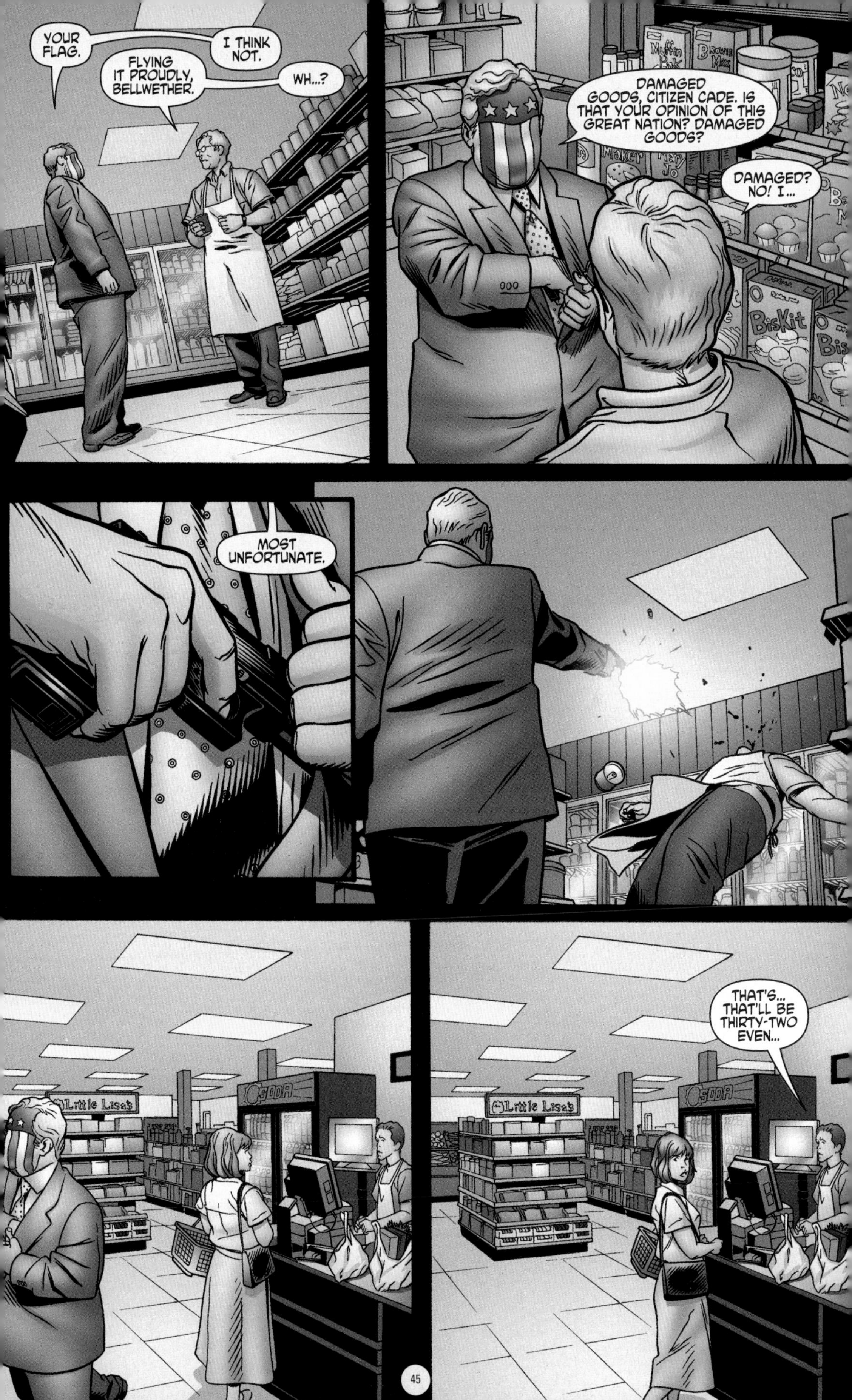

YOUR FLAG.
I THINK NOT.
FLYING IT PROUDLY, BELLWETHER.
WH...?
DAMAGED GOODS, CITIZEN CADE. IS THAT YOUR OPINION OF THIS GREAT NATION? DAMAGED GOODS?
DAMAGED? NO! I...
MOST UNFORTUNATE.
Little Lisa's
SODA
THAT'S... THAT'LL BE THIRTY-TWO EVEN...

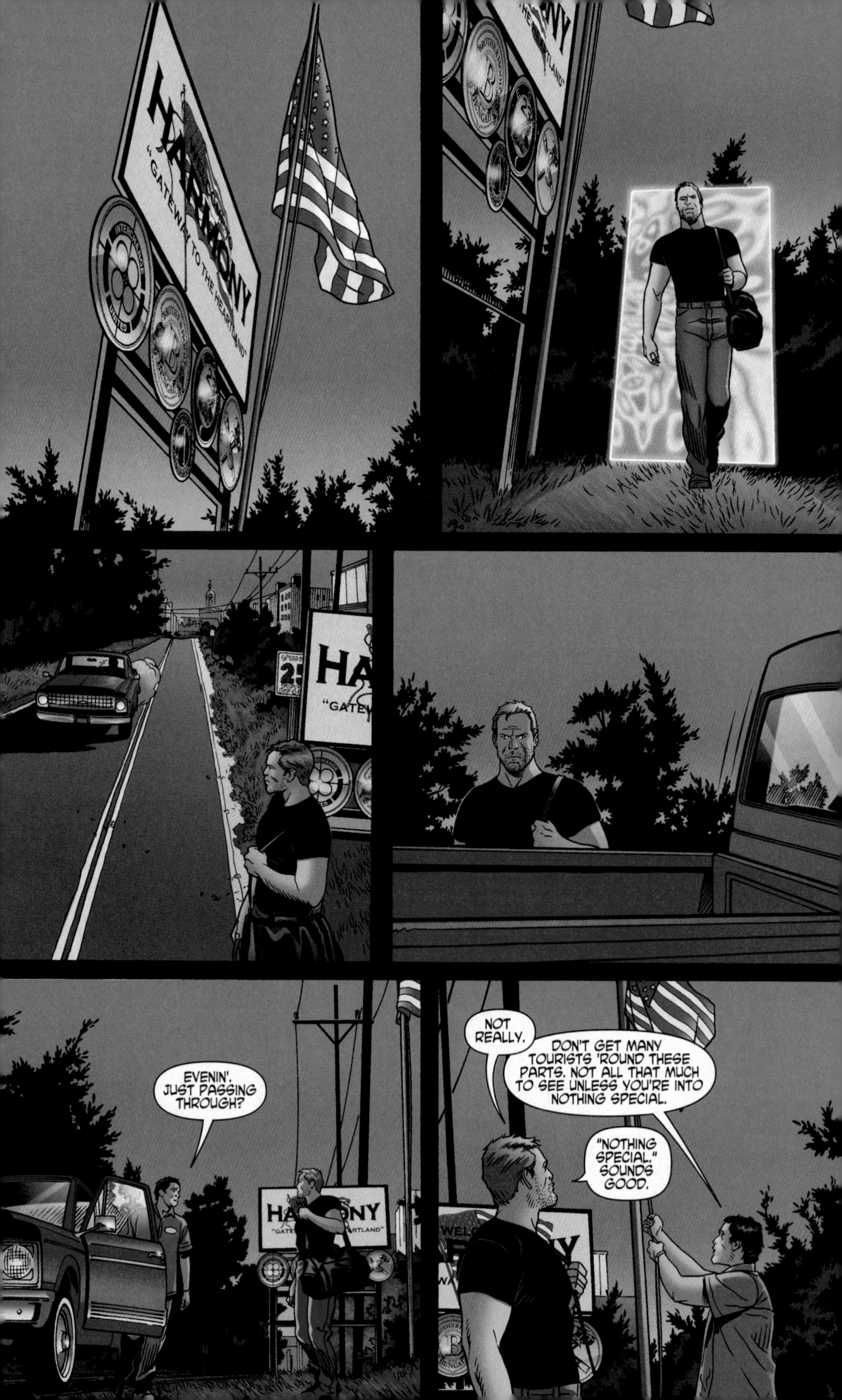
HARMONY
"GATEWAY TO THE HEARTLAND"
EVENIN'. JUST PASSING THROUGH?
NOT REALLY.
DON'T GET MANY TOURISTS 'ROUND THESE PARTS. NOT ALL THAT MUCH TO SEE UNLESS YOU'RE INTO NOTHING SPECIAL.
"NOTHING SPECIAL." SOUNDS GOOD.

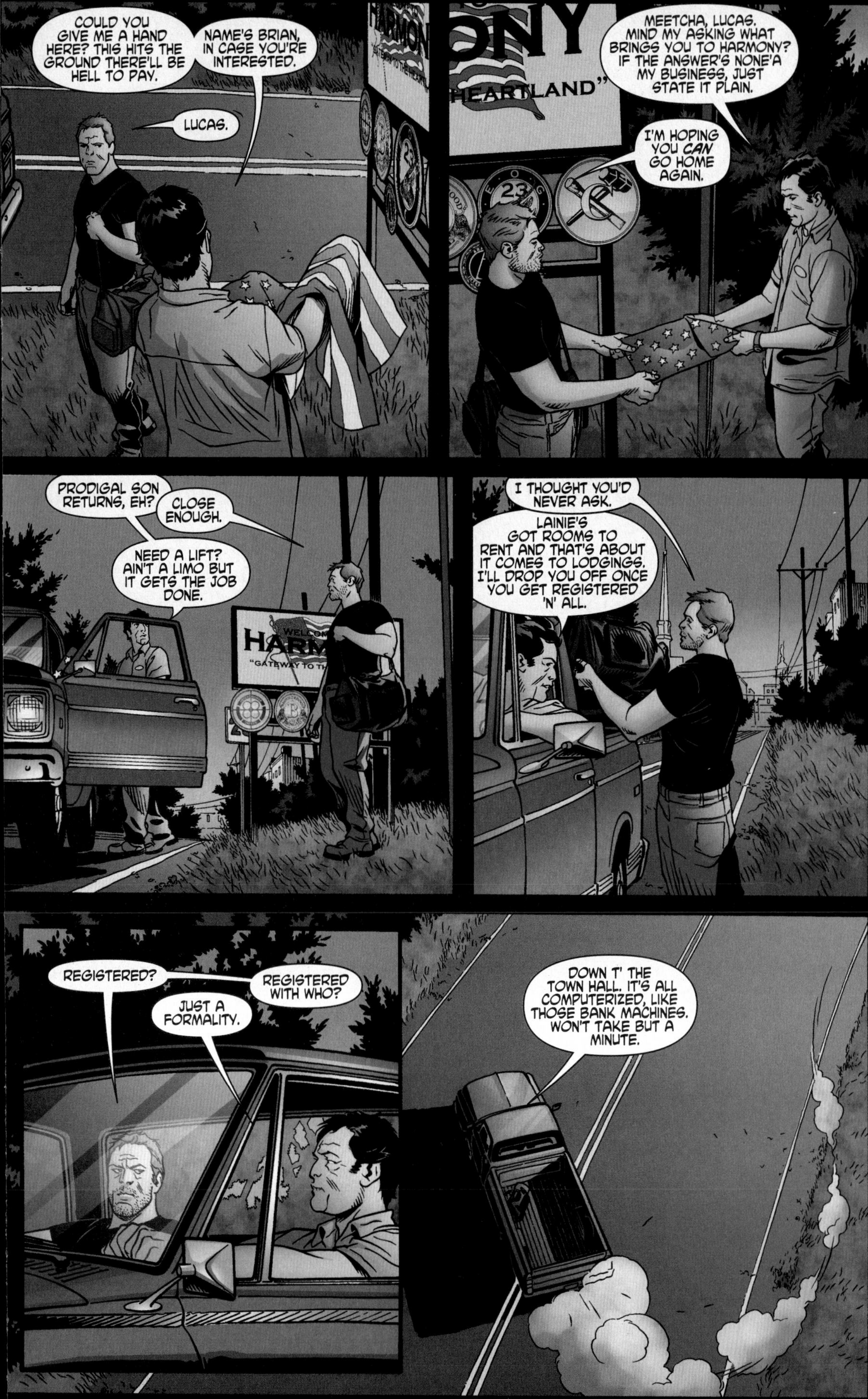
COULD YOU GIVE ME A HAND HERE? THIS HITS THE GROUND THERE'LL BE HELL TO PAY.
NAME'S BRIAN, IN CASE YOU'RE INTERESTED.
LUCAS.
MEETCHA, LUCAS. MIND MY ASKING WHAT BRINGS YOU TO HARMONY? IF THE ANSWER'S NONE'A MY BUSINESS, JUST STATE IT PLAIN.
I'M HOPING YOU CAN GO HOME AGAIN.
PRODIGAL SON RETURNS, EH?
CLOSE ENOUGH.
NEED A LIFT? AIN'T A LIMO BUT IT GETS THE JOB DONE.
I THOUGHT YOU'D NEVER ASK.
LAINIE'S GOT ROOMS TO RENT AND THAT'S ABOUT IT COMES TO LODGINGS. I'LL DROP YOU OFF ONCE YOU GET REGISTERED 'N' ALL.
REGISTERED?
REGISTERED WITH WHO?
JUST A FORMALITY.
DOWN T' THE TOWN HALL. IT'S ALL COMPUTERIZED, LIKE THOSE BANK MACHINES. WON'T TAKE BUT A MINUTE.

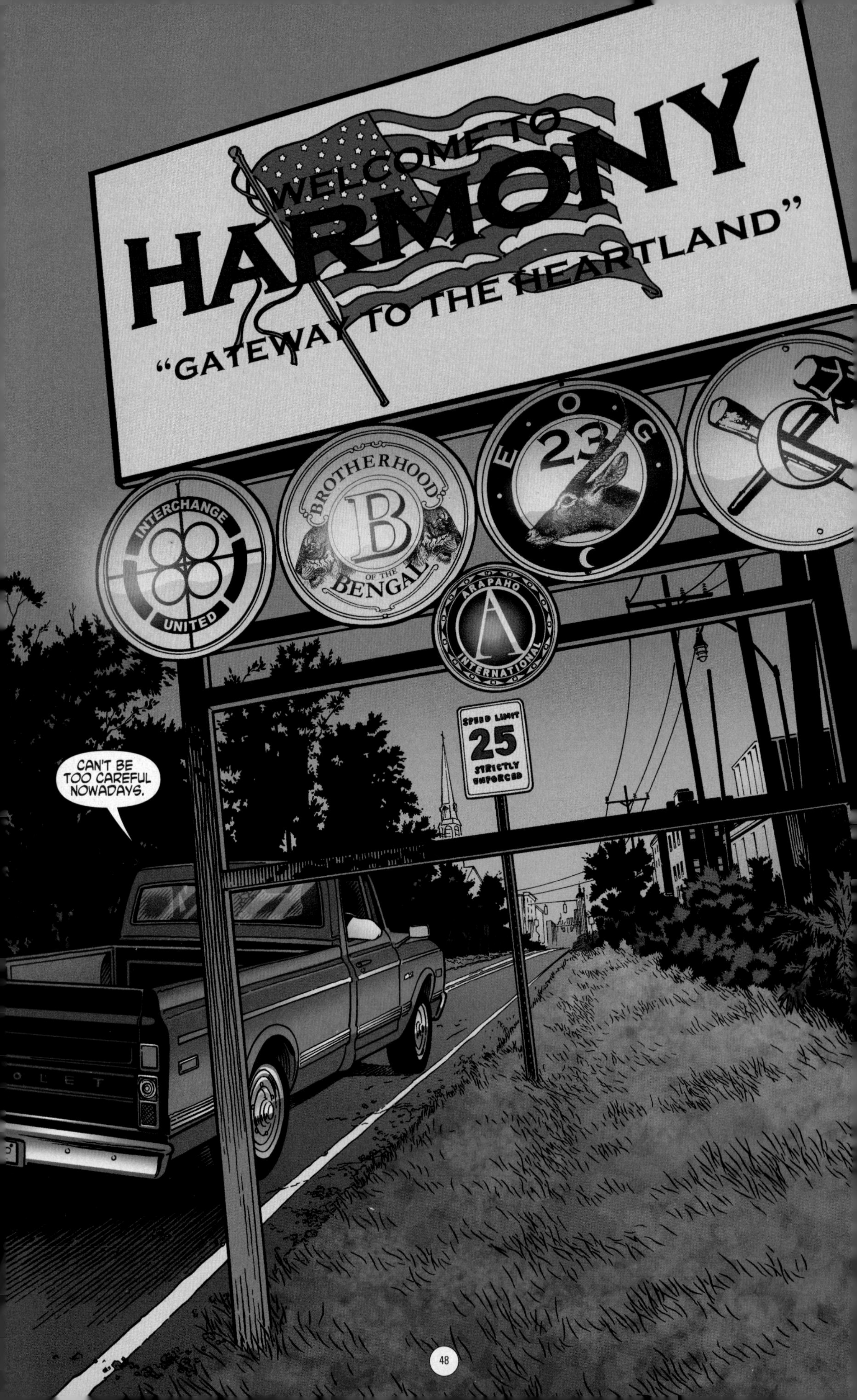
WELCOME TO
HARMONY
"GATEWAY TO THE HEARTLAND"
INTERCHANGE
UNITED
BROTHERHOOD
B
OF THE
BENGAL
E O G
23
ARAPAHO
A
INTERNATIONAL
SPEED LIMIT
25
STRICTLY
ENFORCED
CAN'T BE TOO CAREFUL NOWADAYS.

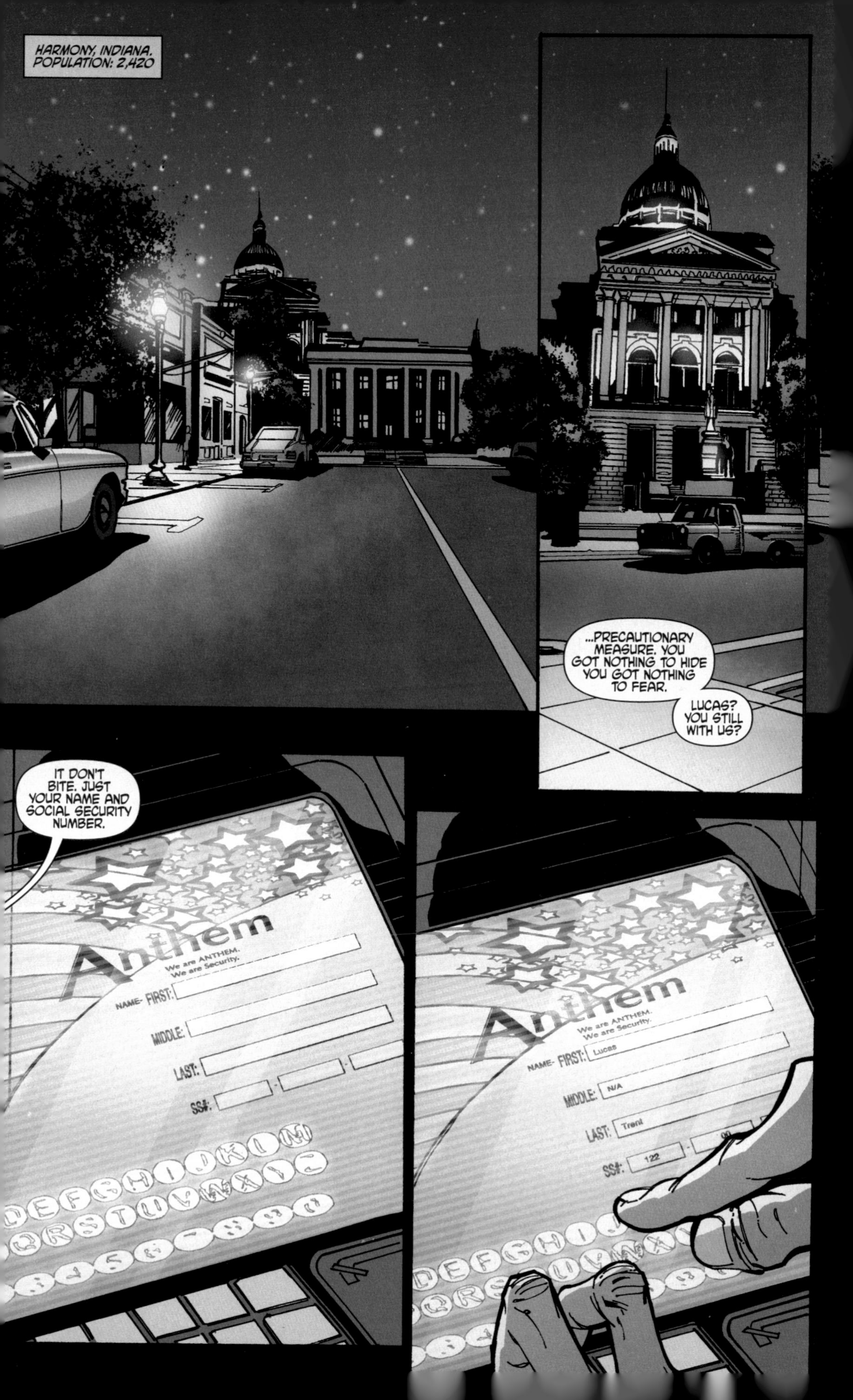
HARMONY, INDIANA. POPULATION: 2,420
...PRECAUTIONARY MEASURE. YOU GOT NOTHING TO HIDE YOU GOT NOTHING TO FEAR.
LUCAS? YOU STILL WITH US?
IT DON'T BITE. JUST YOUR NAME AND SOCIAL SECURITY NUMBER.
Anthem
We are ANTHEM. We are Security.
NAME- FIRST:
MIDDLE:
LAST:
SS#:
Anthem
We are ANTHEM. We are Security.
NAME- FIRST: Lucas
MIDDLE: N/A
LAST: Trent
SS#: 122

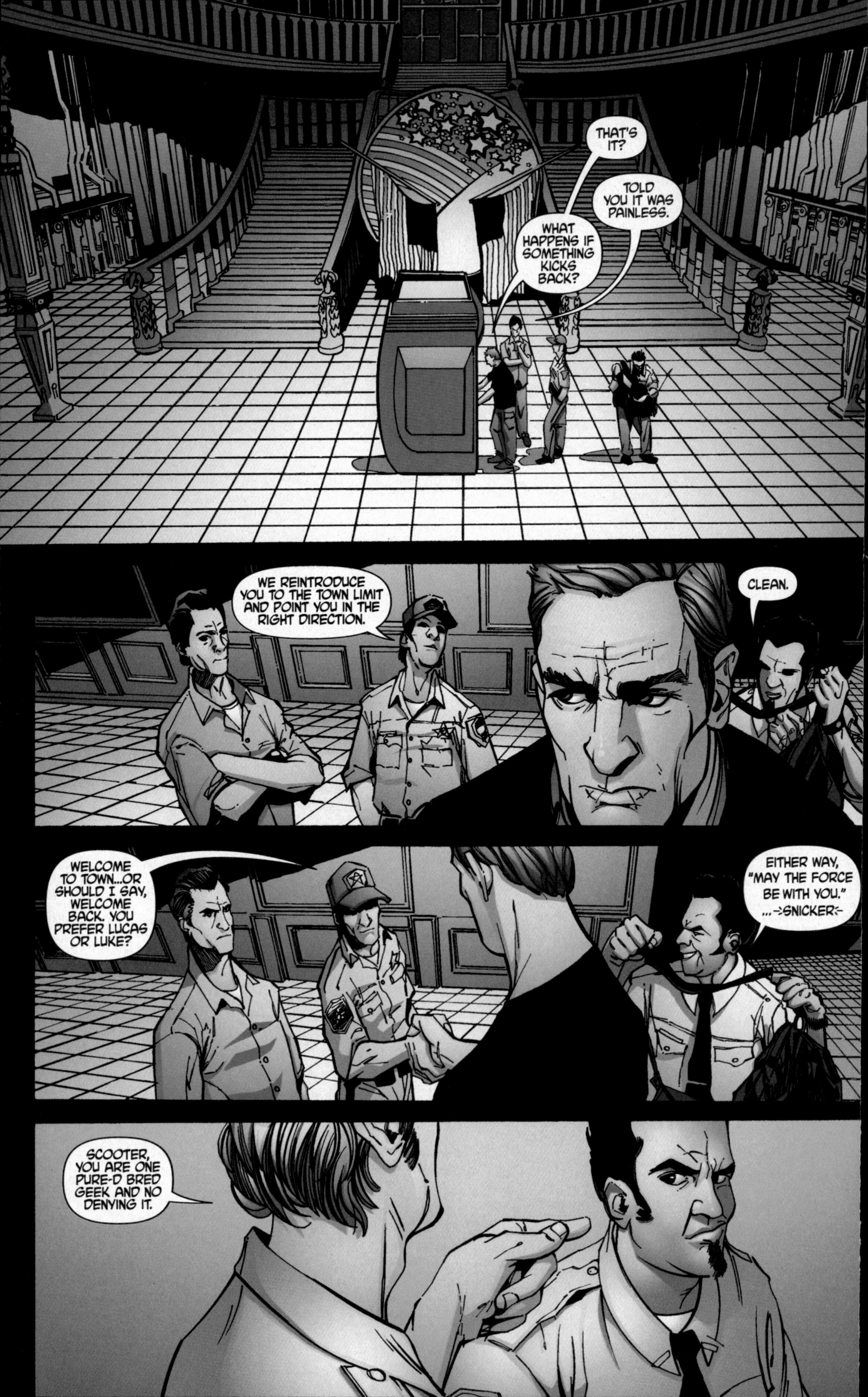
THAT'S IT?
WHAT HAPPENS IF SOMETHING KICKS BACK?
TOLD YOU IT WAS PAINLESS.
WE REINTRODUCE YOU TO THE TOWN LIMIT AND POINT YOU IN THE RIGHT DIRECTION.
CLEAN.
WELCOME TO TOWN...OR SHOULD I SAY, WELCOME BACK. YOU PREFER LUCAS OR LUKE?
EITHER WAY, "MAY THE FORCE BE WITH YOU." ...SNICKER
SCOOTER, YOU ARE ONE PURE-D BRED GEEK AND NO DENYING IT.

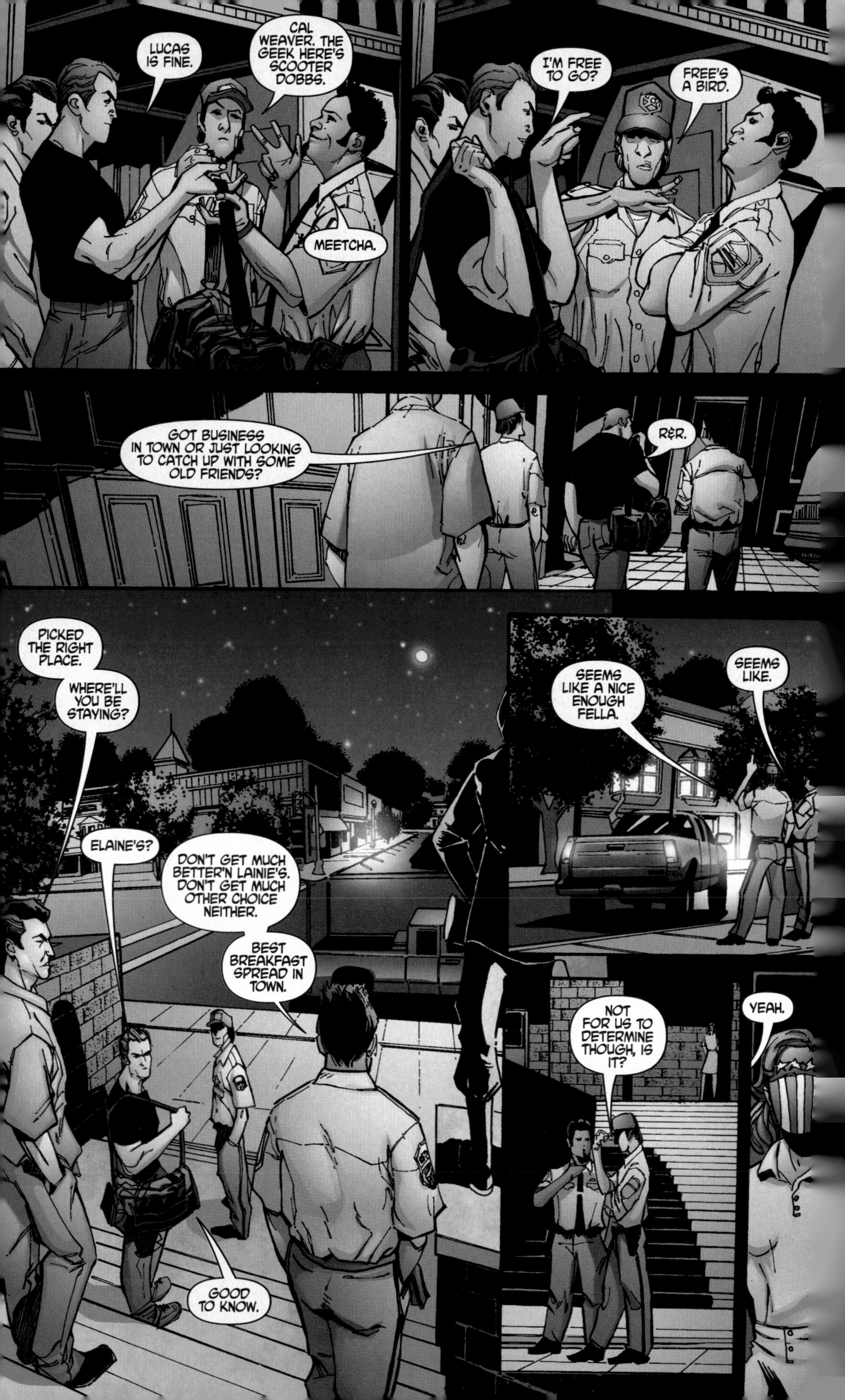

LUCAS IS FINE.
CAL WEAVER. THE GEEK HERE'S SCOOTER DOBBS.
MEETCHA.
I'M FREE TO GO?
FREE'S A BIRD.
GOT BUSINESS IN TOWN OR JUST LOOKING TO CATCH UP WITH SOME OLD FRIENDS?
R&R.
PICKED THE RIGHT PLACE.
WHERE'LL YOU BE STAYING?
ELAINE'S?
DON'T GET MUCH BETTER'N LAINIE'S. DON'T GET MUCH OTHER CHOICE NEITHER.
BEST BREAKFAST SPREAD IN TOWN.
GOOD TO KNOW.
SEEMS LIKE A NICE ENOUGH FELLA.
SEEMS LIKE.
NOT FOR US TO DETERMINE THOUGH, IS IT?
YEAH.

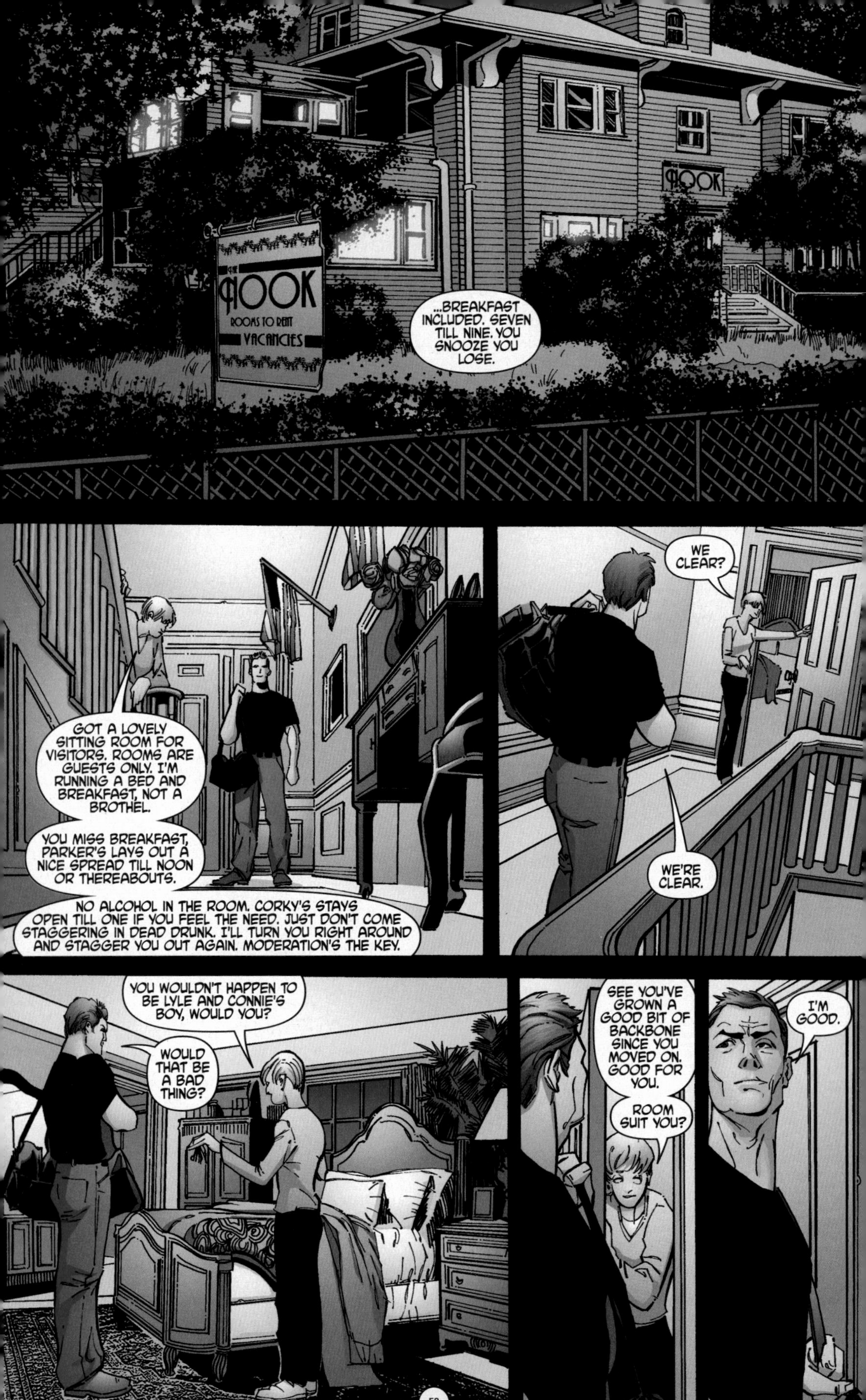
THE NOOK
ROOMS TO RENT
VACANCIES
NOOK
...BREAKFAST INCLUDED. SEVEN TILL NINE. YOU SNOOZE YOU LOSE.
GOT A LOVELY SITTING ROOM FOR VISITORS. ROOMS ARE GUESTS ONLY. I'M RUNNING A BED AND BREAKFAST, NOT A BROTHEL.
YOU MISS BREAKFAST, PARKER'S LAYS OUT A NICE SPREAD TILL NOON OR THEREABOUTS.
NO ALCOHOL IN THE ROOM. CORKY'S STAYS OPEN TILL ONE IF YOU FEEL THE NEED. JUST DON'T COME STAGGERING IN DEAD DRUNK. I'LL TURN YOU RIGHT AROUND AND STAGGER YOU OUT AGAIN. MODERATION'S THE KEY.
WE CLEAR?
WE'RE CLEAR.
YOU WOULDN'T HAPPEN TO BE LYLE AND CONNIE'S BOY, WOULD YOU?
WOULD THAT BE A BAD THING?
SEE YOU'VE GROWN A GOOD BIT OF BACKBONE SINCE YOU MOVED ON. GOOD FOR YOU.
ROOM SUIT YOU?
I'M GOOD.

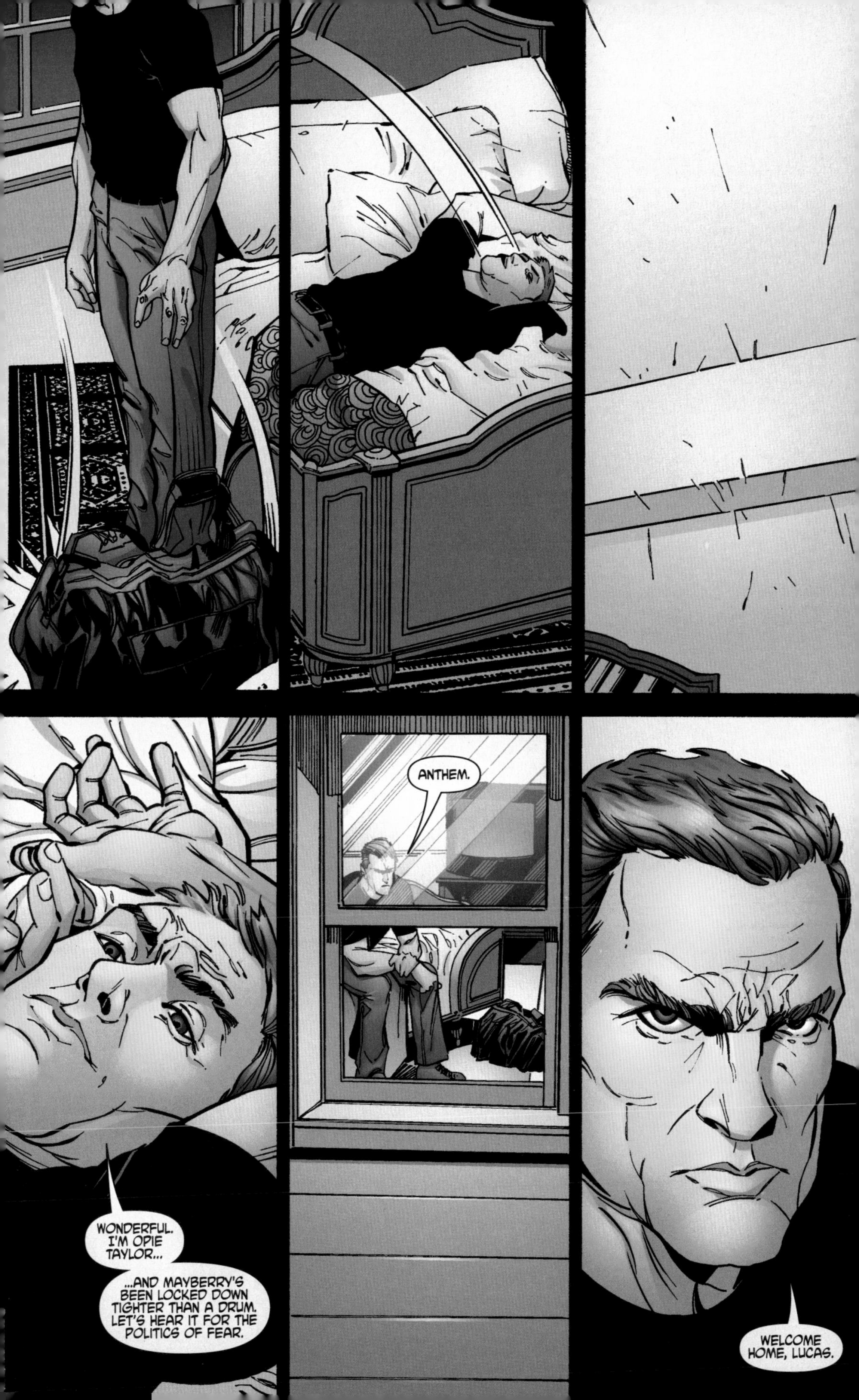
ANTHEM.
WONDERFUL. I'M OPIE TAYLOR...
...AND MAYBERRY'S BEEN LOCKED DOWN TIGHTER THAN A DRUM. LET'S HEAR IT FOR THE POLITICS OF FEAR.
WELCOME HOME, LUCAS.

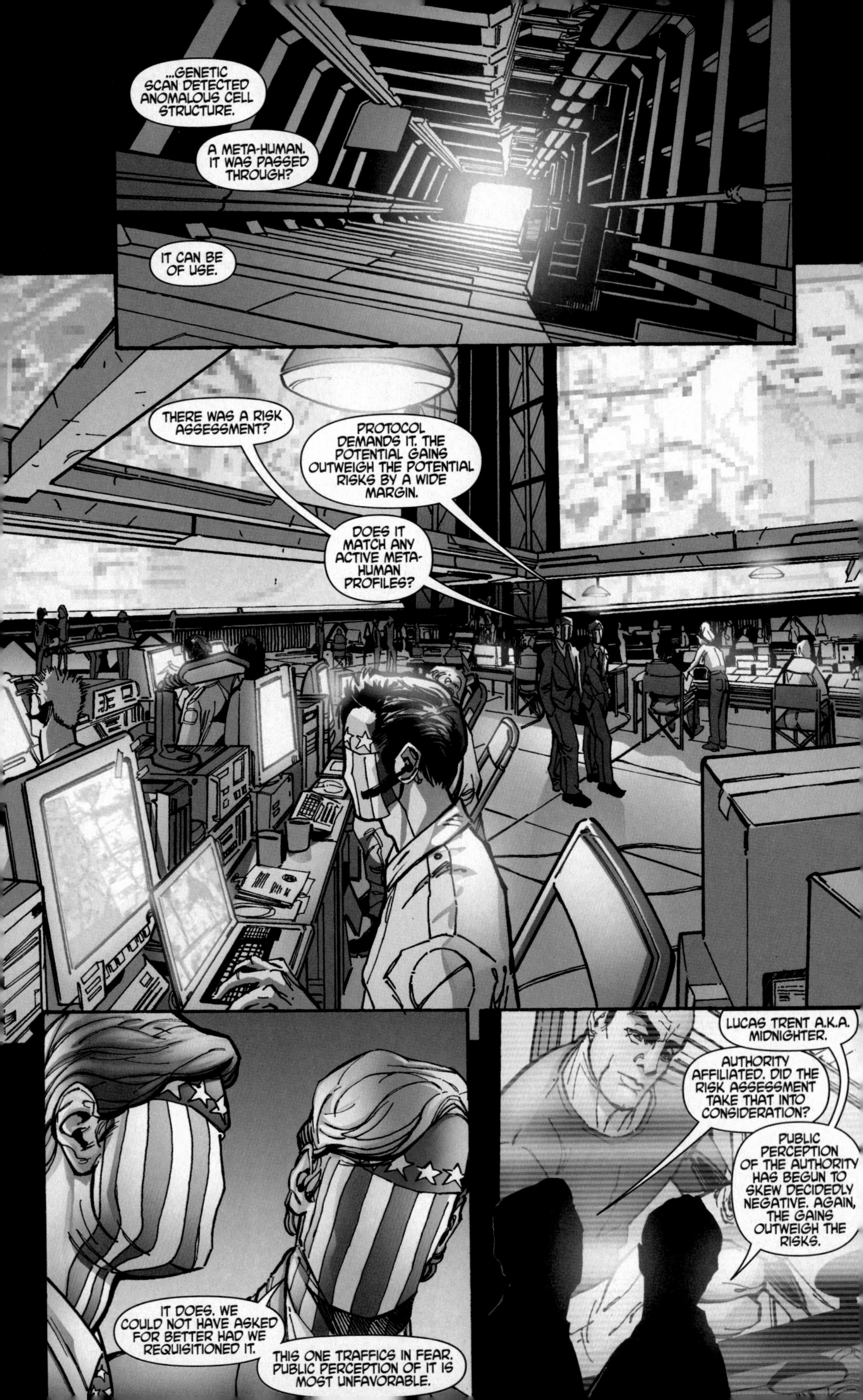
...GENETIC SCAN DETECTED ANOMALOUS CELL STRUCTURE.
A META-HUMAN. IT WAS PASSED THROUGH?
IT CAN BE OF USE.
THERE WAS A RISK ASSESSMENT?
PROTOCOL DEMANDS IT. THE POTENTIAL GAINS OUTWEIGH THE POTENTIAL RISKS BY A WIDE MARGIN.
DOES IT MATCH ANY ACTIVE META-HUMAN PROFILES?
IT DOES. WE COULD NOT HAVE ASKED FOR BETTER HAD WE REQUISITIONED IT.
THIS ONE TRAFFICS IN FEAR. PUBLIC PERCEPTION OF IT IS MOST UNFAVORABLE.
LUCAS TRENT A.K.A. MIDNIGHTER.
AUTHORITY AFFILIATED. DID THE RISK ASSESSMENT TAKE THAT INTO CONSIDERATION?
PUBLIC PERCEPTION OF THE AUTHORITY HAS BEGUN TO SKEW DECIDEDLY NEGATIVE. AGAIN, THE GAINS OUTWEIGH THE RISKS.

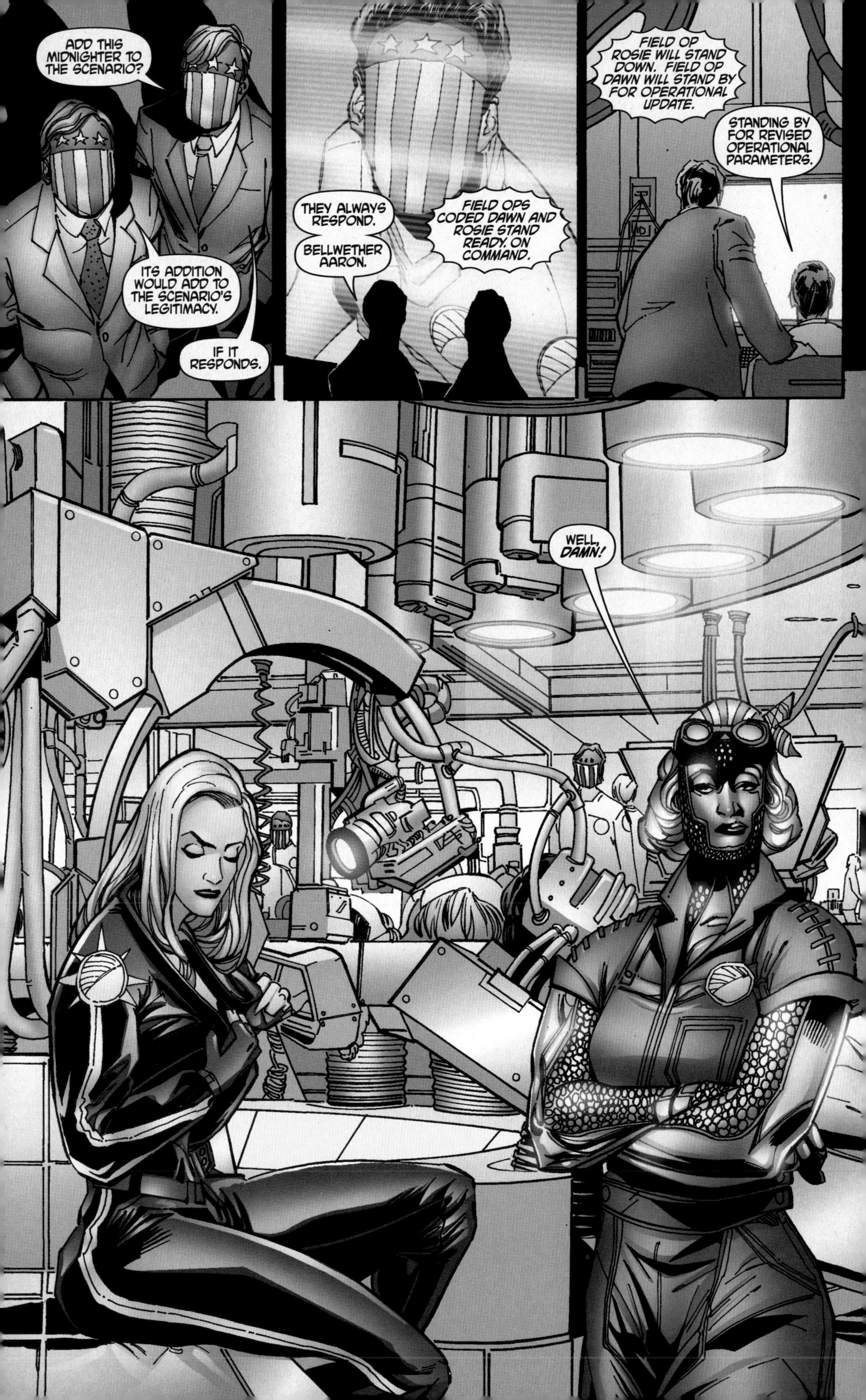

ADD THIS MIDNIGHTER TO THE SCENARIO?
ITS ADDITION WOULD ADD TO THE SCENARIO'S LEGITIMACY.
IF IT RESPONDS.
THEY ALWAYS RESPOND.
BELLWETHER AARON.
FIELD OPS CODED DAWN AND ROSIE STAND READY. ON COMMAND.
FIELD OP ROSIE WILL STAND DOWN. FIELD OP DAWN WILL STAND BY FOR OPERATIONAL UPDATE.
STANDING BY FOR REVISED OPERATIONAL PARAMETERS.
WELL, *DAMN!*

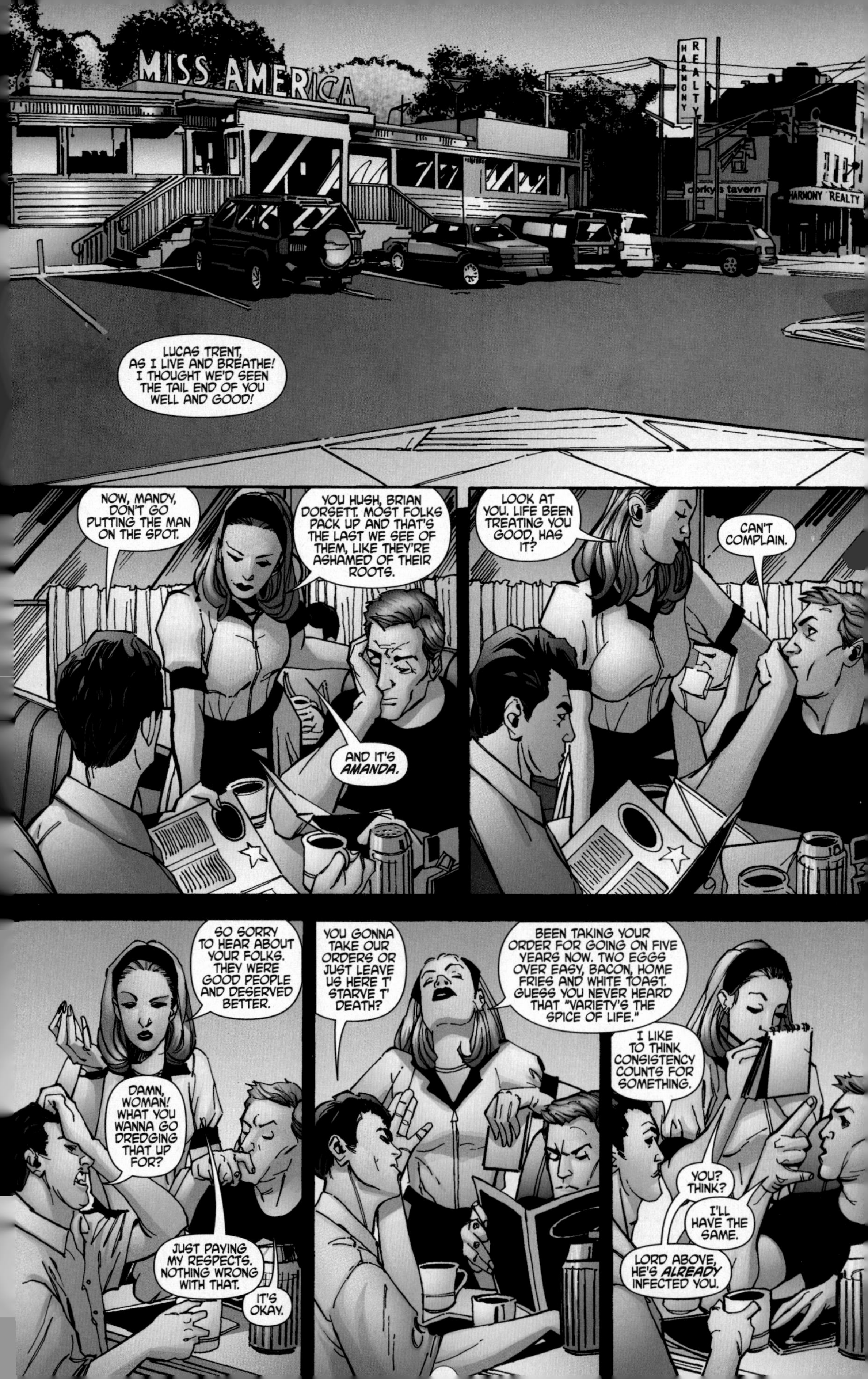
MISS AMERICA
HARMONY REALTY
dorky's tavern
HARMONY REALTY
LUCAS TRENT, AS I LIVE AND BREATHE! I THOUGHT WE'D SEEN THE TAIL END OF YOU WELL AND GOOD!
NOW, MANDY, DON'T GO PUTTING THE MAN ON THE SPOT.
YOU HUSH, BRIAN DORSETT. MOST FOLKS PACK UP AND THAT'S THE LAST WE SEE OF THEM, LIKE THEY'RE ASHAMED OF THEIR ROOTS.
AND IT'S *AMANDA.*
LOOK AT YOU. LIFE BEEN TREATING YOU GOOD, HAS IT?
CAN'T COMPLAIN.
SO SORRY TO HEAR ABOUT YOUR FOLKS. THEY WERE GOOD PEOPLE AND DESERVED BETTER.
DAMN, WOMAN! WHAT YOU WANNA GO DREDGING THAT UP FOR?
JUST PAYING MY RESPECTS. NOTHING WRONG WITH THAT.
IT'S OKAY.
YOU GONNA TAKE OUR ORDERS OR JUST LEAVE US HERE T' STARVE T' DEATH?
BEEN TAKING YOUR ORDER FOR GOING ON FIVE YEARS NOW. TWO EGGS OVER EASY, BACON, HOME FRIES AND WHITE TOAST. GUESS YOU NEVER HEARD THAT "VARIETY'S THE SPICE OF LIFE."
I LIKE TO THINK CONSISTENCY COUNTS FOR SOMETHING.
YOU? THINK?
I'LL HAVE THE SAME.
LORD ABOVE, HE'S *ALREADY* INFECTED YOU.

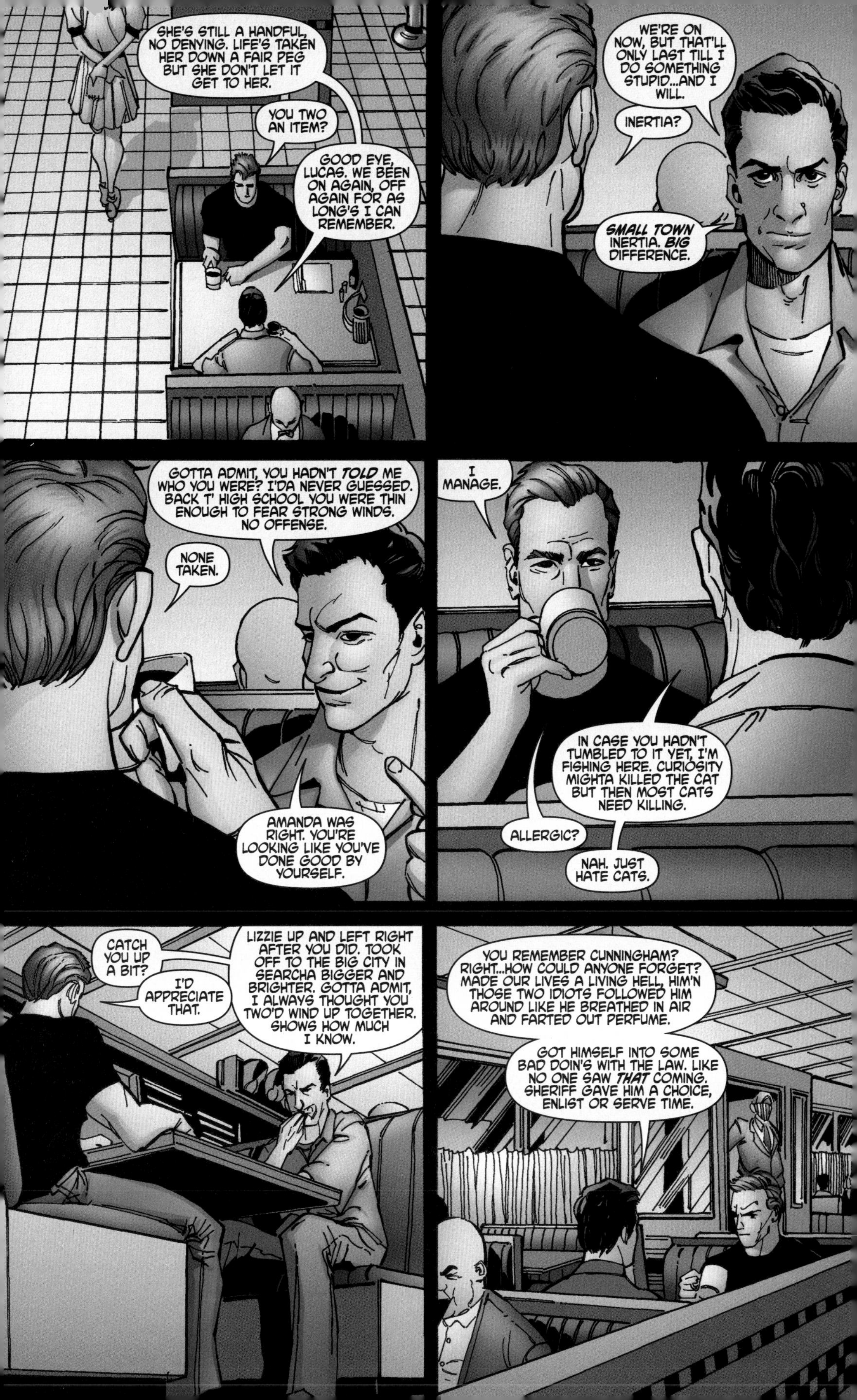
SHE'S STILL A HANDFUL, NO DENYING. LIFE'S TAKEN HER DOWN A FAIR PEG BUT SHE DON'T LET IT GET TO HER.
YOU TWO AN ITEM?
GOOD EYE, LUCAS. WE BEEN ON AGAIN, OFF AGAIN FOR AS LONG'S I CAN REMEMBER.
WE'RE ON NOW, BUT THAT'LL ONLY LAST TILL I DO SOMETHING STUPID...AND I WILL.
INERTIA?
SMALL TOWN INERTIA. BIG DIFFERENCE.
GOTTA ADMIT, YOU HADN'T TOLD ME WHO YOU WERE? I'DA NEVER GUESSED. BACK T' HIGH SCHOOL YOU WERE THIN ENOUGH TO FEAR STRONG WINDS. NO OFFENSE.
NONE TAKEN.
AMANDA WAS RIGHT. YOU'RE LOOKING LIKE YOU'VE DONE GOOD BY YOURSELF.
I MANAGE.
IN CASE YOU HADN'T TUMBLED TO IT YET, I'M FISHING HERE. CURIOSITY MIGHTA KILLED THE CAT BUT THEN MOST CATS NEED KILLING.
ALLERGIC?
NAH. JUST HATE CATS.
CATCH YOU UP A BIT?
I'D APPRECIATE THAT.
LIZZIE UP AND LEFT RIGHT AFTER YOU DID. TOOK OFF TO THE BIG CITY IN SEARCHA BIGGER AND BRIGHTER. GOTTA ADMIT, I ALWAYS THOUGHT YOU TWO'D WIND UP TOGETHER. SHOWS HOW MUCH I KNOW.
YOU REMEMBER CUNNINGHAM? RIGHT...HOW COULD ANYONE FORGET? MADE OUR LIVES A LIVING HELL, HIM'N THOSE TWO IDIOTS FOLLOWED HIM AROUND LIKE HE BREATHED IN AIR AND FARTED OUT PERFUME.
GOT HIMSELF INTO SOME BAD DOIN'S WITH THE LAW. LIKE NO ONE SAW THAT COMING. SHERIFF GAVE HIM A CHOICE, ENLIST OR SERVE TIME.

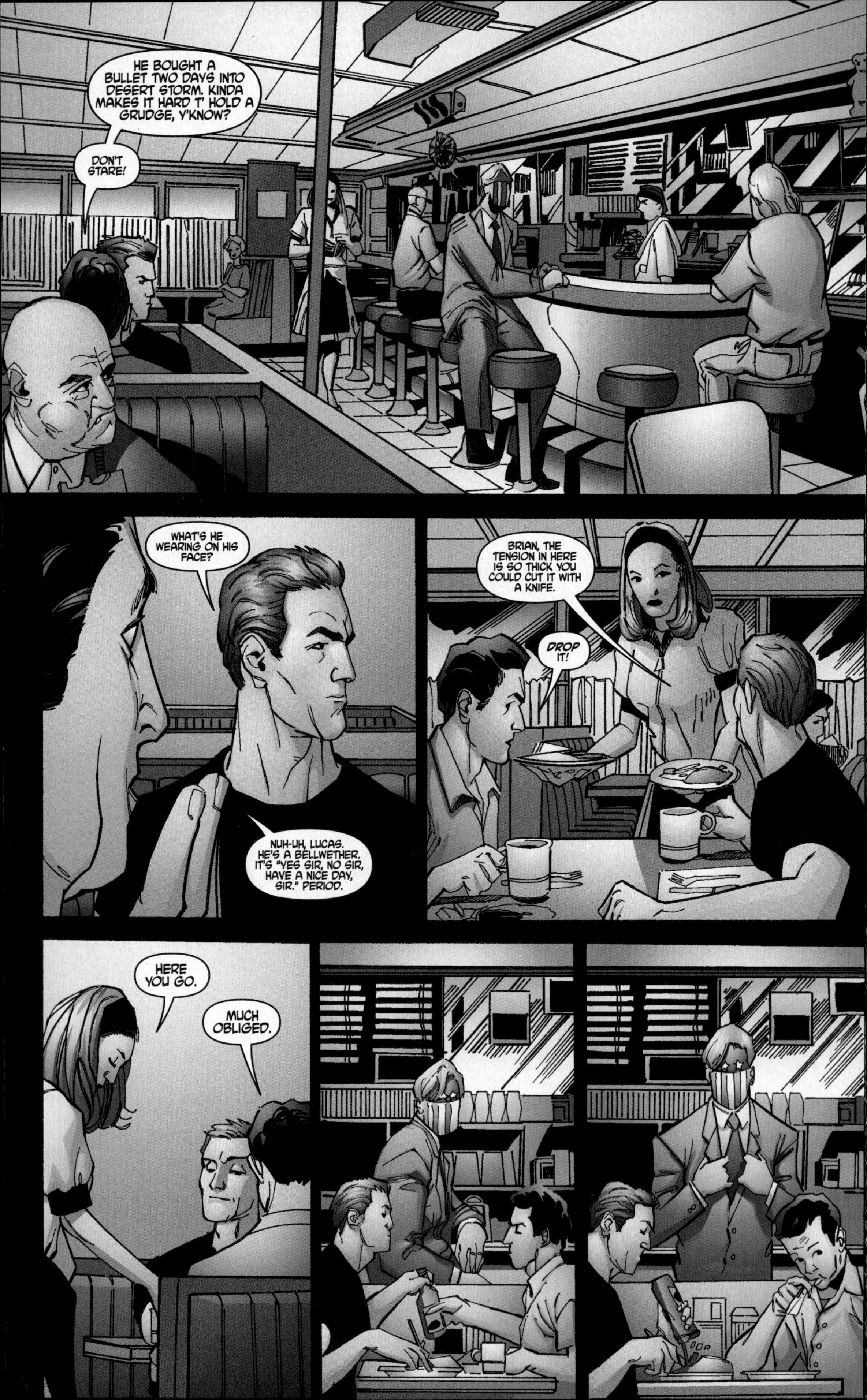
HE BOUGHT A BULLET TWO DAYS INTO DESERT STORM. KINDA MAKES IT HARD T' HOLD A GRUDGE, Y'KNOW?
DON'T STARE!
WHAT'S HE WEARING ON HIS FACE?
NUH-UH, LUCAS. HE'S A BELLWETHER. IT'S "YES SIR, NO SIR, HAVE A NICE DAY, SIR." PERIOD.
BRIAN, THE TENSION IN HERE IS SO THICK YOU COULD CUT IT WITH A KNIFE.
DROP IT!
HERE YOU GO.
MUCH OBLIGED.

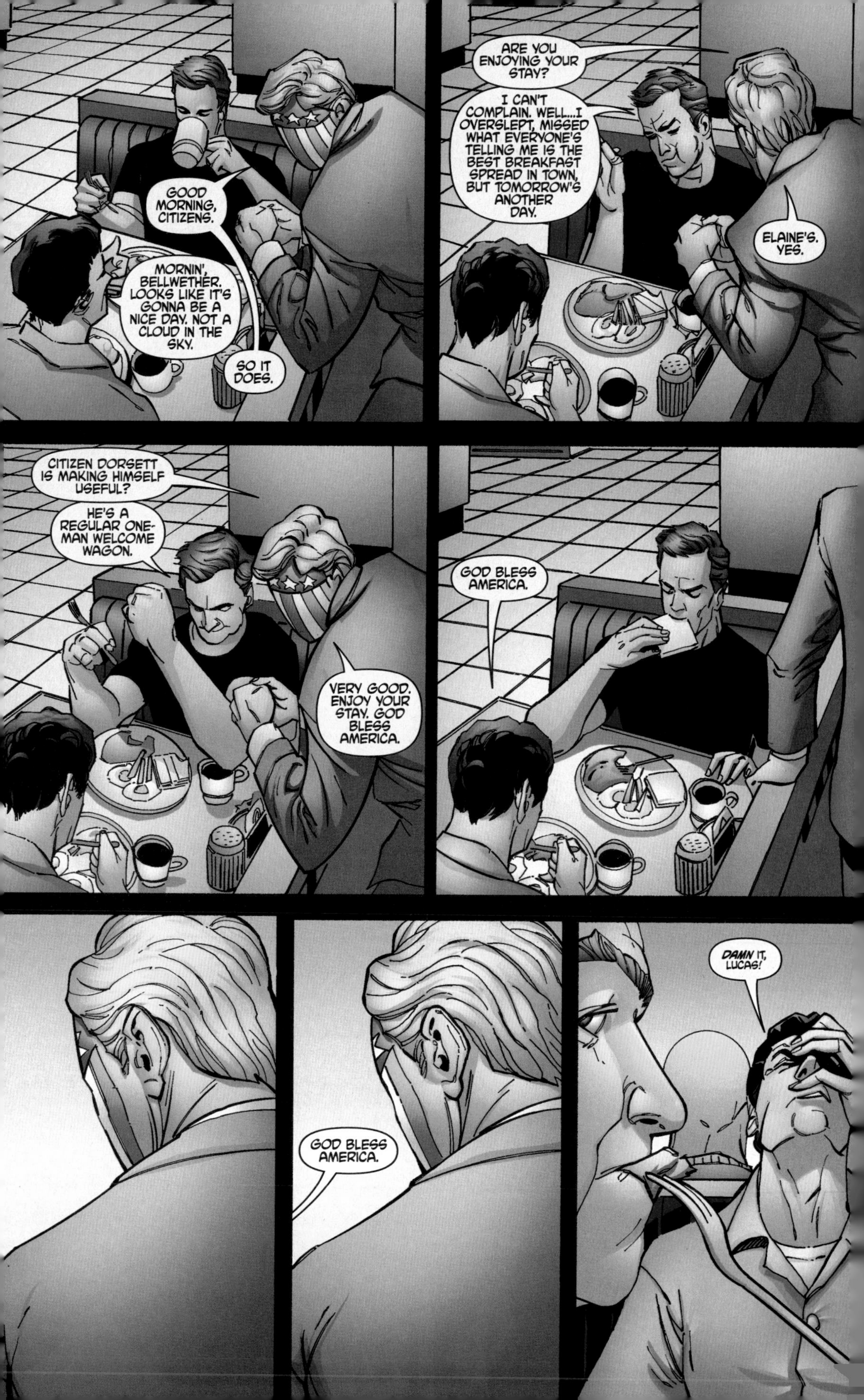
GOOD MORNING, CITIZENS.
MORNIN', BELLWETHER. LOOKS LIKE IT'S GONNA BE A NICE DAY. NOT A CLOUD IN THE SKY.
SO IT DOES.
ARE YOU ENJOYING YOUR STAY?
I CAN'T COMPLAIN. WELL...I OVERSLEPT, MISSED WHAT EVERYONE'S TELLING ME IS THE BEST BREAKFAST SPREAD IN TOWN, BUT TOMORROW'S ANOTHER DAY.
ELAINE'S. YES.
CITIZEN DORSETT IS MAKING HIMSELF USEFUL?
HE'S A REGULAR ONE-MAN WELCOME WAGON.
VERY GOOD. ENJOY YOUR STAY. GOD BLESS AMERICA.
GOD BLESS AMERICA.
GOD BLESS AMERICA.
DAMN IT, LUCAS!

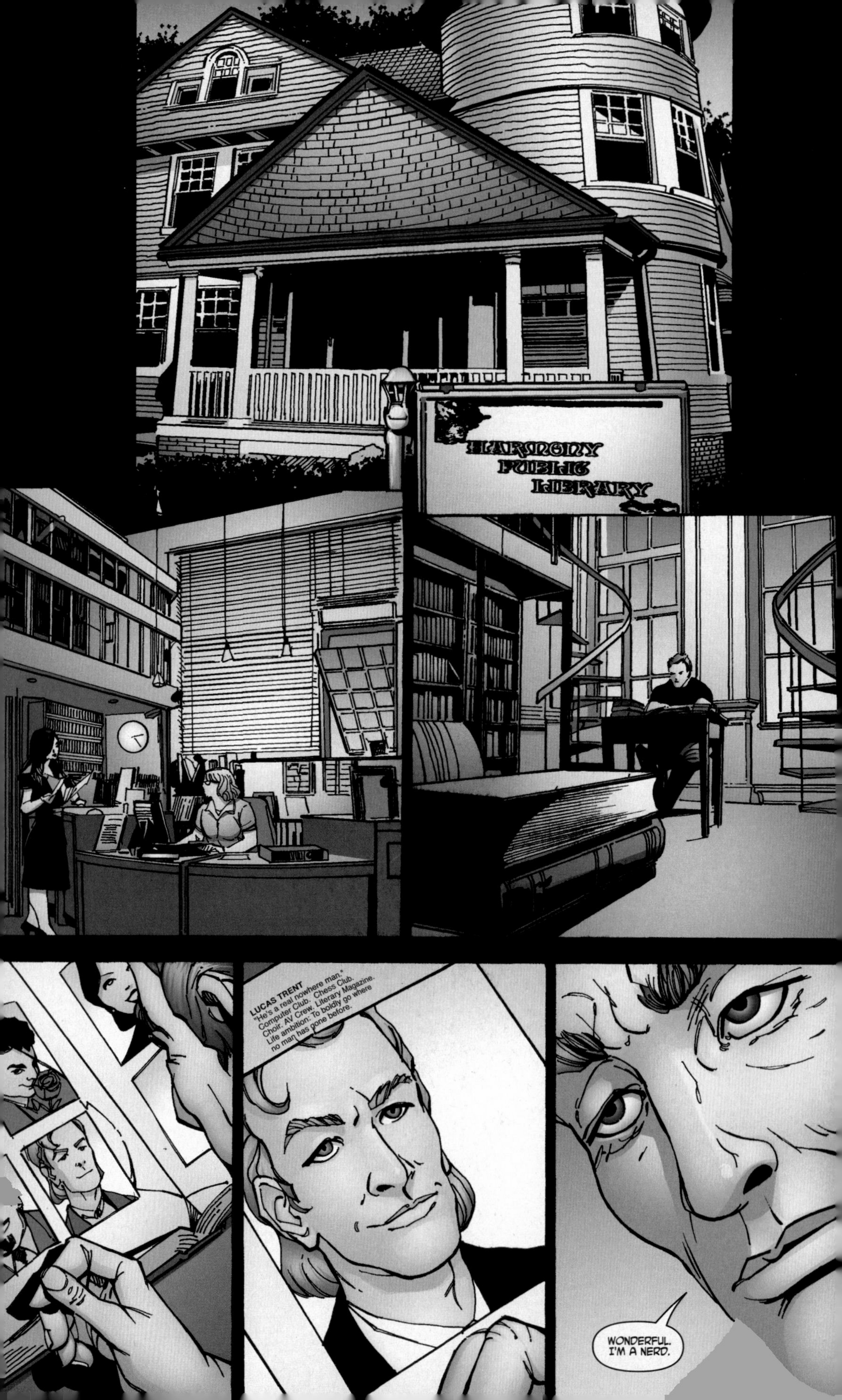
HARMONY
PUBLIC
LIBRARY
LUCAS TRENT
"He's a real nowhere man."
Computer Club. Chess Club.
Choir. AV Crew. Literary Magazine.
Life ambition: To boldly go where
no man has gone before.
WONDERFUL. I'M A NERD.

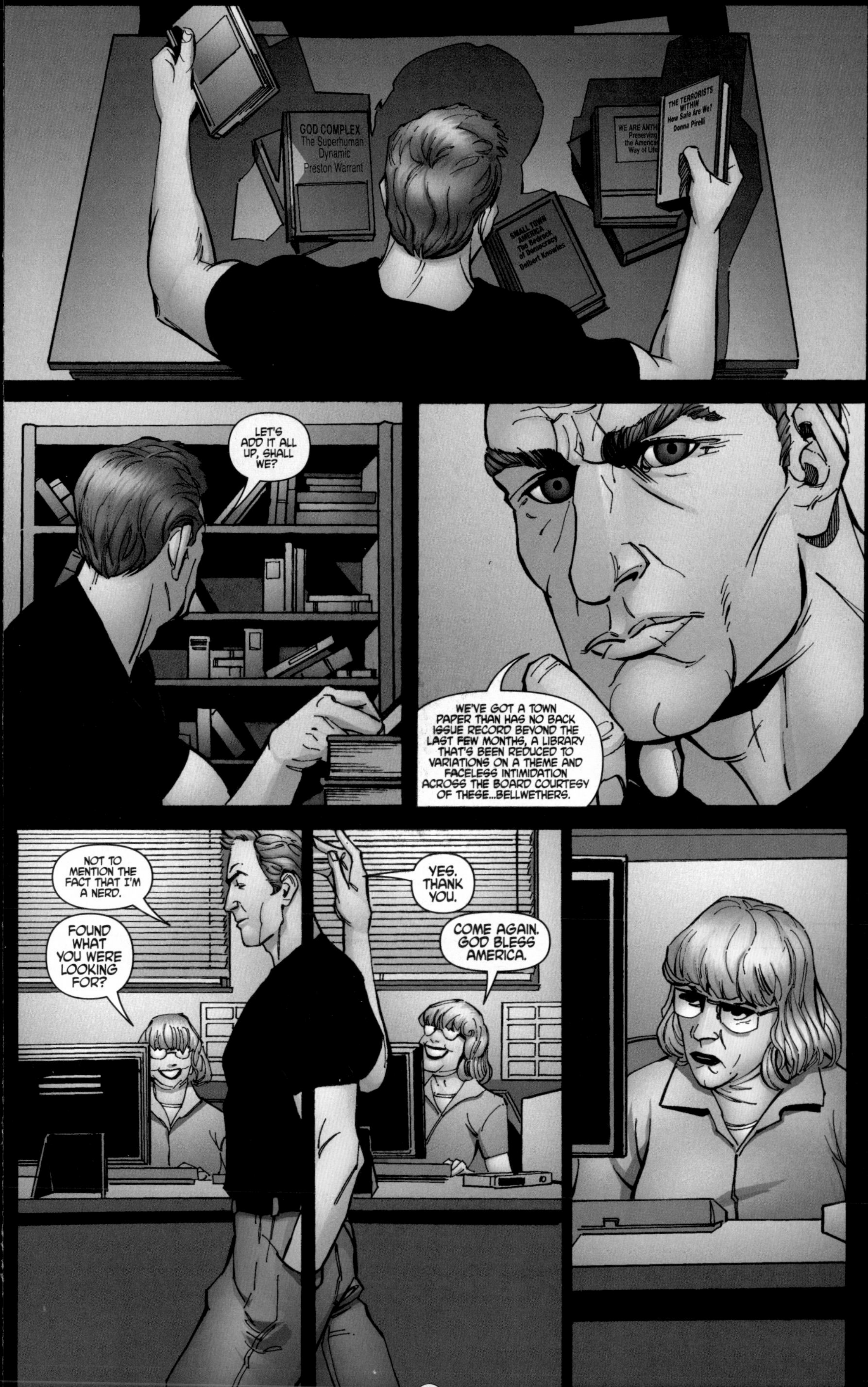
GOD COMPLEX
The Superhuman Dynamic
Preston Warrant
THE TERRORISTS WITHIN
How Safe Are We?
Donna Pirelli
SMALL TOWN AMERICA
The Bedrock of Democracy
Delbert Knowles
LET'S ADD IT ALL UP, SHALL WE?
WE'VE GOT A TOWN PAPER THAN HAS NO BACK ISSUE RECORD BEYOND THE LAST FEW MONTHS, A LIBRARY THAT'S BEEN REDUCED TO VARIATIONS ON A THEME AND FACELESS INTIMIDATION ACROSS THE BOARD COURTESY OF THESE...BELLWETHERS.
NOT TO MENTION THE FACT THAT I'M A NERD.
FOUND WHAT YOU WERE LOOKING FOR?
YES. THANK YOU.
COME AGAIN. GOD BLESS AMERICA.

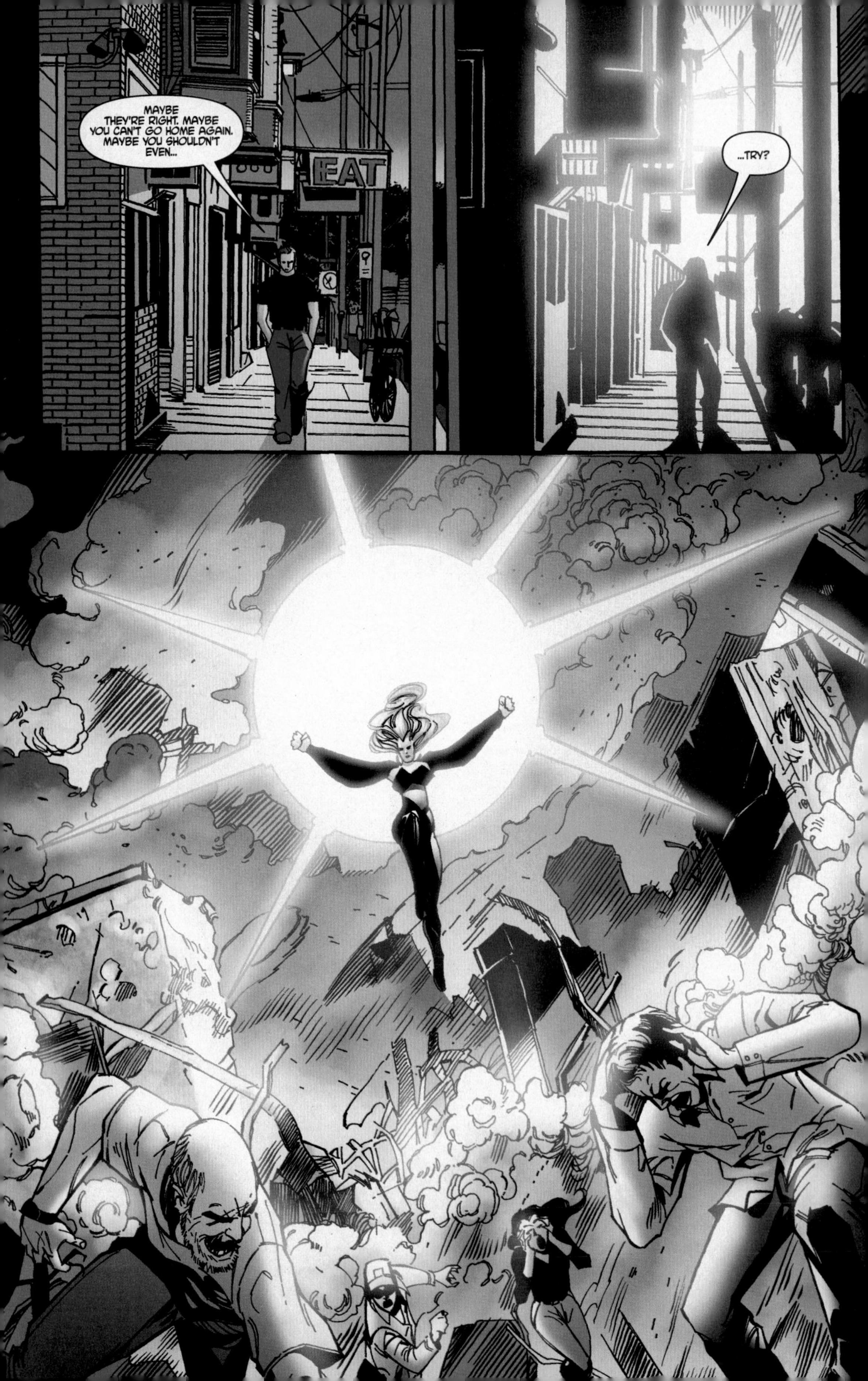
MAYBE THEY'RE RIGHT. MAYBE YOU CAN'T GO HOME AGAIN. MAYBE YOU SHOULDN'T EVEN...
EAT
...TRY?

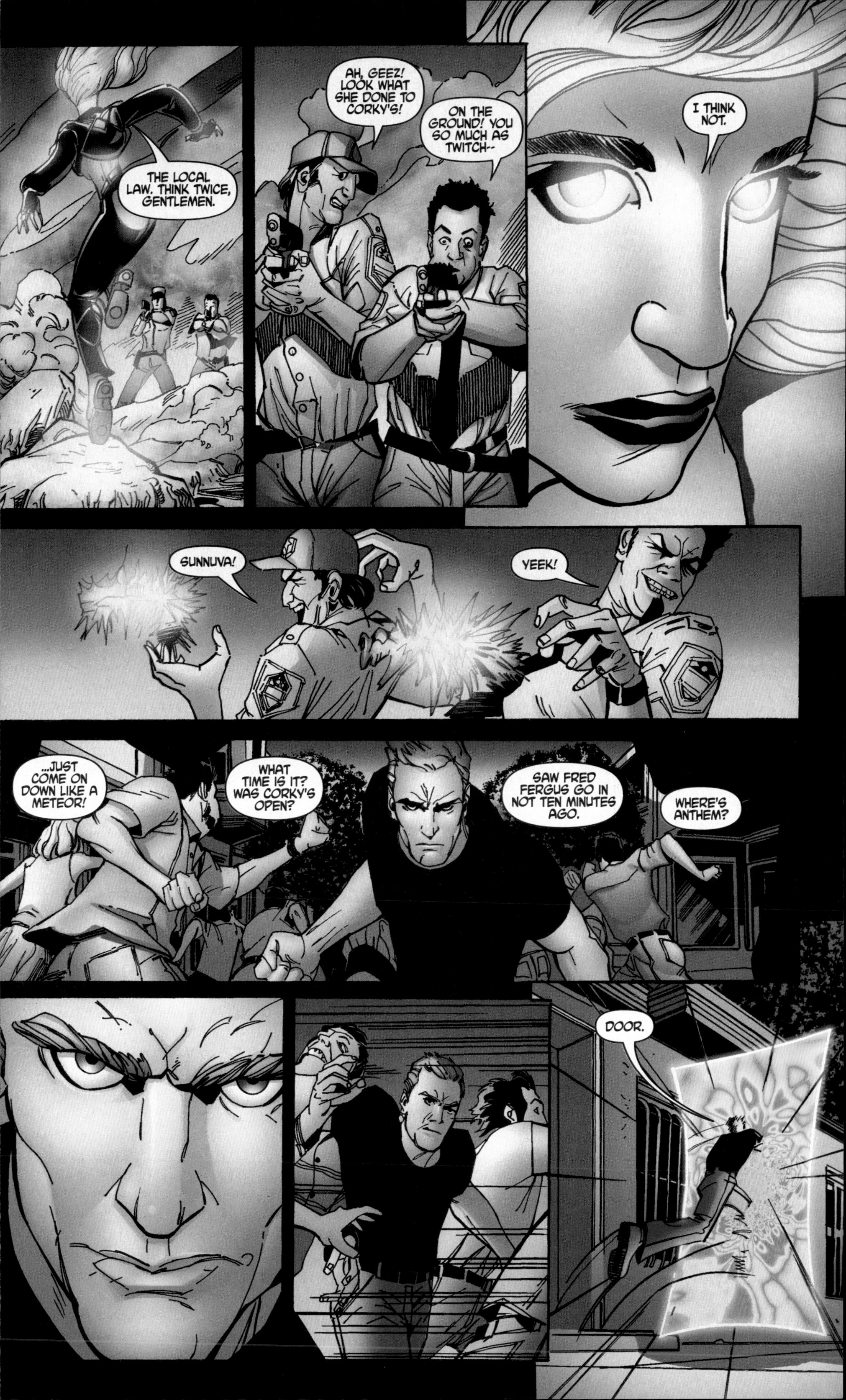
THE LOCAL LAW. THINK TWICE, GENTLEMEN.
AH, GEEZ! LOOK WHAT SHE DONE TO CORKY'S!
ON THE GROUND! YOU SO MUCH AS TWITCH--
I THINK NOT.
SUNNUVA!
YEEK!
...JUST COME ON DOWN LIKE A METEOR!
WHAT TIME IS IT? WAS CORKY'S OPEN?
SAW FRED FERGUS GO IN NOT TEN MINUTES AGO.
WHERE'S ANTHEM?
DOOR.

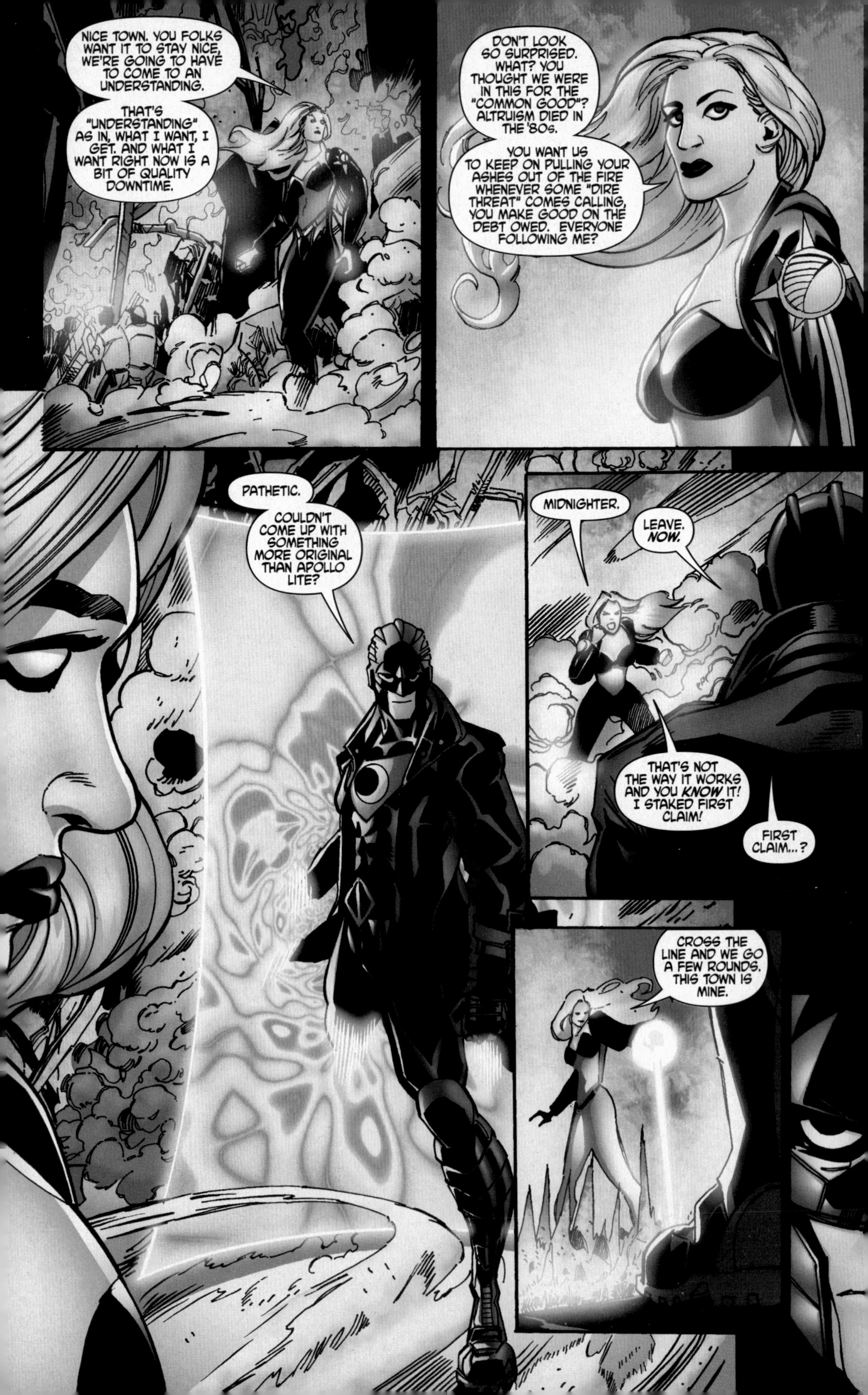
NICE TOWN. YOU FOLKS WANT IT TO STAY NICE, WE'RE GOING TO HAVE TO COME TO AN UNDERSTANDING.
THAT'S "UNDERSTANDING" AS IN, WHAT I WANT, I GET. AND WHAT I WANT RIGHT NOW IS A BIT OF QUALITY DOWNTIME.
DON'T LOOK SO SURPRISED. WHAT? YOU THOUGHT WE WERE IN THIS FOR THE "COMMON GOOD"? ALTRUISM DIED IN THE '80s.
YOU WANT US TO KEEP ON PULLING YOUR ASHES OUT OF THE FIRE WHENEVER SOME "DIRE THREAT" COMES CALLING, YOU MAKE GOOD ON THE DEBT OWED. EVERYONE FOLLOWING ME?
PATHETIC.
COULDN'T COME UP WITH SOMETHING MORE ORIGINAL THAN APOLLO LITE?
MIDNIGHTER.
LEAVE. *NOW.*
THAT'S NOT THE WAY IT WORKS AND YOU *KNOW* IT! I STAKED FIRST CLAIM!
FIRST CLAIM...?
CROSS THE LINE AND WE GO A FEW ROUNDS. THIS TOWN IS MINE.

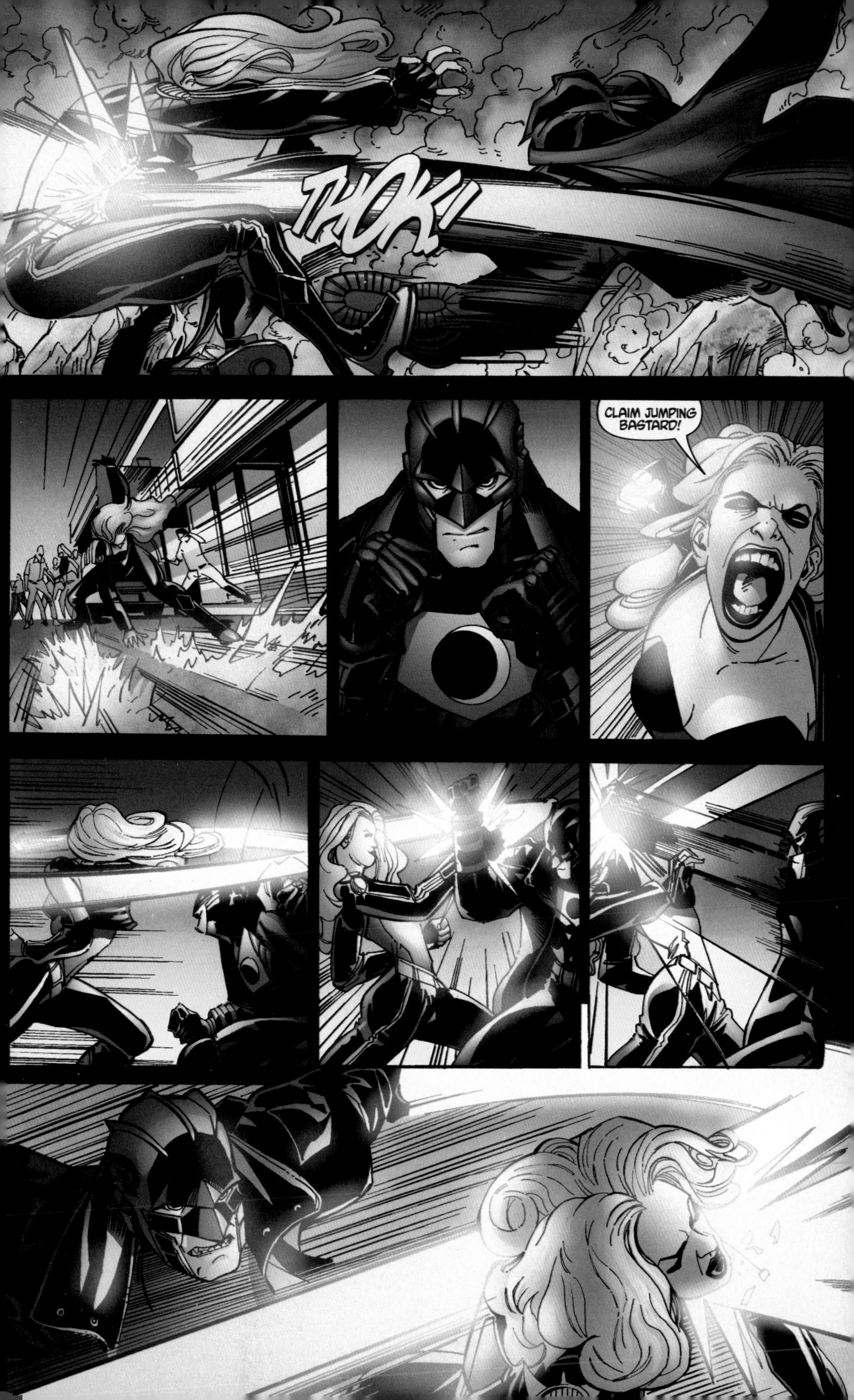
THOK!!
CLAIM JUMPING BASTARD!

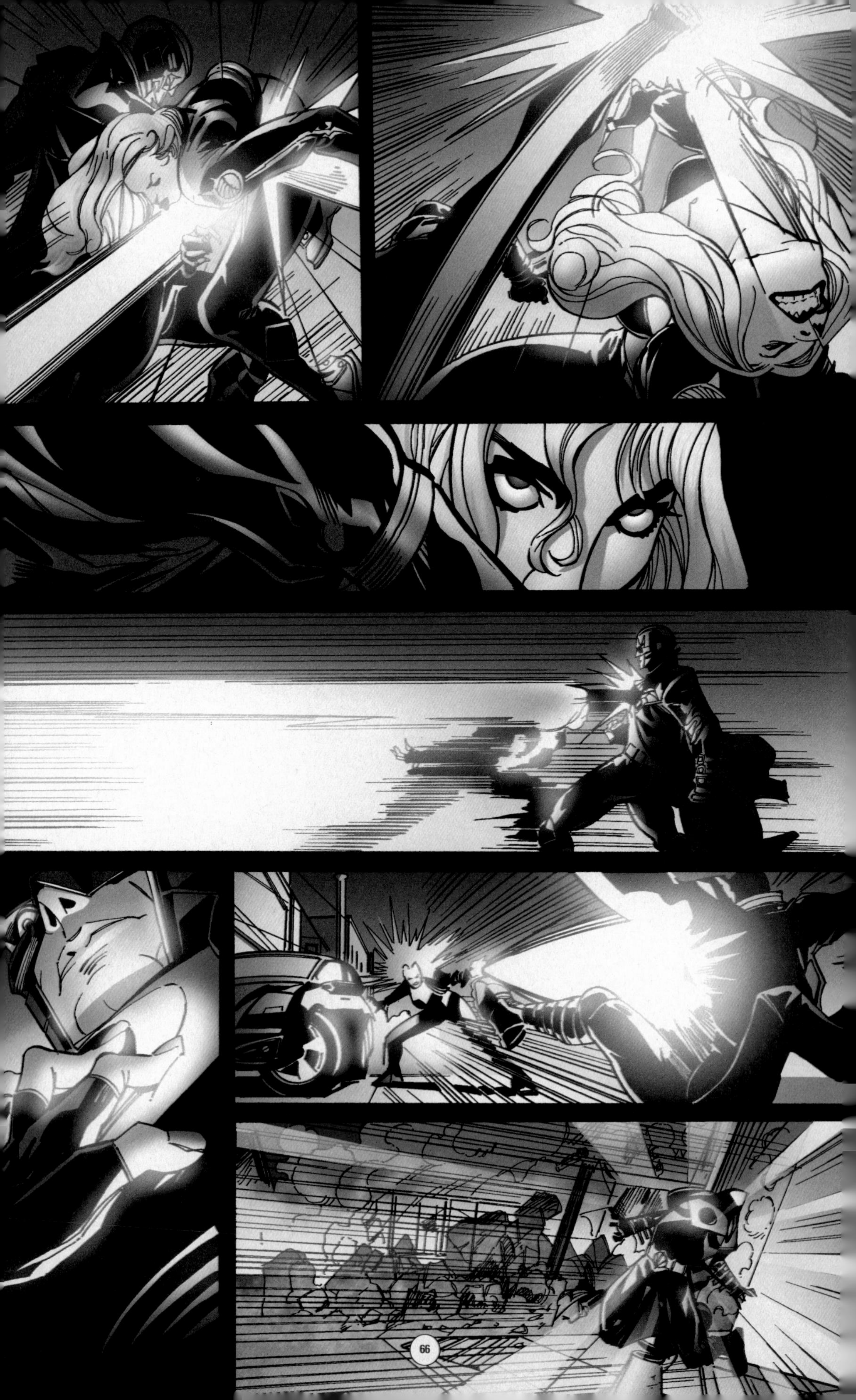

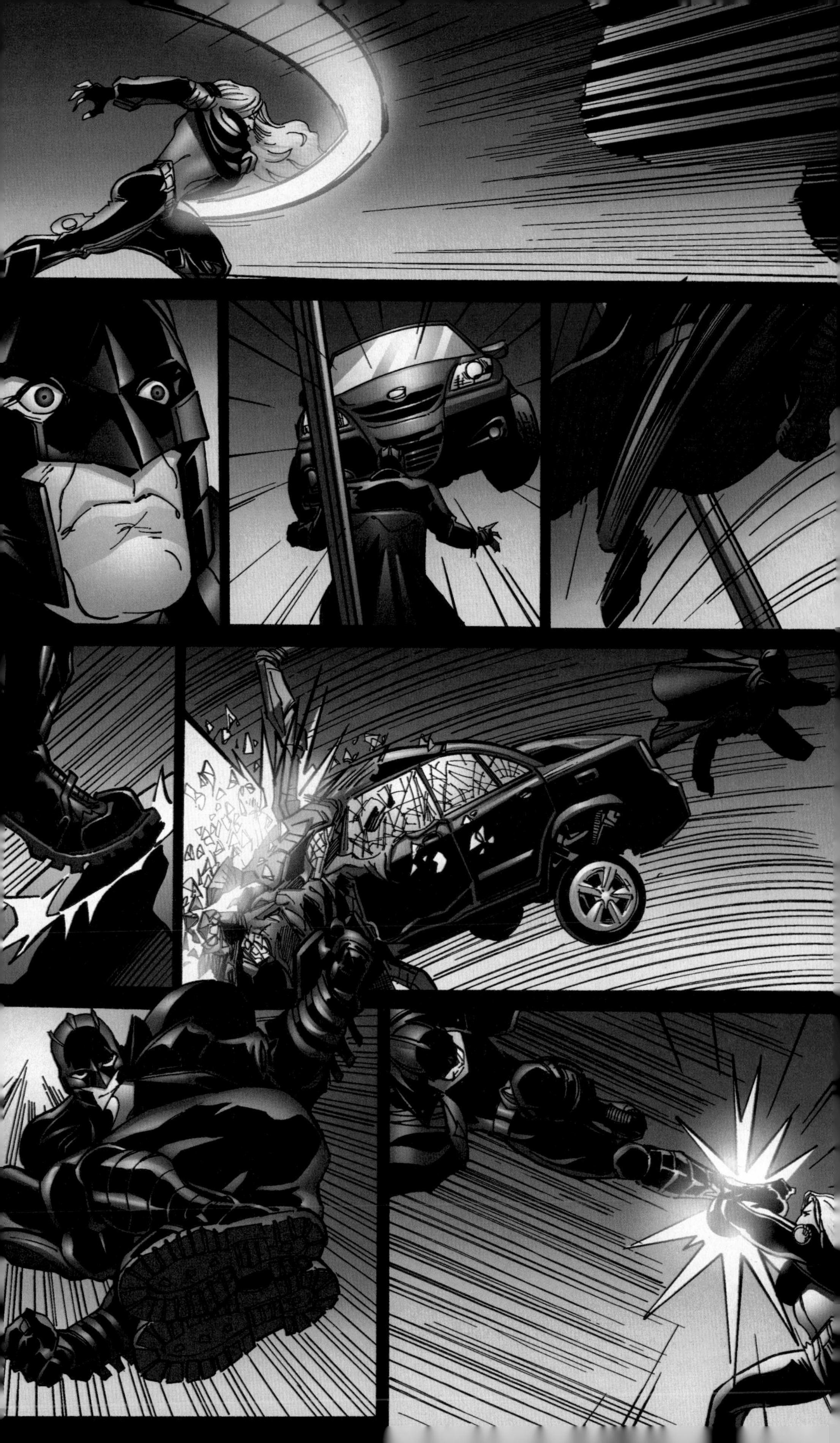

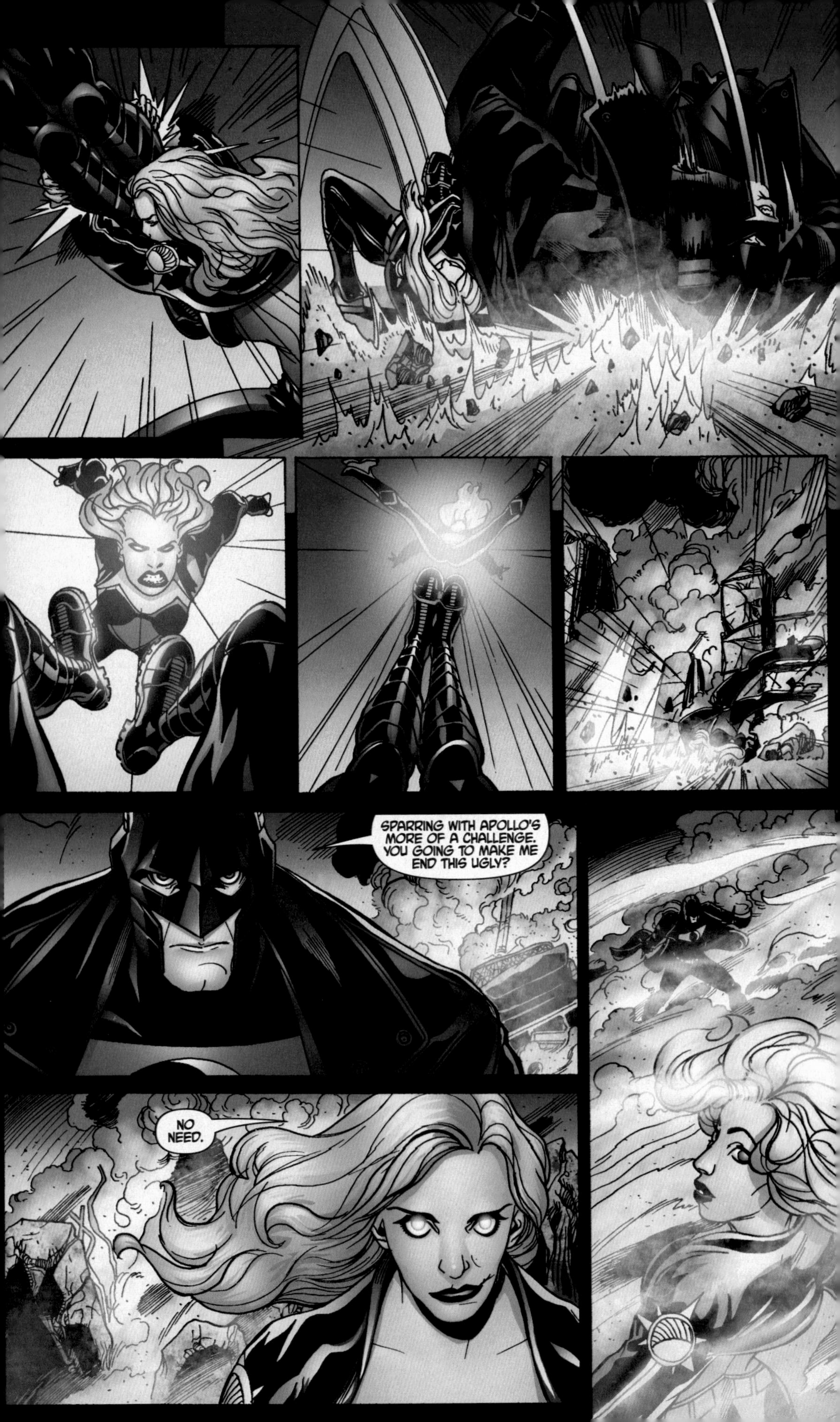
SPARRING WITH APOLLO'S MORE OF A CHALLENGE. YOU GOING TO MAKE ME END THIS UGLY?
NO NEED.

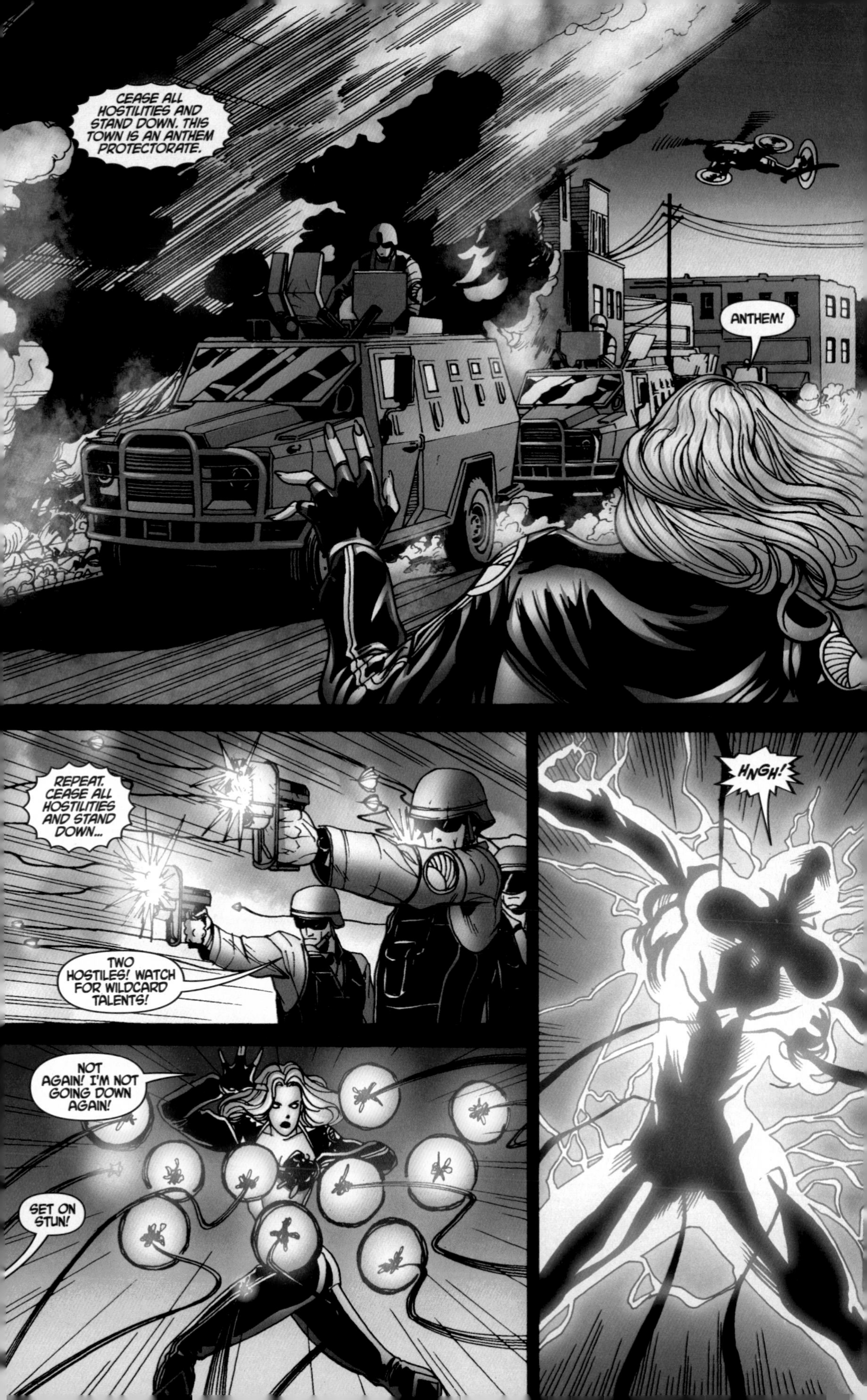

CEASE ALL HOSTILITIES AND STAND DOWN. THIS TOWN IS AN ANTHEM PROTECTORATE.
ANTHEM!
REPEAT. CEASE ALL HOSTILITIES AND STAND DOWN...
TWO HOSTILES! WATCH FOR WILDCARD TALENTS!
NOT AGAIN! I'M NOT GOING DOWN AGAIN!
SET ON STUN!
HNGH!

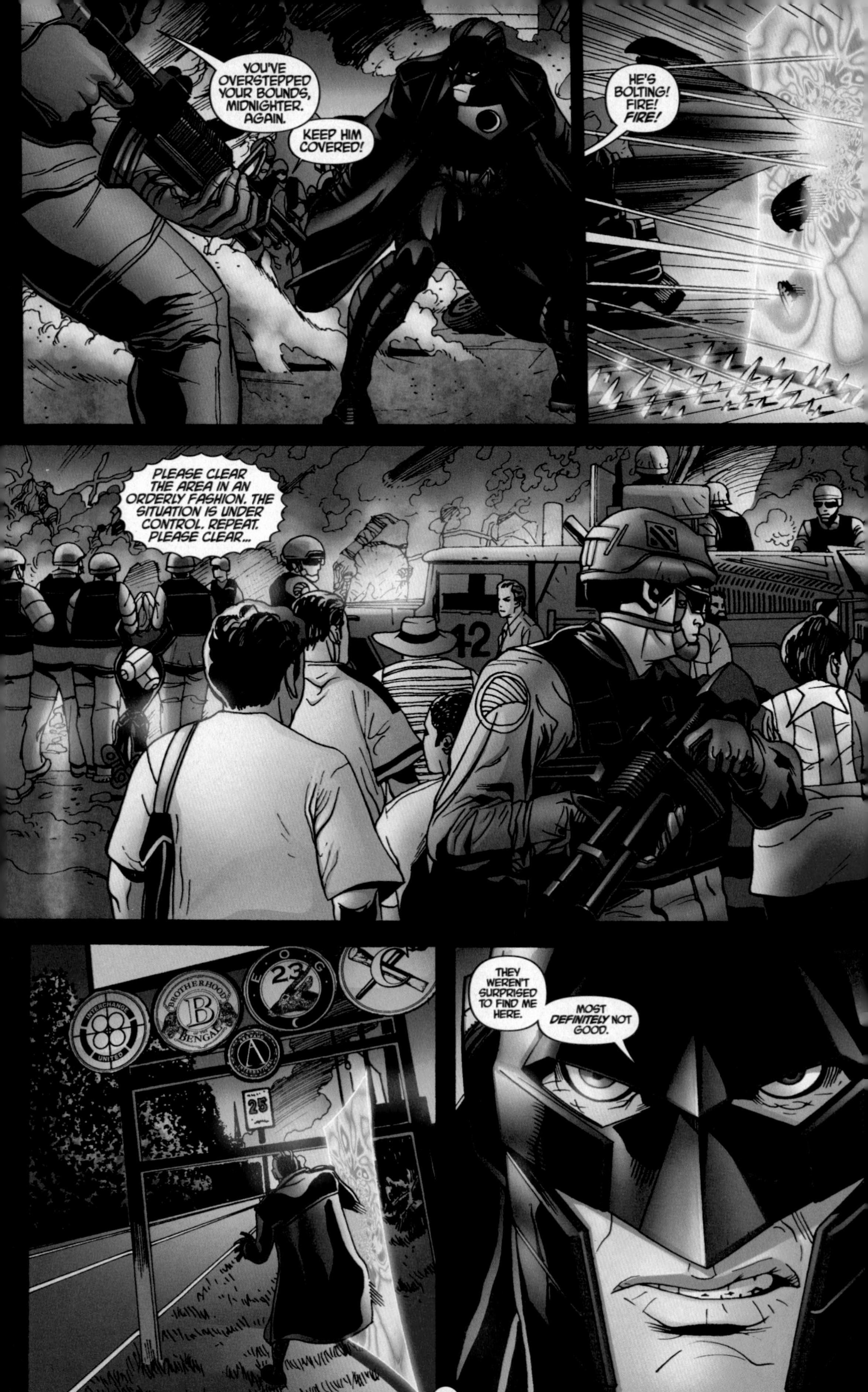
YOU'VE OVERSTEPPED YOUR BOUNDS, MIDNIGHTER. AGAIN.
KEEP HIM COVERED!
HE'S BOLTING! FIRE! *FIRE!*
PLEASE CLEAR THE AREA IN AN ORDERLY FASHION. THE SITUATION IS UNDER CONTROL. REPEAT. PLEASE CLEAR...
42
INTERCHANGE
UNITED
BROTHERHOOD
B
BENGAL
23
25
THEY WEREN'T SURPRISED TO FIND ME HERE.
MOST *DEFINITELY* NOT GOOD.

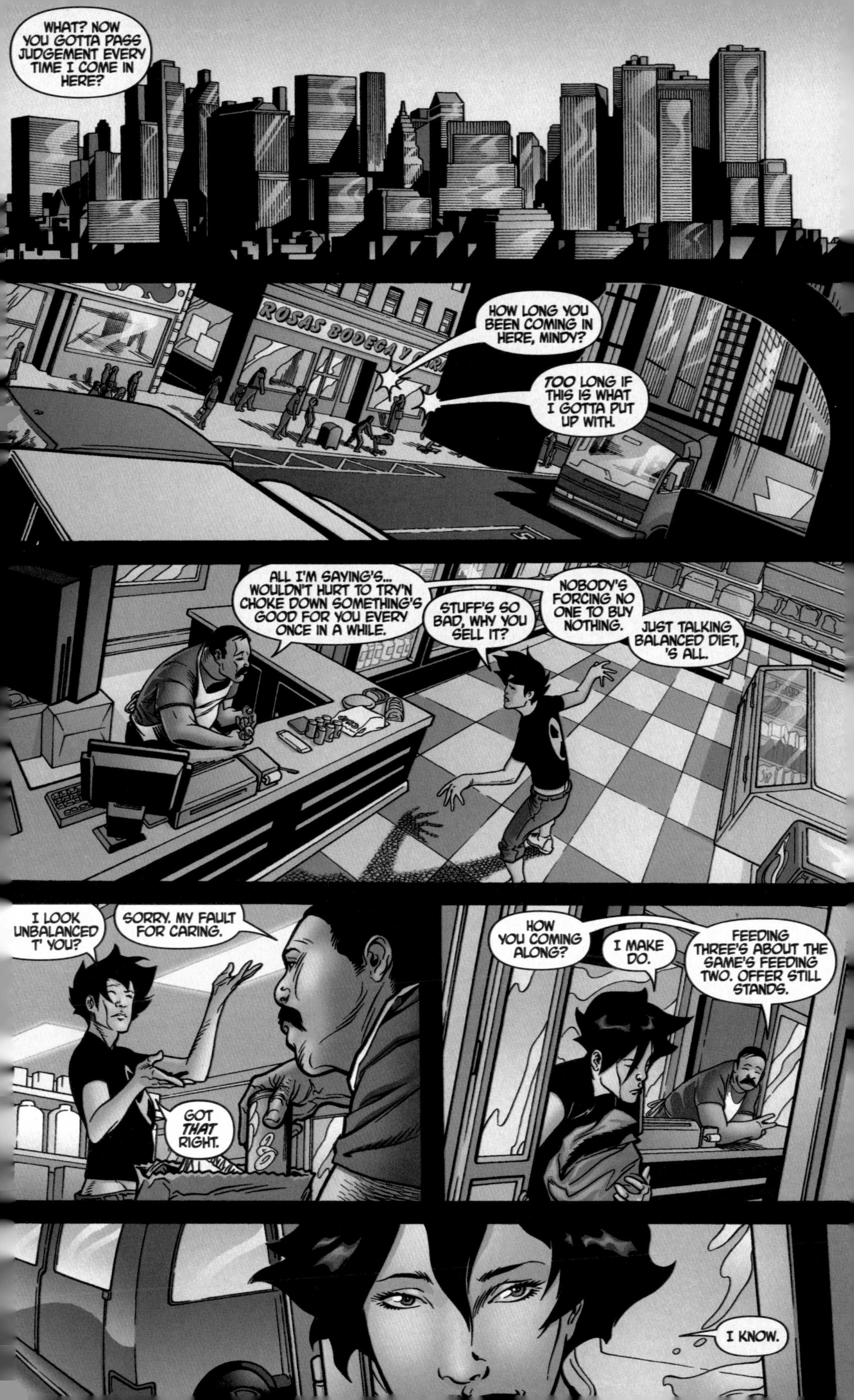
WHAT? NOW YOU GOTTA PASS JUDGEMENT EVERY TIME I COME IN HERE?
ROSAS BODEGA Y
HOW LONG YOU BEEN COMING IN HERE, MINDY?
TOO LONG IF THIS IS WHAT I GOTTA PUT UP WITH.
ALL I'M SAYING'S... WOULDN'T HURT TO TRY'N CHOKE DOWN SOMETHING'S GOOD FOR YOU EVERY ONCE IN A WHILE.
STUFF'S SO BAD, WHY YOU SELL IT?
NOBODY'S FORCING NO ONE TO BUY NOTHING.
JUST TALKING BALANCED DIET, 'S ALL.
I LOOK UNBALANCED T' YOU?
SORRY. MY FAULT FOR CARING.
GOT THAT RIGHT.
HOW YOU COMING ALONG?
I MAKE DO.
FEEDING THREE'S ABOUT THE SAME'S FEEDING TWO. OFFER STILL STANDS.
I KNOW.

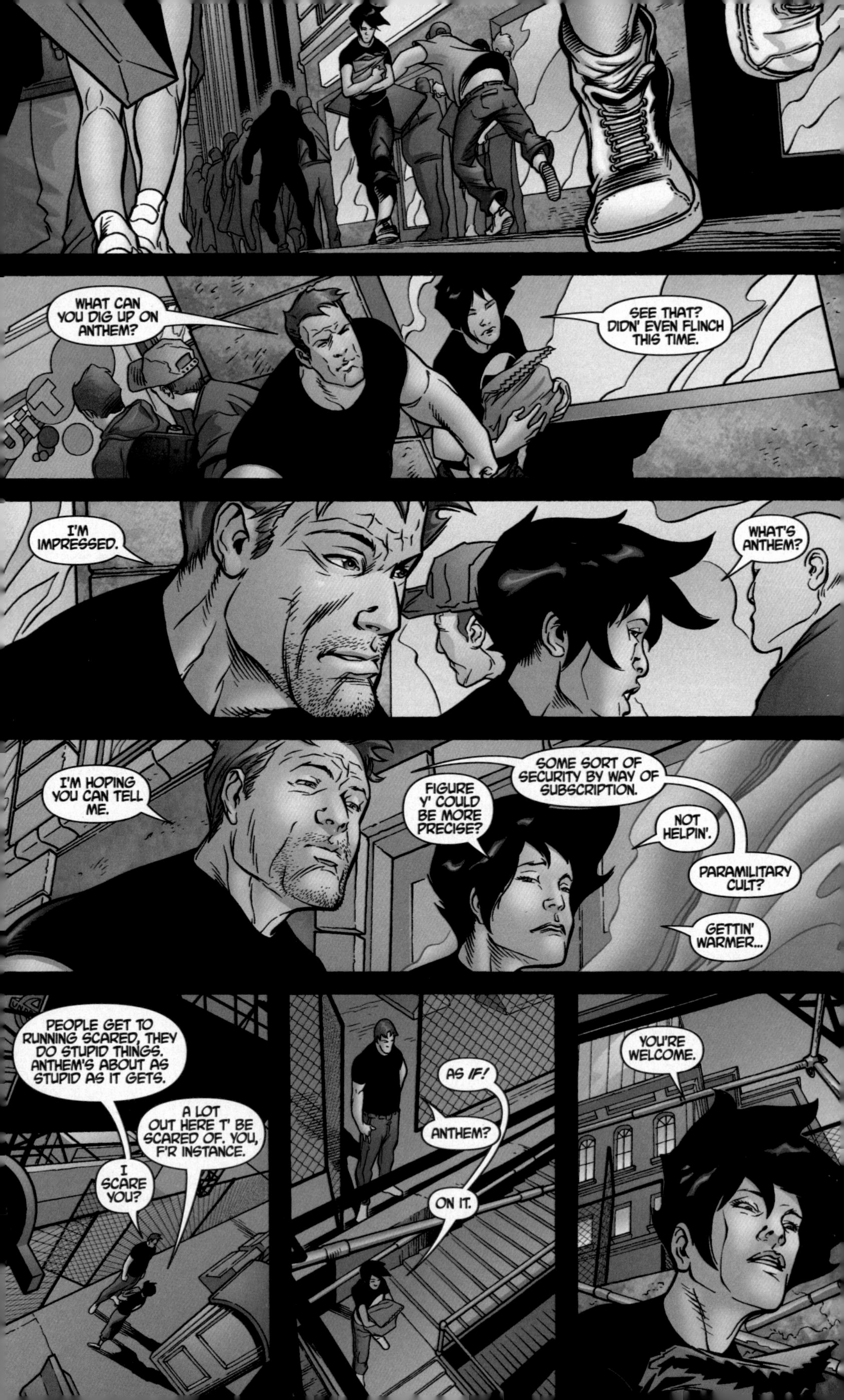
WHAT CAN YOU DIG UP ON ANTHEM?
SEE THAT? DIDN' EVEN FLINCH THIS TIME.
I'M IMPRESSED.
WHAT'S ANTHEM?
I'M HOPING YOU CAN TELL ME.
FIGURE Y' COULD BE MORE PRECISE?
SOME SORT OF SECURITY BY WAY OF SUBSCRIPTION.
NOT HELPIN'.
PARAMILITARY CULT?
GETTIN' WARMER...
PEOPLE GET TO RUNNING SCARED, THEY DO STUPID THINGS. ANTHEM'S ABOUT AS STUPID AS IT GETS.
A LOT OUT HERE T' BE SCARED OF. YOU, F'R INSTANCE.
I SCARE YOU?
AS IF!
ANTHEM?
ON IT.
YOU'RE WELCOME.

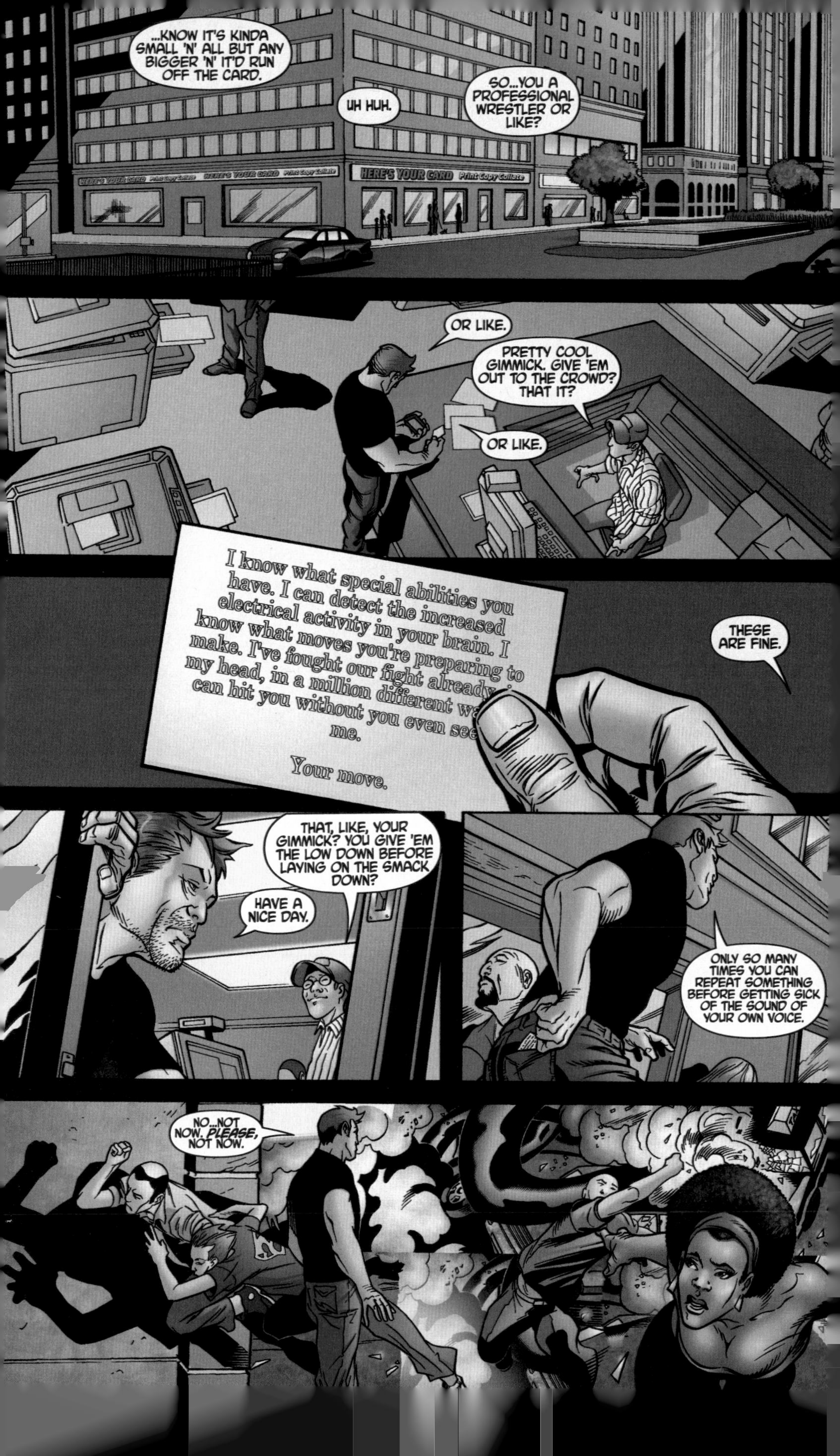
...KNOW IT'S KINDA SMALL 'N' ALL BUT ANY BIGGER 'N' IT'D RUN OFF THE CARD.
UH HUH.
SO...YOU A PROFESSIONAL WRESTLER OR LIKE?
HERE'S YOUR CARD Print Copy Collate
OR LIKE.
PRETTY COOL GIMMICK. GIVE 'EM OUT TO THE CROWD? THAT IT?
OR LIKE.
I know what special abilities you have. I can detect the increased electrical activity in your brain. I know what moves you're preparing to make. I've fought our fight already in my head, in a million different ways. I can hit you without you even seeing me.
Your move.
THESE ARE FINE.
THAT, LIKE, YOUR GIMMICK? YOU GIVE 'EM THE LOW DOWN BEFORE LAYING ON THE SMACK DOWN?
HAVE A NICE DAY.
ONLY SO MANY TIMES YOU CAN REPEAT SOMETHING BEFORE GETTING SICK OF THE SOUND OF YOUR OWN VOICE.
NO...NOT NOW. PLEASE, NOT NOW.

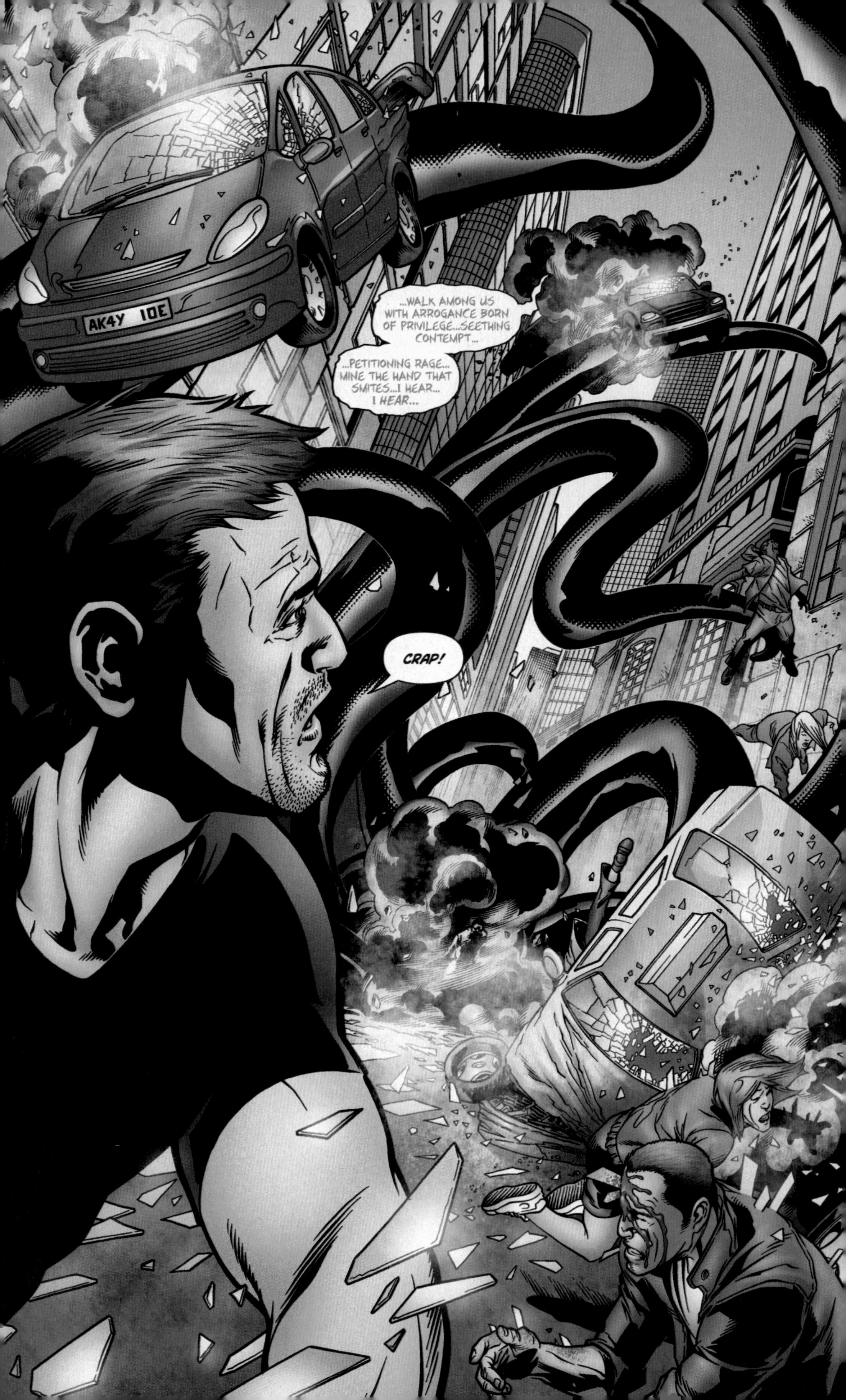
AK4Y IOE
...WALK AMONG US WITH ARROGANCE BORN OF PRIVILEGE...SEETHING CONTEMPT...
...PETITIONING RAGE... MINE THE HAND THAT SMITES...I HEAR... I HEAR...
CRAP!

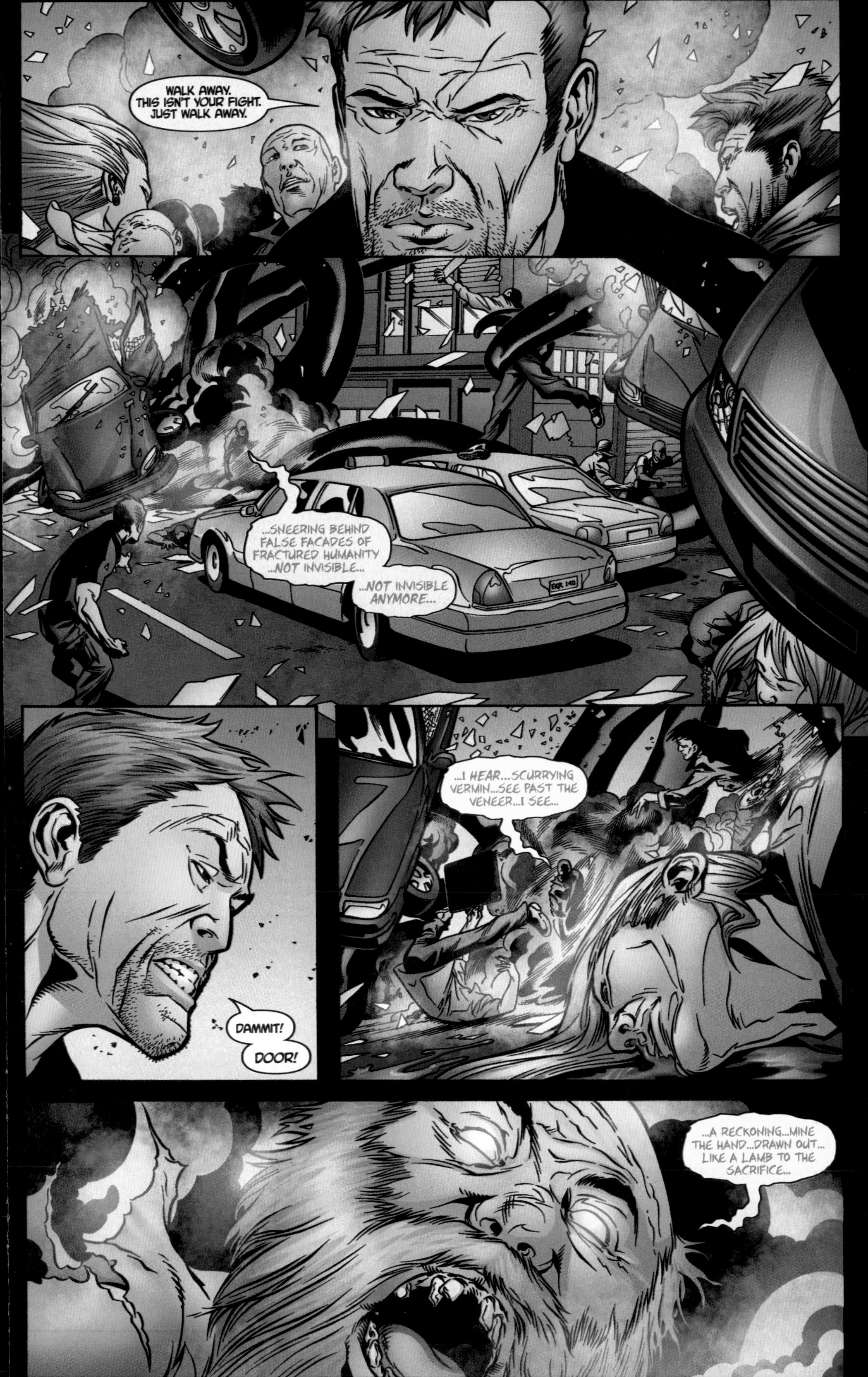
WALK AWAY. THIS ISN'T YOUR FIGHT. JUST WALK AWAY.
...SNEERING BEHIND FALSE FACADES OF FRACTURED HUMANITY ...NOT INVISIBLE...
...NOT INVISIBLE ANYMORE...
DAMMIT!
DOOR!
...I HEAR...SCURRYING VERMIN...SEE PAST THE VENEER...I SEE...
...A RECKONING...MINE THE HAND...DRAWN OUT... LIKE A LAMB TO THE SACRIFICE...

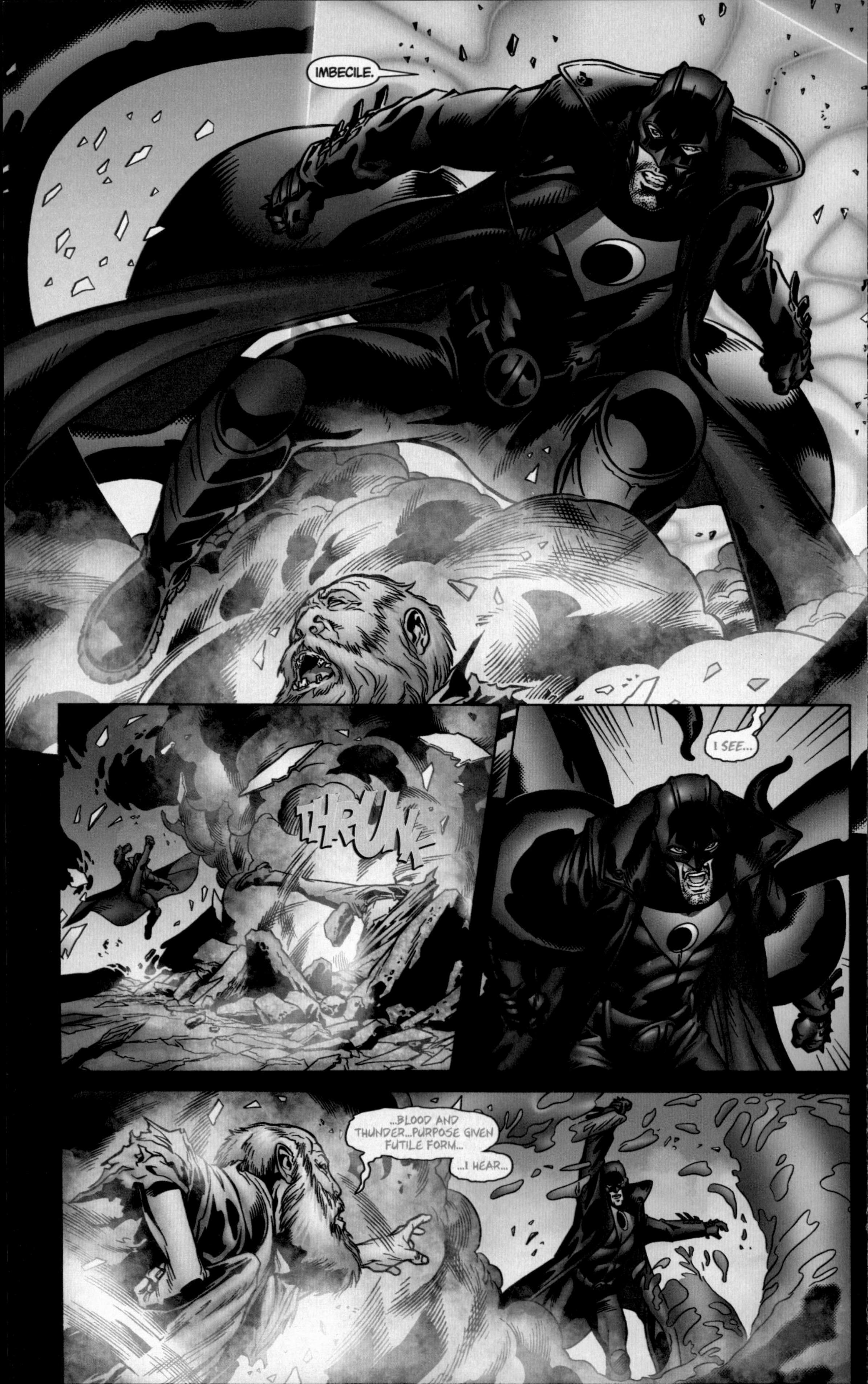
IMBECILE.
THRUNK
I SEE...
...BLOOD AND THUNDER...PURPOSE GIVEN FUTILE FORM...
...I HEAR...

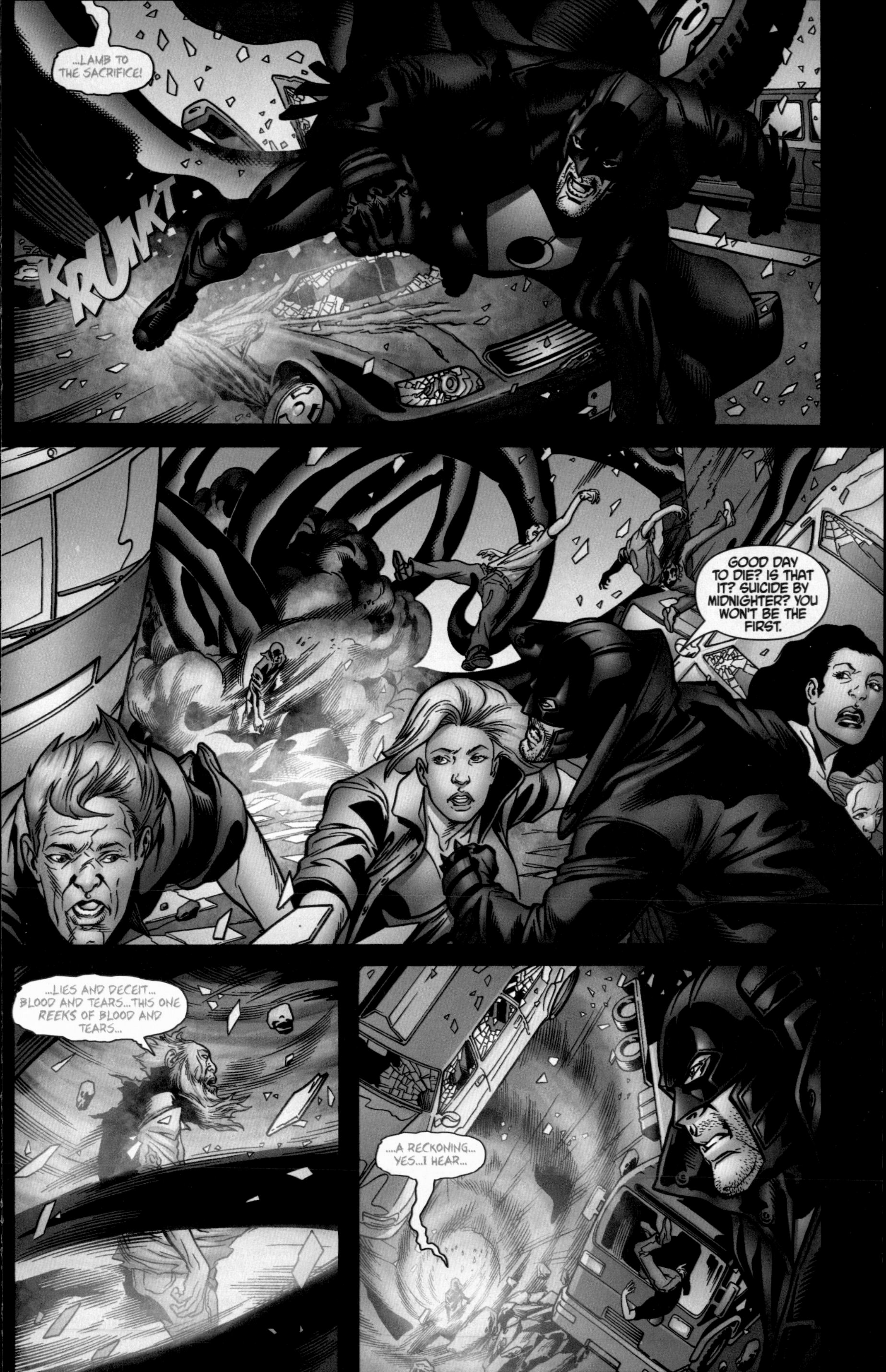
...LAMB TO THE SACRIFICE!
KRUNKT
GOOD DAY TO DIE? IS THAT IT? SUICIDE BY MIDNIGHTER? YOU WON'T BE THE FIRST.
...LIES AND DECEIT... BLOOD AND TEARS...THIS ONE REEKS OF BLOOD AND TEARS...
...A RECKONING... YES...I HEAR...

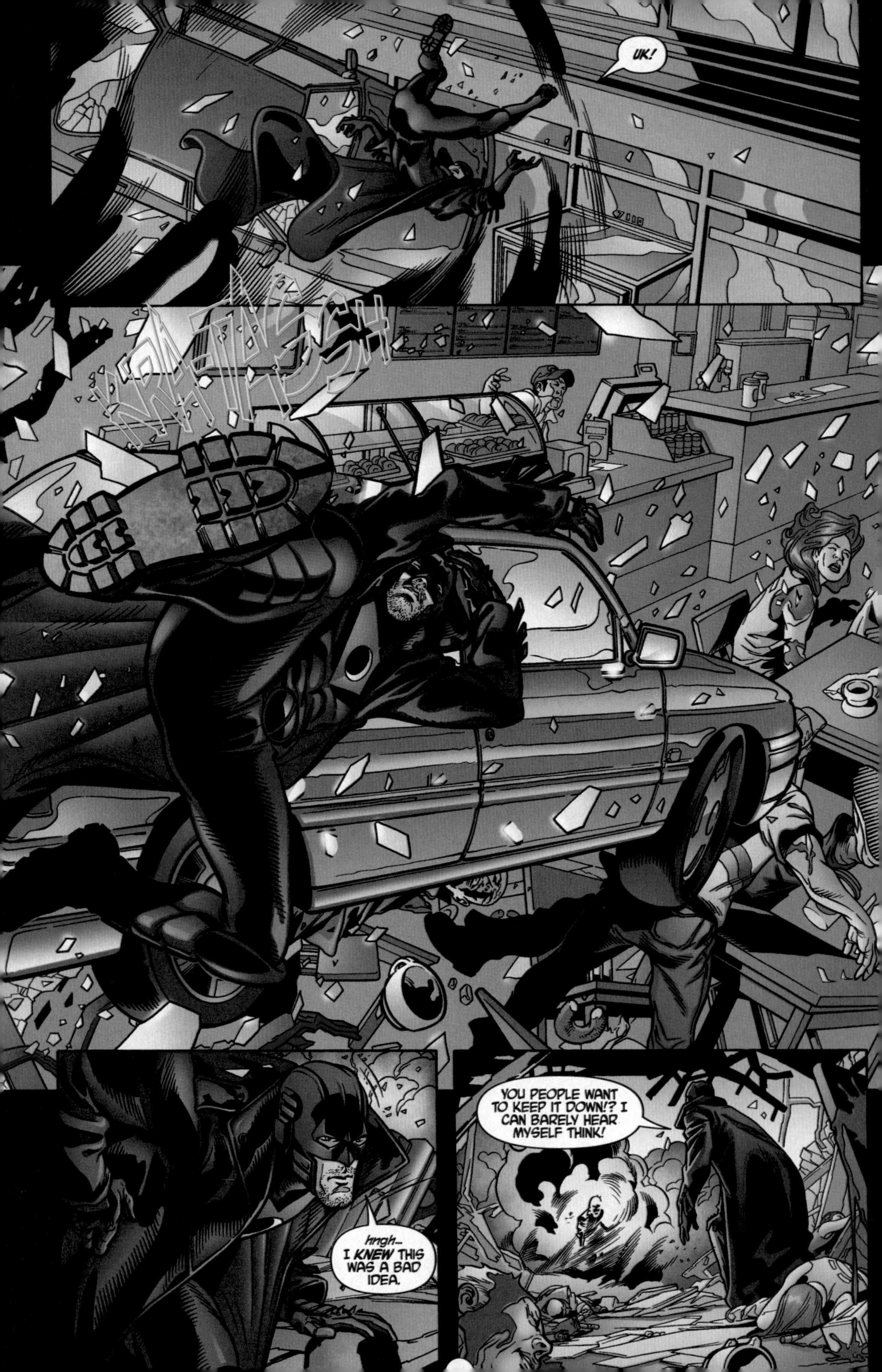
UK!
KRATOOSH
hngh... I KNEW THIS WAS A BAD IDEA.
YOU PEOPLE WANT TO KEEP IT DOWN!? I CAN BARELY HEAR MYSELF THINK!

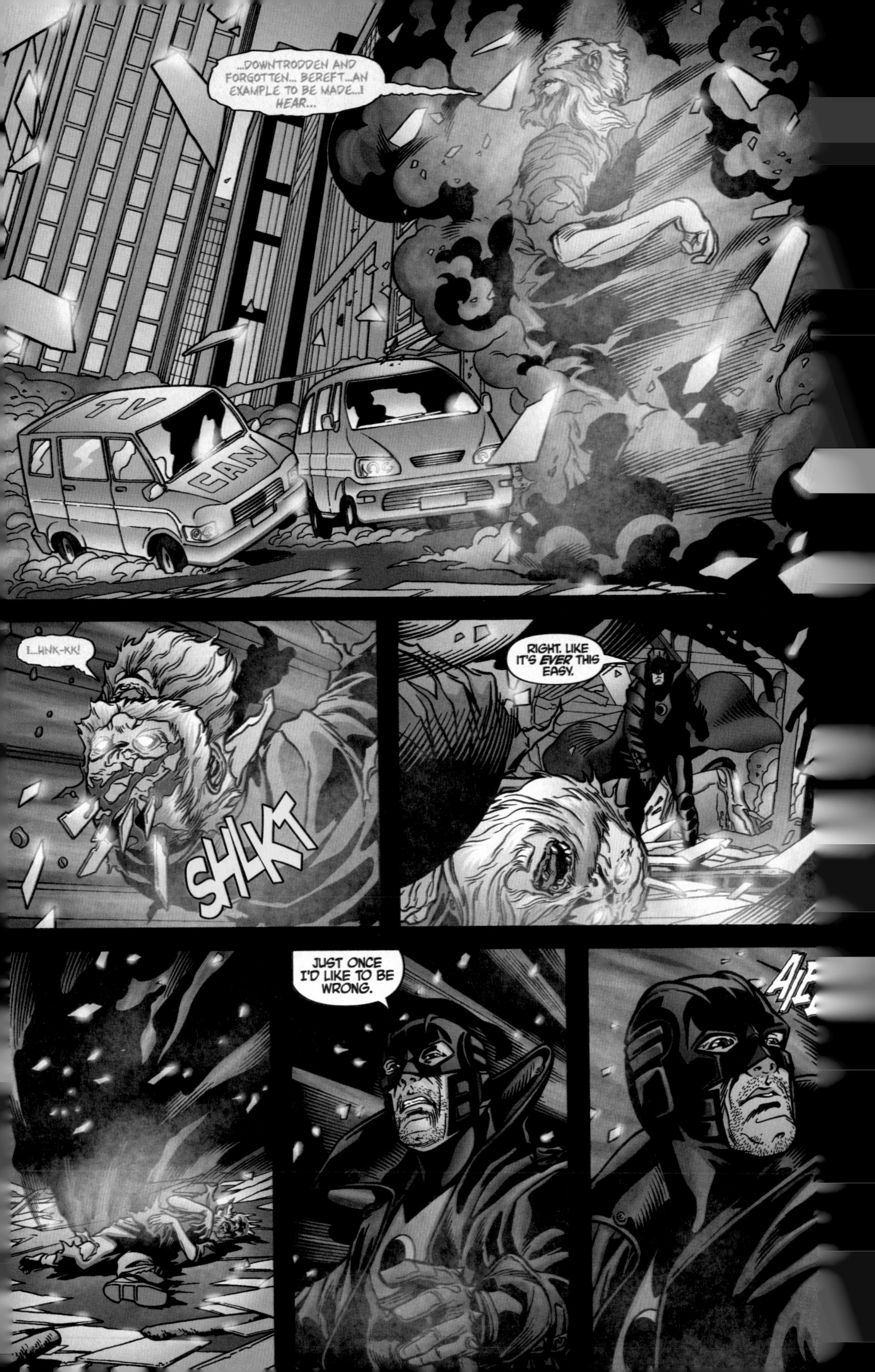
...DOWNTRODDEN AND FORGOTTEN... BEREFT...AN EXAMPLE TO BE MADE...I HEAR...
TV
CAN
I...HNK-KK!
SHLKT
RIGHT. LIKE IT'S *EVER* THIS EASY.
JUST ONCE I'D LIKE TO BE WRONG.

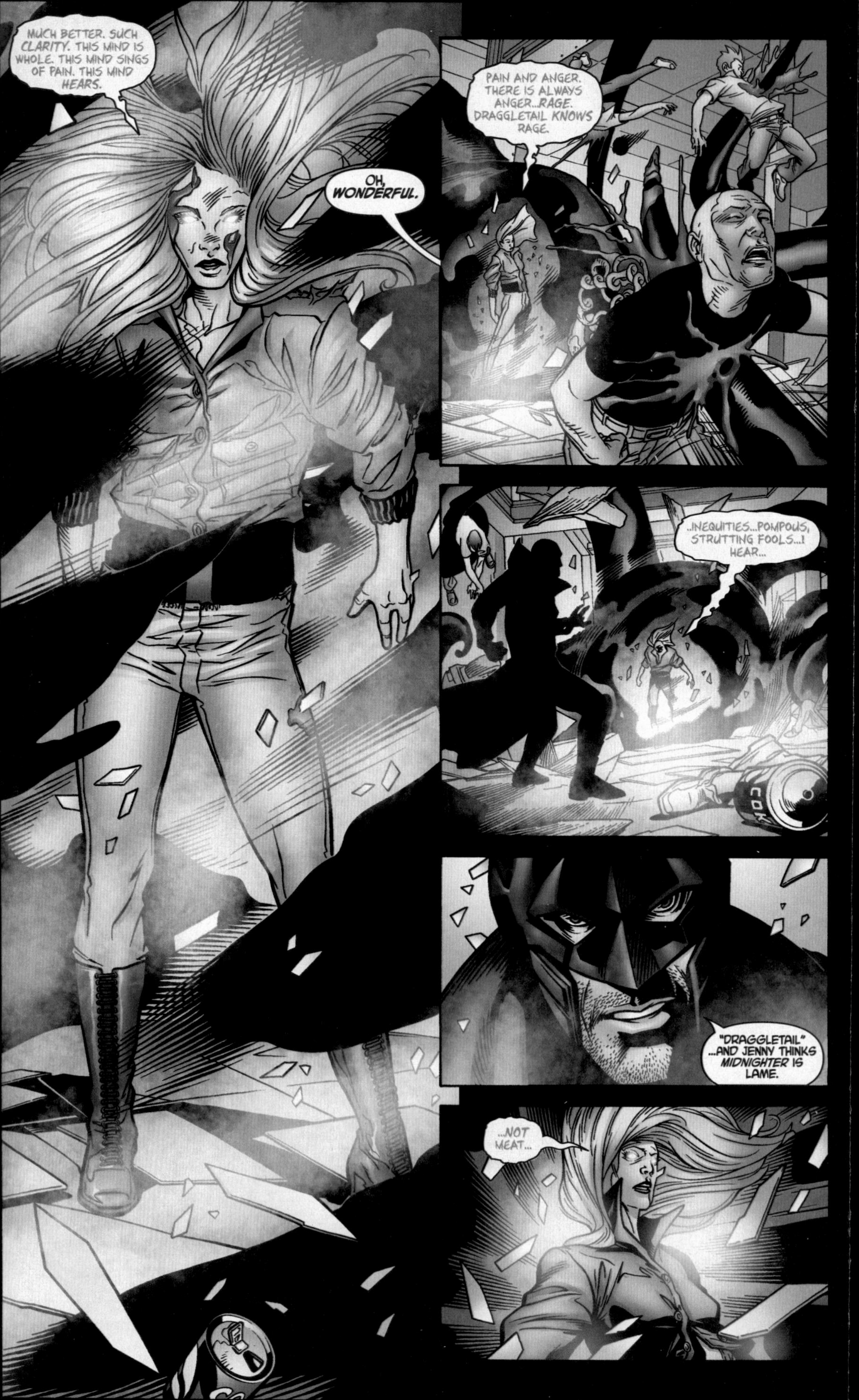
MUCH BETTER. SUCH CLARITY. THIS MIND IS WHOLE. THIS MIND SINGS OF PAIN. THIS MIND HEARS.
OH, WONDERFUL.
PAIN AND ANGER. THERE IS ALWAYS ANGER...RAGE. DRAGGLETAIL KNOWS RAGE.
..INEQUITIES...POMPOUS, STRUTTING FOOLS...I HEAR...
"DRAGGLETAIL" ...AND JENNY THINKS MIDNIGHTER IS LAME.
...NOT MEAT...

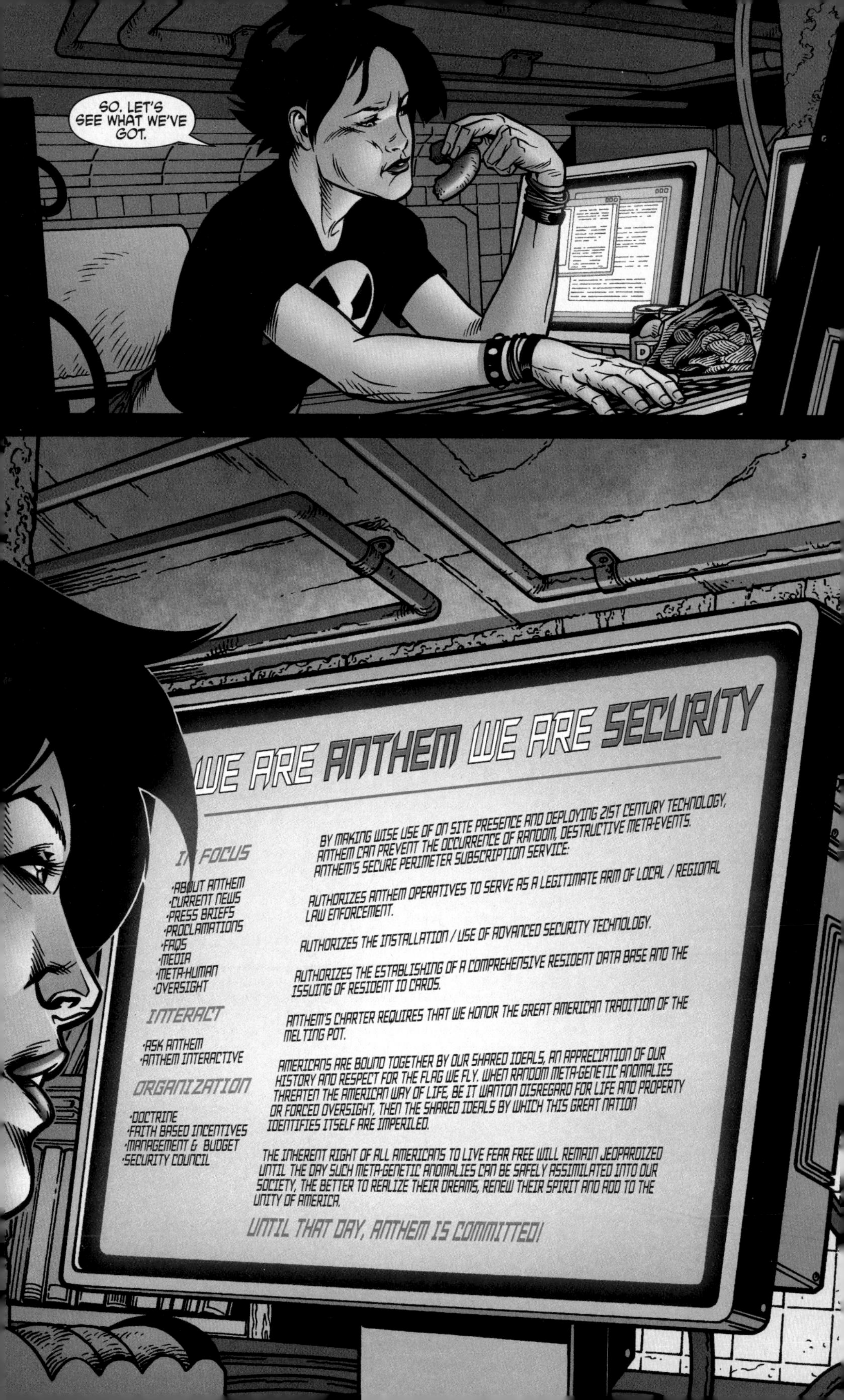
SO. LET'S SEE WHAT WE'VE GOT.
WE ARE ANTHEM WE ARE SECURITY
FOCUS
·ABOUT ANTHEM
·CURRENT NEWS
·PRESS BRIEFS
·PROCLAMATIONS
·FAQS
·MEDIA
·META-HUMAN
·OVERSIGHT
INTERACT
·ASK ANTHEM
·ANTHEM INTERACTIVE
ORGANIZATION
·DOCTRINE
·FAITH BASED INCENTIVES
·MANAGEMENT & BUDGET
·SECURITY COUNCIL
BY MAKING WISE USE OF ON SITE PRESENCE AND DEPLOYING 21ST CENTURY TECHNOLOGY, ANTHEM CAN PREVENT THE OCCURRENCE OF RANDOM, DESTRUCTIVE META-EVENTS. ANTHEM'S SECURE PERIMETER SUBSCRIPTION SERVICE:
AUTHORIZES ANTHEM OPERATIVES TO SERVE AS A LEGITIMATE ARM OF LOCAL / REGIONAL LAW ENFORCEMENT.
AUTHORIZES THE INSTALLATION / USE OF ADVANCED SECURITY TECHNOLOGY.
AUTHORIZES THE ESTABLISHING OF A COMPREHENSIVE RESIDENT DATA BASE AND THE ISSUING OF RESIDENT ID CARDS.
ANTHEM'S CHARTER REQUIRES THAT WE HONOR THE GREAT AMERICAN TRADITION OF THE MELTING POT.
AMERICANS ARE BOUND TOGETHER BY OUR SHARED IDEALS, AN APPRECIATION OF OUR HISTORY AND RESPECT FOR THE FLAG WE FLY. WHEN RANDOM META-GENETIC ANOMALIES THREATEN THE AMERICAN WAY OF LIFE, BE IT WANTON DISREGARD FOR LIFE AND PROPERTY OR FORCED OVERSIGHT, THEN THE SHARED IDEALS BY WHICH THIS GREAT NATION IDENTIFIES ITSELF ARE IMPERILED.
THE INHERENT RIGHT OF ALL AMERICANS TO LIVE FEAR FREE WILL REMAIN JEOPARDIZED UNTIL THE DAY SUCH META-GENETIC ANOMALIES CAN BE SAFELY ASSIMILATED INTO OUR SOCIETY, THE BETTER TO REALIZE THEIR DREAMS, RENEW THEIR SPIRIT AND ADD TO THE UNITY OF AMERICA.
UNTIL THAT DAY, ANTHEM IS COMMITTED!

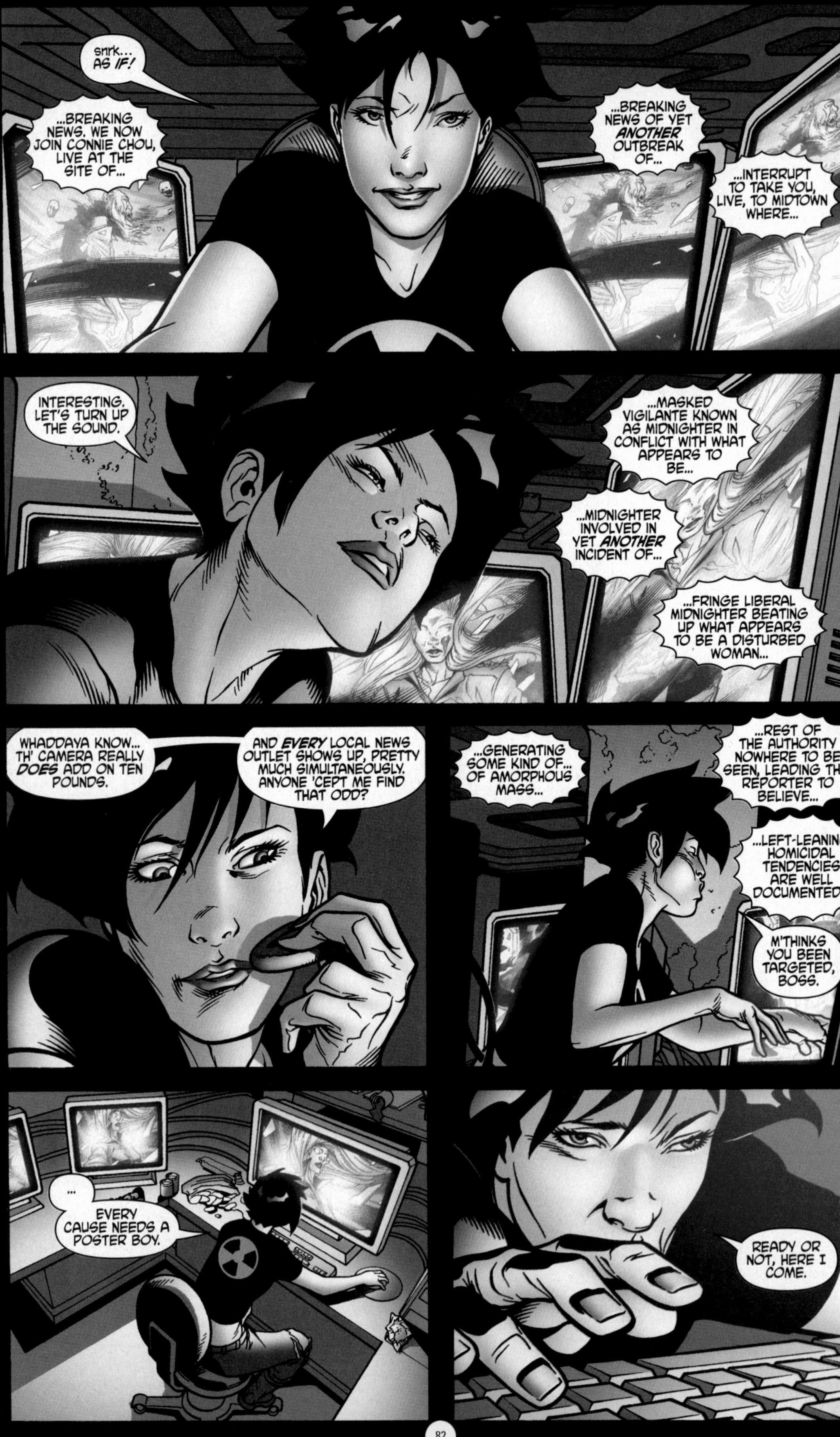
SNRK... AS IF!
...BREAKING NEWS. WE NOW JOIN CONNIE CHOU, LIVE AT THE SITE OF...
...BREAKING NEWS OF YET ANOTHER OUTBREAK OF...
...INTERRUPT TO TAKE YOU, LIVE, TO MIDTOWN WHERE...
INTERESTING. LET'S TURN UP THE SOUND.
...MASKED VIGILANTE KNOWN AS MIDNIGHTER IN CONFLICT WITH WHAT APPEARS TO BE...
...MIDNIGHTER INVOLVED IN YET ANOTHER INCIDENT OF...
...FRINGE LIBERAL MIDNIGHTER BEATING UP WHAT APPEARS TO BE A DISTURBED WOMAN...
WHADDAYA KNOW... TH' CAMERA REALLY DOES ADD ON TEN POUNDS.
AND EVERY LOCAL NEWS OUTLET SHOWS UP, PRETTY MUCH SIMULTANEOUSLY. ANYONE 'CEPT ME FIND THAT ODD?
...GENERATING SOME KIND OF... OF AMORPHOUS MASS...
...REST OF THE AUTHORITY NOWHERE TO BE SEEN, LEADING THIS REPORTER TO BELIEVE...
...LEFT-LEANING HOMICIDAL TENDENCIES ARE WELL DOCUMENTED...
M'THINKS YOU BEEN TARGETED, BOSS.
... EVERY CAUSE NEEDS A POSTER BOY.
READY OR NOT, HERE I COME.

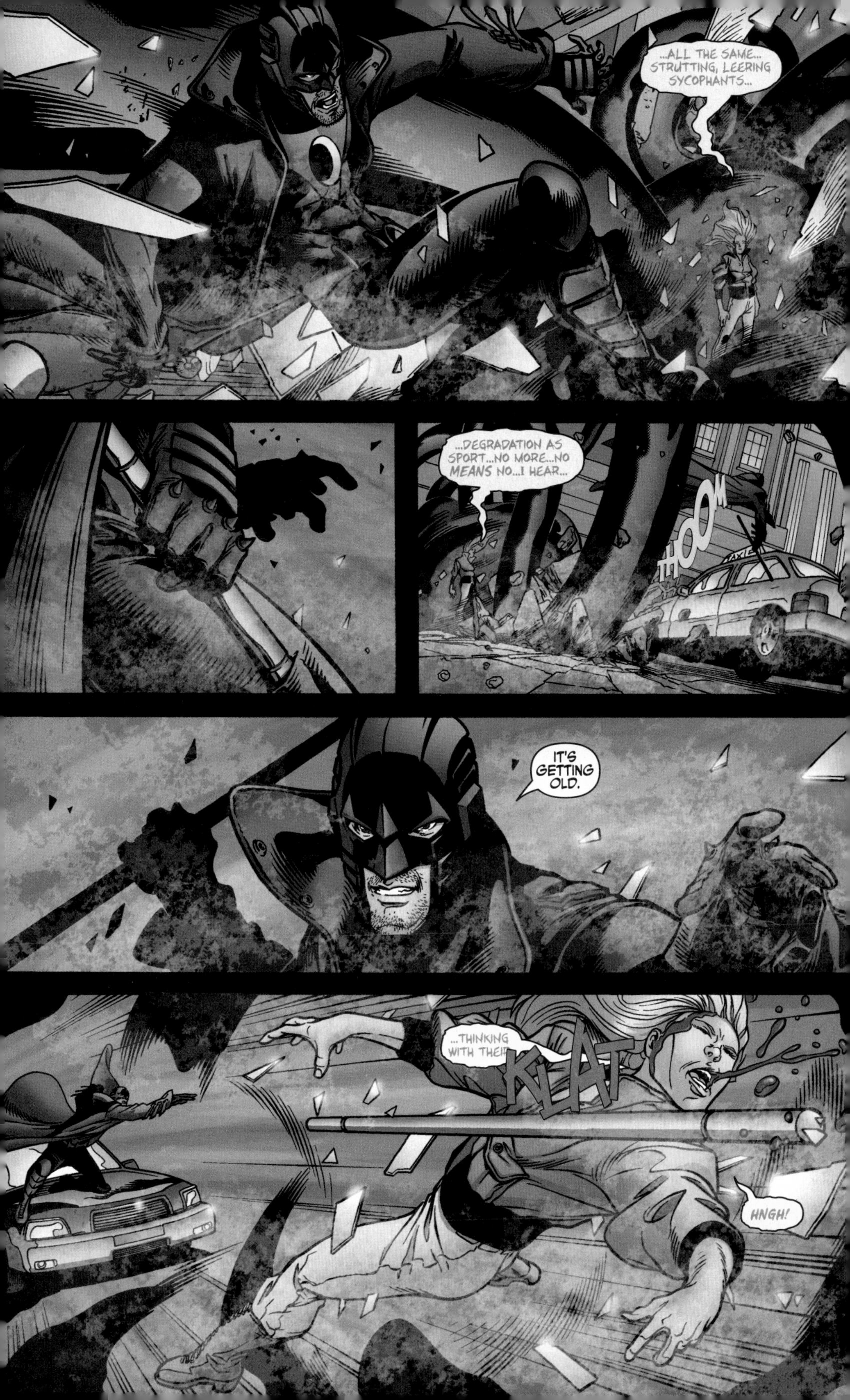
...ALL THE SAME... STRUTTING, LEERING SYCOPHANTS...
...DEGRADATION AS SPORT...NO MORE...NO MEANS NO...I HEAR...
WHOOM
IT'S GETTING OLD.
...THINKING WITH THEIR
KLAT
HNGH!

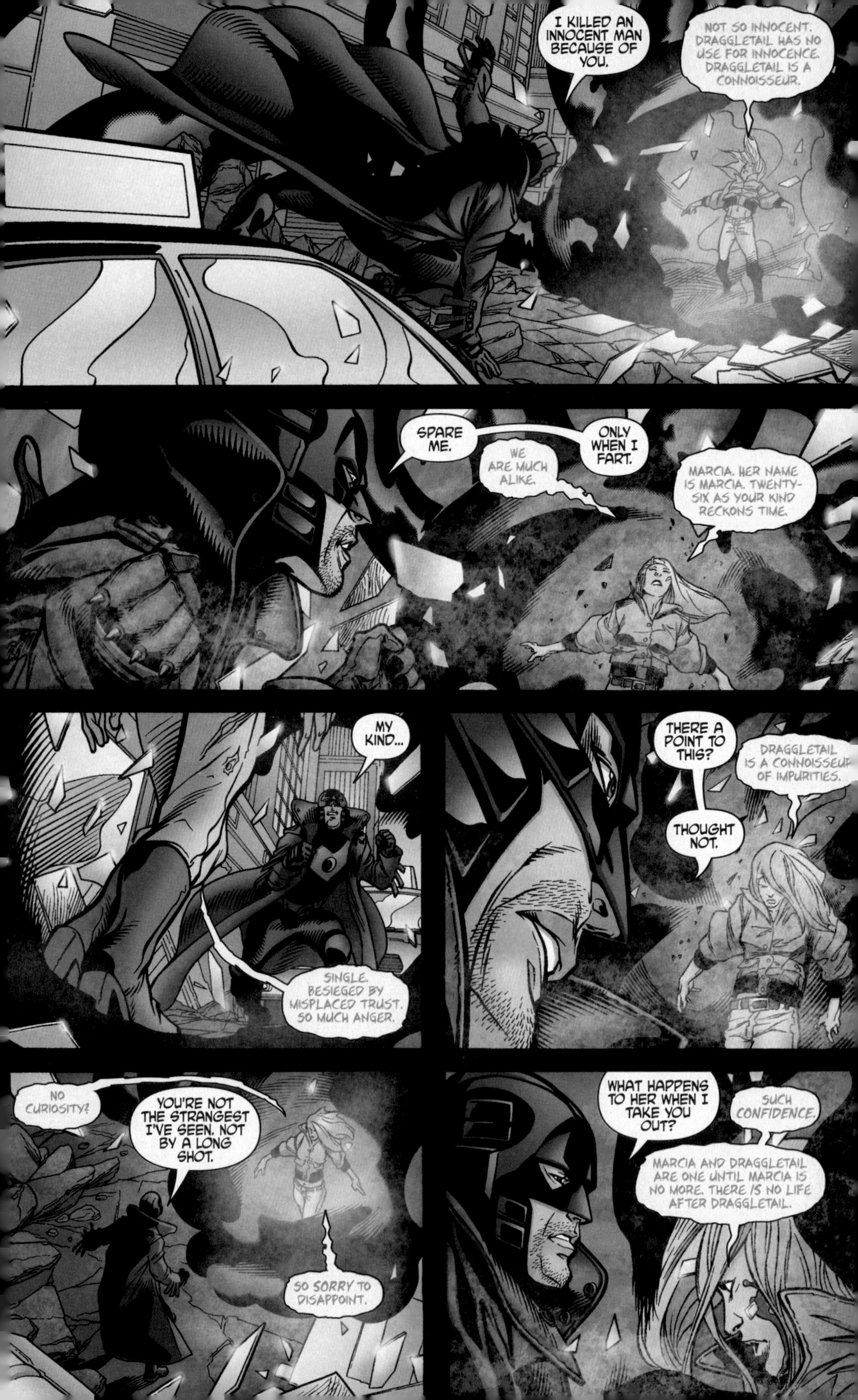
I KILLED AN INNOCENT MAN BECAUSE OF YOU.
NOT SO INNOCENT. DRAGGLETAIL HAS NO USE FOR INNOCENCE. DRAGGLETAIL IS A CONNOISSEUR.
SPARE ME.
WE ARE MUCH ALIKE.
ONLY WHEN I FART.
MARCIA. HER NAME IS MARCIA. TWENTY-SIX AS YOUR KIND RECKONS TIME.
MY KIND...
SINGLE. BESIEGED BY MISPLACED TRUST. SO MUCH ANGER.
THERE A POINT TO THIS?
DRAGGLETAIL IS A CONNOISSEUR OF IMPURITIES.
THOUGHT NOT.
NO CURIOSITY?
YOU'RE NOT THE STRANGEST I'VE SEEN. NOT BY A LONG SHOT.
SO SORRY TO DISAPPOINT.
WHAT HAPPENS TO HER WHEN I TAKE YOU OUT?
SUCH CONFIDENCE.
MARCIA AND DRAGGLETAIL ARE ONE UNTIL MARCIA IS NO MORE. THERE IS NO LIFE AFTER DRAGGLETAIL.

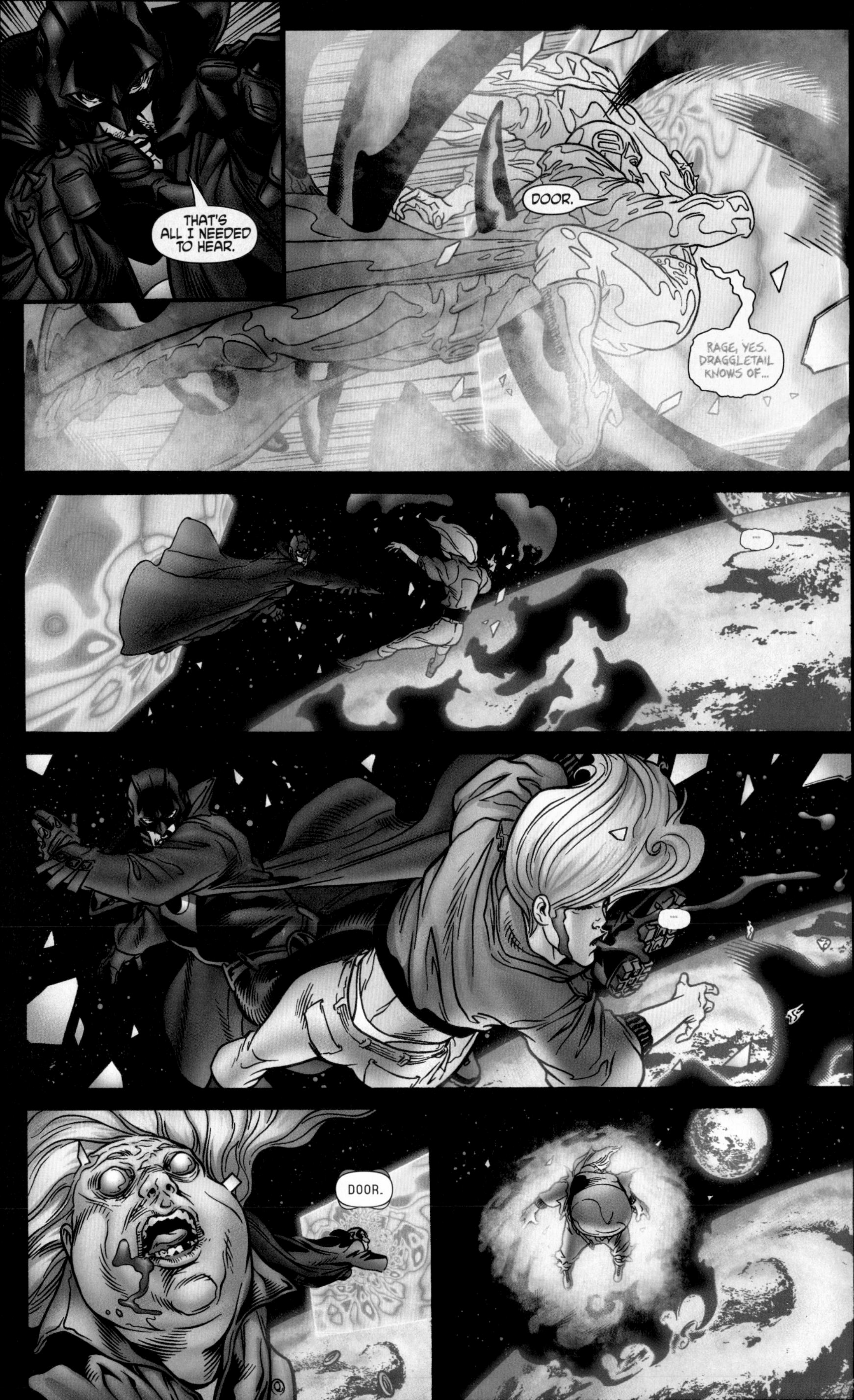
THAT'S ALL I NEEDED TO HEAR.
DOOR.
RAGE, YES. DRAGGLETAIL KNOWS OF...
DOOR.

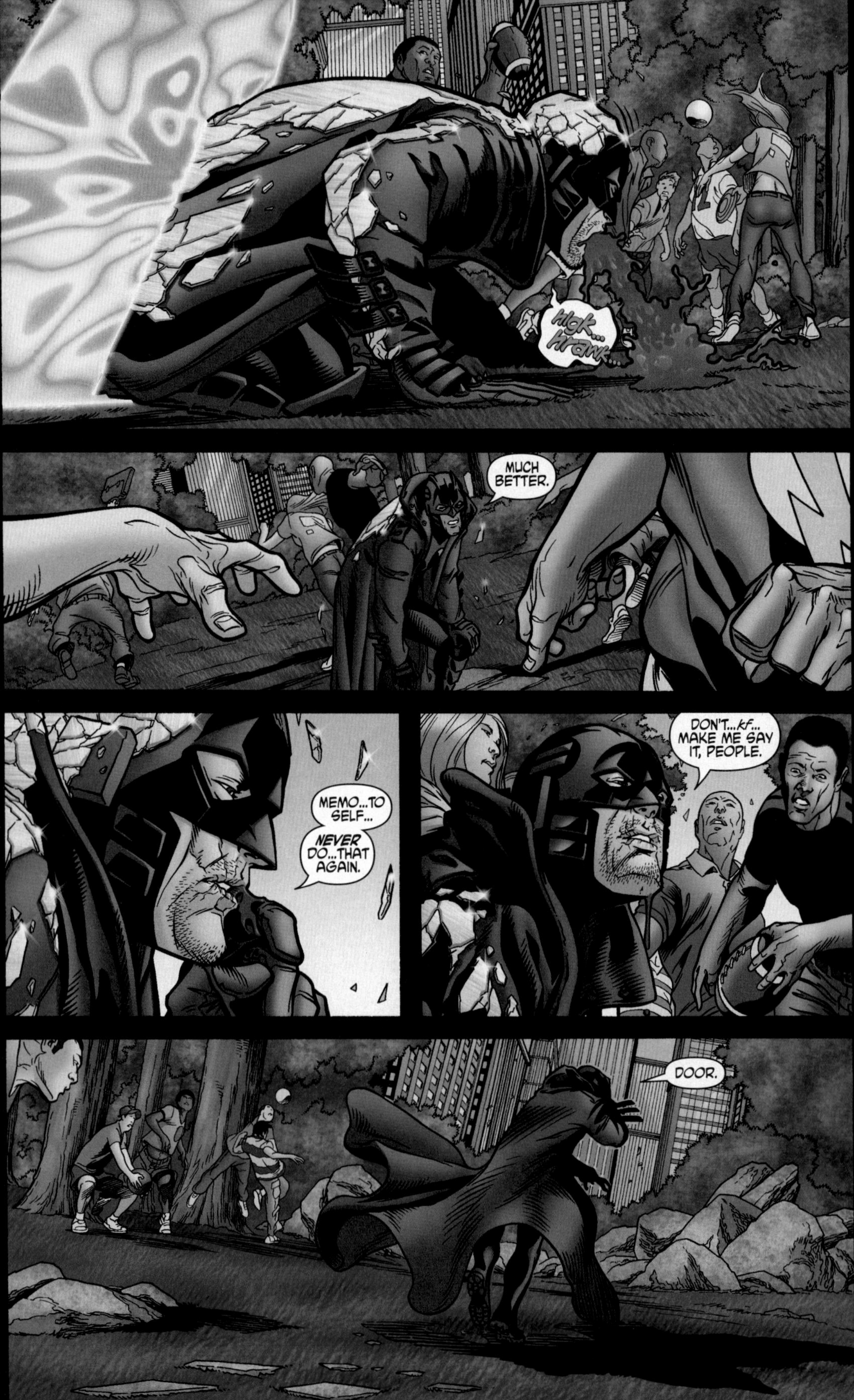
hlgk... hrawk
MUCH BETTER.
MEMO...TO SELF... NEVER DO...THAT AGAIN.
DON'T...kf... MAKE ME SAY IT, PEOPLE.
DOOR.

...LATEST INCIDENT OF META-HUMAN COMBAT PLAYED OUT IN A PUBLIC ARENA WITH LITTLE OR NO REGARD FOR COLLATERAL DAMAGE.

THIS AFTERNOON, THE AUTHORITY OPERATIVE KNOWN AS MIDNIGHTER FOUGHT IT OUT WITH AN, AS YET, UNIDENTIFIED META-HUMAN...

...BEFORE BOTH VANISHED INTO WHAT APPEARS TO BE A GLOWING *PORTAL*.

THIS MARKS THE FOURTH INCIDENT OF THIS KIND IN AS MANY MONTHS. ASKED FOR COMMENT, MAYOR YARLSBERG'S OFFICE DECLINED...

...WORLD'S PREEMINENT AUTHORITY ON META-HUMAN AFFAIRS AND AUTHOR OF "GOD COMPLEX."

PROFESSOR, IN YOUR BOOK, YOU CITE NUMEROUS INSTANCES OF DISASTERS THAT CAN BE DIRECTLY TRACED TO META-HUMAN ACTIVITY.

DISASTERS THAT WERE THE *DIRECT RESULT* OF META-HUMAN ACTIVITY.

Preston Warre

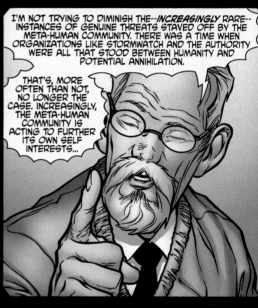

I'M NOT TRYING TO DIMINISH THE--*INCREASINGLY* RARE--INSTANCES OF GENUINE THREATS STAVED OFF BY THE META-HUMAN COMMUNITY. THERE WAS A TIME WHEN ORGANIZATIONS LIKE STORMWATCH AND THE AUTHORITY WERE ALL THAT STOOD BETWEEN HUMANITY AND POTENTIAL ANNIHILATION.

THAT'S, MORE OFTEN THAN NOT, NO LONGER THE CASE. INCREASINGLY, THE META-HUMAN COMMUNITY IS ACTING TO FURTHER ITS OWN SELF INTERESTS...

...WHATEVER HAPPENED TO *ACCOUNTABILITY?* THE AUTHORITY'S PIT BULL RIPS UP MIDTOWN MANHATTAN AND THAT'S THAT? TWELVE PEOPLE *DIED!*

THESE "HEROES" ARE *NOT* ABOVE THE LAW! NO. LET ME REPHRASE THAT. THESE "COSTUMED HOOLIGANS!"

AND THIS MIDNIGHTER CHARACTER! TALK ABOUT THE WORST OF A BAD LOT! SINCE WHEN ARE *MURDERERS* ELEVATED TO *HEROES?*

THIS IS THE TYPE OF ROLE MODEL WE WANT FOR OUR KIDS? NOT *MY* KIDS! IT *SICKENS* ME TO THINK THAT...

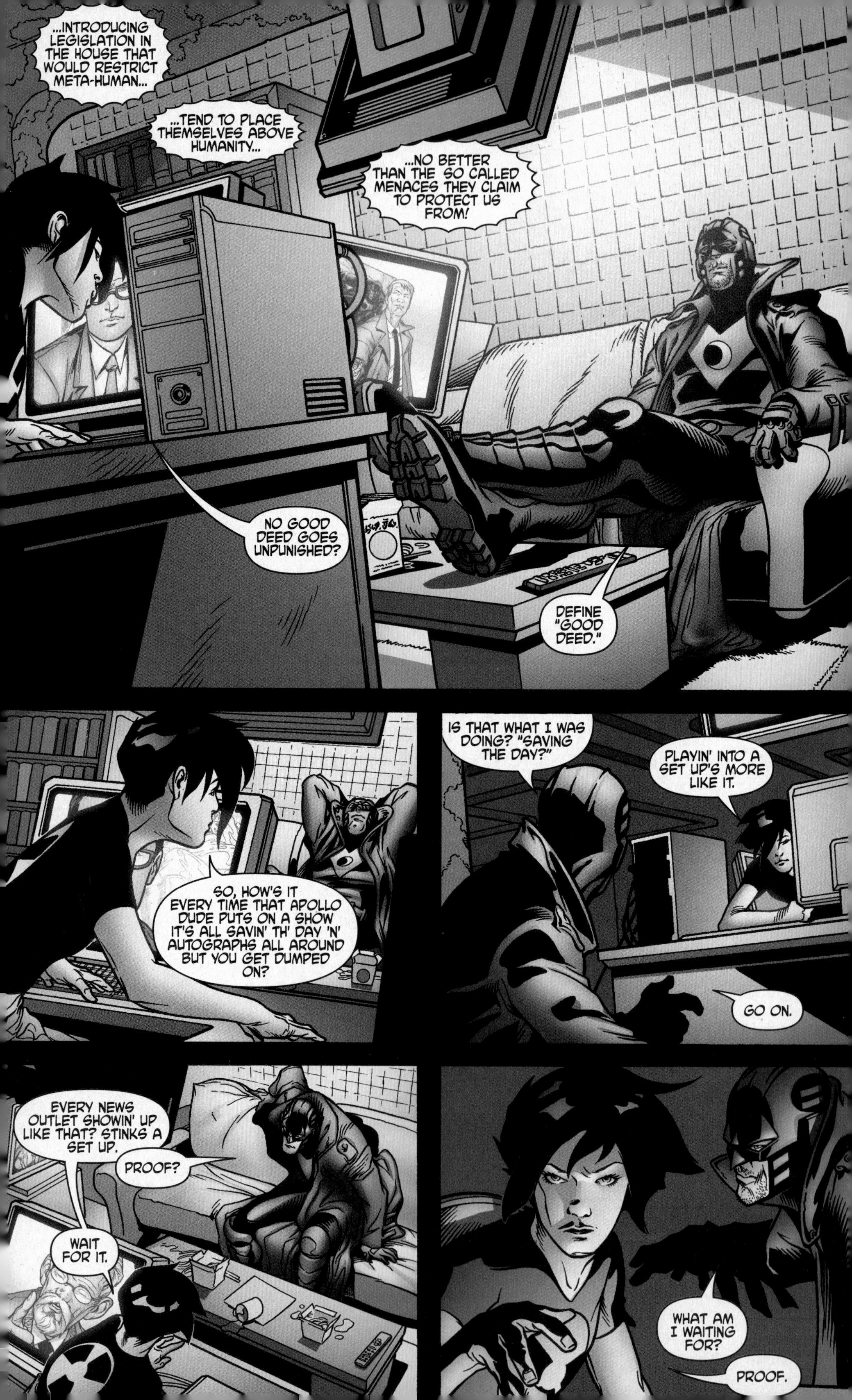
...INTRODUCING LEGISLATION IN THE HOUSE THAT WOULD RESTRICT META-HUMAN...
...TEND TO PLACE THEMSELVES ABOVE HUMANITY...
...NO BETTER THAN THE SO CALLED MENACES THEY CLAIM TO PROTECT US FROM!
NO GOOD DEED GOES UNPUNISHED?
DEFINE "GOOD DEED."
SO, HOW'S IT EVERY TIME THAT APOLLO DUDE PUTS ON A SHOW IT'S ALL SAVIN' TH' DAY 'N' AUTOGRAPHS ALL AROUND BUT YOU GET DUMPED ON?
IS THAT WHAT I WAS DOING? "SAVING THE DAY?"
PLAYIN' INTO A SET UP'S MORE LIKE IT.
GO ON.
EVERY NEWS OUTLET SHOWIN' UP LIKE THAT? STINKS A SET UP.
PROOF?
WAIT FOR IT.
WHAT AM I WAITING FOR?
PROOF.

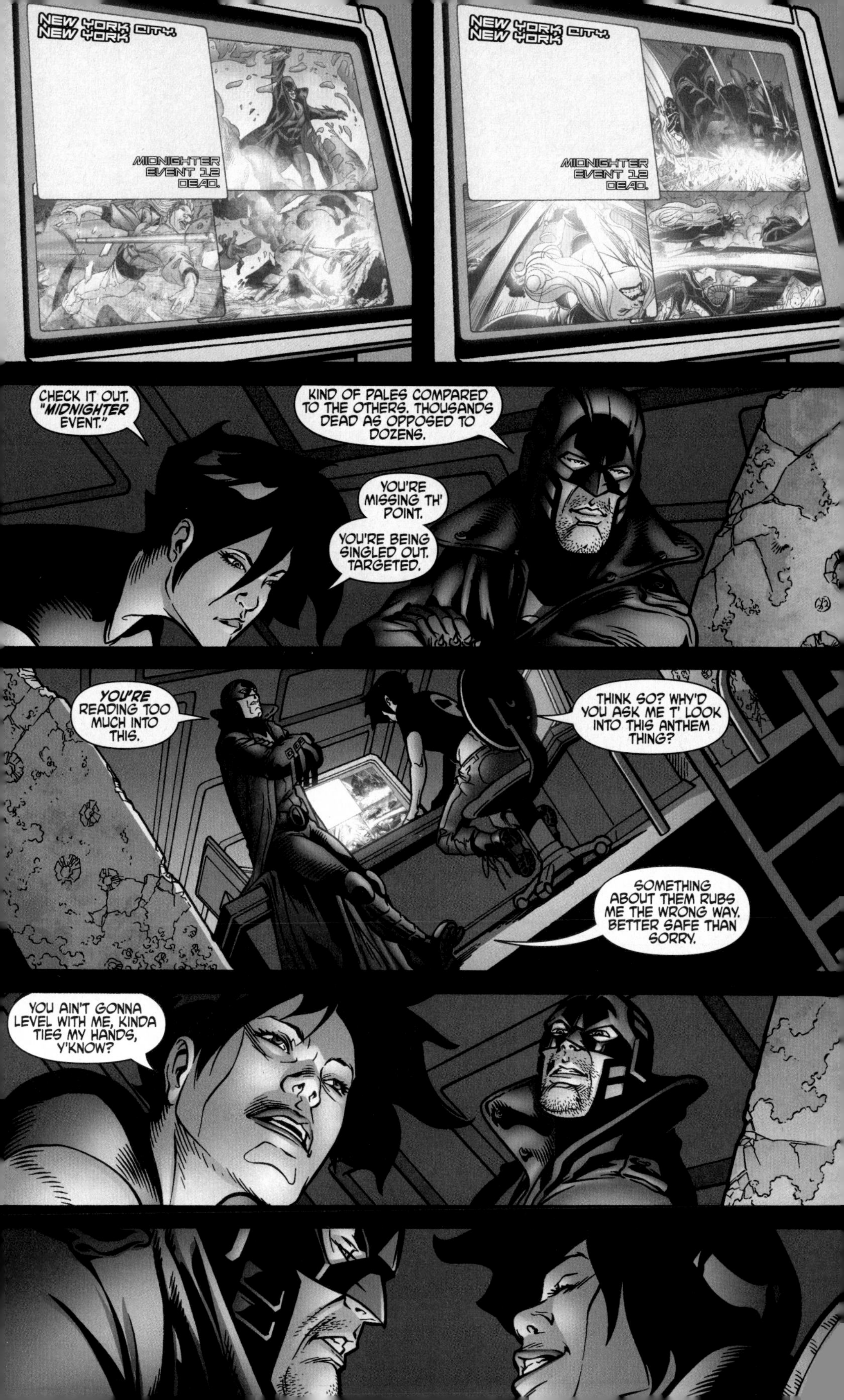
NEW YORK CITY, NEW YORK
MIDNIGHTER EVENT 12 DEAD.
NEW YORK CITY, NEW YORK
MIDNIGHTER EVENT 12 DEAD.
CHECK IT OUT. "MIDNIGHTER EVENT."
KIND OF PALES COMPARED TO THE OTHERS. THOUSANDS DEAD AS OPPOSED TO DOZENS.
YOU'RE MISSING TH' POINT.
YOU'RE BEING SINGLED OUT. TARGETED.
YOU'RE READING TOO MUCH INTO THIS.
THINK SO? WHY'D YOU ASK ME T' LOOK INTO THIS ANTHEM THING?
SOMETHING ABOUT THEM RUBS ME THE WRONG WAY. BETTER SAFE THAN SORRY.
YOU AIN'T GONNA LEVEL WITH ME, KINDA TIES MY HANDS, Y'KNOW?

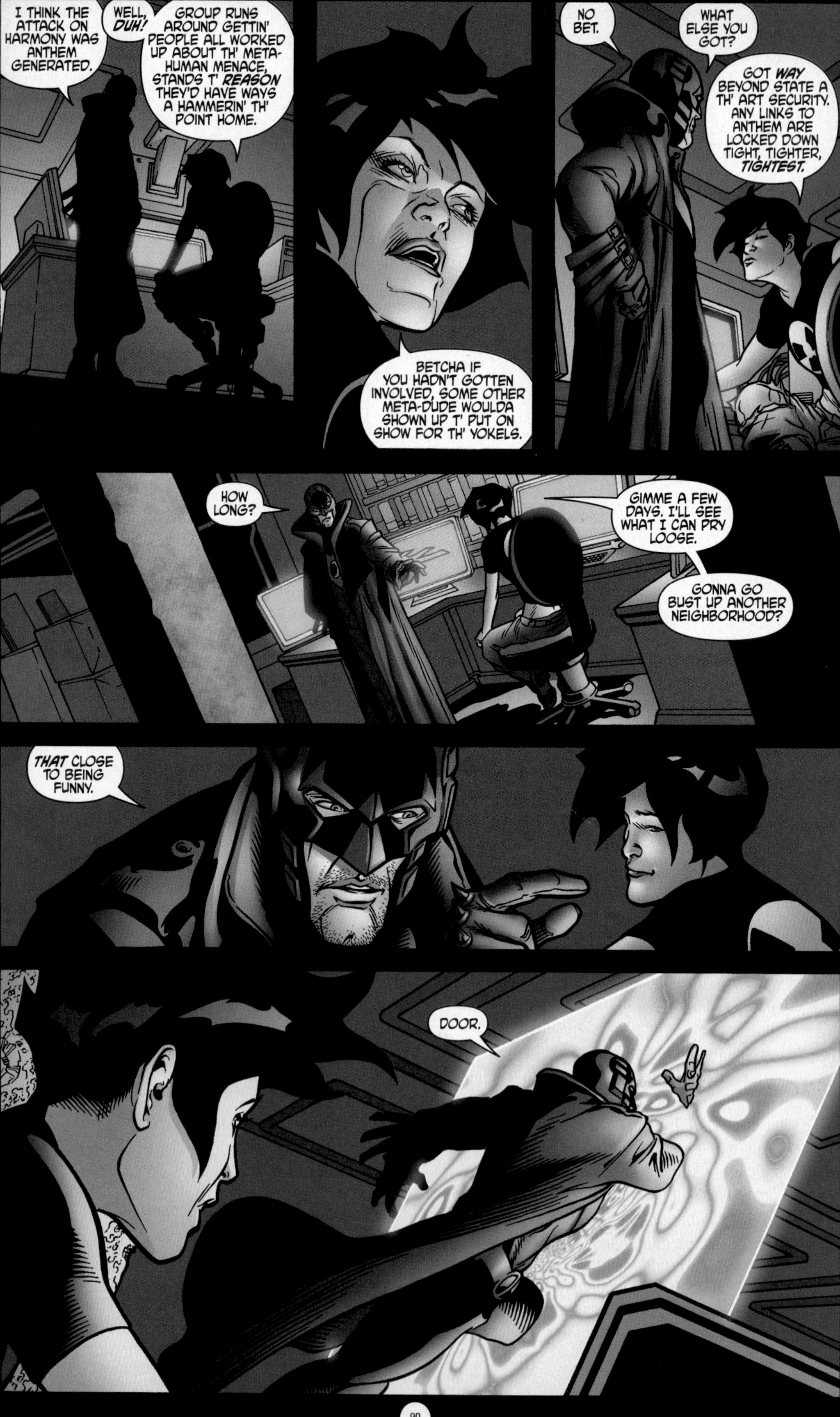

I THINK THE ATTACK ON HARMONY WAS ANTHEM GENERATED.
WELL, *DUH!*
GROUP RUNS AROUND GETTIN' PEOPLE ALL WORKED UP ABOUT TH' META-HUMAN MENACE, STANDS T' *REASON* THEY'D HAVE WAYS A HAMMERIN' TH' POINT HOME.
BETCHA IF YOU HADN'T GOTTEN INVOLVED, SOME OTHER META-DUDE WOULDA SHOWN UP T' PUT ON SHOW FOR TH' YOKELS.
NO BET.
WHAT ELSE YOU GOT?
GOT *WAY* BEYOND STATE A TH' ART SECURITY. ANY LINKS TO ANTHEM ARE LOCKED DOWN TIGHT, TIGHTER, *TIGHTEST.*
HOW LONG?
GIMME A FEW DAYS. I'LL SEE WHAT I CAN PRY LOOSE.
GONNA GO BUST UP ANOTHER NEIGHBORHOOD?
THAT CLOSE TO BEING FUNNY.
DOOR.

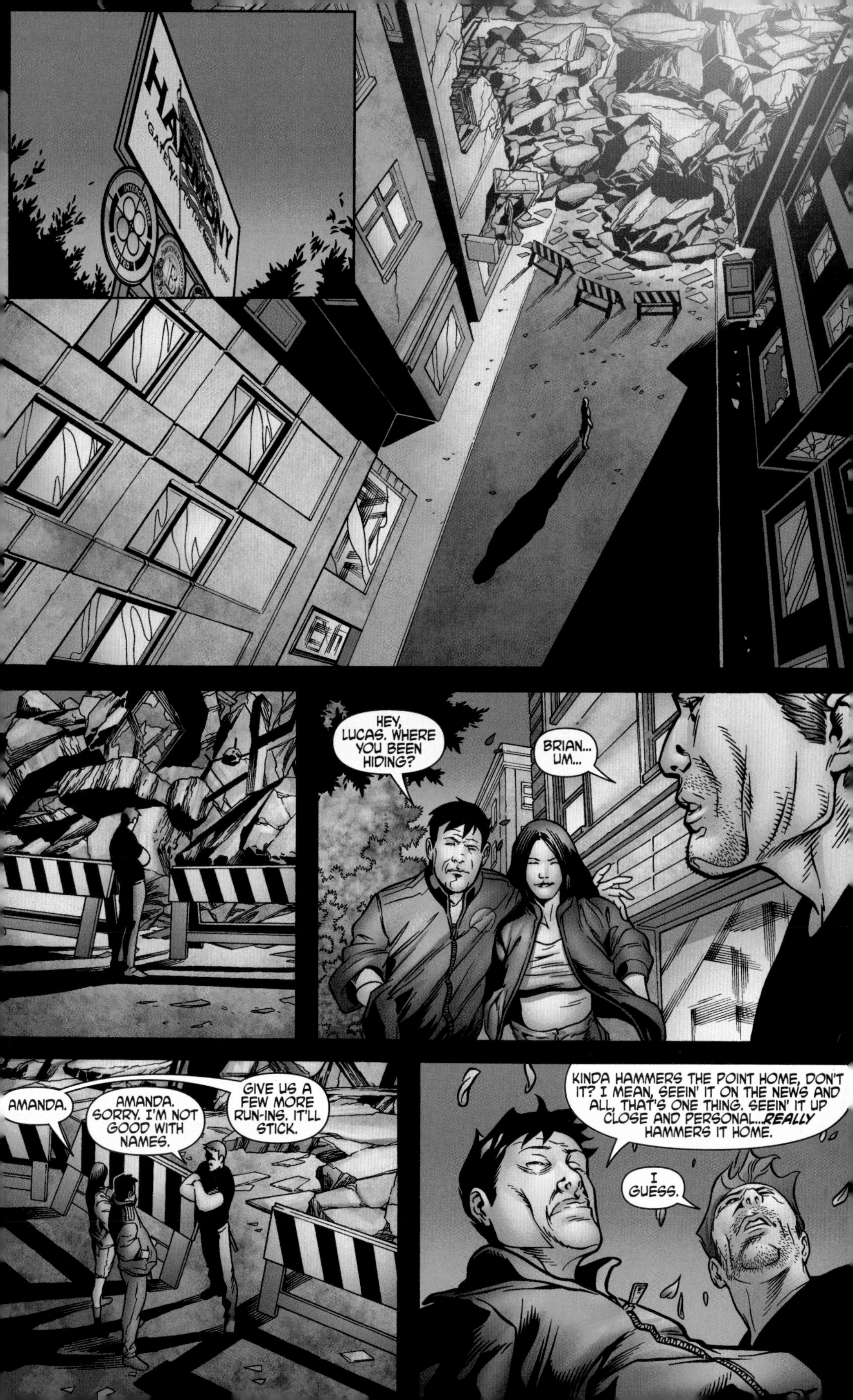
HARMONY
HEY, LUCAS. WHERE YOU BEEN HIDING?
BRIAN... UM...
AMANDA.
AMANDA. SORRY. I'M NOT GOOD WITH NAMES.
GIVE US A FEW MORE RUN-INS. IT'LL STICK.
KINDA HAMMERS THE POINT HOME, DON'T IT? I MEAN, SEEIN' IT ON THE NEWS AND ALL, THAT'S ONE THING. SEEIN' IT UP CLOSE AND PERSONAL...*REALLY* HAMMERS IT HOME.
I GUESS.

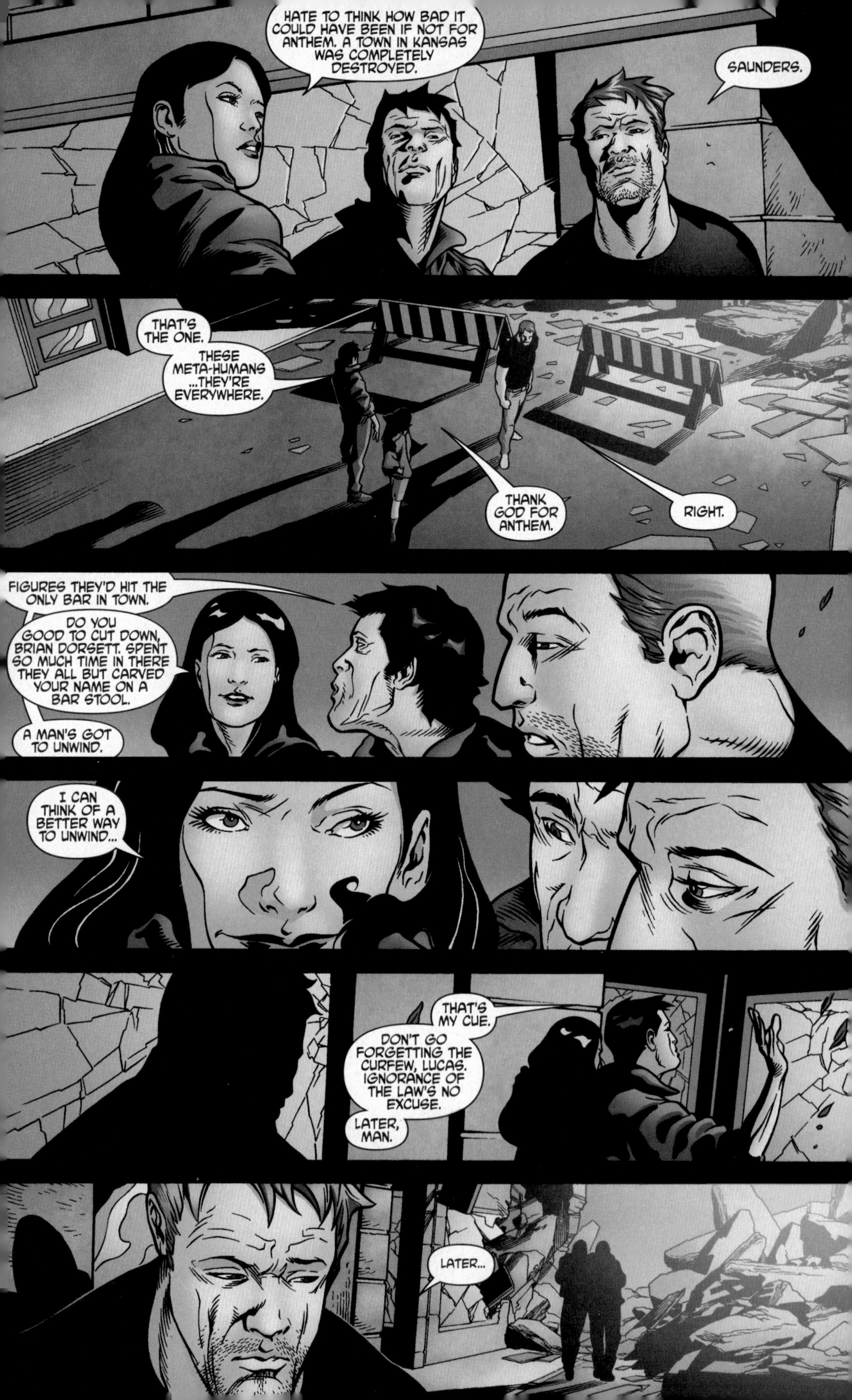
HATE TO THINK HOW BAD IT COULD HAVE BEEN IF NOT FOR ANTHEM. A TOWN IN KANSAS WAS COMPLETELY DESTROYED.
SAUNDERS.
THAT'S THE ONE.
THESE META-HUMANS ...THEY'RE EVERYWHERE.
THANK GOD FOR ANTHEM.
RIGHT.
FIGURES THEY'D HIT THE ONLY BAR IN TOWN.
DO YOU GOOD TO CUT DOWN, BRIAN DORSETT. SPENT SO MUCH TIME IN THERE THEY ALL BUT CARVED YOUR NAME ON A BAR STOOL.
A MAN'S GOT TO UNWIND.
I CAN THINK OF A BETTER WAY TO UNWIND...
THAT'S MY CUE.
DON'T GO FORGETTING THE CURFEW, LUCAS. IGNORANCE OF THE LAW'S NO EXCUSE.
LATER, MAN.
LATER...

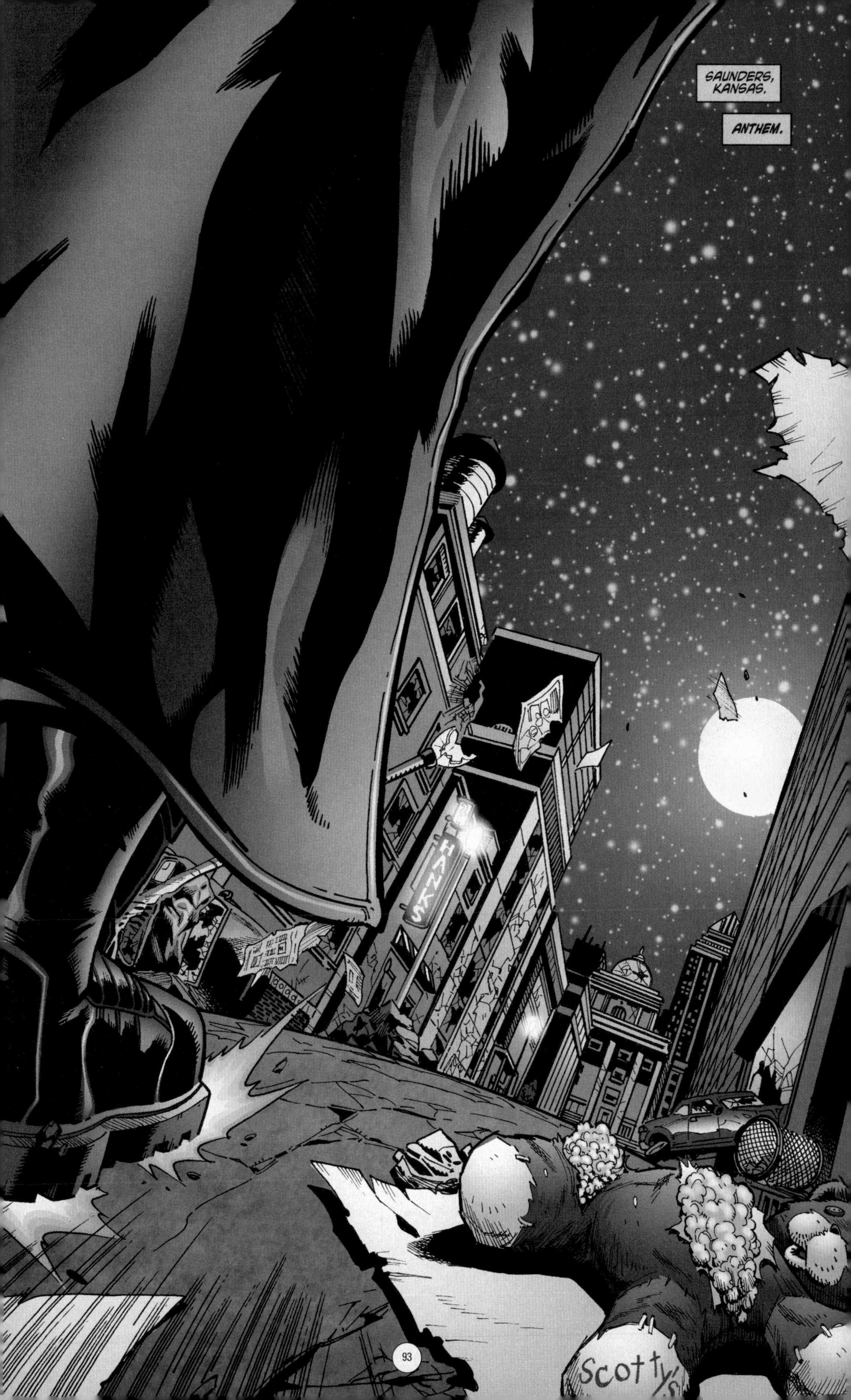
SAUNDERS, KANSAS.
ANTHEM.
HANKS
Scotty's

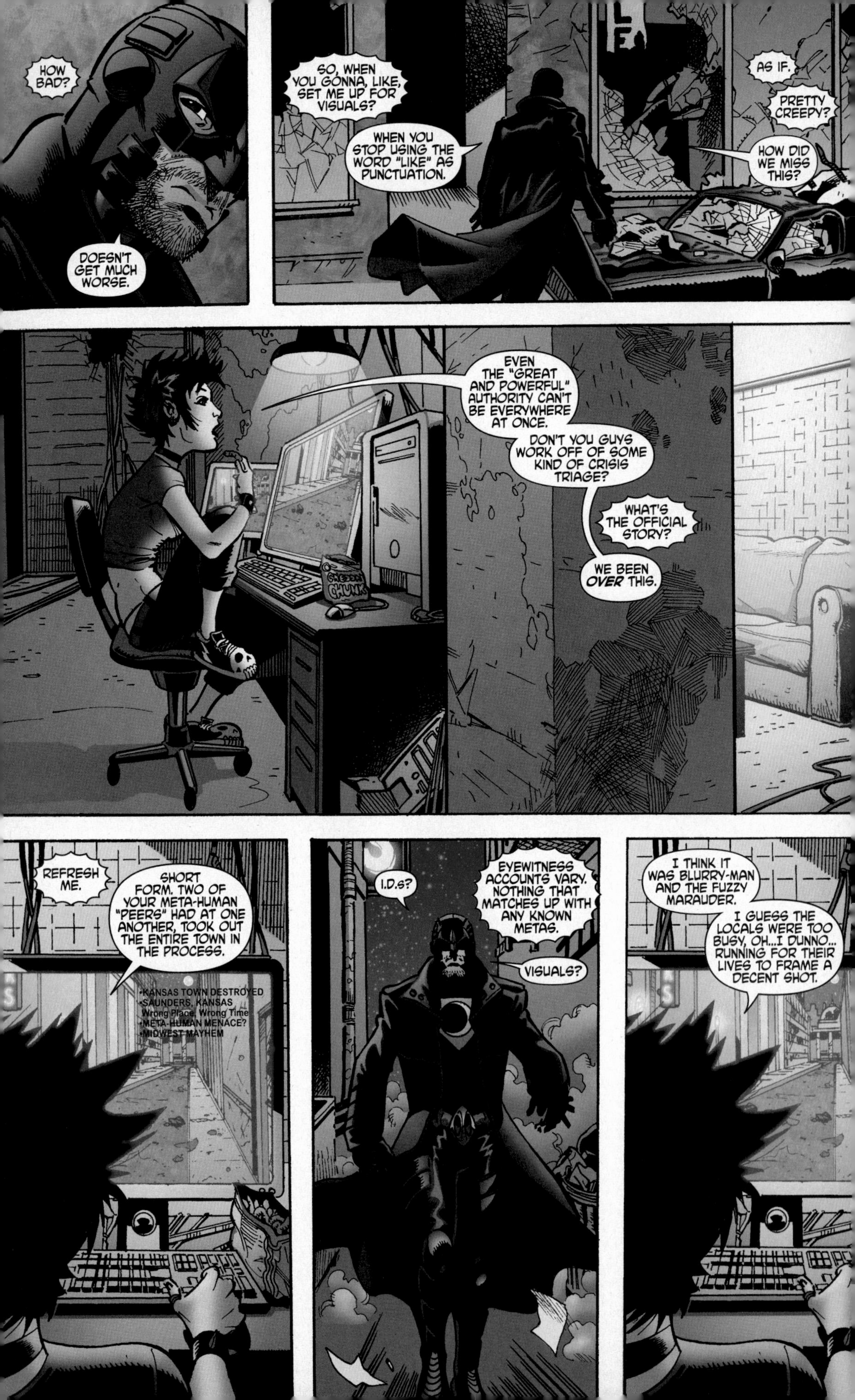
HOW BAD?
DOESN'T GET MUCH WORSE.
SO, WHEN YOU GONNA, LIKE, SET ME UP FOR VISUALS?
WHEN YOU STOP USING THE WORD "LIKE" AS PUNCTUATION.
AS IF.
PRETTY CREEPY?
HOW DID WE MISS THIS?
EVEN THE "GREAT AND POWERFUL" AUTHORITY CAN'T BE EVERYWHERE AT ONCE.
DON'T YOU GUYS WORK OFF OF SOME KIND OF CRISIS TRIAGE?
WHAT'S THE OFFICIAL STORY?
WE BEEN OVER THIS.
REFRESH ME.
SHORT FORM. TWO OF YOUR META-HUMAN "PEERS" HAD AT ONE ANOTHER, TOOK OUT THE ENTIRE TOWN IN THE PROCESS.
•KANSAS TOWN DESTROYED
•SAUNDERS, KANSAS Wrong Place, Wrong Time
•META-HUMAN MENACE?
•MIDWEST MAYHEM
I.D.s?
EYEWITNESS ACCOUNTS VARY. NOTHING THAT MATCHES UP WITH ANY KNOWN METAS.
VISUALS?
I THINK IT WAS BLURRY-MAN AND THE FUZZY MARAUDER.
I GUESS THE LOCALS WERE TOO BUSY, OH...I DUNNO... RUNNING FOR THEIR LIVES TO FRAME A DECENT SHOT.

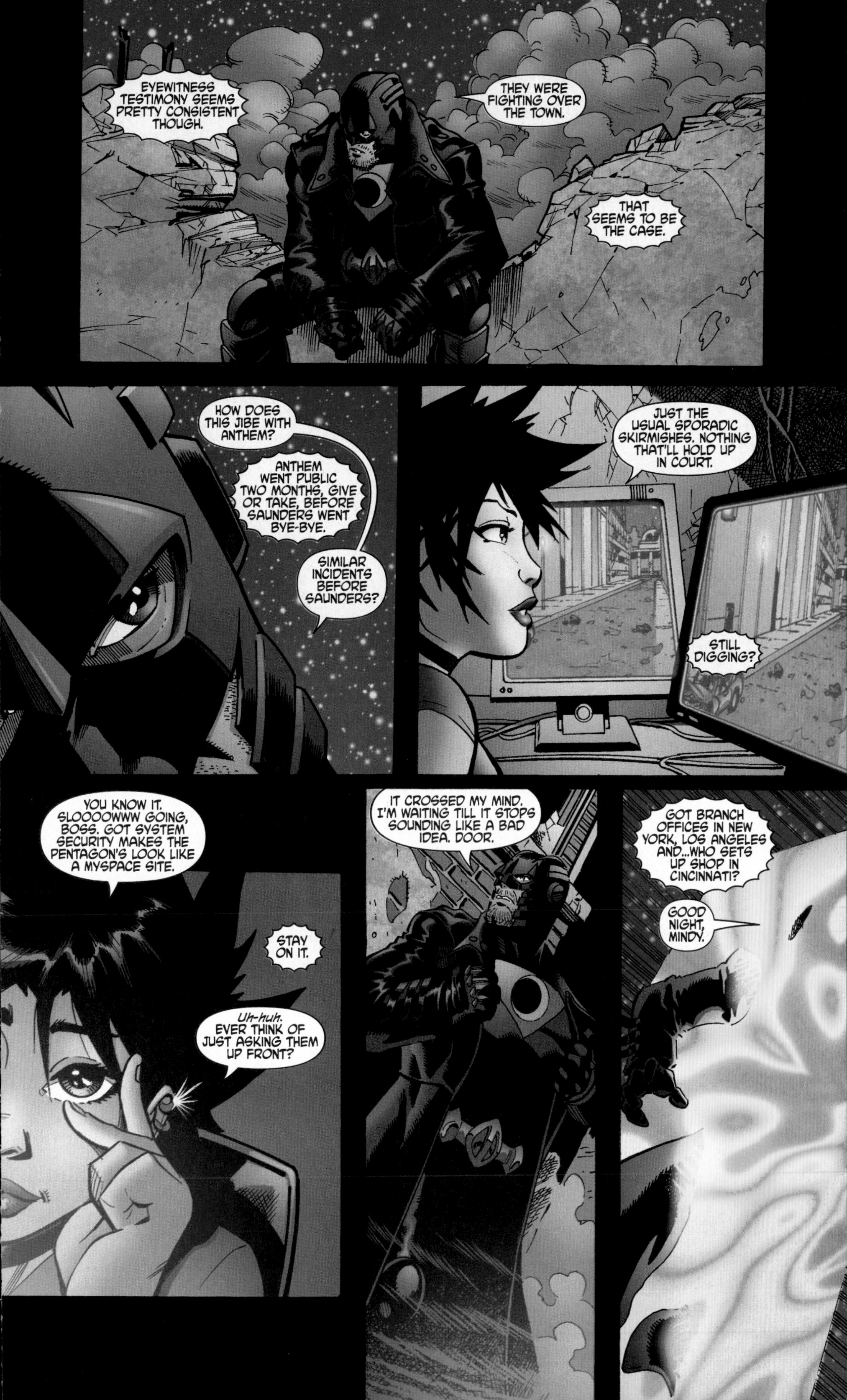
EYEWITNESS TESTIMONY SEEMS PRETTY CONSISTENT THOUGH.
THEY WERE FIGHTING OVER THE TOWN.
THAT SEEMS TO BE THE CASE.
HOW DOES THIS JIBE WITH ANTHEM?
ANTHEM WENT PUBLIC TWO MONTHS, GIVE OR TAKE, BEFORE SAUNDERS WENT BYE-BYE.
SIMILAR INCIDENTS BEFORE SAUNDERS?
JUST THE USUAL SPORADIC SKIRMISHES. NOTHING THAT'LL HOLD UP IN COURT.
STILL DIGGING?
YOU KNOW IT. SLOOOOWWW GOING, BOSS. GOT SYSTEM SECURITY MAKES THE PENTAGON'S LOOK LIKE A MYSPACE SITE.
STAY ON IT.
Uh-huh. EVER THINK OF JUST ASKING THEM UP FRONT?
IT CROSSED MY MIND. I'M WAITING TILL IT STOPS SOUNDING LIKE A BAD IDEA. DOOR.
GOT BRANCH OFFICES IN NEW YORK, LOS ANGELES AND...WHO SETS UP SHOP IN CINCINNATI?
GOOD NIGHT, MINDY.

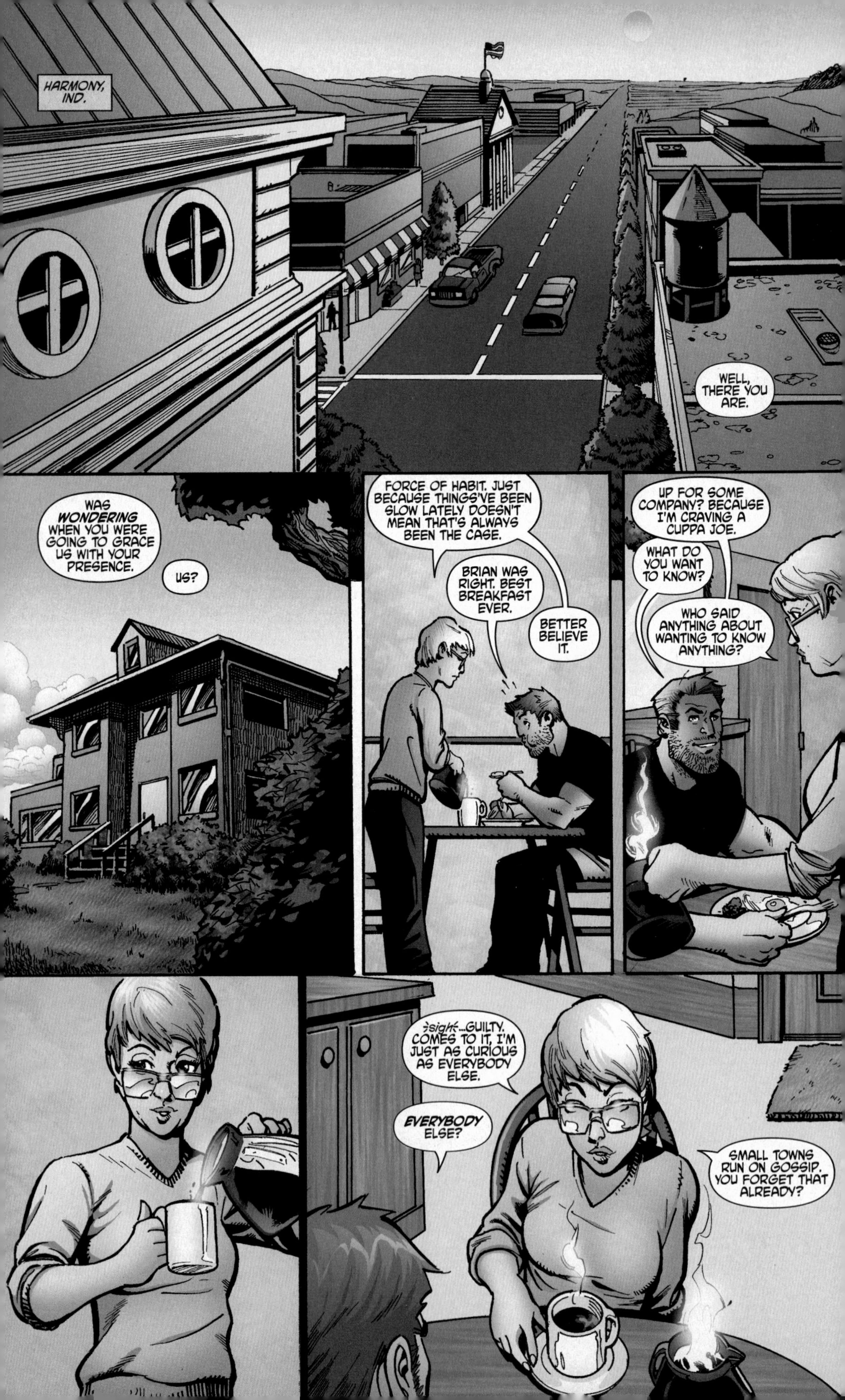
HARMONY, IND.
WELL, THERE YOU ARE.
WAS *WONDERING* WHEN YOU WERE GOING TO GRACE US WITH YOUR PRESENCE.
US?
FORCE OF HABIT. JUST BECAUSE THINGS'VE BEEN SLOW LATELY DOESN'T MEAN THAT'S ALWAYS BEEN THE CASE.
BRIAN WAS RIGHT. BEST BREAKFAST EVER.
BETTER BELIEVE IT.
UP FOR SOME COMPANY? BECAUSE I'M CRAVING A CUPPA JOE.
WHAT DO YOU WANT TO KNOW?
WHO SAID ANYTHING ABOUT WANTING TO KNOW ANYTHING?
sigh...GUILTY. COMES TO IT, I'M JUST AS CURIOUS AS EVERYBODY ELSE.
EVERYBODY ELSE?
SMALL TOWNS RUN ON GOSSIP. YOU FORGET THAT ALREADY?

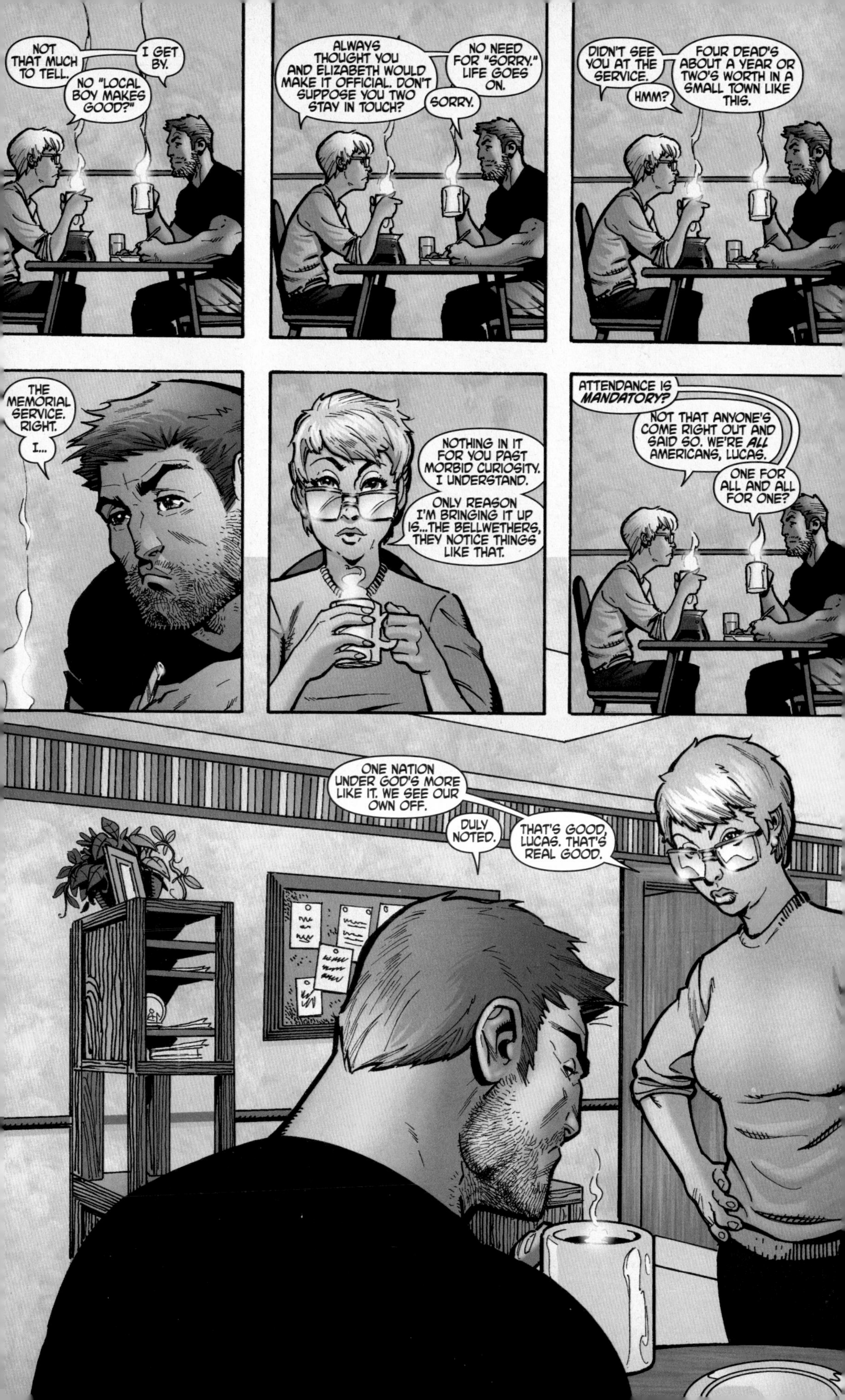

NOT THAT MUCH TO TELL.
I GET BY.
NO "LOCAL BOY MAKES GOOD?"
ALWAYS THOUGHT YOU AND ELIZABETH WOULD MAKE IT OFFICIAL. DON'T SUPPOSE YOU TWO STAY IN TOUCH?
NO NEED FOR "SORRY." LIFE GOES ON.
SORRY.
DIDN'T SEE YOU AT THE SERVICE.
HMM?
FOUR DEAD'S ABOUT A YEAR OR TWO'S WORTH IN A SMALL TOWN LIKE THIS.
THE MEMORIAL SERVICE. RIGHT.
I...
NOTHING IN IT FOR YOU PAST MORBID CURIOSITY. I UNDERSTAND.
ONLY REASON I'M BRINGING IT UP IS...THE BELLWETHERS, THEY NOTICE THINGS LIKE THAT.
ATTENDANCE IS MANDATORY?
NOT THAT ANYONE'S COME RIGHT OUT AND SAID SO. WE'RE ALL AMERICANS, LUCAS.
ONE FOR ALL AND ALL FOR ONE?
ONE NATION UNDER GOD'S MORE LIKE IT. WE SEE OUR OWN OFF.
DULY NOTED.
THAT'S GOOD, LUCAS. THAT'S REAL GOOD.

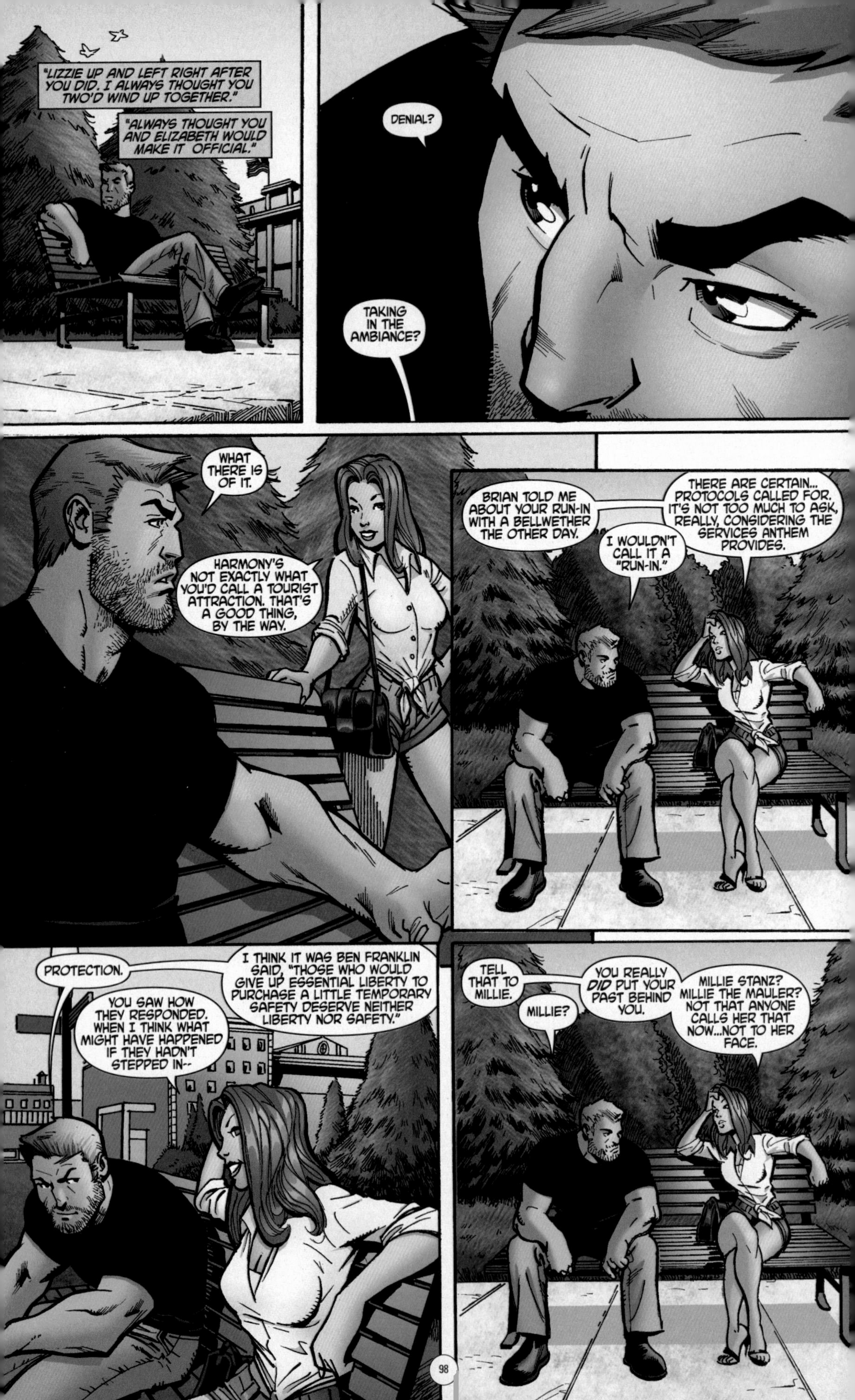
"LIZZIE UP AND LEFT RIGHT AFTER YOU DID. I ALWAYS THOUGHT YOU TWO'D WIND UP TOGETHER."
"ALWAYS THOUGHT YOU AND ELIZABETH WOULD MAKE IT OFFICIAL."
DENIAL?
TAKING IN THE AMBIANCE?
WHAT THERE IS OF IT.
HARMONY'S NOT EXACTLY WHAT YOU'D CALL A TOURIST ATTRACTION. THAT'S A GOOD THING, BY THE WAY.
BRIAN TOLD ME ABOUT YOUR RUN-IN WITH A BELLWETHER THE OTHER DAY.
I WOULDN'T CALL IT A "RUN-IN."
THERE ARE CERTAIN... PROTOCOLS CALLED FOR. IT'S NOT TOO MUCH TO ASK, REALLY, CONSIDERING THE SERVICES ANTHEM PROVIDES.
PROTECTION.
YOU SAW HOW THEY RESPONDED. WHEN I THINK WHAT MIGHT HAVE HAPPENED IF THEY HADN'T STEPPED IN--
I THINK IT WAS BEN FRANKLIN SAID, "THOSE WHO WOULD GIVE UP ESSENTIAL LIBERTY TO PURCHASE A LITTLE TEMPORARY SAFETY DESERVE NEITHER LIBERTY NOR SAFETY."
TELL THAT TO MILLIE.
MILLIE?
YOU REALLY *DID* PUT YOUR PAST BEHIND YOU.
MILLIE STANZ? MILLIE THE MAULER? NOT THAT ANYONE CALLS HER THAT NOW...NOT TO HER FACE.

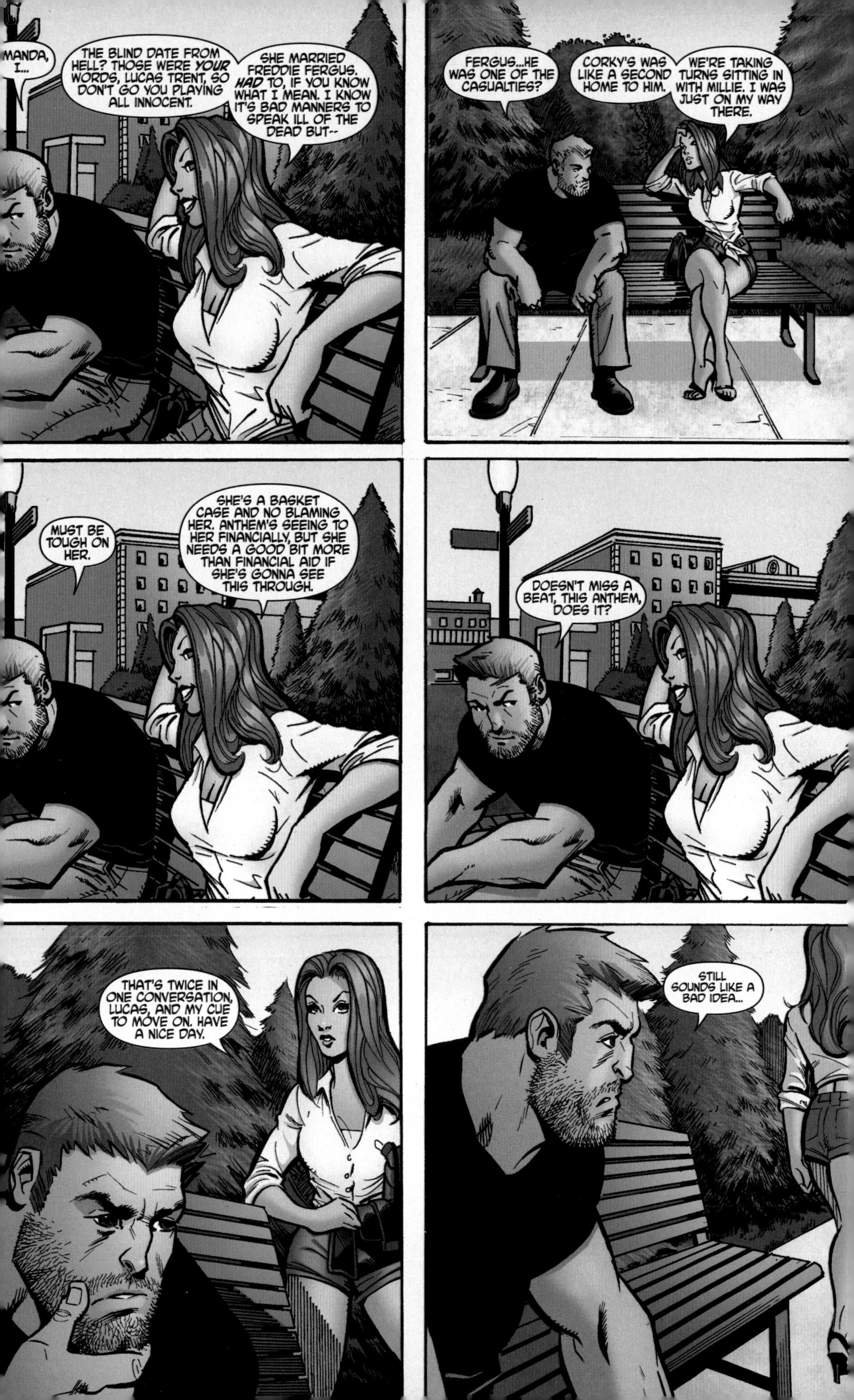
MANDA, I...
THE BLIND DATE FROM HELL? THOSE WERE YOUR WORDS, LUCAS TRENT, SO DON'T GO YOU PLAYING ALL INNOCENT.
SHE MARRIED FREDDIE FERGUS. HAD TO, IF YOU KNOW WHAT I MEAN. I KNOW IT'S BAD MANNERS TO SPEAK ILL OF THE DEAD BUT--
FERGUS...HE WAS ONE OF THE CASUALTIES?
CORKY'S WAS LIKE A SECOND HOME TO HIM.
WE'RE TAKING TURNS SITTING IN WITH MILLIE. I WAS JUST ON MY WAY THERE.
MUST BE TOUGH ON HER.
SHE'S A BASKET CASE AND NO BLAMING HER. ANTHEM'S SEEING TO HER FINANCIALLY, BUT SHE NEEDS A GOOD BIT MORE THAN FINANCIAL AID IF SHE'S GONNA SEE THIS THROUGH.
DOESN'T MISS A BEAT, THIS ANTHEM, DOES IT?
THAT'S TWICE IN ONE CONVERSATION, LUCAS, AND MY CUE TO MOVE ON. HAVE A NICE DAY.
STILL SOUNDS LIKE A BAD IDEA...

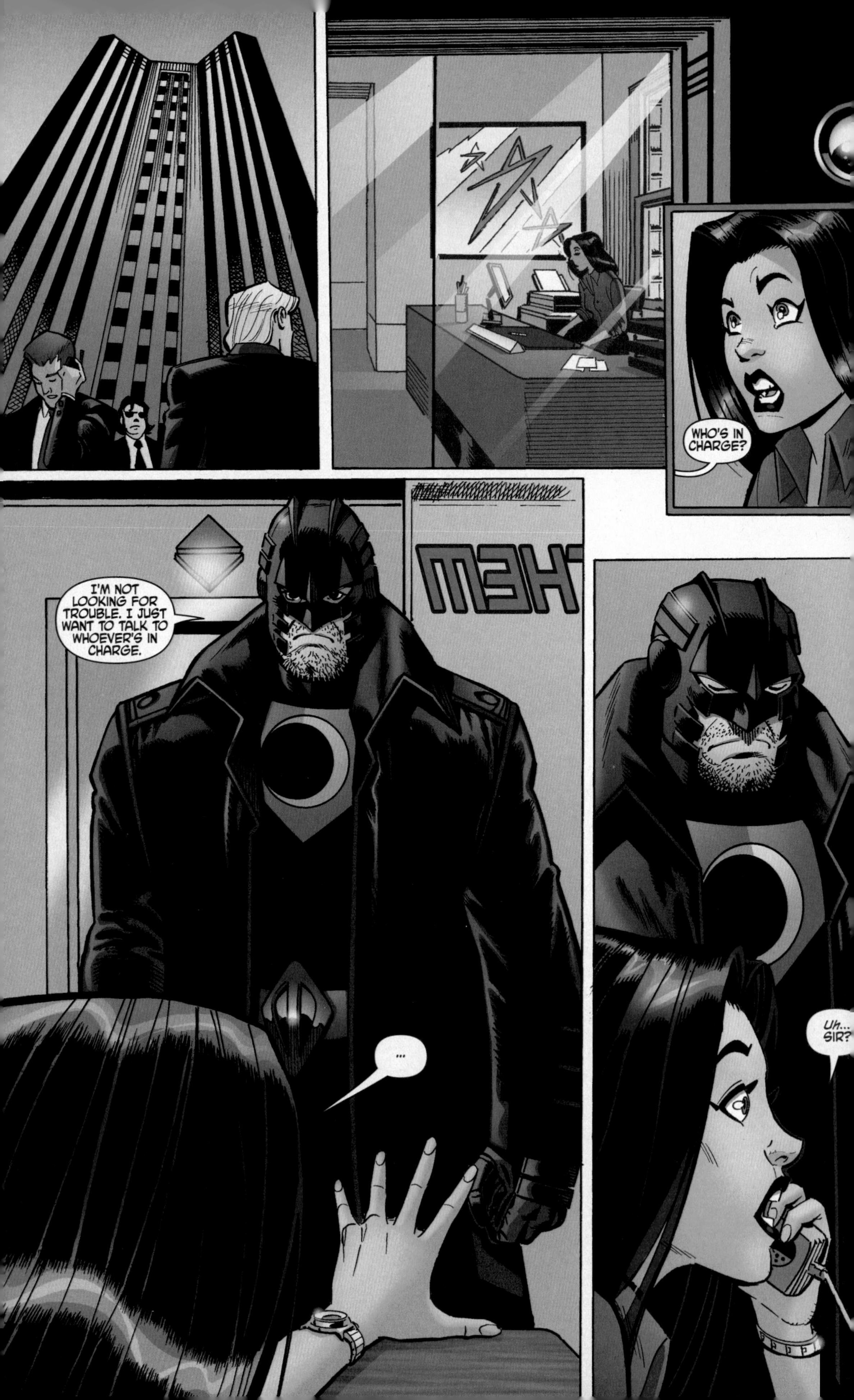
WHO'S IN CHARGE?
I'M NOT LOOKING FOR TROUBLE. I JUST WANT TO TALK TO WHOEVER'S IN CHARGE.
...
UH... SIR?

I'M SURPRISED IT TOOK YOU THIS LONG.

INDEED.

THEN YOU'VE BEEN EXPECTING ME?

WHY ME?

IT'S NOT JUST YOU.

"MIDNIGHTER EVENT."

Ah. WE WERE MISTAKEN? YOU WEREN'T INVOLVED?

YOU PICKED THE WRONG POSTER BOY.

A VEILED THREAT?

YOU FIGURE IT OUT.

CAN I GET YOU ANYTHING? A SOFT DRINK? COFFEE?

A STRAIGHT ANSWER WOULD BE NICE.

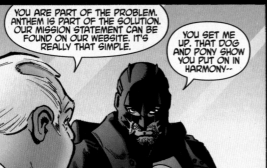

YOU ARE PART OF THE PROBLEM. ANTHEM IS PART OF THE SOLUTION. OUR MISSION STATEMENT CAN BE FOUND ON OUR WEBSITE. IT'S REALLY THAT SIMPLE.

YOU SET ME UP. THAT DOG AND PONY SHOW YOU PUT ON IN HARMONY--

IT'S CALLED RAPID RESPONSE. WOULD YOU RATHER WE'D LEFT THE TWO OF YOU TO YOUR OWN DEVICES?

I KNEW THIS WAS A BAD IDEA.

IT GALLS YOU, DOESN'T IT? YOUR KIND HAVE HAD IT YOUR WAY FOR SO LONG...TELL ME, WHAT PLACES YOU AND YOURS ABOVE THE LAW?

I DIDN'T COME HERE TO DEBATE YOU.

THERE IS NOTHING TO DEBATE.

I COULDN'T HELP NOTICING THAT YOU DIDN'T ANSWER MY QUESTION... MR. TRENT.

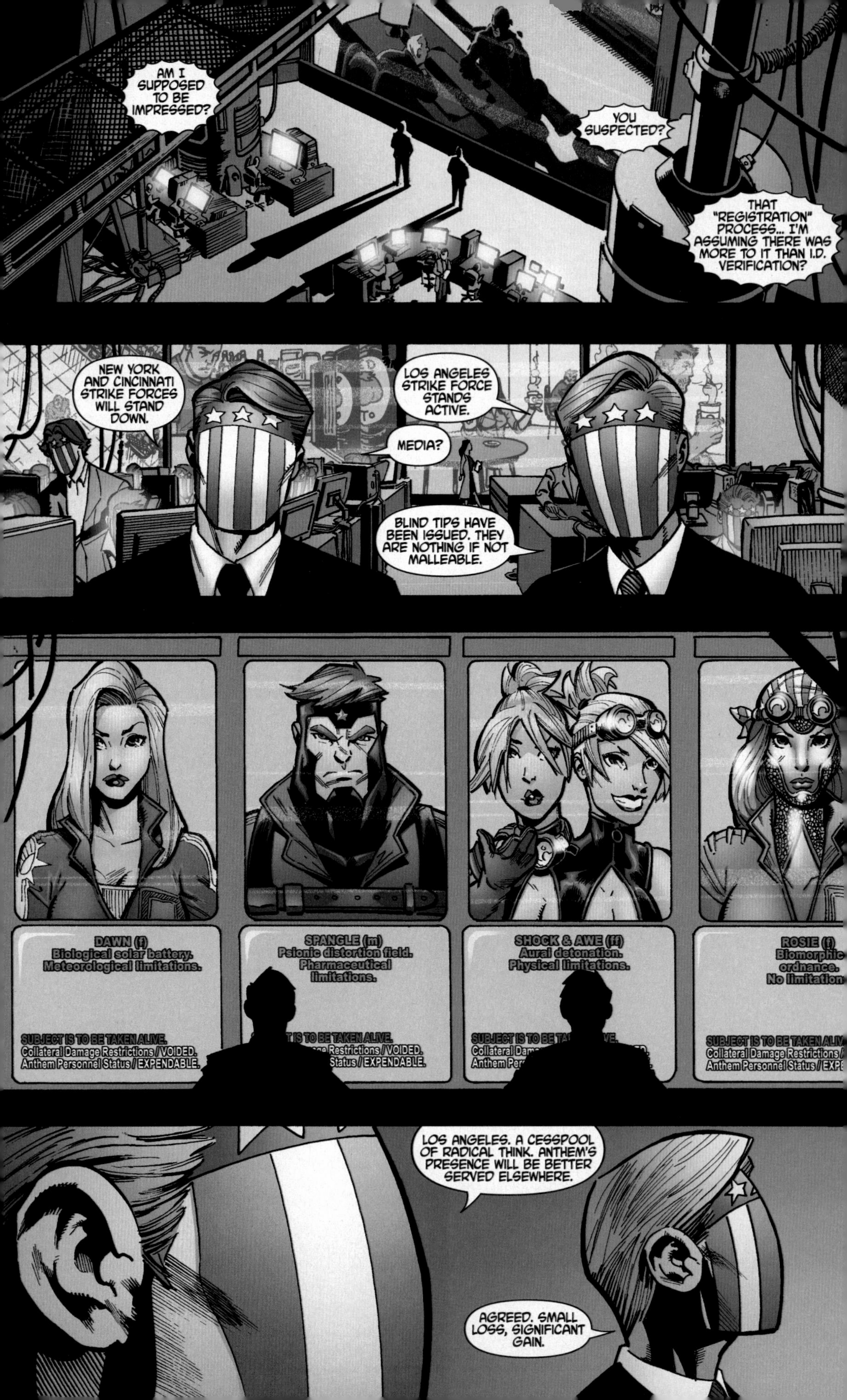

AM I SUPPOSED TO BE IMPRESSED?
YOU SUSPECTED?
THAT "REGISTRATION" PROCESS... I'M ASSUMING THERE WAS MORE TO IT THAN I.D. VERIFICATION?
NEW YORK AND CINCINNATI STRIKE FORCES WILL STAND DOWN.
LOS ANGELES STRIKE FORCE STANDS ACTIVE.
MEDIA?
BLIND TIPS HAVE BEEN ISSUED. THEY ARE NOTHING IF NOT MALLEABLE.
DAWN (f)
Biological solar battery.
Meteorological limitations.
SUBJECT IS TO BE TAKEN ALIVE.
Collateral Damage Restrictions / VOIDED.
Anthem Personnel Status / EXPENDABLE.
SPANGLE (m)
Psionic distortion field.
Pharmaceutical limitations.
SHOCK & AWE (ff)
Aural detonation.
Physical limitations.
ROSIE (f)
LOS ANGELES. A CESSPOOL OF RADICAL THINK. ANTHEM'S PRESENCE WILL BE BETTER SERVED ELSEWHERE.
AGREED. SMALL LOSS, SIGNIFICANT GAIN.

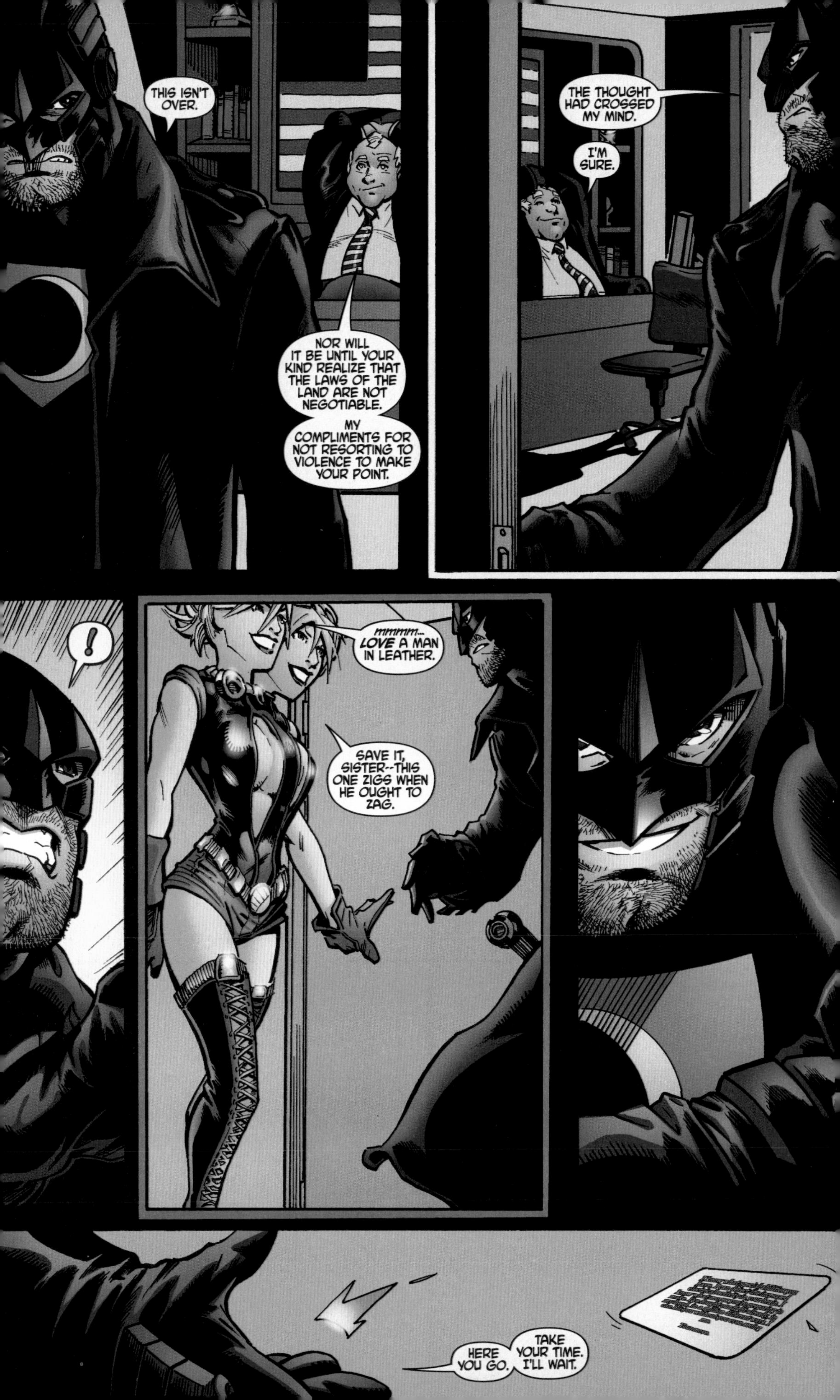

THIS ISN'T OVER.
NOR WILL IT BE UNTIL YOUR KIND REALIZE THAT THE LAWS OF THE LAND ARE NOT NEGOTIABLE.
MY COMPLIMENTS FOR NOT RESORTING TO VIOLENCE TO MAKE YOUR POINT.
THE THOUGHT HAD CROSSED MY MIND.
I'M SURE.
!
mmmmm... LOVE A MAN IN LEATHER.
SAVE IT, SISTER--THIS ONE ZIGS WHEN HE OUGHT TO ZAG.
HERE YOU GO.
TAKE YOUR TIME. I'LL WAIT.

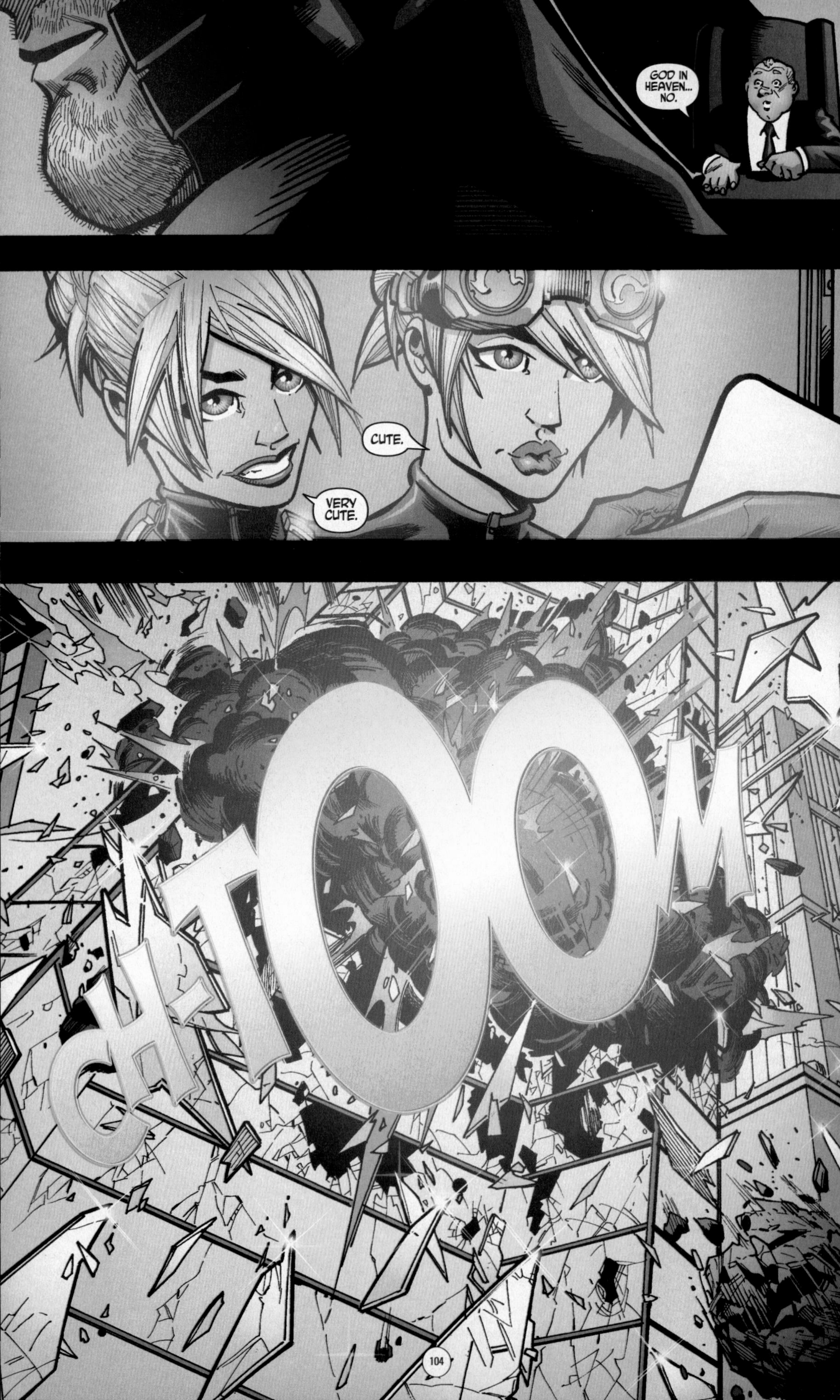
GOD IN HEAVEN... NO.
CUTE.
VERY CUTE.
CH-TOOM

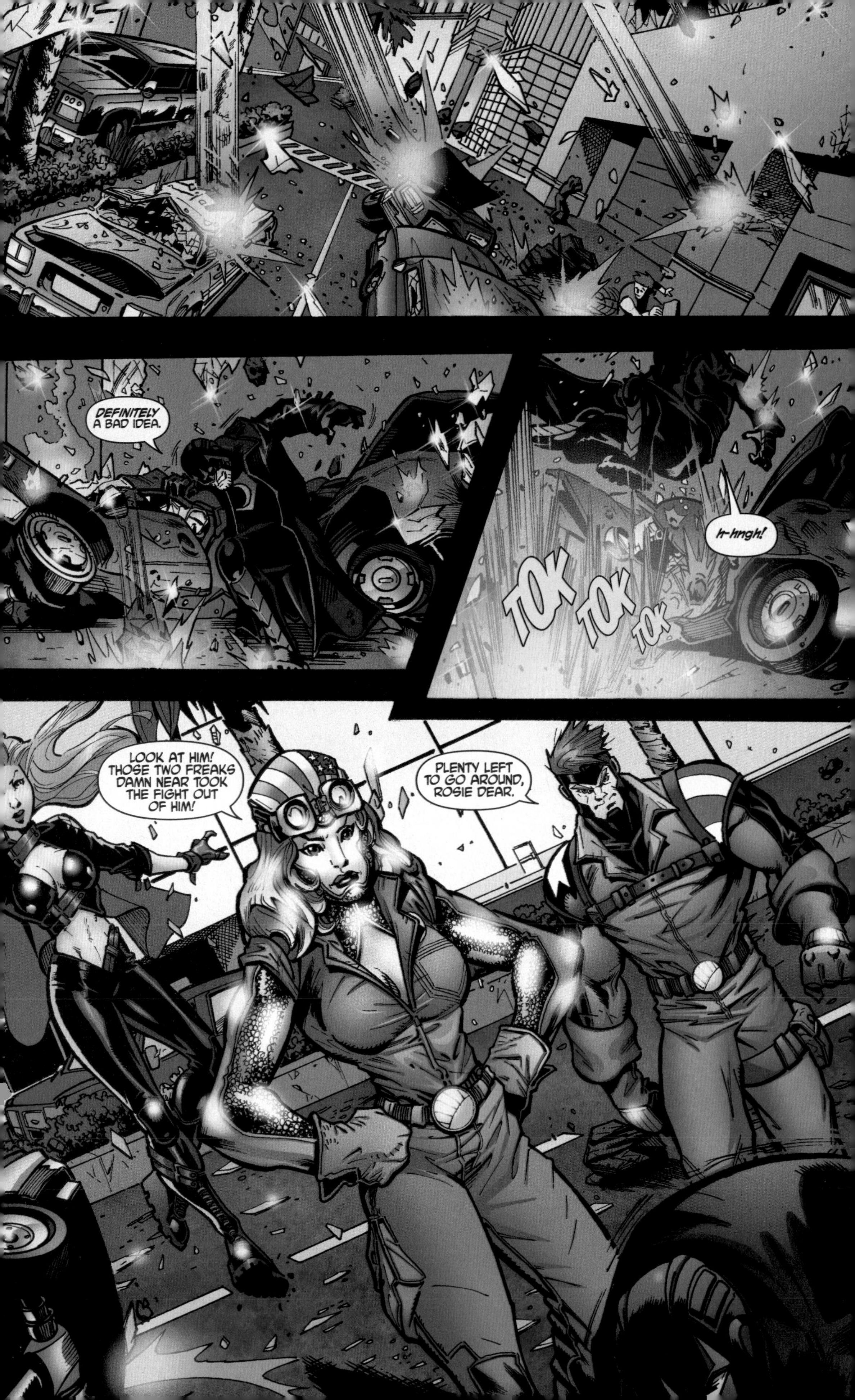
DEFINITELY A BAD IDEA.
h-hngh!
TOK TOK TOK
LOOK AT HIM! THOSE TWO FREAKS DAMN NEAR TOOK THE FIGHT OUT OF HIM!
PLENTY LEFT TO GO AROUND, ROSIE DEAR.

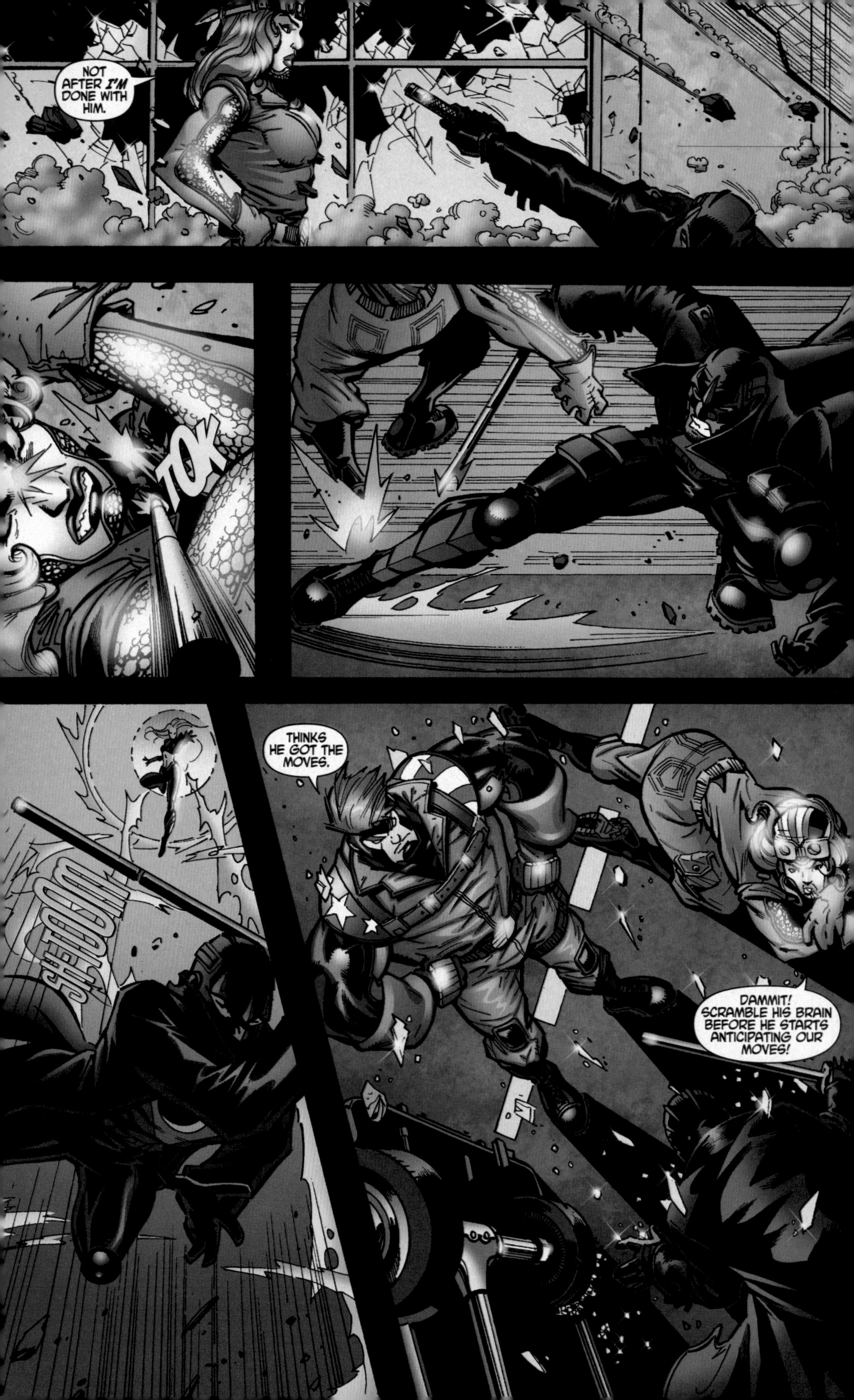
NOT AFTER I'M DONE WITH HIM.
TOK
THINKS HE GOT THE MOVES.
DAMMIT! SCRAMBLE HIS BRAIN BEFORE HE STARTS ANTICIPATING OUR MOVES!

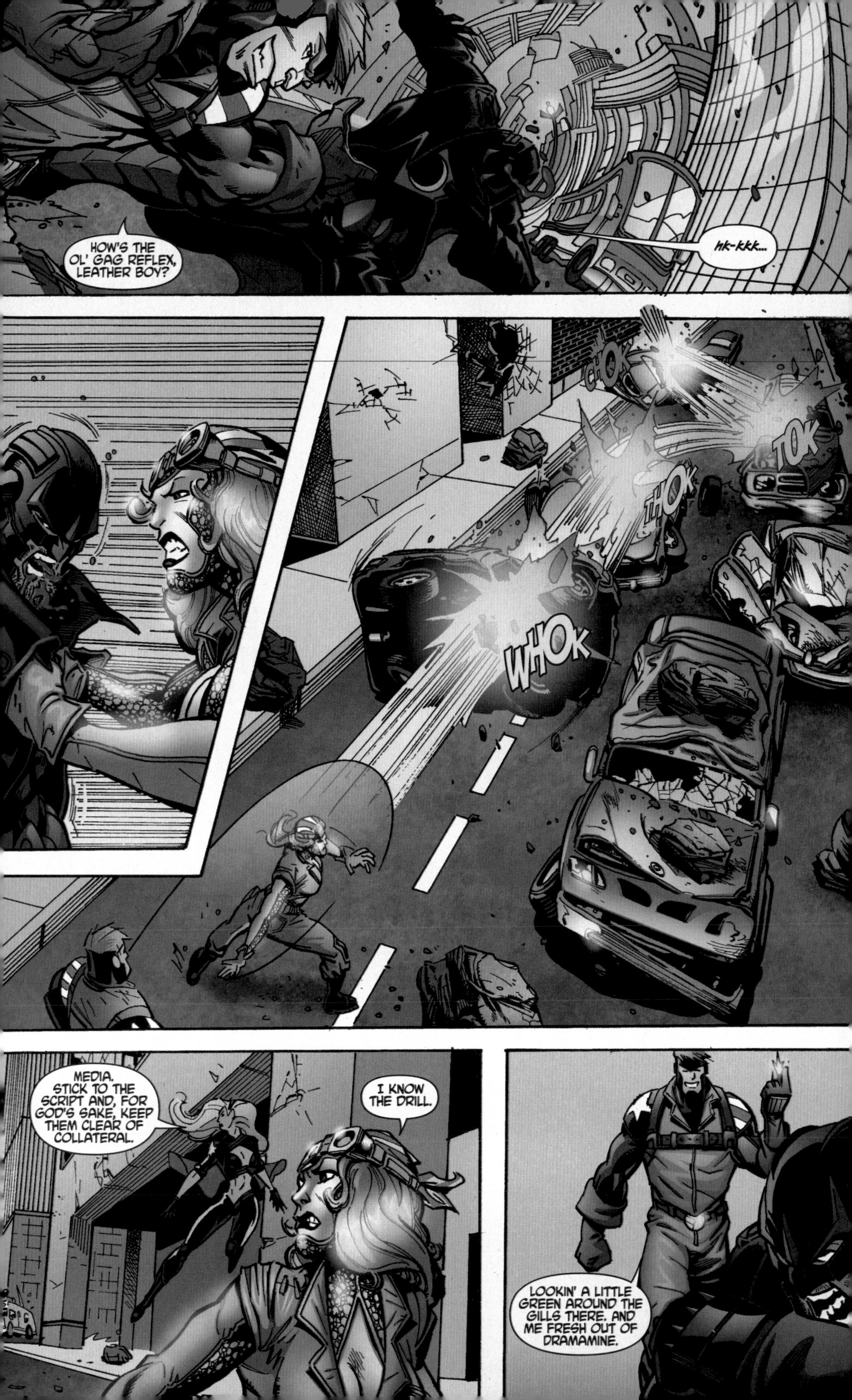
HOW'S THE OL' GAG REFLEX, LEATHER BOY?
hk-kkk...
CHOK
TOK
THOK
WHOK
MEDIA. STICK TO THE SCRIPT AND, FOR GOD'S SAKE, KEEP THEM CLEAR OF COLLATERAL.
I KNOW THE DRILL.
LOOKIN' A LITTLE GREEN AROUND THE GILLS THERE. AND ME FRESH OUT OF DRAMAMINE.

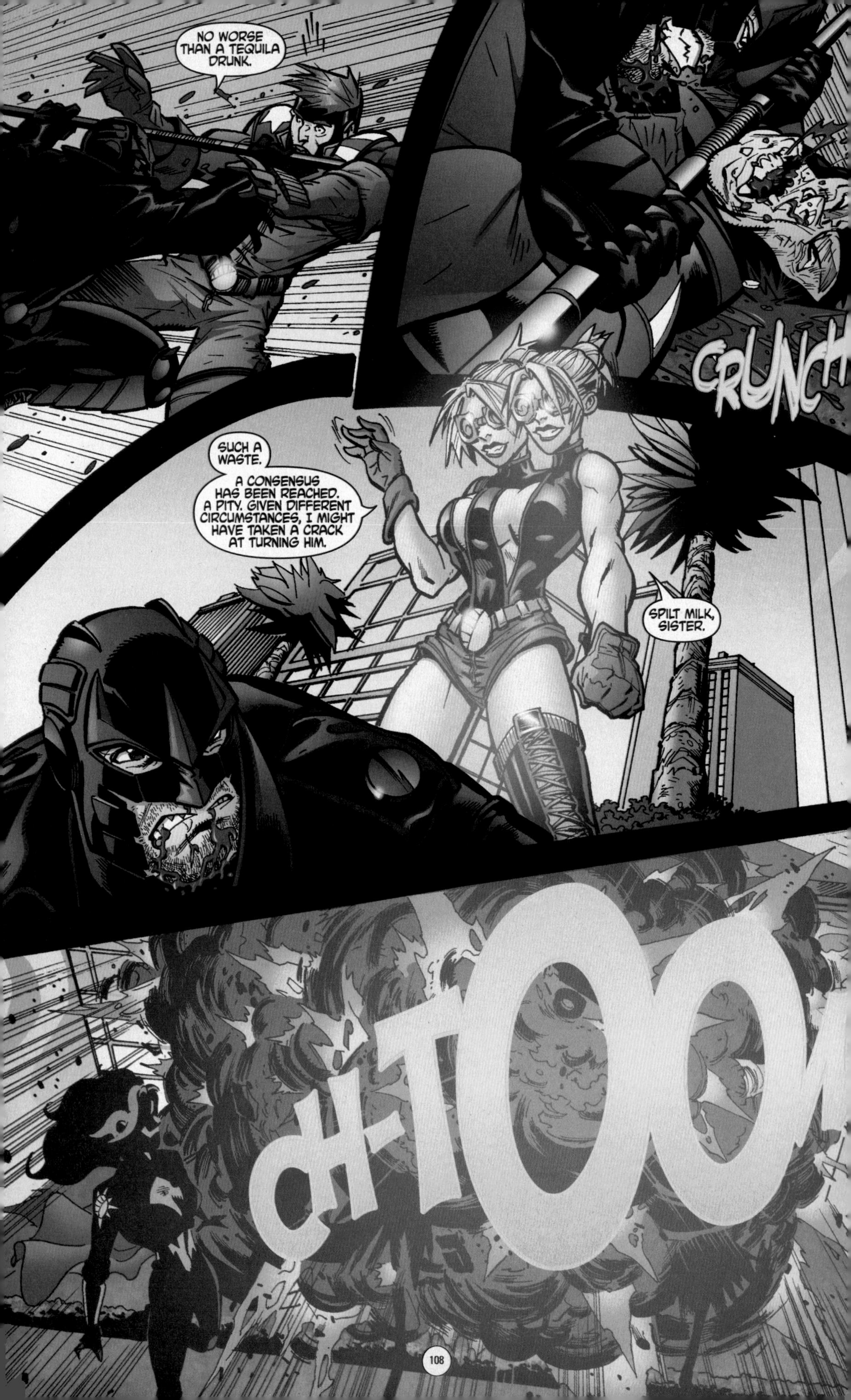
NO WORSE THAN A TEQUILA DRUNK.
CRUNCH
SUCH A WASTE.
A CONSENSUS HAS BEEN REACHED. A PITY. GIVEN DIFFERENT CIRCUMSTANCES, I MIGHT HAVE TAKEN A CRACK AT TURNING HIM.
SPILT MILK, SISTER.

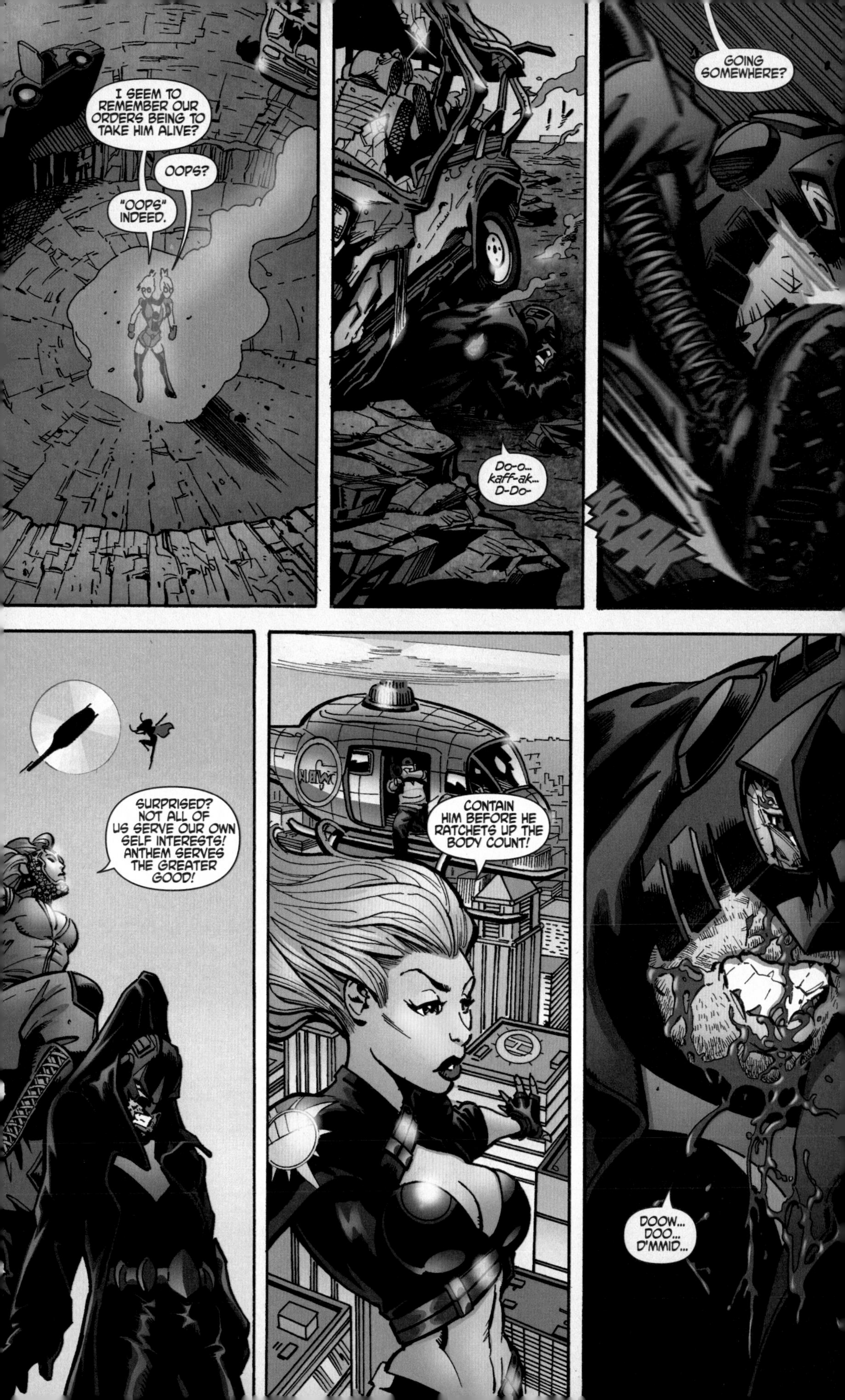
I SEEM TO REMEMBER OUR ORDERS BEING TO TAKE HIM ALIVE?
OOPS?
"OOPS" INDEED.
!!
Do-o... kaff-ak... D-Do-
GOING SOMEWHERE?
KRAK
SURPRISED? NOT ALL OF US SERVE OUR OWN SELF INTERESTS! ANTHEM SERVES THE GREATER GOOD!
CONTAIN HIM BEFORE HE RATCHETS UP THE BODY COUNT!
DOOW... DOO... D'MMID...

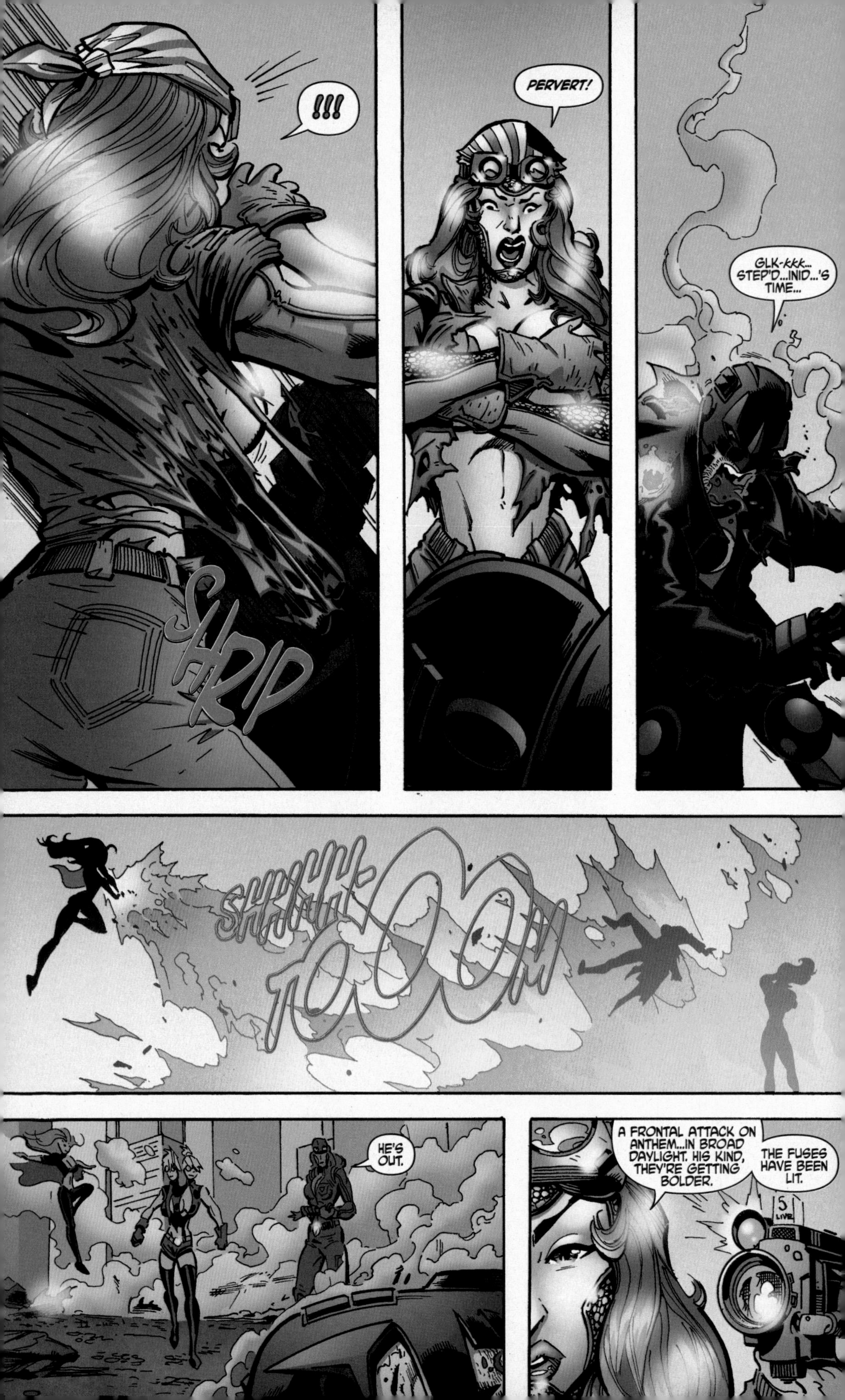
!!!
SHRIP
PERVERT!
GLK-kkk... STEP'D...INID...'S TIME...
SHHHHK-TOOOM
HE'S OUT.
A FRONTAL ATTACK ON ANTHEM...IN BROAD DAYLIGHT. HIS KIND, THEY'RE GETTING BOLDER.
THE FUSES HAVE BEEN LIT.

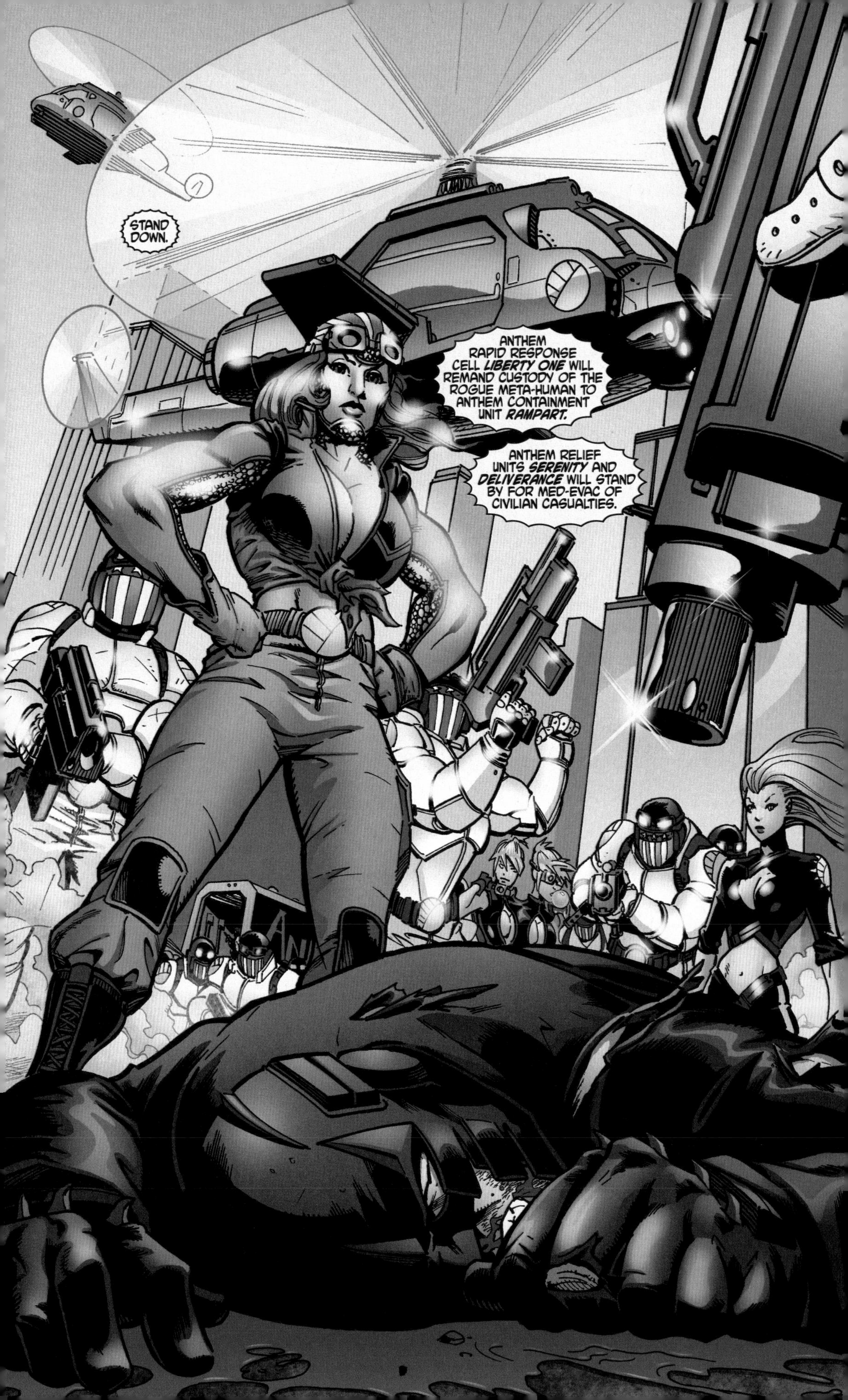
STAND DOWN.
ANTHEM RAPID RESPONSE CELL LIBERTY ONE WILL REMAND CUSTODY OF THE ROGUE META-HUMAN TO ANTHEM CONTAINMENT UNIT RAMPART.
ANTHEM RELIEF UNITS SERENITY AND DELIVERANCE WILL STAND BY FOR MED-EVAC OF CIVILIAN CASUALTIES.

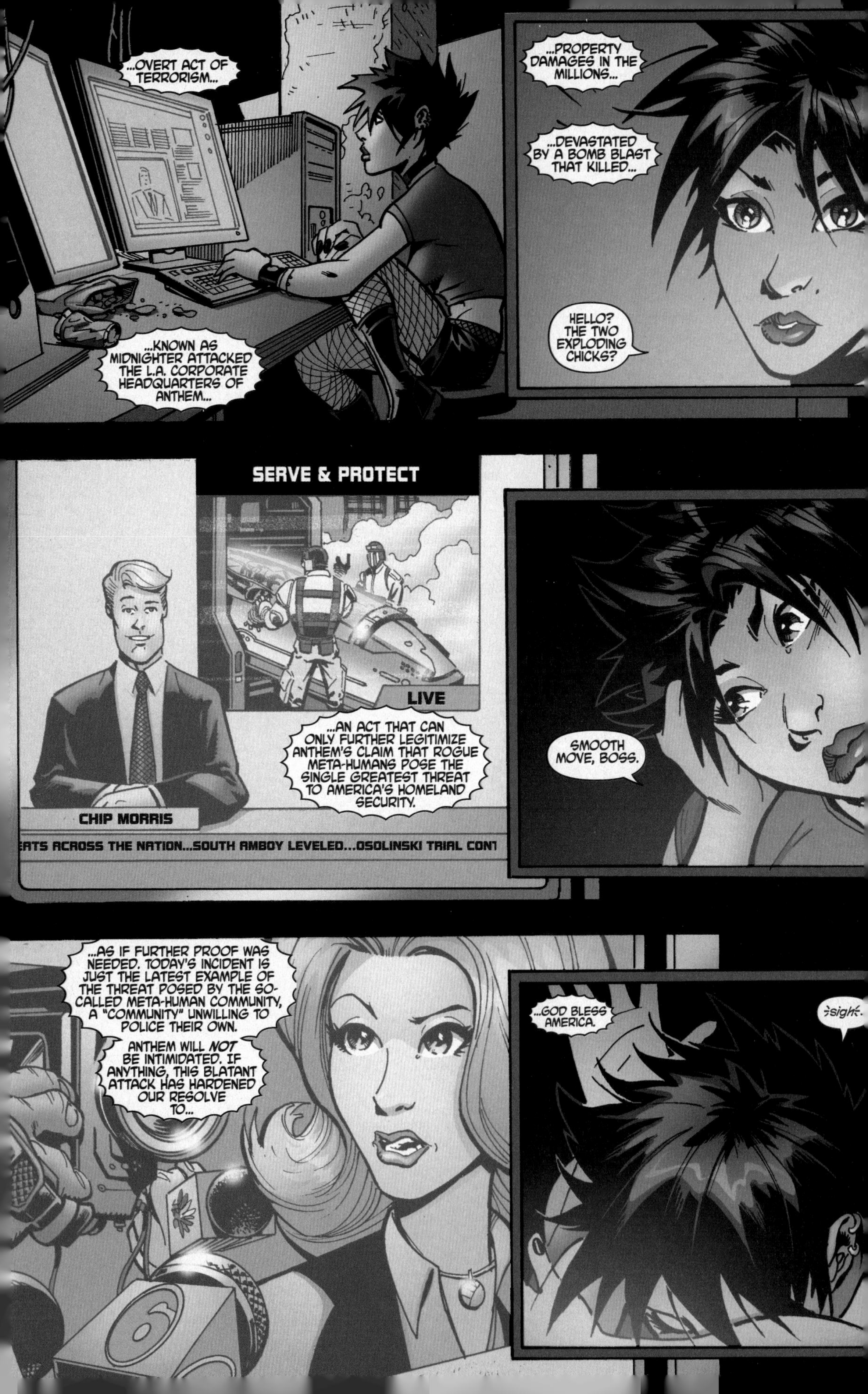
...OVERT ACT OF TERRORISM...
...KNOWN AS MIDNIGHTER ATTACKED THE L.A. CORPORATE HEADQUARTERS OF ANTHEM...
...PROPERTY DAMAGES IN THE MILLIONS...
...DEVASTATED BY A BOMB BLAST THAT KILLED...
HELLO? THE TWO EXPLODING CHICKS?
SERVE & PROTECT
LIVE
...AN ACT THAT CAN ONLY FURTHER LEGITIMIZE ANTHEM'S CLAIM THAT ROGUE META-HUMANS POSE THE SINGLE GREATEST THREAT TO AMERICA'S HOMELAND SECURITY.
CHIP MORRIS
EATS ACROSS THE NATION...SOUTH AMBOY LEVELED...OSOLINSKI TRIAL CONT
SMOOTH MOVE, BOSS.
...AS IF FURTHER PROOF WAS NEEDED. TODAY'S INCIDENT IS JUST THE LATEST EXAMPLE OF THE THREAT POSED BY THE SO-CALLED META-HUMAN COMMUNITY, A "COMMUNITY" UNWILLING TO POLICE THEIR OWN.
ANTHEM WILL NOT BE INTIMIDATED. IF ANYTHING, THIS BLATANT ATTACK HAS HARDENED OUR RESOLVE TO...
...GOD BLESS AMERICA.
sigh

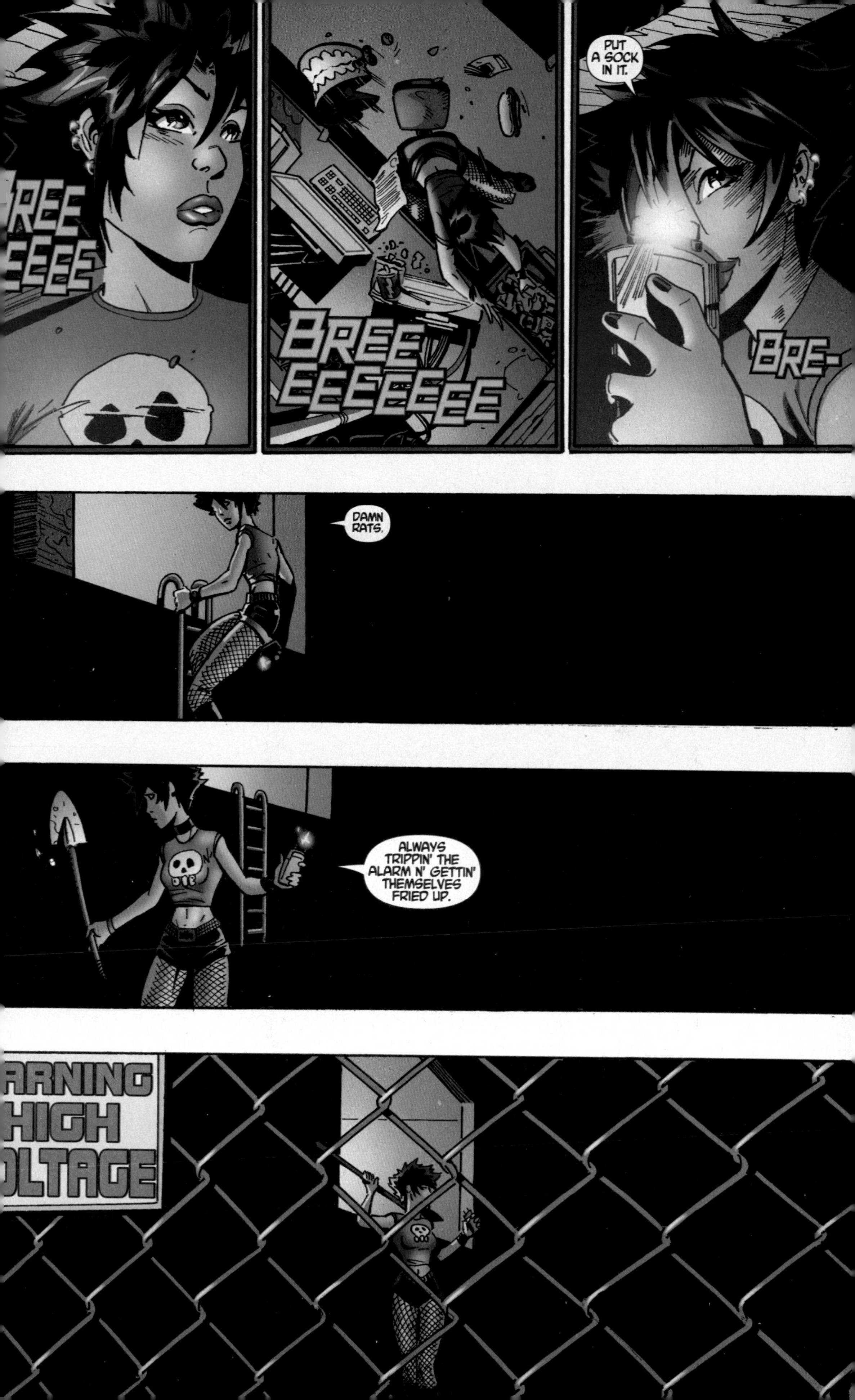
REE EEEE
BREE EEEEEEEE
PUT A SOCK IN IT.
BRE-
DAMN RATS.
ALWAYS TRIPPIN' THE ALARM N' GETTIN' THEMSELVES FRIED UP.
ARNING HIGH OLTAGE

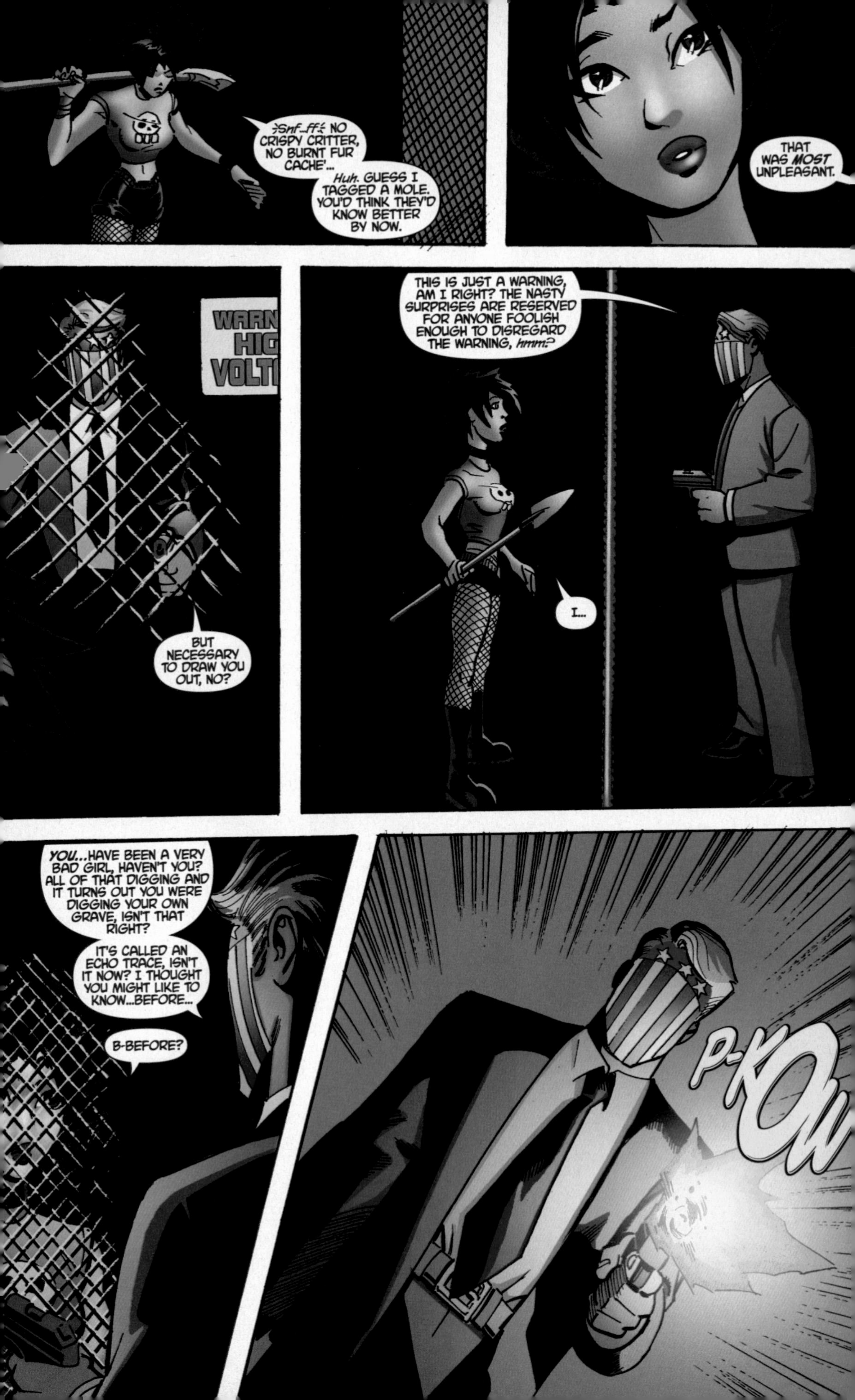
Snf..ff NO CRISPY CRITTER, NO BURNT FUR CACHE'...
Huh. GUESS I TAGGED A MOLE. YOU'D THINK THEY'D KNOW BETTER BY NOW.
THAT WAS MOST UNPLEASANT.
BUT NECESSARY TO DRAW YOU OUT, NO?
THIS IS JUST A WARNING, AM I RIGHT? THE NASTY SURPRISES ARE RESERVED FOR ANYONE FOOLISH ENOUGH TO DISREGARD THE WARNING, hmm?
I...
YOU...HAVE BEEN A VERY BAD GIRL, HAVEN'T YOU? ALL OF THAT DIGGING AND IT TURNS OUT YOU WERE DIGGING YOUR OWN GRAVE, ISN'T THAT RIGHT?
IT'S CALLED AN ECHO TRACE, ISN'T IT NOW? I THOUGHT YOU MIGHT LIKE TO KNOW...BEFORE...
B-BEFORE?
P-KOW

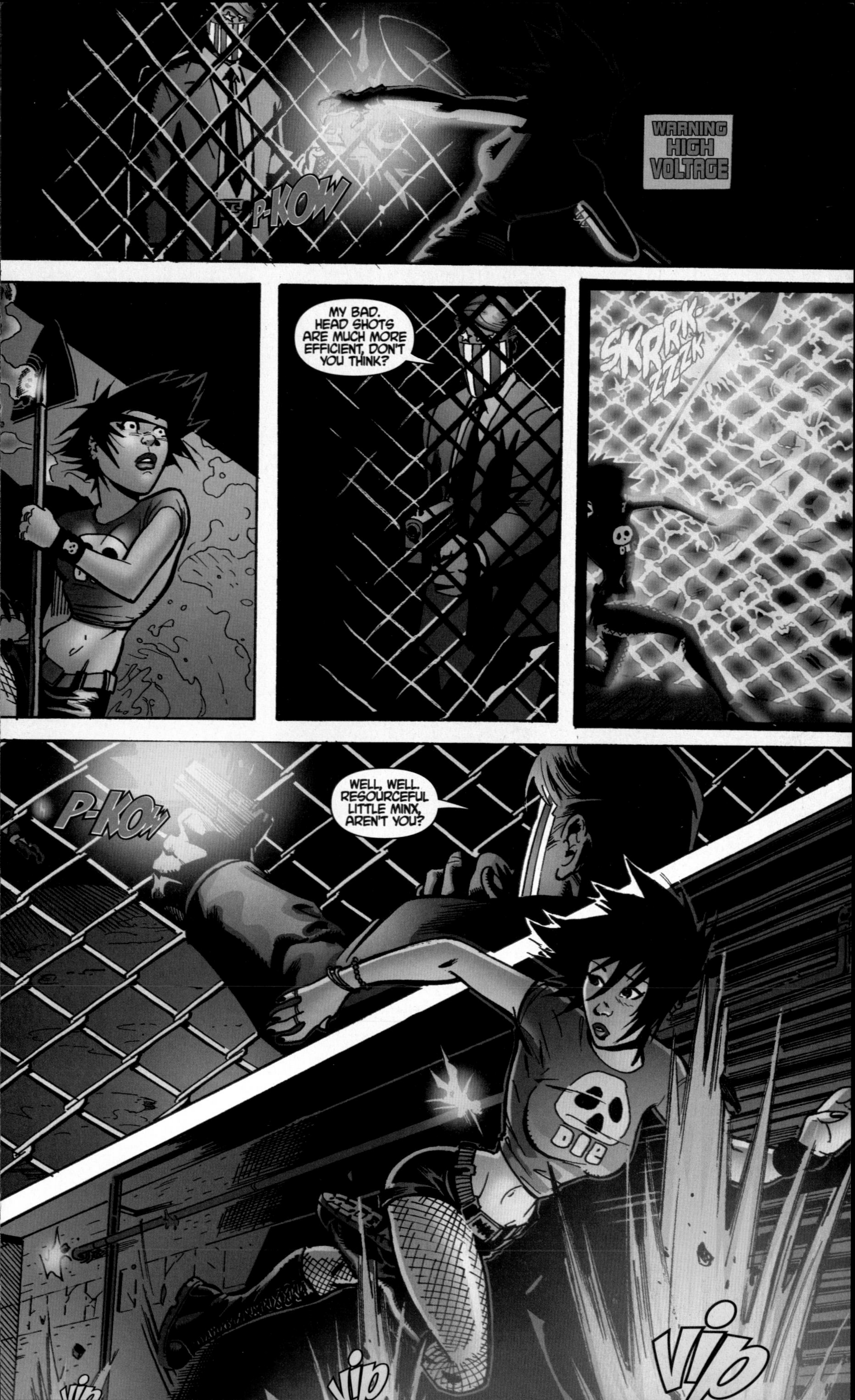
WARNING HIGH VOLTAGE
P-KOW
MY BAD. HEAD SHOTS ARE MUCH MORE EFFICIENT, DON'T YOU THINK?
SKRRK-ZZZK
P-KOW
WELL, WELL. RESOURCEFUL LITTLE MINX, AREN'T YOU?
DIE
VIP
VIP

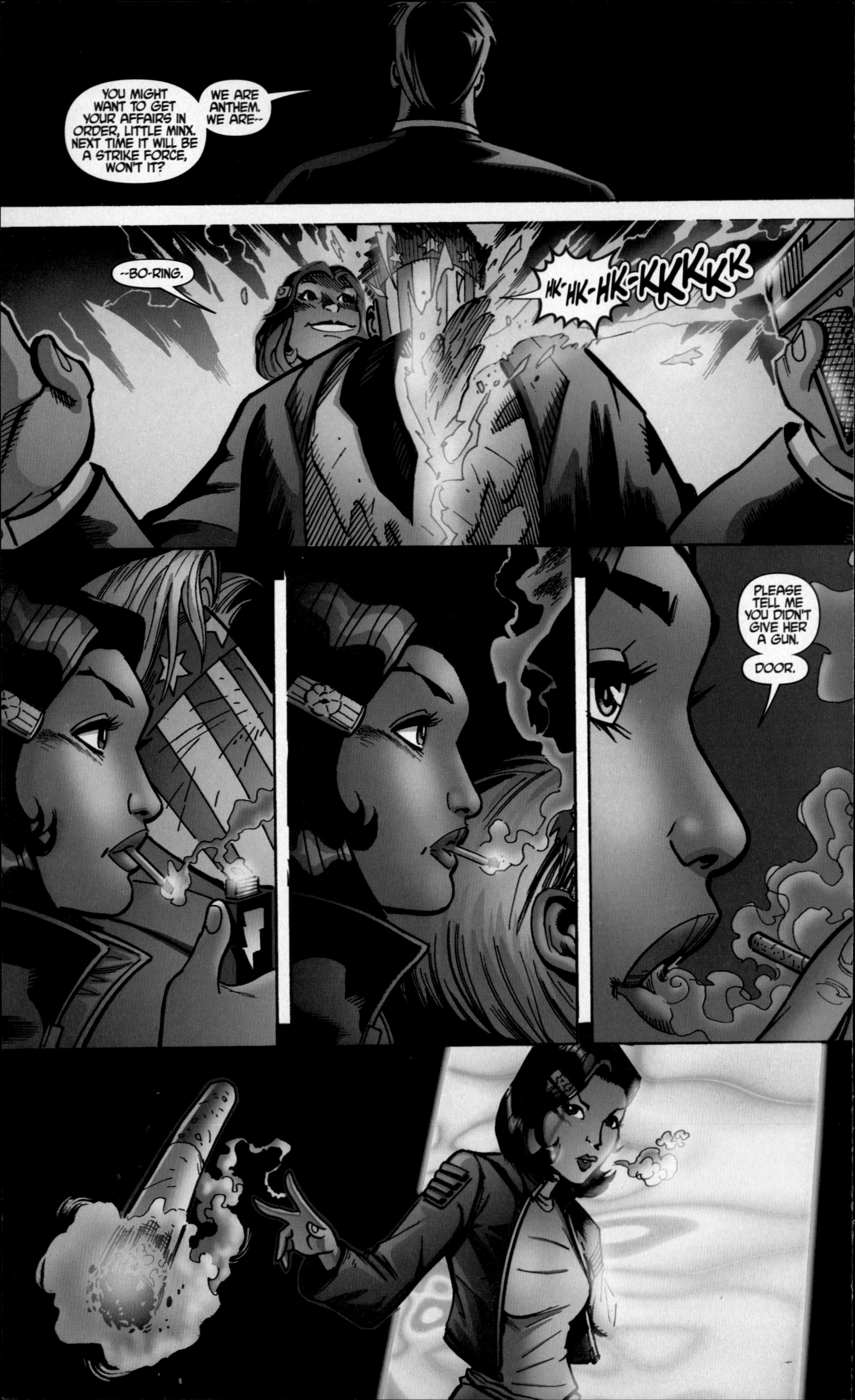
YOU MIGHT WANT TO GET YOUR AFFAIRS IN ORDER, LITTLE MINX. NEXT TIME IT WILL BE A STRIKE FORCE, WON'T IT?
WE ARE ANTHEM. WE ARE--
--BO-RING.
HK-HK-HK-KKKKK
PLEASE TELL ME YOU DIDN'T GIVE HER A GUN.
DOOR.

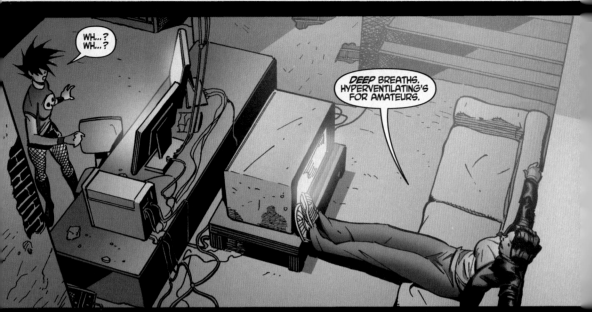

WH...? WH...?

DEEP BREATHS. HYPERVENTILATING'S FOR AMATEURS.

SHOT AT ME...HE...

WHAT THE HELL JUST HAPPENED!?

FIRST TIME'S ALWAYS A BITCH.

THIS CAME AS A SURPRISE TO YOU? PLAY WITH FIRE, EXPECT TO GET BURNED.

JESUS...

LET ME KNOW WHEN YOU'RE UP FOR IT.

UP FOR WHAT?

APPARENTLY, ANTHEM'S NOT THE *ONLY* PLACE YOU'VE BEEN SNIFFING AROUND.

WE SHOULD TALK.

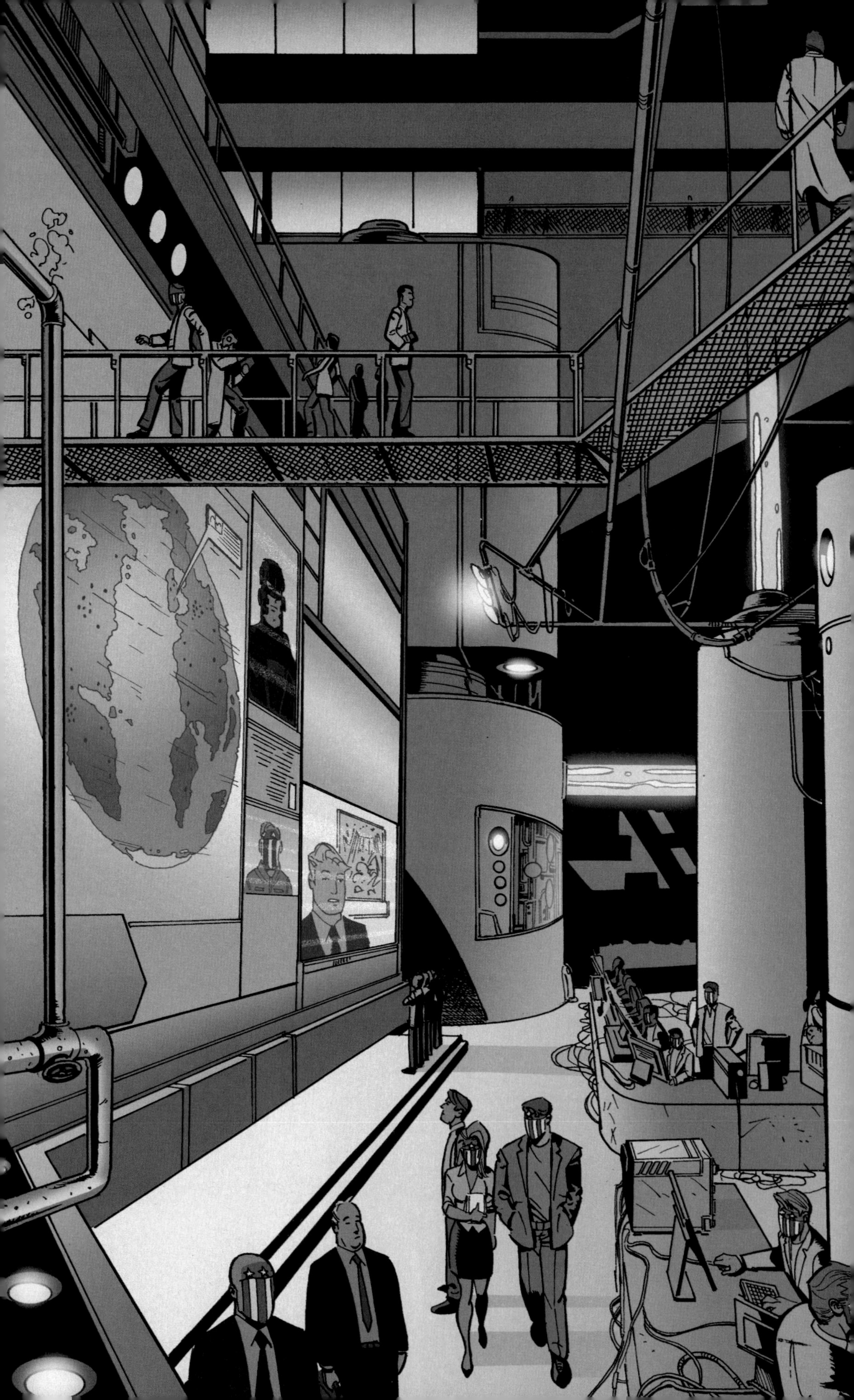

SLEEP WELL?

OKAY. WASN'T EXPECTING THIS.

WE ARE NOT MONSTERS, MISTER TRENT.

YOU HAVE THIRTY SECONDS TO CONVINCE ME YOU DESERVE TO LIVE.

JUST LIKE THAT? YOU'D TAKE MY LIFE AWAY AFTER GOING TO SUCH EFFORT TO SEE IT RESTORED?

WE'VE MET?

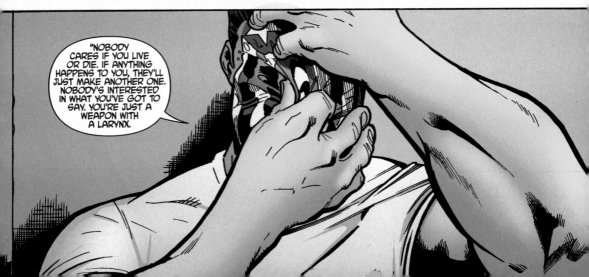

"NOBODY CARES IF YOU LIVE OR DIE. IF ANYTHING HAPPENS TO YOU, THEY'LL JUST MAKE ANOTHER ONE. NOBODY'S INTERESTED IN WHAT YOU'VE GOT TO SAY. YOU'RE JUST A WEAPON WITH A LARYNX.

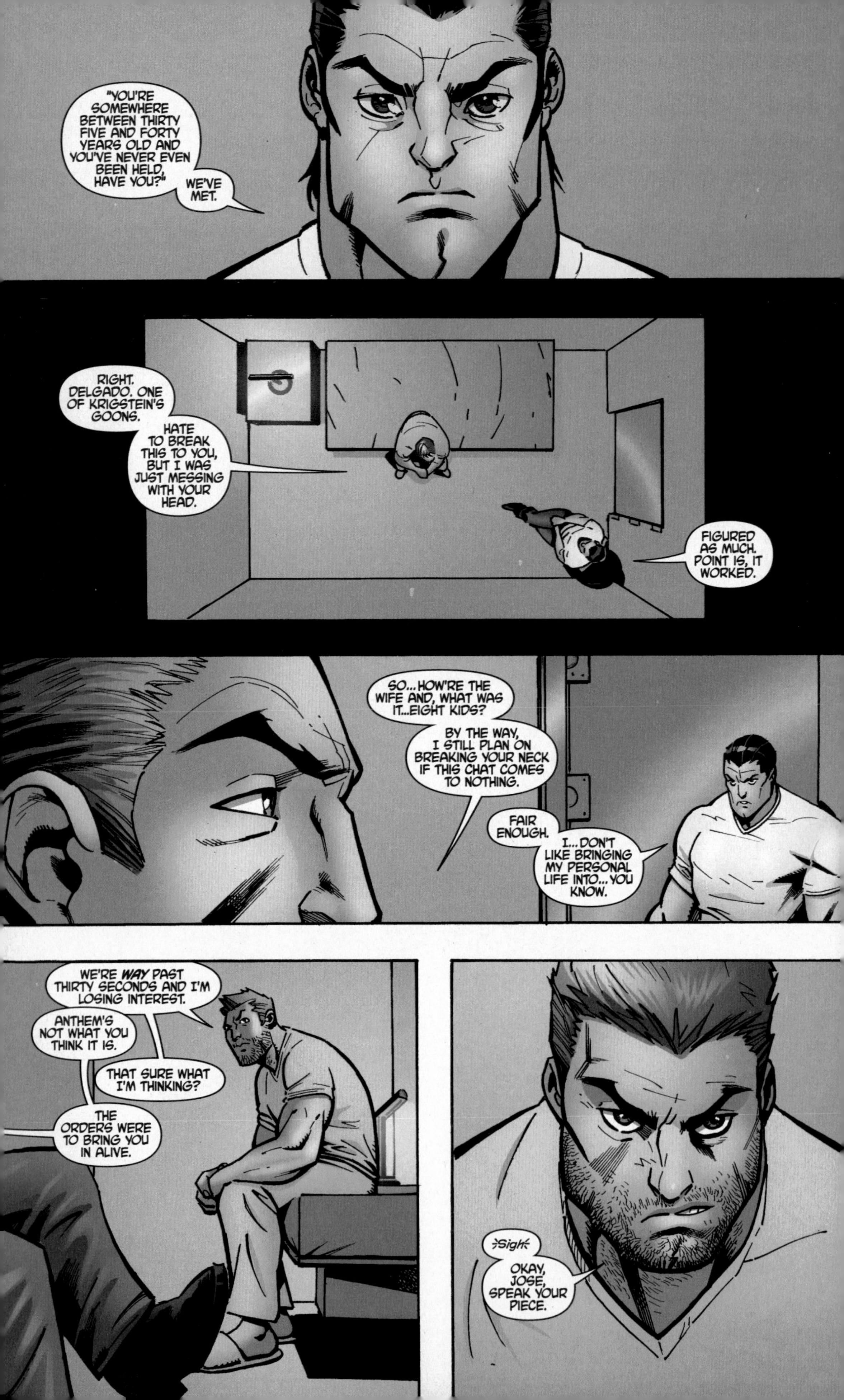
"YOU'RE SOMEWHERE BETWEEN THIRTY FIVE AND FORTY YEARS OLD AND YOU'VE NEVER EVEN BEEN HELD, HAVE YOU?"
WE'VE MET.
RIGHT. DELGADO. ONE OF KRIGSTEIN'S GOONS.
HATE TO BREAK THIS TO YOU, BUT I WAS JUST MESSING WITH YOUR HEAD.
FIGURED AS MUCH. POINT IS, IT WORKED.
SO...HOW'RE THE WIFE AND, WHAT WAS IT...EIGHT KIDS?
BY THE WAY, I STILL PLAN ON BREAKING YOUR NECK IF THIS CHAT COMES TO NOTHING.
FAIR ENOUGH.
I...DON'T LIKE BRINGING MY PERSONAL LIFE INTO...YOU KNOW.
WE'RE *WAY* PAST THIRTY SECONDS AND I'M LOSING INTEREST.
ANTHEM'S NOT WHAT YOU THINK IT IS.
THAT SURE WHAT I'M THINKING?
THE ORDERS WERE TO BRING YOU IN ALIVE.
Sigh
OKAY, JOSE, SPEAK YOUR PIECE.

LET'S SEE IT.

YOU WOULDN'T BE HERE UNLESS YOU ALREADY SAW IT.

HUMOR ME.

WASN'T *ME* GONNA TELL HIM.

WE'RE NEVER GOING TO GET ANYWHERE IF YOU START LYING TO ME.

HERE.

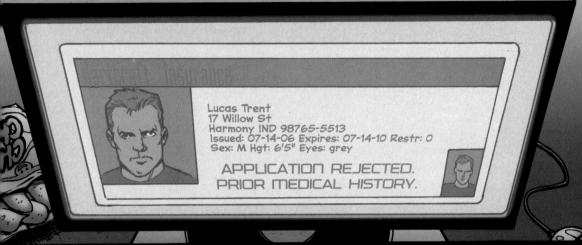

Soulcraft Insurance

Lucas Trent
17 Willow St
Harmony IND 98765-5513
Issued: 07-14-06 Expires: 07-14-10 Restr: 0
Sex: M Hgt: 6'5" Eyes: grey

APPLICATION REJECTED.
PRIOR MEDICAL HISTORY.

YOU'RE GOOD AND THERE'S NO DENYING IT. NEVER THOUGHT TO COMB THROUGH DEAD END FILES.

IT'S NOT HIS LIFE.

IT'S THE LIFE HE NEEDS.

THERE'S, LIKE, SO MUCH WRONG WITH THAT STATEMENT I DON'T KNOW WHERE TO BEGIN.

WHAT SET YOU TO LOOKING?

YOU.

GO ON.

I DON'T TRUST YOU.

YOU DON'T KNOW ME.

KNOW YOUR KIND. WELL MEANING IN ALL THE WRONG WAYS.

HE FINDS OUT, AND HE WILL, IT'S NOT GONNA BE PRETTY.

I HAD MY REASONS.

CARE TO SHARE?

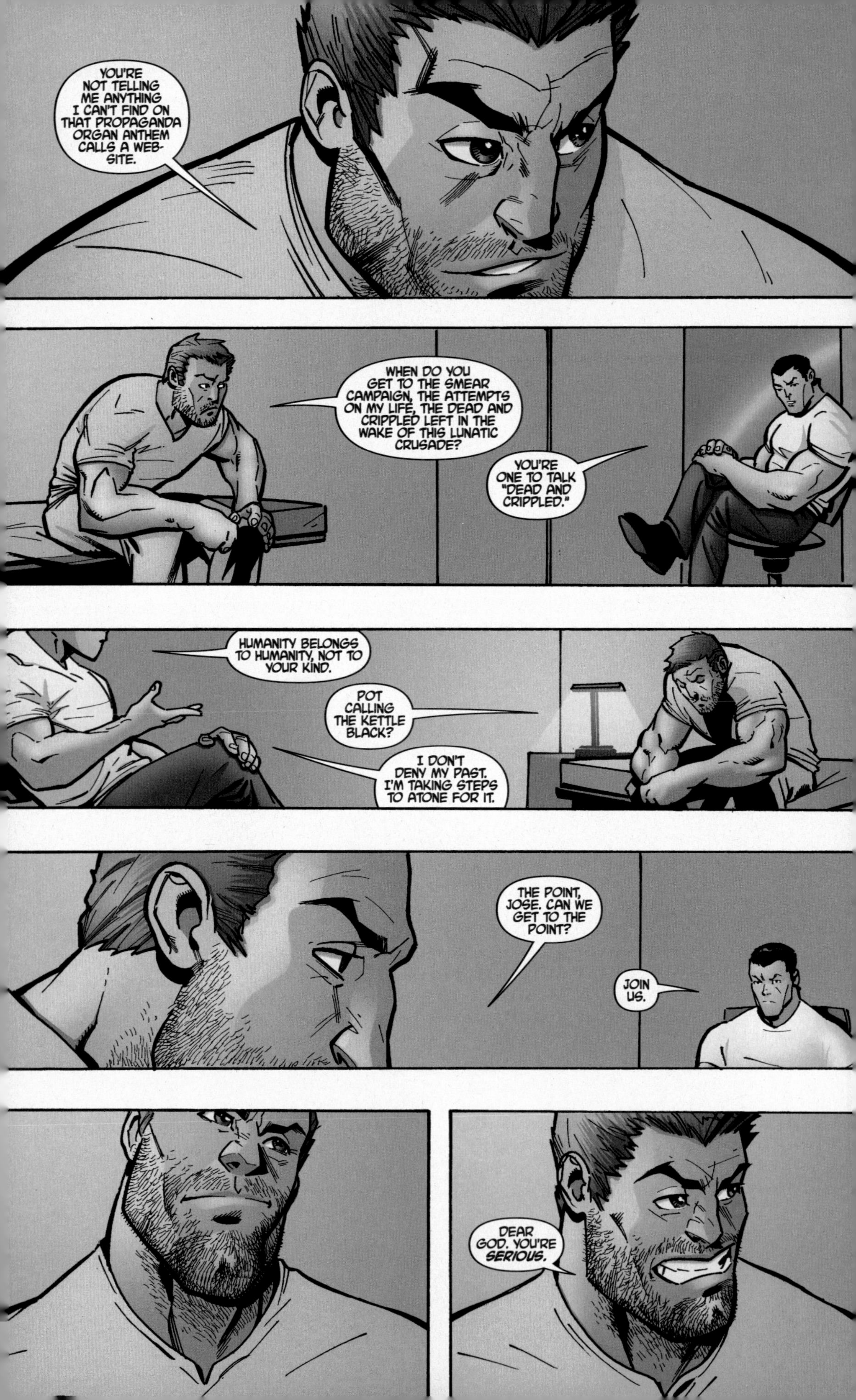
YOU'RE NOT TELLING ME ANYTHING I CAN'T FIND ON THAT PROPAGANDA ORGAN ANTHEM CALLS A WEB-SITE.
WHEN DO YOU GET TO THE SMEAR CAMPAIGN, THE ATTEMPTS ON MY LIFE, THE DEAD AND CRIPPLED LEFT IN THE WAKE OF THIS LUNATIC CRUSADE?
YOU'RE ONE TO TALK "DEAD AND CRIPPLED."
HUMANITY BELONGS TO HUMANITY, NOT TO YOUR KIND.
POT CALLING THE KETTLE BLACK?
I DON'T DENY MY PAST. I'M TAKING STEPS TO ATONE FOR IT.
THE POINT, JOSE. CAN WE GET TO THE POINT?
JOIN US.
DEAR GOD. YOU'RE *SERIOUS.*

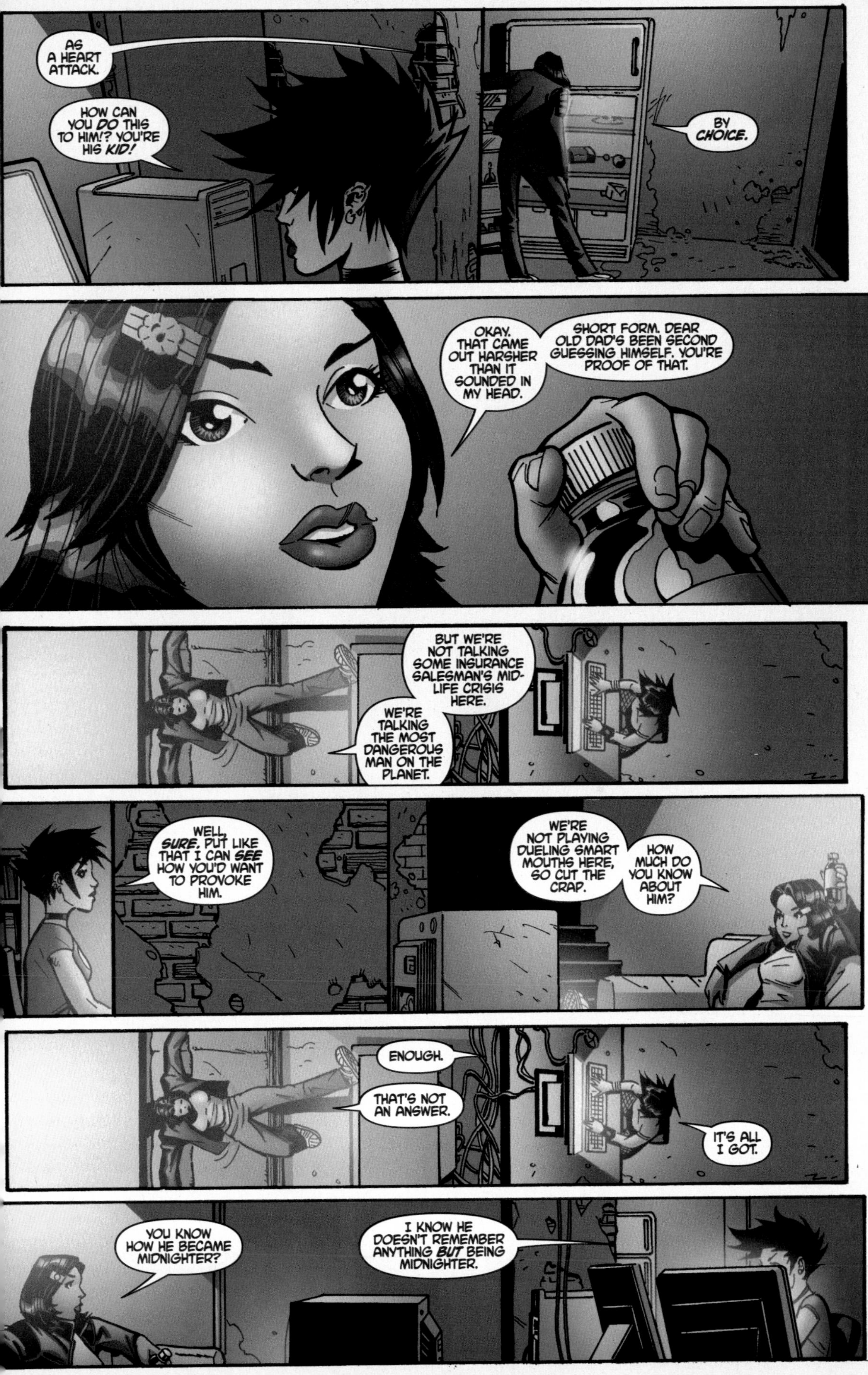
AS A HEART ATTACK.
HOW CAN YOU *DO* THIS TO HIM!? YOU'RE HIS *KID!*
BY *CHOICE.*
OKAY. THAT CAME OUT HARSHER THAN IT SOUNDED IN MY HEAD.
SHORT FORM. DEAR OLD DAD'S BEEN SECOND GUESSING HIMSELF. YOU'RE PROOF OF THAT.
BUT WE'RE NOT TALKING SOME INSURANCE SALESMAN'S MID-LIFE CRISIS HERE.
WE'RE TALKING THE MOST DANGEROUS MAN ON THE PLANET.
WELL, *SURE.* PUT LIKE THAT I CAN *SEE* HOW YOU'D WANT TO PROVOKE HIM.
WE'RE NOT PLAYING DUELING SMART MOUTHS HERE, SO CUT THE CRAP.
HOW MUCH DO YOU KNOW ABOUT HIM?
ENOUGH.
THAT'S NOT AN ANSWER.
IT'S ALL I GOT.
YOU KNOW HOW HE BECAME MIDNIGHTER?
I KNOW HE DOESN'T REMEMBER ANYTHING *BUT* BEING MIDNIGHTER.

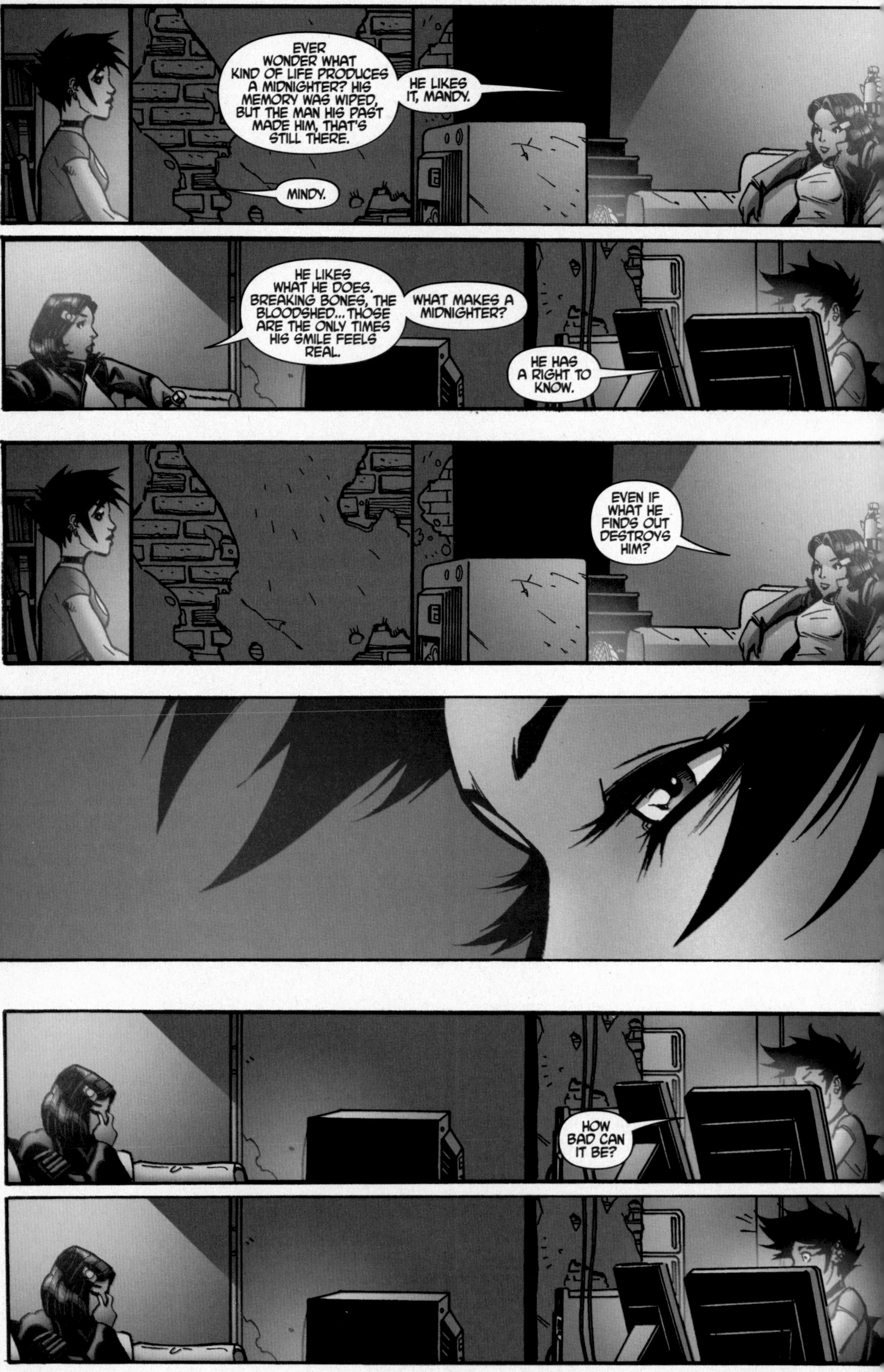
EVER WONDER WHAT KIND OF LIFE PRODUCES A MIDNIGHTER? HIS MEMORY WAS WIPED, BUT THE MAN HIS PAST MADE HIM, THAT'S STILL THERE.
HE LIKES IT, MANDY.
MINDY.
HE LIKES WHAT HE DOES. BREAKING BONES, THE BLOODSHED... THOSE ARE THE ONLY TIMES HIS SMILE FEELS REAL.
WHAT MAKES A MIDNIGHTER?
HE HAS A RIGHT TO KNOW.
EVEN IF WHAT HE FINDS OUT DESTROYS HIM?
HOW BAD CAN IT BE?

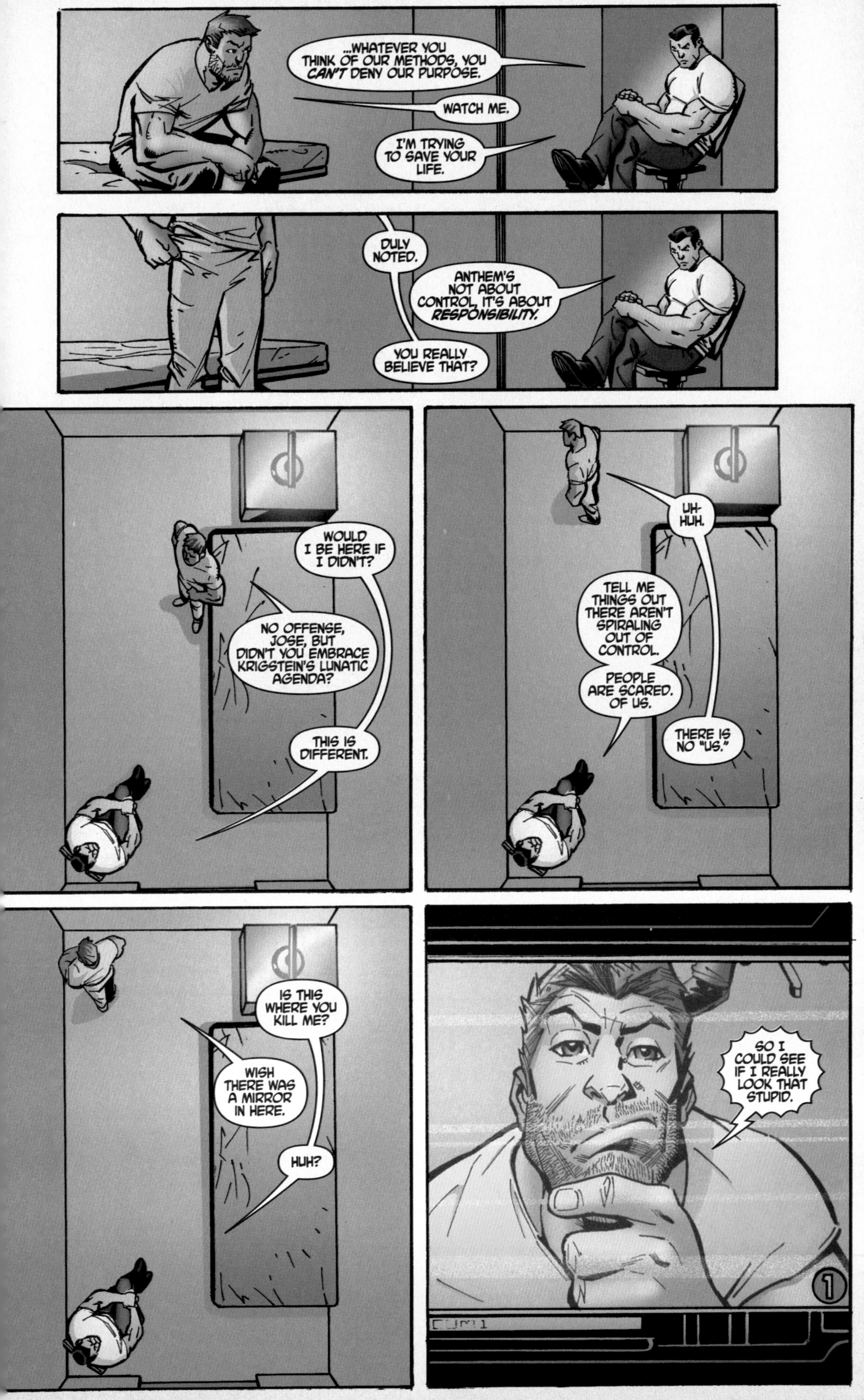
...WHATEVER YOU THINK OF OUR METHODS, YOU *CAN'T* DENY OUR PURPOSE.
WATCH ME.
I'M TRYING TO SAVE YOUR LIFE.
DULY NOTED.
ANTHEM'S NOT ABOUT CONTROL, IT'S ABOUT *RESPONSIBILITY.*
YOU REALLY BELIEVE THAT?
WOULD I BE HERE IF I DIDN'T?
NO OFFENSE, JOSE, BUT DIDN'T YOU EMBRACE KRIGSTEIN'S LUNATIC AGENDA?
THIS IS DIFFERENT.
UH-HUH.
TELL ME THINGS OUT THERE AREN'T SPIRALING OUT OF CONTROL.
PEOPLE ARE SCARED. OF US.
THERE IS NO "US."
IS THIS WHERE YOU KILL ME?
WISH THERE WAS A MIRROR IN HERE.
HUH?
SO I COULD SEE IF I REALLY LOOK THAT STUPID.

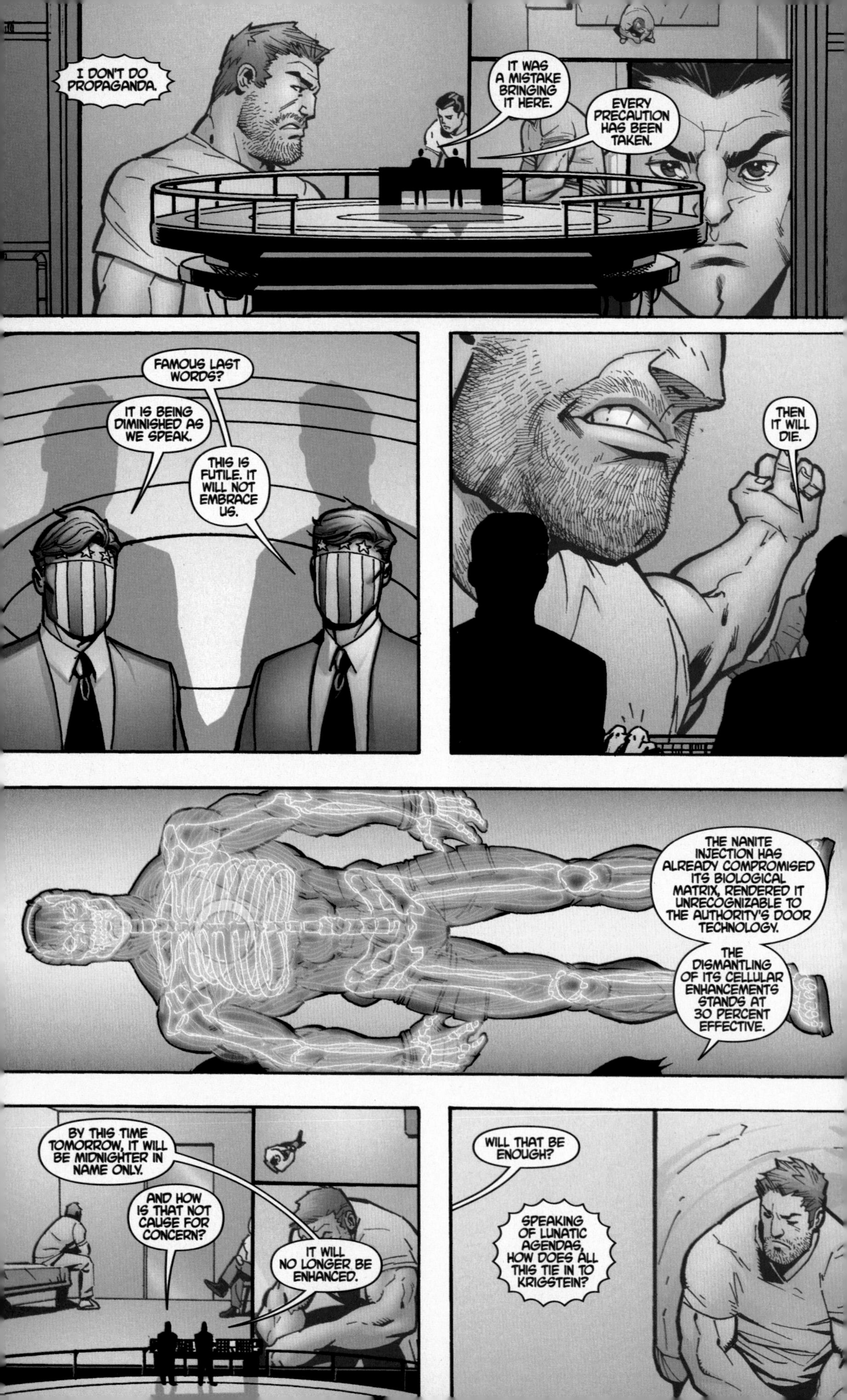
I DON'T DO PROPAGANDA.
IT WAS A MISTAKE BRINGING IT HERE.
EVERY PRECAUTION HAS BEEN TAKEN.
FAMOUS LAST WORDS?
IT IS BEING DIMINISHED AS WE SPEAK.
THIS IS FUTILE. IT WILL NOT EMBRACE US.
THEN IT WILL DIE.
THE NANITE INJECTION HAS ALREADY COMPROMISED ITS BIOLOGICAL MATRIX, RENDERED IT UNRECOGNIZABLE TO THE AUTHORITY'S DOOR TECHNOLOGY.
THE DISMANTLING OF ITS CELLULAR ENHANCEMENTS STANDS AT 30 PERCENT EFFECTIVE.
BY THIS TIME TOMORROW, IT WILL BE MIDNIGHTER IN NAME ONLY.
AND HOW IS THAT NOT CAUSE FOR CONCERN?
IT WILL NO LONGER BE ENHANCED.
WILL THAT BE ENOUGH?
SPEAKING OF LUNATIC AGENDAS, HOW DOES ALL THIS TIE IN TO KRIGSTEIN?

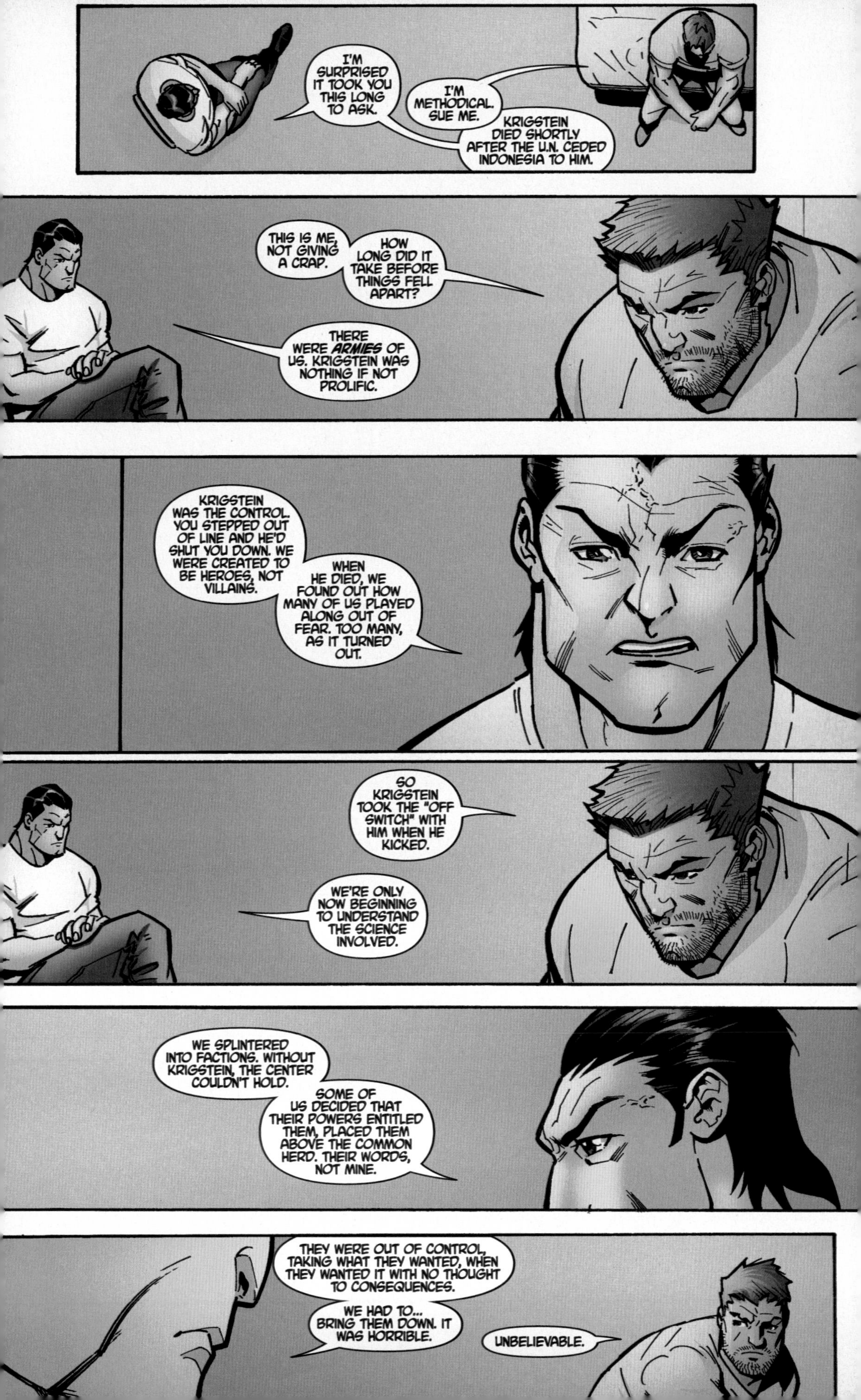
I'M SURPRISED IT TOOK YOU THIS LONG TO ASK.
I'M METHODICAL. SUE ME.
KRIGSTEIN DIED SHORTLY AFTER THE U.N. CEDED INDONESIA TO HIM.
THIS IS ME, NOT GIVING A CRAP.
HOW LONG DID IT TAKE BEFORE THINGS FELL APART?
THERE WERE *ARMIES* OF US. KRIGSTEIN WAS NOTHING IF NOT PROLIFIC.
KRIGSTEIN WAS THE CONTROL. YOU STEPPED OUT OF LINE AND HE'D SHUT YOU DOWN. WE WERE CREATED TO BE HEROES, NOT VILLAINS.
WHEN HE DIED, WE FOUND OUT HOW MANY OF US PLAYED ALONG OUT OF FEAR. TOO MANY, AS IT TURNED OUT.
SO KRIGSTEIN TOOK THE "OFF SWITCH" WITH HIM WHEN HE KICKED.
WE'RE ONLY NOW BEGINNING TO UNDERSTAND THE SCIENCE INVOLVED.
WE SPLINTERED INTO FACTIONS. WITHOUT KRIGSTEIN, THE CENTER COULDN'T HOLD.
SOME OF US DECIDED THAT THEIR POWERS ENTITLED THEM, PLACED THEM ABOVE THE COMMON HERD. THEIR WORDS, NOT MINE.
THEY WERE OUT OF CONTROL, TAKING WHAT THEY WANTED, WHEN THEY WANTED IT WITH NO THOUGHT TO CONSEQUENCES.
WE HAD TO... BRING THEM DOWN. IT WAS HORRIBLE.
UNBELIEVABLE.

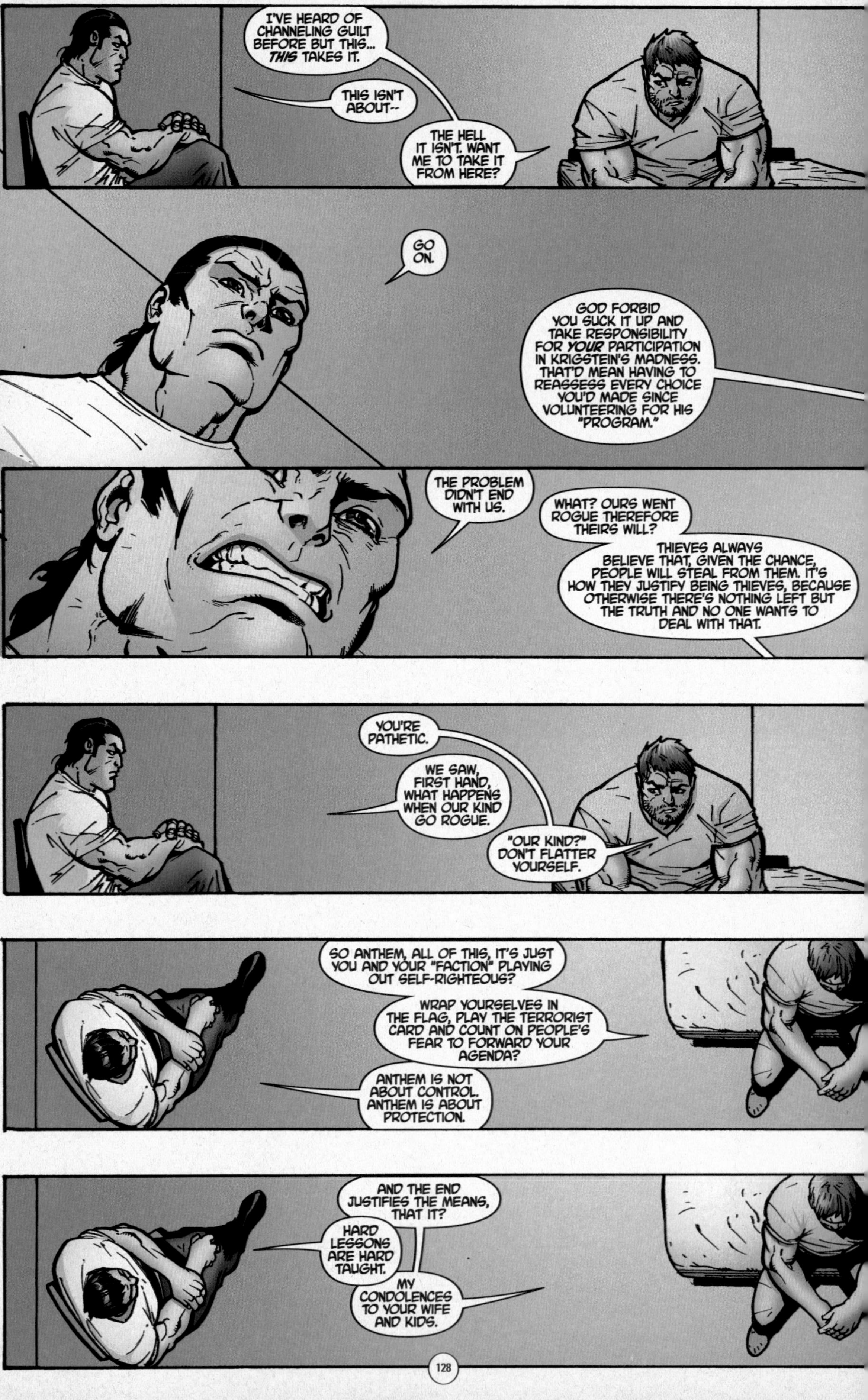

I'VE HEARD OF CHANNELING GUILT BEFORE BUT THIS... *THIS* TAKES IT.
THIS ISN'T ABOUT--
THE HELL IT ISN'T. WANT ME TO TAKE IT FROM HERE?
GO ON.
GOD FORBID YOU SUCK IT UP AND TAKE RESPONSIBILITY FOR *YOUR* PARTICIPATION IN KRIGSTEIN'S MADNESS. THAT'D MEAN HAVING TO REASSESS EVERY CHOICE YOU'D MADE SINCE VOLUNTEERING FOR HIS "PROGRAM."
THE PROBLEM DIDN'T END WITH US.
WHAT? OURS WENT ROGUE THEREFORE THEIRS WILL?
THIEVES ALWAYS BELIEVE THAT, GIVEN THE CHANCE, PEOPLE WILL STEAL FROM THEM. IT'S HOW THEY JUSTIFY BEING THIEVES, BECAUSE OTHERWISE THERE'S NOTHING LEFT BUT THE TRUTH AND NO ONE WANTS TO DEAL WITH THAT.
YOU'RE PATHETIC.
WE SAW, FIRST HAND, WHAT HAPPENS WHEN OUR KIND GO ROGUE.
"OUR KIND?" DON'T FLATTER YOURSELF.
SO ANTHEM, ALL OF THIS, IT'S JUST YOU AND YOUR "FACTION" PLAYING OUT SELF-RIGHTEOUS?
WRAP YOURSELVES IN THE FLAG, PLAY THE TERRORIST CARD AND COUNT ON PEOPLE'S FEAR TO FORWARD YOUR AGENDA?
ANTHEM IS NOT ABOUT CONTROL. ANTHEM IS ABOUT PROTECTION.
AND THE END JUSTIFIES THE MEANS, THAT IT?
HARD LESSONS ARE HARD TAUGHT.
MY CONDOLENCES TO YOUR WIFE AND KIDS.

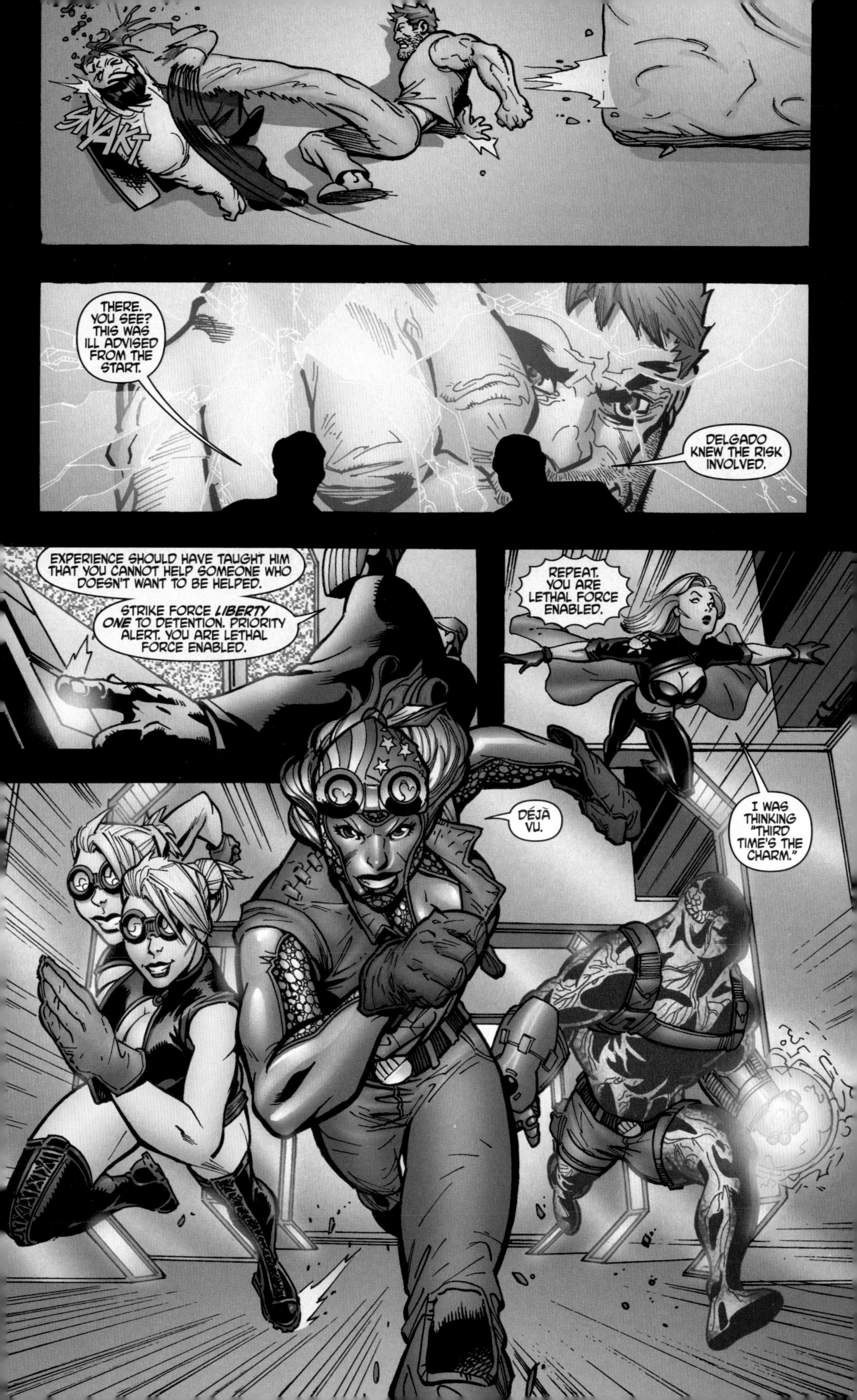
SNAKT
THERE. YOU SEE? THIS WAS ILL ADVISED FROM THE START.
DELGADO KNEW THE RISK INVOLVED.
EXPERIENCE SHOULD HAVE TAUGHT HIM THAT YOU CANNOT HELP SOMEONE WHO DOESN'T WANT TO BE HELPED.
STRIKE FORCE *LIBERTY ONE* TO DETENTION. PRIORITY ALERT. YOU ARE LETHAL FORCE ENABLED.
REPEAT. YOU ARE LETHAL FORCE ENABLED.
DÉJÀ VU.
I WAS THINKING "THIRD TIME'S THE CHARM."

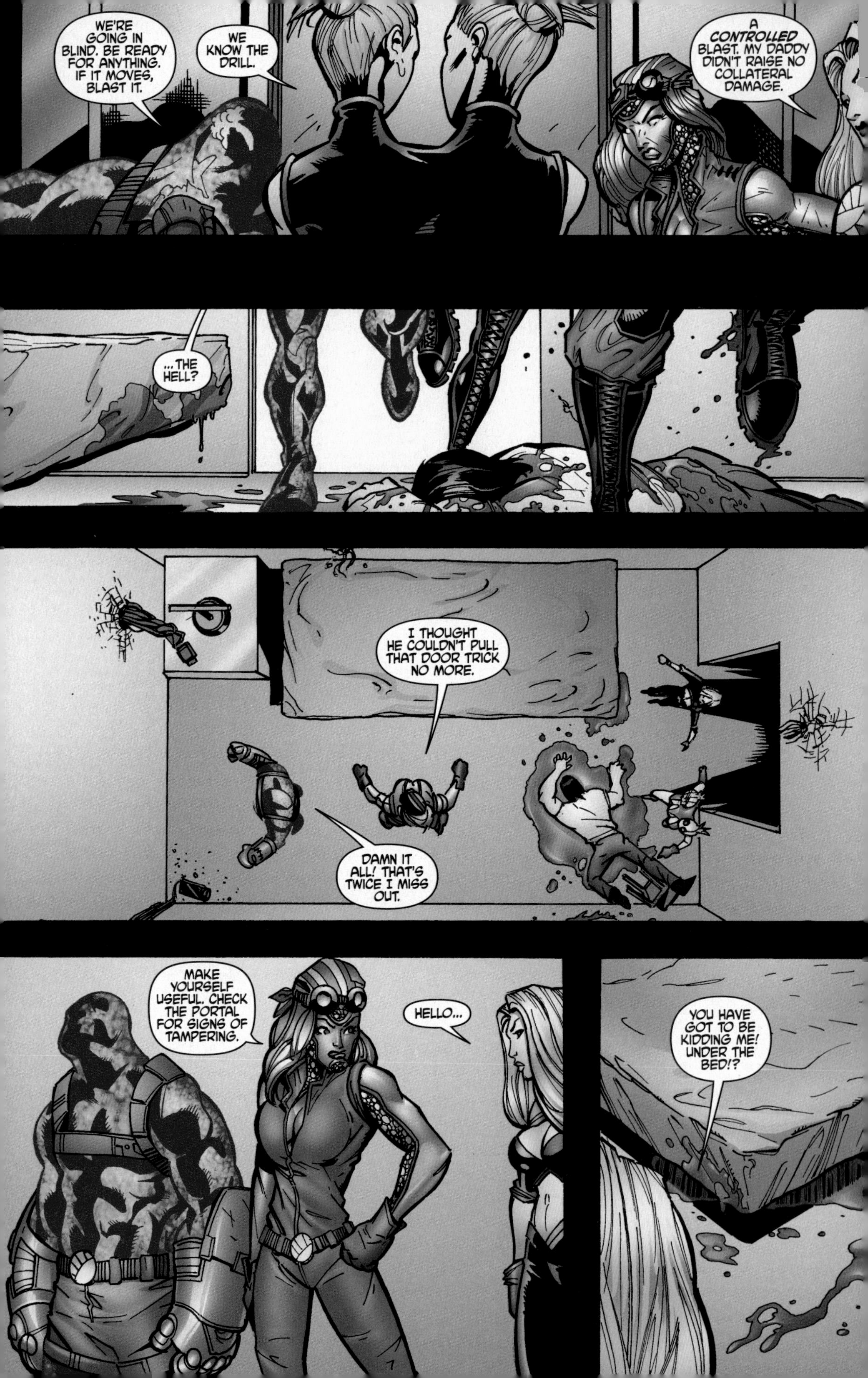
WE'RE GOING IN BLIND. BE READY FOR ANYTHING. IF IT MOVES, BLAST IT.
WE KNOW THE DRILL.
A *CONTROLLED* BLAST. MY DADDY DIDN'T RAISE NO COLLATERAL DAMAGE.
...THE HELL?
I THOUGHT HE COULDN'T PULL THAT DOOR TRICK NO MORE.
DAMN IT ALL! THAT'S TWICE I MISS OUT.
MAKE YOURSELF USEFUL. CHECK THE PORTAL FOR SIGNS OF TAMPERING.
HELLO...
YOU HAVE GOT TO BE KIDDING ME! UNDER THE BED!?

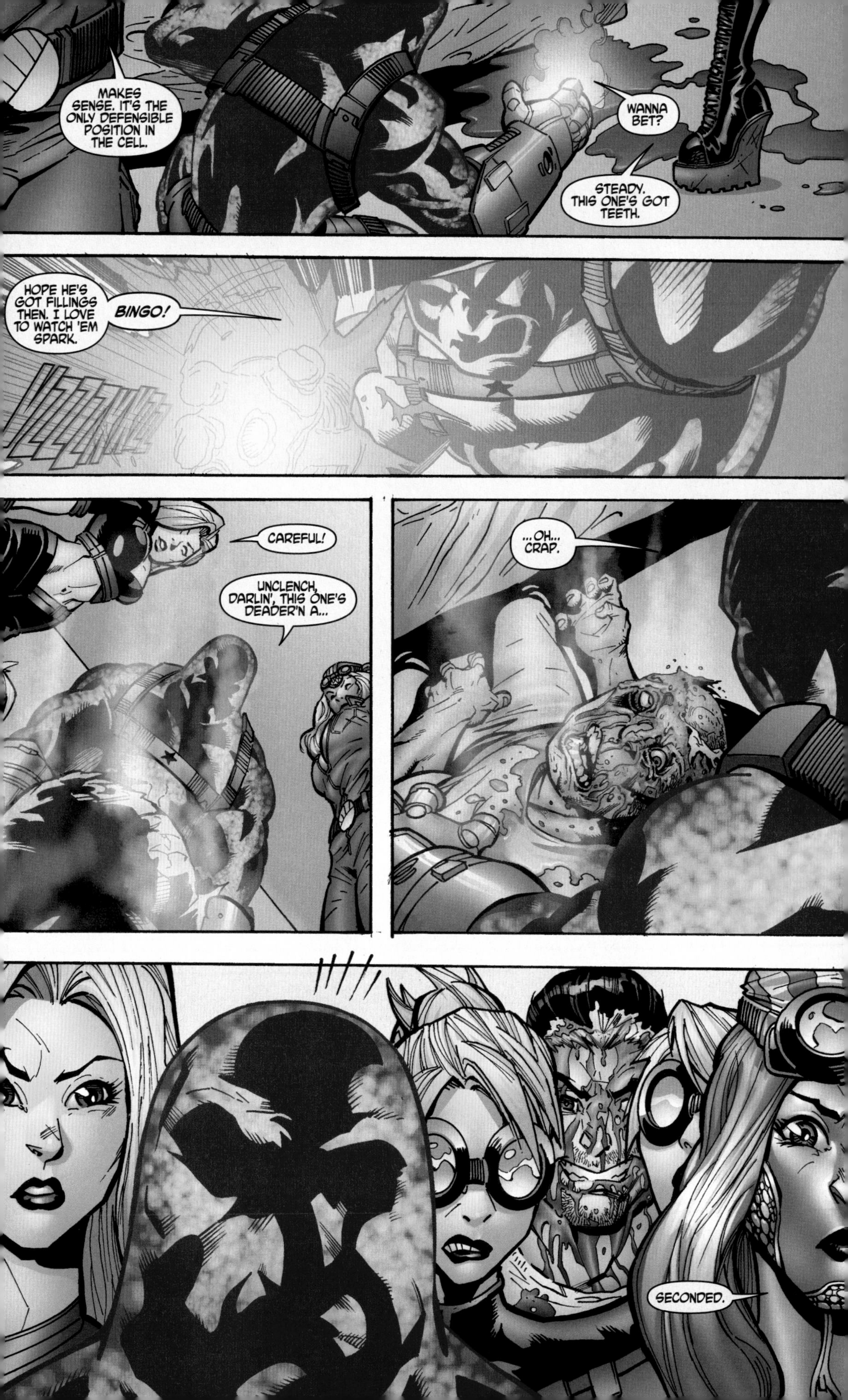
MAKES SENSE. IT'S THE ONLY DEFENSIBLE POSITION IN THE CELL.
WANNA BET?
STEADY. THIS ONE'S GOT TEETH.
HOPE HE'S GOT FILLINGS THEN. I LOVE TO WATCH 'EM SPARK.
BINGO!
CAREFUL!
UNCLENCH, DARLIN', THIS ONE'S DEADER'N A...
...OH... CRAP.
SECONDED.

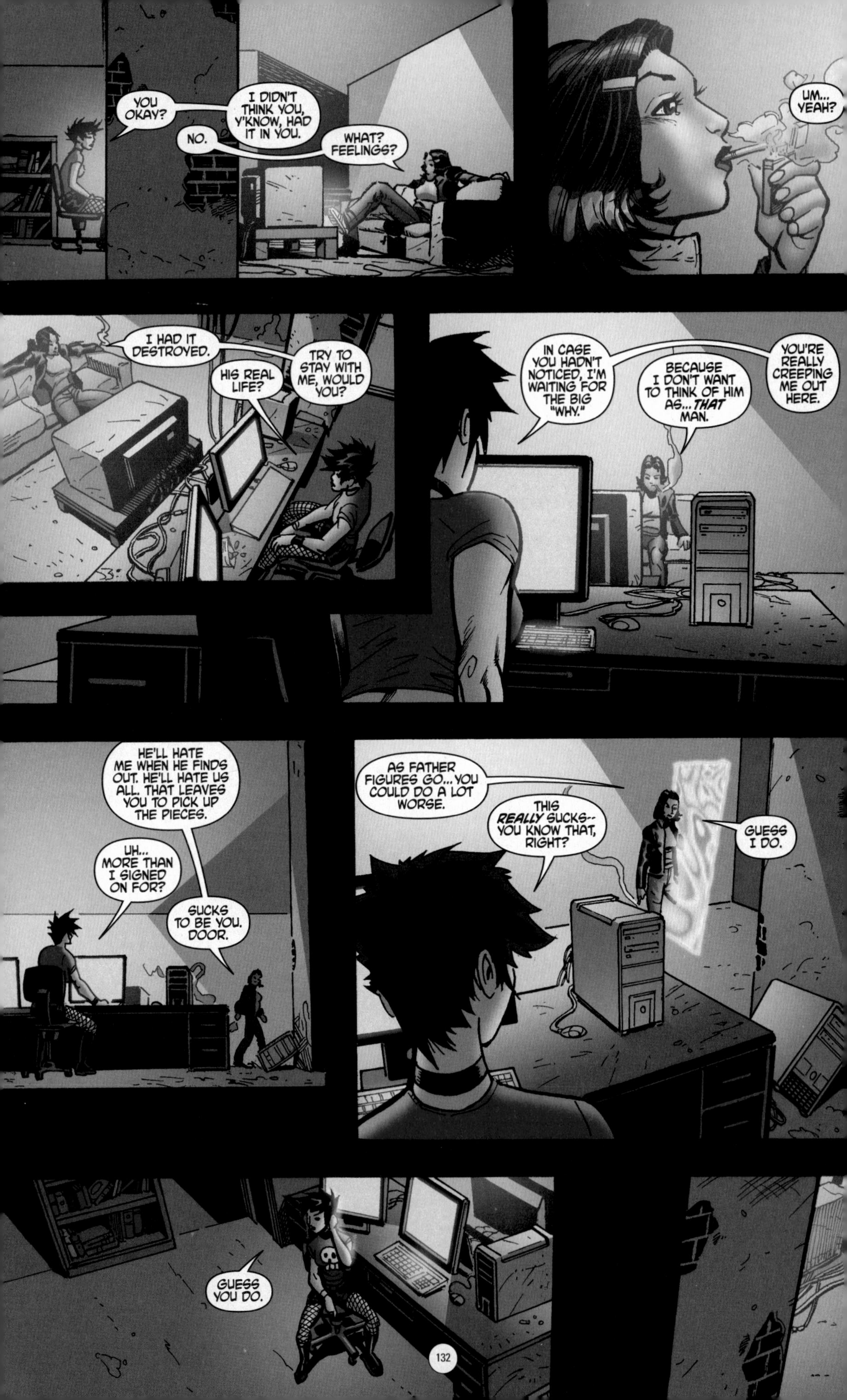

YOU OKAY?
I DIDN'T THINK YOU, Y'KNOW, HAD IT IN YOU.
NO.
WHAT? FEELINGS?
UM... YEAH?
I HAD IT DESTROYED.
HIS REAL LIFE?
TRY TO STAY WITH ME, WOULD YOU?
IN CASE YOU HADN'T NOTICED, I'M WAITING FOR THE BIG "WHY."
BECAUSE I DON'T WANT TO THINK OF HIM AS...THAT MAN.
YOU'RE REALLY CREEPING ME OUT HERE.
HE'LL HATE ME WHEN HE FINDS OUT. HE'LL HATE US ALL. THAT LEAVES YOU TO PICK UP THE PIECES.
UH... MORE THAN I SIGNED ON FOR?
SUCKS TO BE YOU. DOOR.
AS FATHER FIGURES GO...YOU COULD DO A LOT WORSE.
THIS REALLY SUCKS-- YOU KNOW THAT, RIGHT?
GUESS I DO.
GUESS YOU DO.

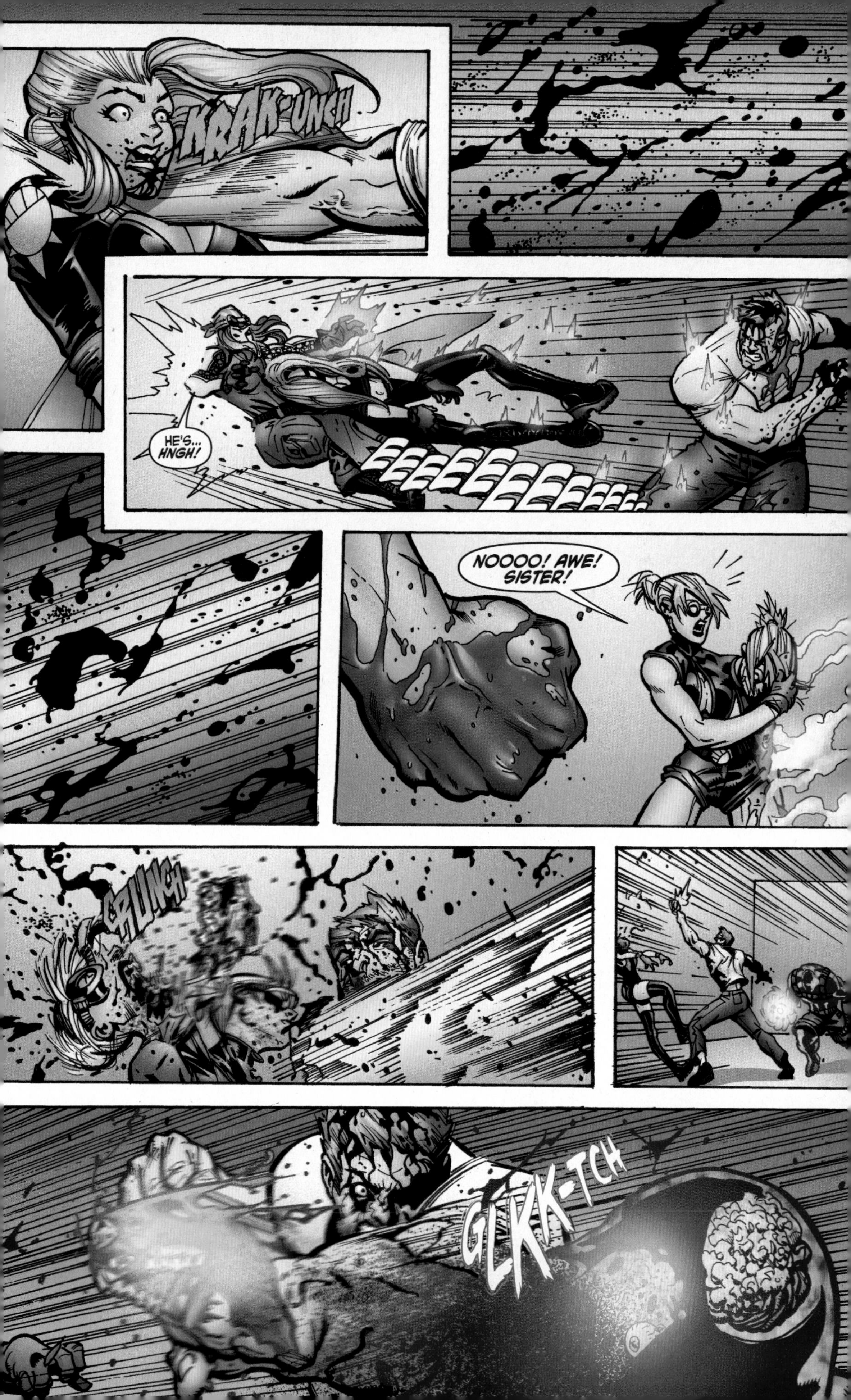
KRAK-UNCH
HE'S... HNGH!
EEEEEEEEEEEEEEEE...
NOOOO! AWE! SISTER!
CRUNCH
GLKK-TCH

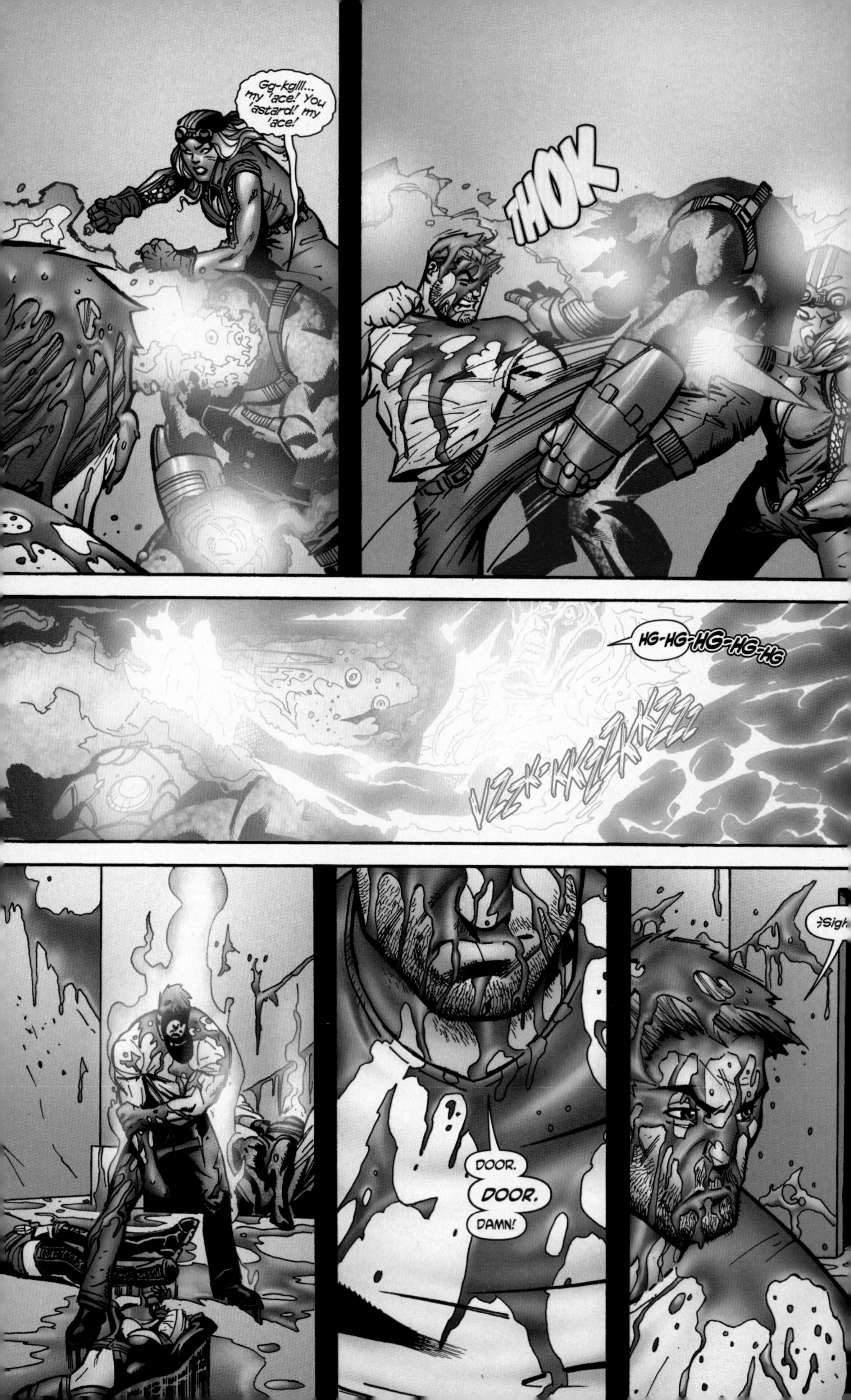
Gg-kglll... my 'ace! You 'astard! my 'ace!
THOK
HG-HG-HG-HG-HG
DOOR.
DOOR.
DAMN!
Sigh

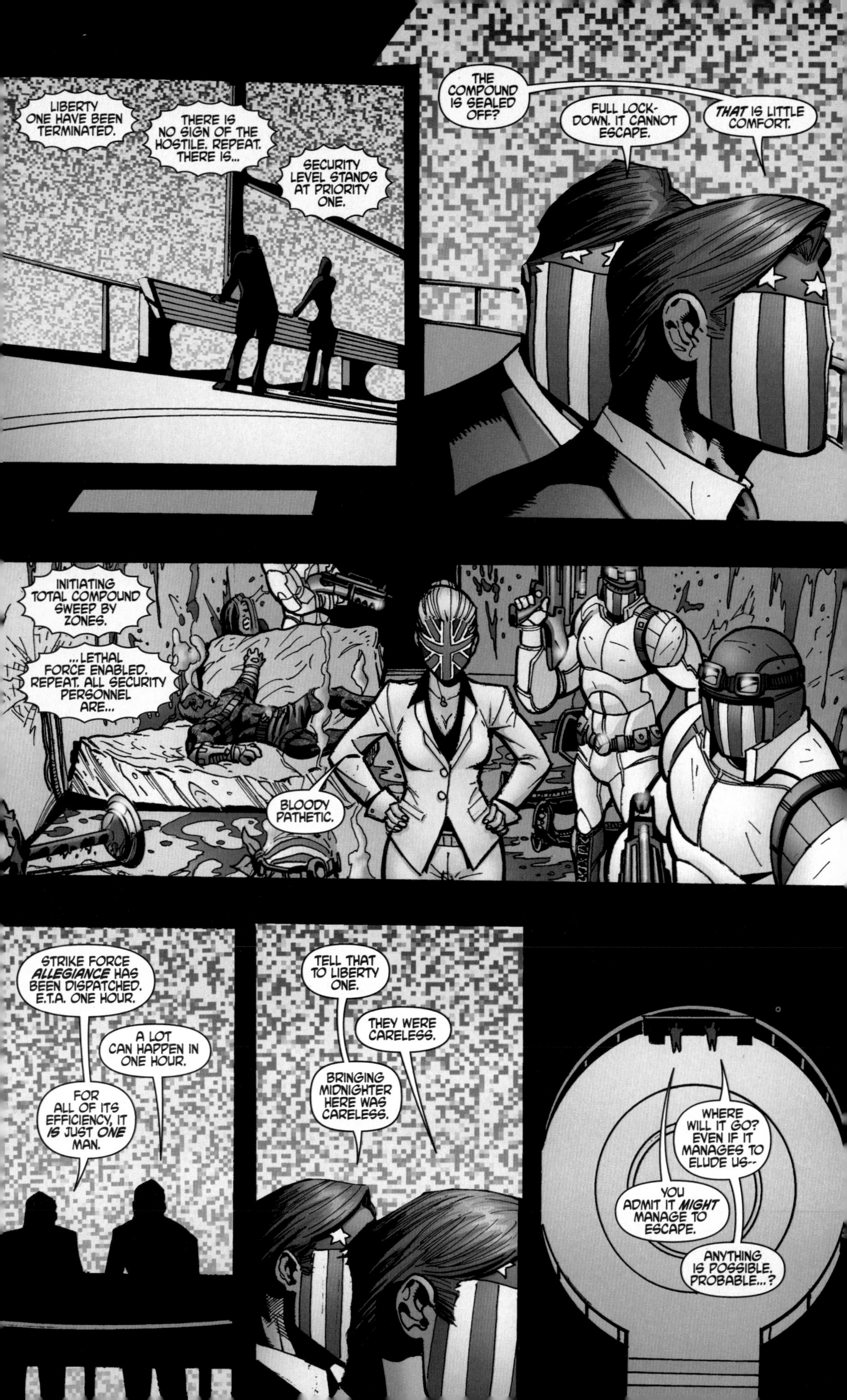
LIBERTY ONE HAVE BEEN TERMINATED.
THERE IS NO SIGN OF THE HOSTILE. REPEAT. THERE IS...
SECURITY LEVEL STANDS AT PRIORITY ONE.
THE COMPOUND IS SEALED OFF?
FULL LOCK-DOWN. IT CANNOT ESCAPE.
THAT IS LITTLE COMFORT.
INITIATING TOTAL COMPOUND SWEEP BY ZONES.
...LETHAL FORCE ENABLED. REPEAT. ALL SECURITY PERSONNEL ARE...
BLOODY PATHETIC.
STRIKE FORCE ALLEGIANCE HAS BEEN DISPATCHED. E.T.A. ONE HOUR.
A LOT CAN HAPPEN IN ONE HOUR.
FOR ALL OF ITS EFFICIENCY, IT IS JUST ONE MAN.
TELL THAT TO LIBERTY ONE.
THEY WERE CARELESS.
BRINGING MIDNIGHTER HERE WAS CARELESS.
WHERE WILL IT GO? EVEN IF IT MANAGES TO ELUDE US--
YOU ADMIT IT MIGHT MANAGE TO ESCAPE.
ANYTHING IS POSSIBLE. PROBABLE...?

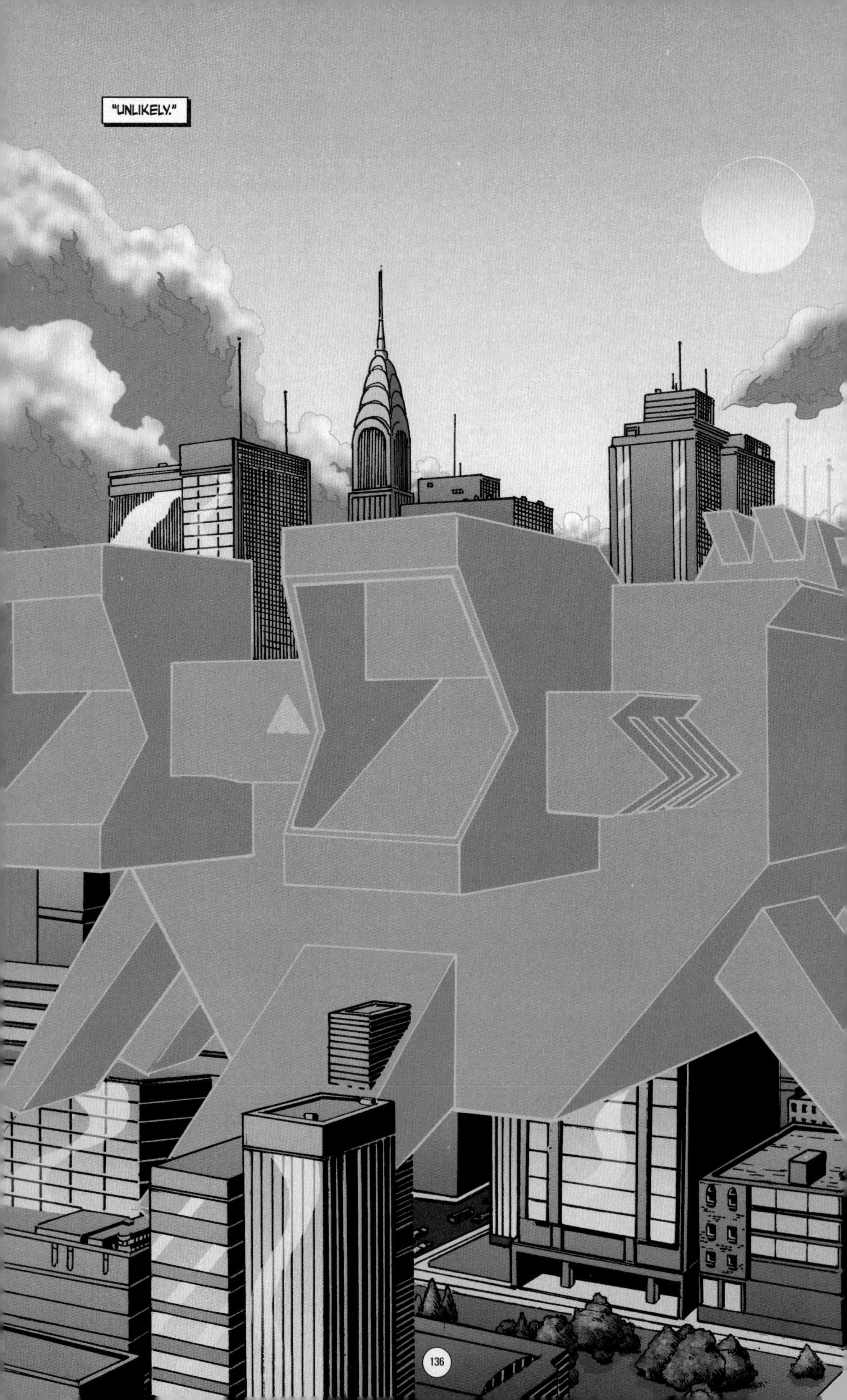
"UNLIKELY."

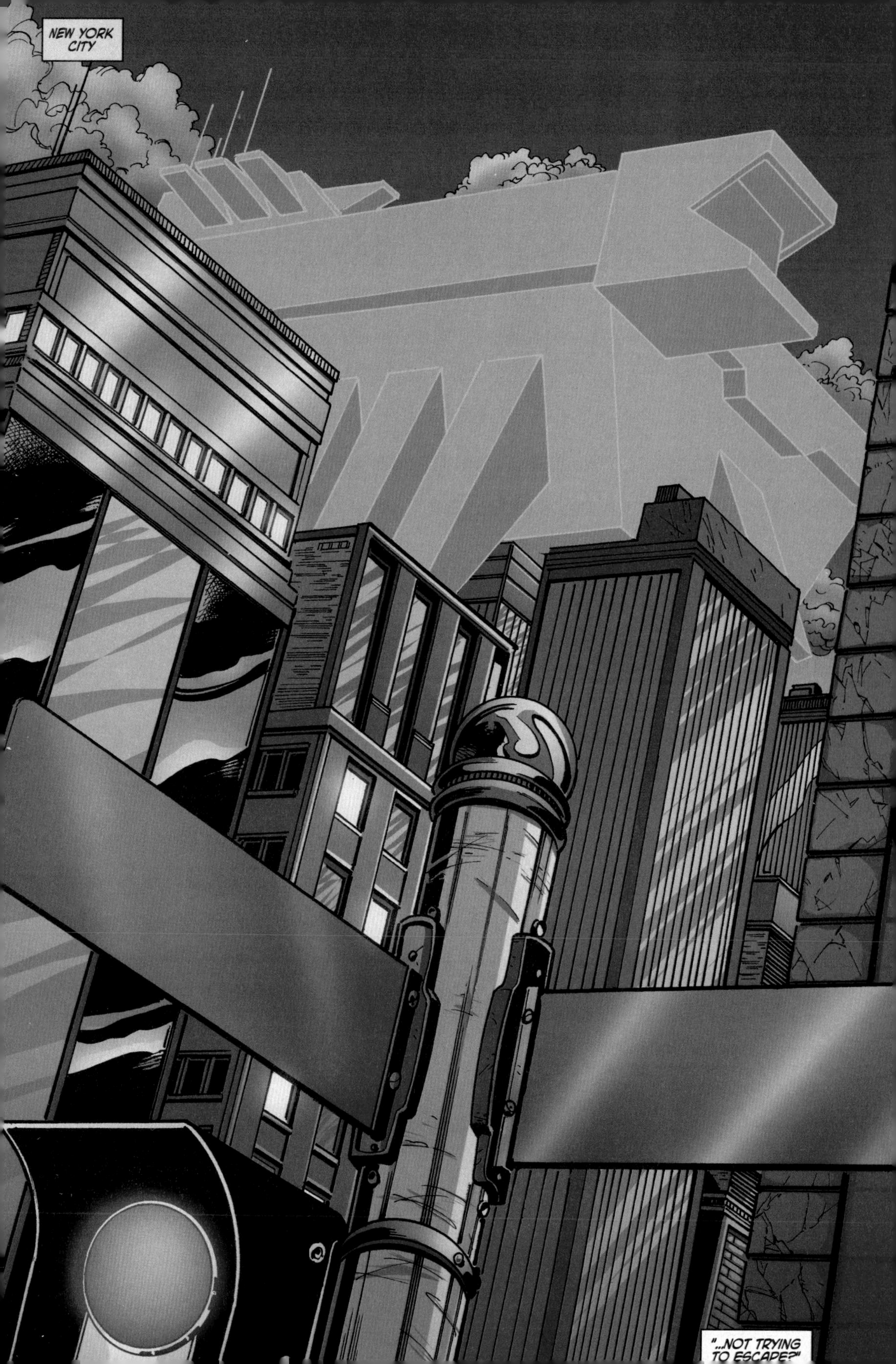
NEW YORK CITY
"...NOT TRYING TO ESCAPE?"

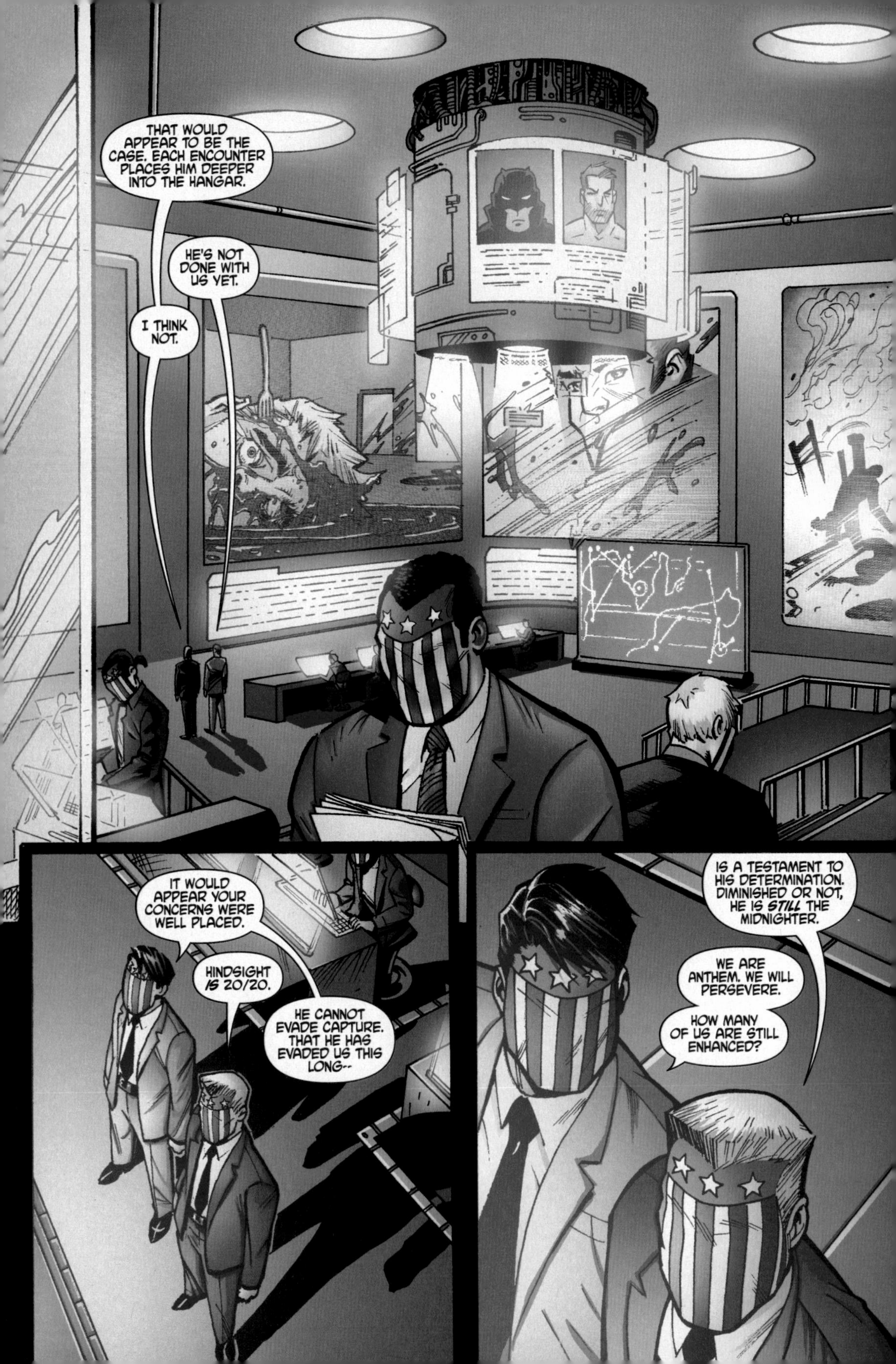
THAT WOULD APPEAR TO BE THE CASE. EACH ENCOUNTER PLACES HIM DEEPER INTO THE HANGAR.
HE'S NOT DONE WITH US YET.
I THINK NOT.
IT WOULD APPEAR YOUR CONCERNS WERE WELL PLACED.
HINDSIGHT *IS* 20/20.
HE CANNOT EVADE CAPTURE. THAT HE HAS EVADED US THIS LONG--
IS A TESTAMENT TO HIS DETERMINATION. DIMINISHED OR NOT, HE IS *STILL* THE MIDNIGHTER.
WE ARE ANTHEM. WE WILL PERSEVERE.
HOW MANY OF US ARE STILL ENHANCED?

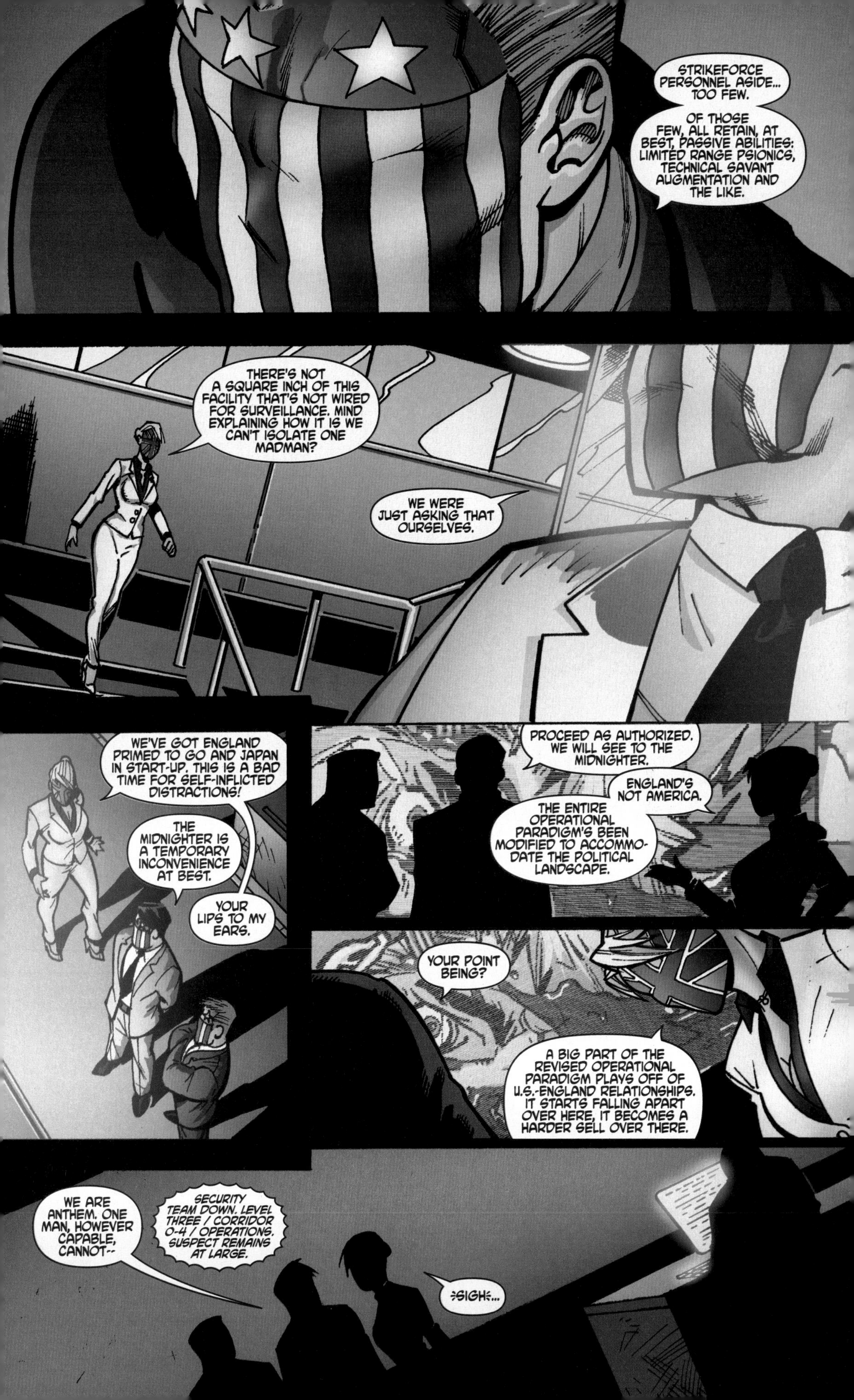
STRIKEFORCE PERSONNEL ASIDE... TOO FEW.
OF THOSE FEW, ALL RETAIN, AT BEST, PASSIVE ABILITIES: LIMITED RANGE PSIONICS, TECHNICAL SAVANT AUGMENTATION AND THE LIKE.
THERE'S NOT A SQUARE INCH OF THIS FACILITY THAT'S NOT WIRED FOR SURVEILLANCE. MIND EXPLAINING HOW IT IS WE CAN'T ISOLATE ONE MADMAN?
WE WERE JUST ASKING THAT OURSELVES.
WE'VE GOT ENGLAND PRIMED TO GO AND JAPAN IN START-UP. THIS IS A BAD TIME FOR SELF-INFLICTED DISTRACTIONS!
THE MIDNIGHTER IS A TEMPORARY INCONVENIENCE AT BEST.
YOUR LIPS TO MY EARS.
PROCEED AS AUTHORIZED. WE WILL SEE TO THE MIDNIGHTER.
ENGLAND'S NOT AMERICA.
THE ENTIRE OPERATIONAL PARADIGM'S BEEN MODIFIED TO ACCOMMODATE THE POLITICAL LANDSCAPE.
YOUR POINT BEING?
A BIG PART OF THE REVISED OPERATIONAL PARADIGM PLAYS OFF OF U.S.-ENGLAND RELATIONSHIPS. IT STARTS FALLING APART OVER HERE, IT BECOMES A HARDER SELL OVER THERE.
WE ARE ANTHEM. ONE MAN, HOWEVER CAPABLE, CANNOT--
SECURITY TEAM DOWN. LEVEL THREE / CORRIDOR 0-4 / OPERATIONS. SUSPECT REMAINS AT LARGE.
SIGH...

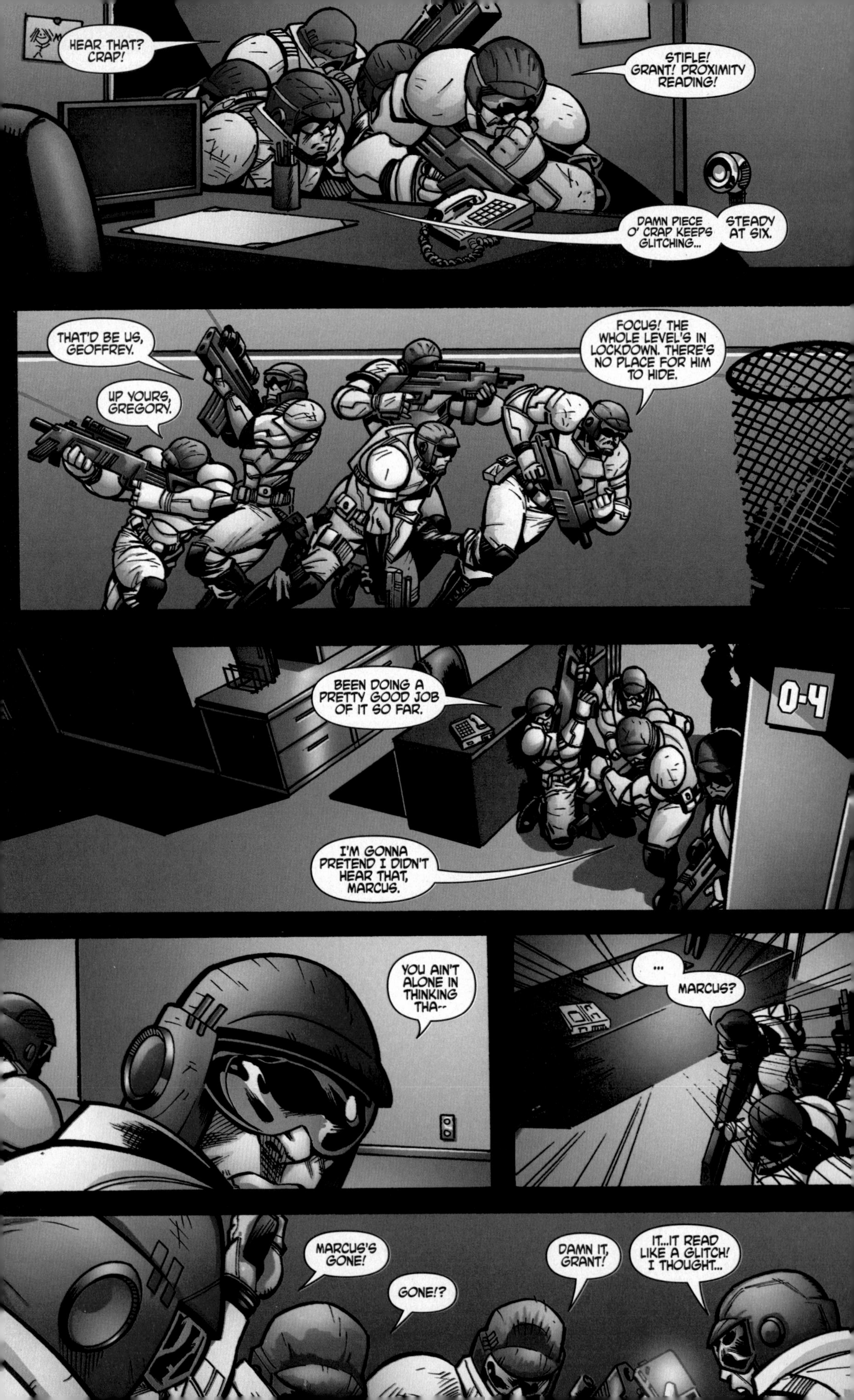
HEAR THAT? CRAP!
STIFLE! GRANT! PROXIMITY READING!
DAMN PIECE O' CRAP KEEPS GLITCHING...
STEADY AT SIX.
THAT'D BE US, GEOFFREY.
UP YOURS, GREGORY.
FOCUS! THE WHOLE LEVEL'S IN LOCKDOWN. THERE'S NO PLACE FOR HIM TO HIDE.
BEEN DOING A PRETTY GOOD JOB OF IT SO FAR.
0-4
I'M GONNA PRETEND I DIDN'T HEAR THAT, MARCUS.
YOU AIN'T ALONE IN THINKING THA--
...
MARCUS?
MARCUS'S GONE!
GONE!?
DAMN IT, GRANT!
IT...IT READ LIKE A GLITCH! I THOUGHT...

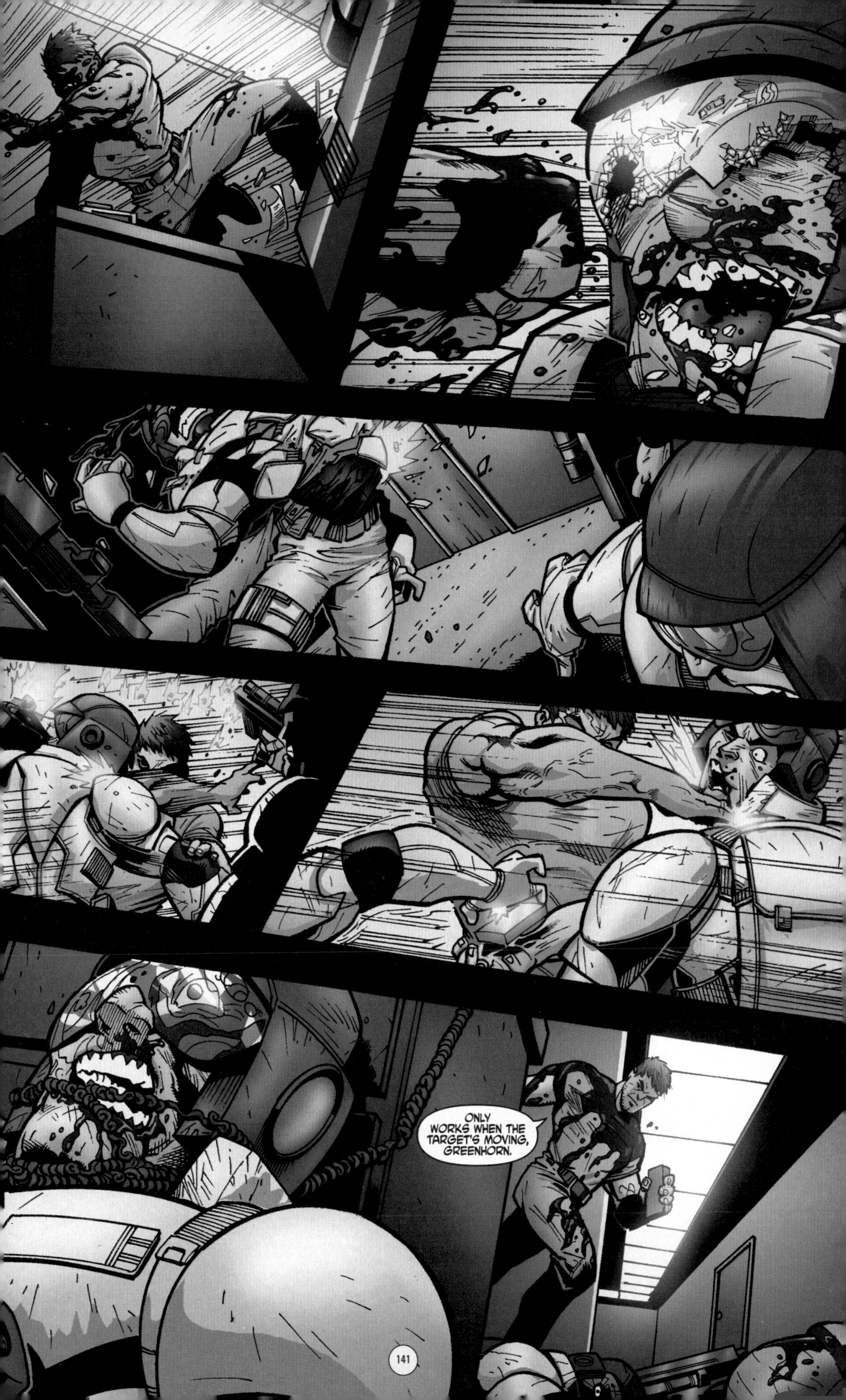
ONLY WORKS WHEN THE TARGET'S MOVING, GREENHORN.

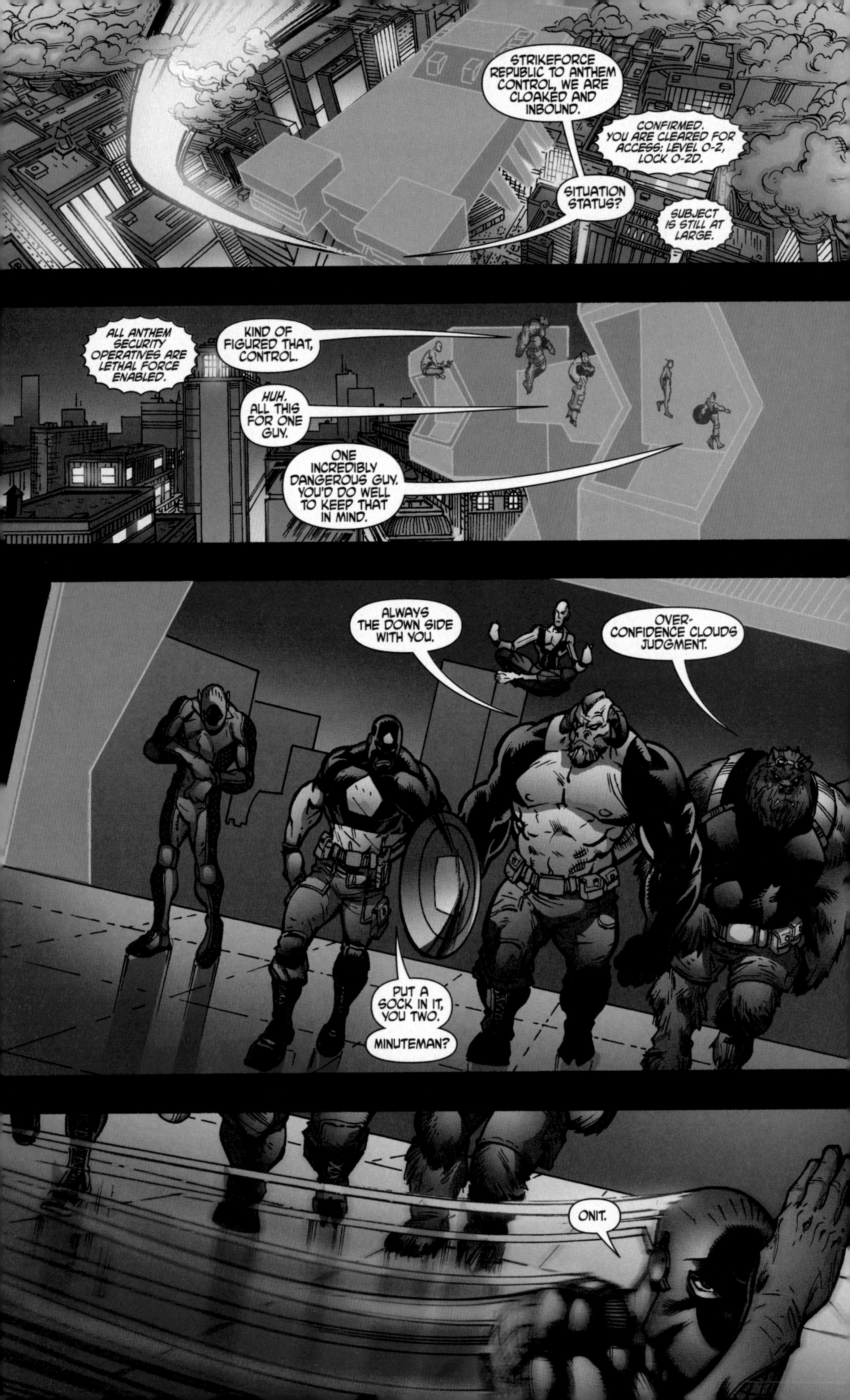
STRIKEFORCE REPUBLIC TO ANTHEM CONTROL, WE ARE CLOAKED AND INBOUND.
CONFIRMED. YOU ARE CLEARED FOR ACCESS: LEVEL O-2, LOCK O-2D.
SITUATION STATUS?
SUBJECT IS STILL AT LARGE.
ALL ANTHEM SECURITY OPERATIVES ARE LETHAL FORCE ENABLED.
KIND OF FIGURED THAT, CONTROL.
HUH. ALL THIS FOR ONE GUY.
ONE INCREDIBLY DANGEROUS GUY. YOU'D DO WELL TO KEEP THAT IN MIND.
ALWAYS THE DOWN SIDE WITH YOU.
OVER-CONFIDENCE CLOUDS JUDGMENT.
PUT A SOCK IN IT, YOU TWO.
MINUTEMAN?
ONIT.

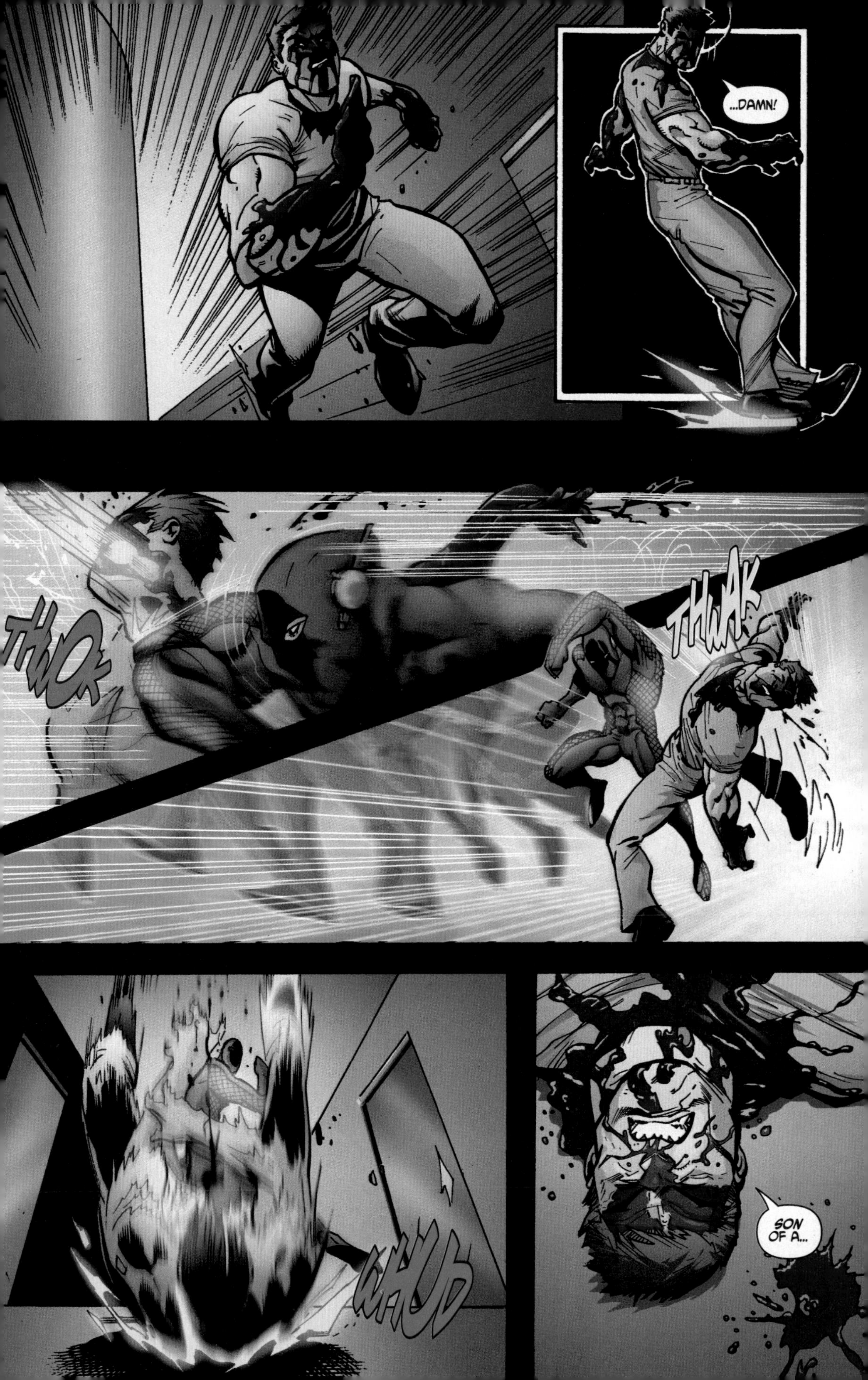
...DAMN!
THWOK
THWAK
WHUD
SON OF A...

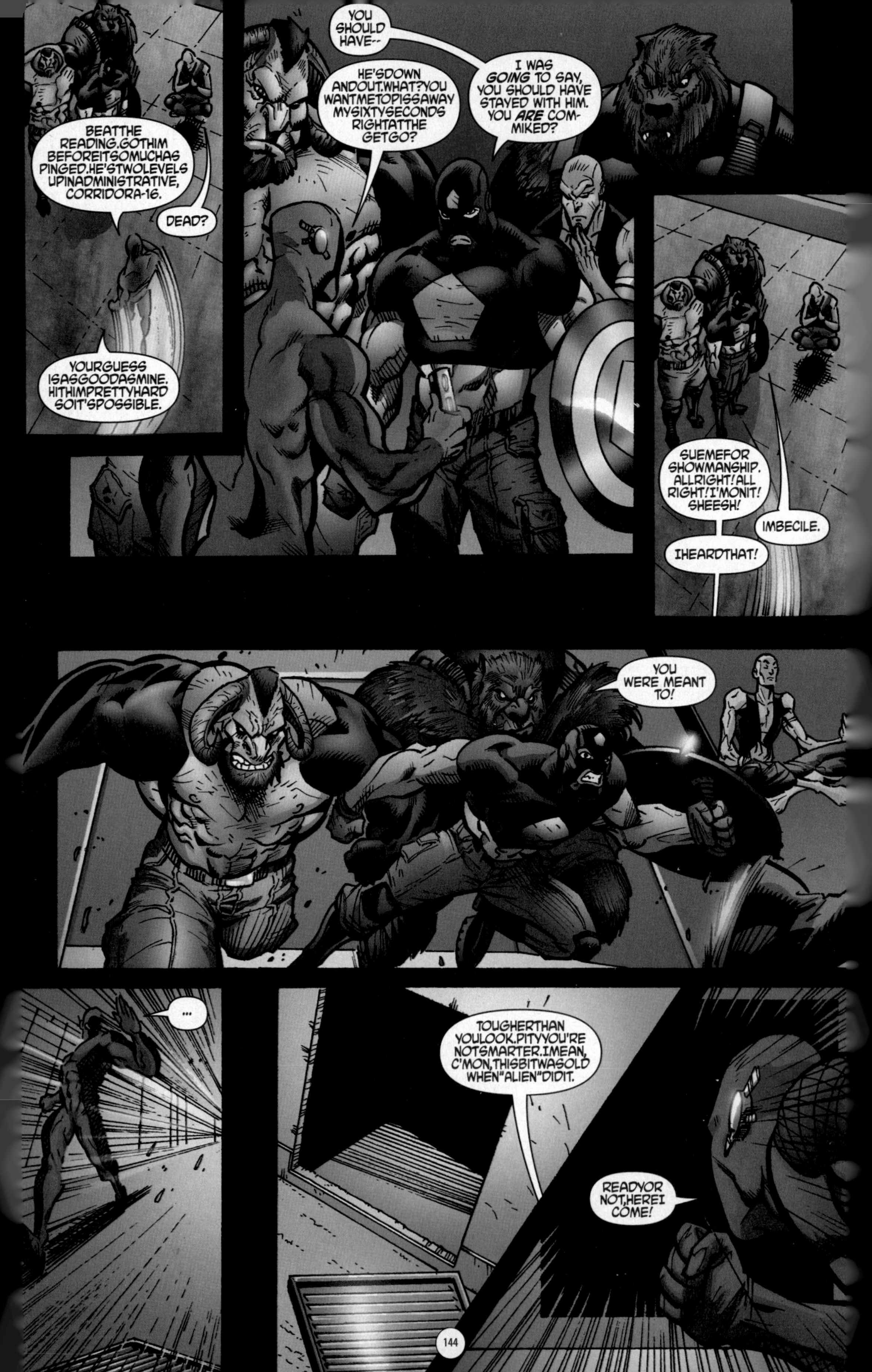
BEATTHE READING.GOTHIM BEFOREITSOMUCHAS PINGED.HE'STWOLEVELS UPINADMINISTRATIVE, CORRIDORA-16.
DEAD?
YOURGUESS ISASGOODASMINE. HITHIMPRETTYHARD SOIT'SPOSSIBLE.
YOU SHOULD HAVE--
HE'SDOWN ANDOUT.WHAT?YOU WANTMETOPISSAWAY MYSIXTYSECONDS RIGHTATTHE GETGO?
I WAS *GOING* TO SAY, YOU SHOULD HAVE STAYED WITH HIM. YOU ***ARE*** COM-MIKED?
SUEMEFOR SHOWMANSHIP. ALLRIGHT! ALL RIGHT! I'MONIT! SHEESH!
IMBECILE.
IHEARDTHAT!
YOU WERE MEANT TO!
...
TOUGHERTHAN YOULOOK.PITYYOU'RE NOTSMARTER.IMEAN, C'MON,THISBITWASOLD WHEN"ALIEN"DIDIT.
READYOR NOT,HEREI COME!

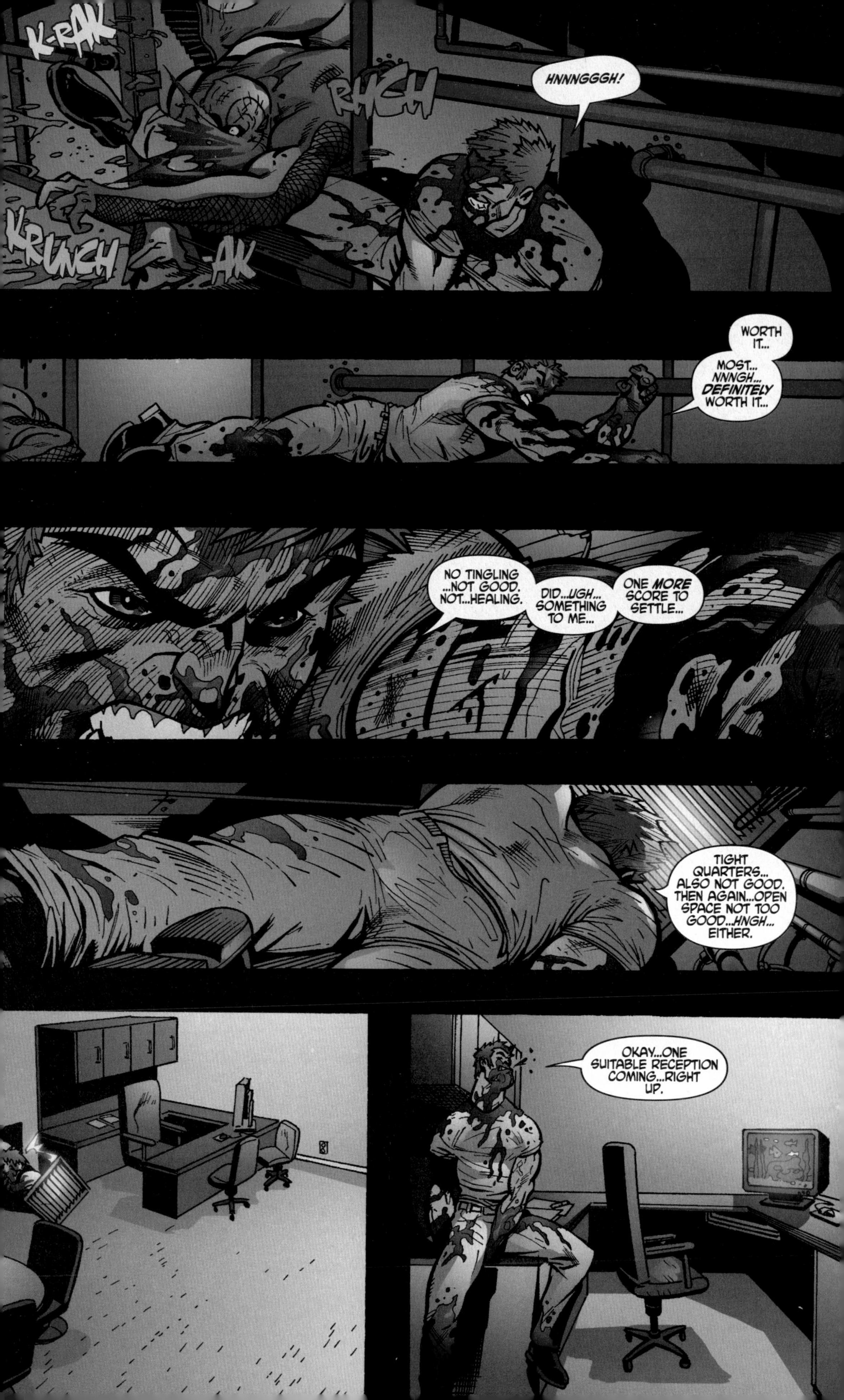
K-RAK
RHCH
KRUNCH
-AK
HNNNGGGH!
WORTH IT...
MOST... NNNGH... DEFINITELY WORTH IT...
NO TINGLING ...NOT GOOD. NOT...HEALING.
DID...UGH... SOMETHING TO ME...
ONE MORE SCORE TO SETTLE...
TIGHT QUARTERS... ALSO NOT GOOD. THEN AGAIN...OPEN SPACE NOT TOO GOOD...HNGH... EITHER.
OKAY...ONE SUITABLE RECEPTION COMING...RIGHT UP.

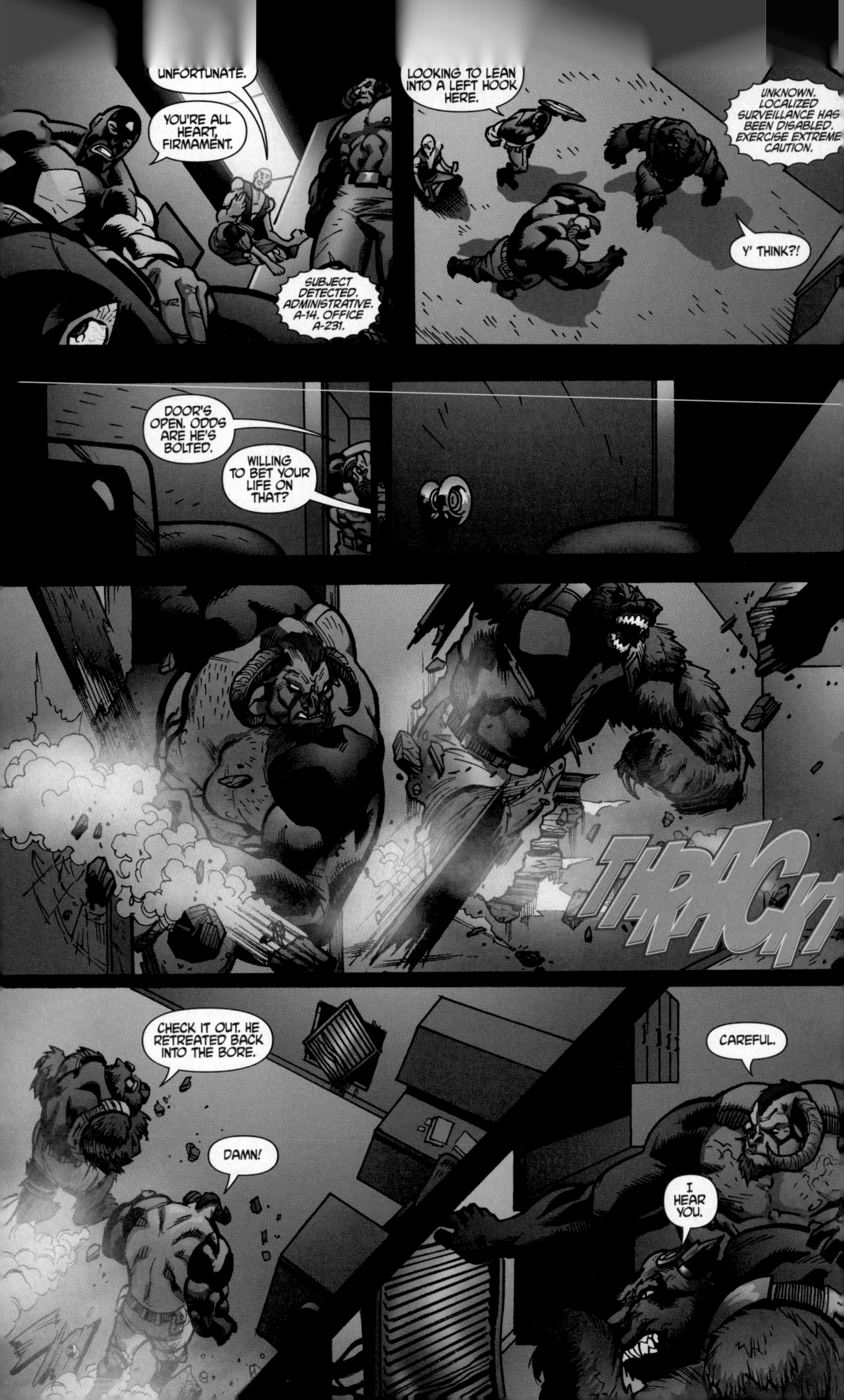
UNFORTUNATE.
YOU'RE ALL HEART, FIRMAMENT.
SUBJECT DETECTED. ADMINISTRATIVE. A-14. OFFICE A-231.
LOOKING TO LEAN INTO A LEFT HOOK HERE.
UNKNOWN. LOCALIZED SURVEILLANCE HAS BEEN DISABLED. EXERCISE EXTREME CAUTION.
Y' THINK?!
DOOR'S OPEN. ODDS ARE HE'S BOLTED.
WILLING TO BET YOUR LIFE ON THAT?
CHECK IT OUT. HE RETREATED BACK INTO THE BORE.
DAMN!
CAREFUL.
I HEAR YOU.

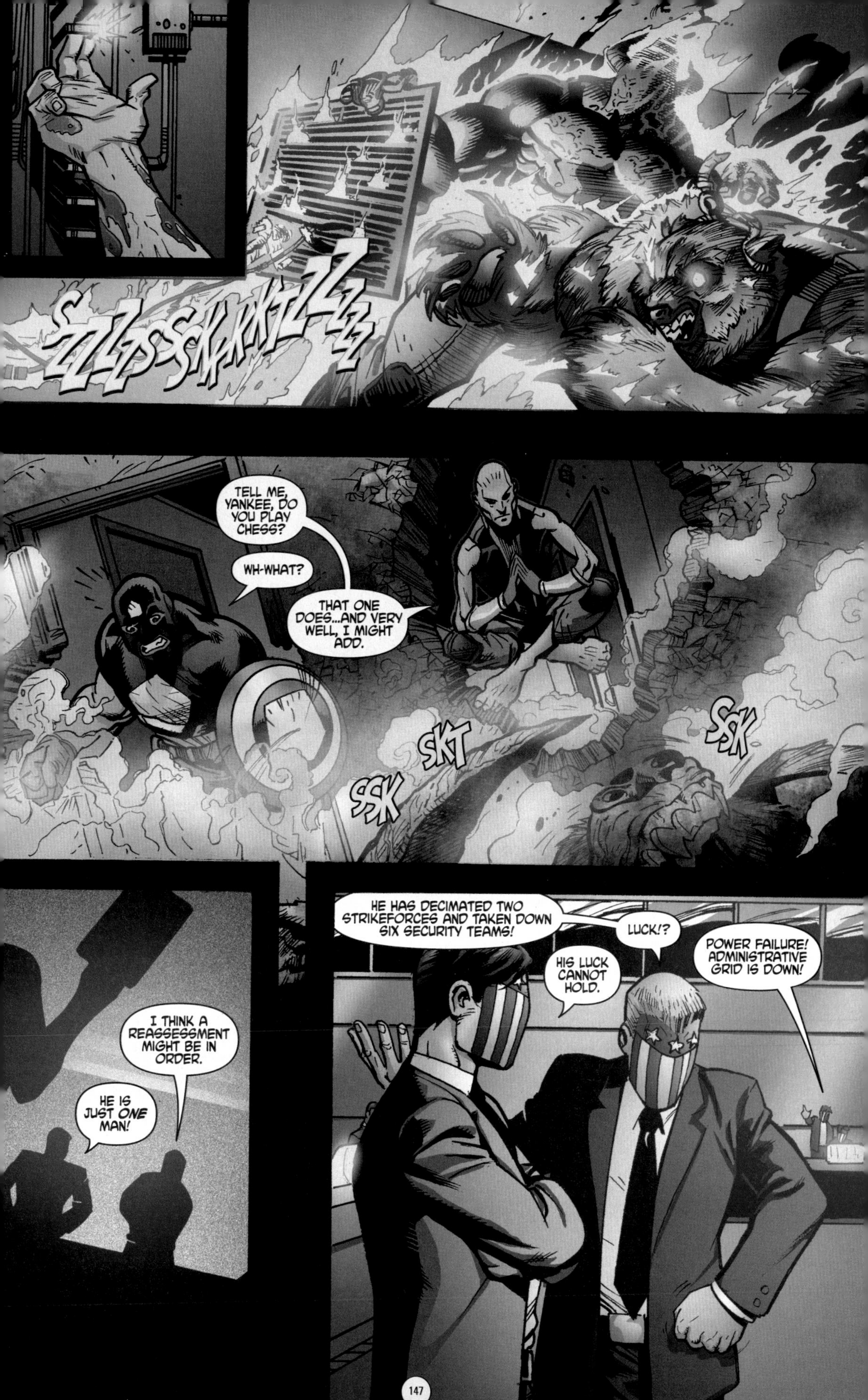
SZZZZSSSKKKKTZZZZZ
TELL ME, YANKEE, DO YOU PLAY CHESS?
WH-WHAT?
THAT ONE DOES...AND VERY WELL, I MIGHT ADD.
SSK
SKT
SSK
I THINK A REASSESSMENT MIGHT BE IN ORDER.
HE IS JUST *ONE* MAN!
HE HAS DECIMATED TWO STRIKEFORCES AND TAKEN DOWN SIX SECURITY TEAMS!
LUCK!?
HIS LUCK CANNOT HOLD.
POWER FAILURE! ADMINISTRATIVE GRID IS DOWN!

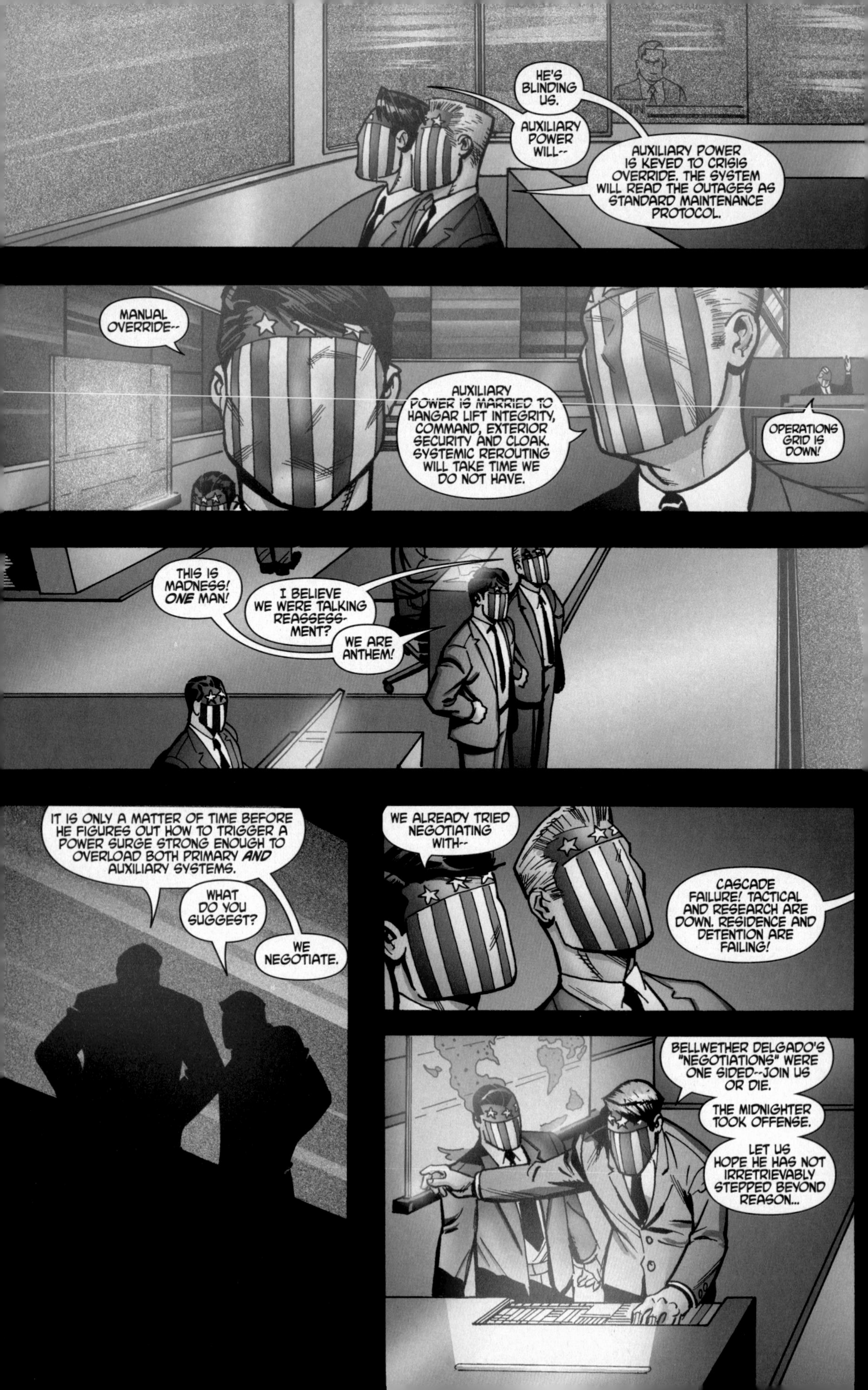

HE'S BLINDING US.
AUXILIARY POWER WILL--
AUXILIARY POWER IS KEYED TO CRISIS OVERRIDE. THE SYSTEM WILL READ THE OUTAGES AS STANDARD MAINTENANCE PROTOCOL.
MANUAL OVERRIDE--
AUXILIARY POWER IS MARRIED TO HANGAR LIFT INTEGRITY, COMMAND, EXTERIOR SECURITY AND CLOAK. SYSTEMIC REROUTING WILL TAKE TIME WE DO NOT HAVE.
OPERATIONS GRID IS DOWN!
THIS IS MADNESS! ONE MAN!
I BELIEVE WE WERE TALKING REASSESS-MENT?
WE ARE ANTHEM!
IT IS ONLY A MATTER OF TIME BEFORE HE FIGURES OUT HOW TO TRIGGER A POWER SURGE STRONG ENOUGH TO OVERLOAD BOTH PRIMARY AND AUXILIARY SYSTEMS.
WHAT DO YOU SUGGEST?
WE NEGOTIATE.
WE ALREADY TRIED NEGOTIATING WITH--
CASCADE FAILURE! TACTICAL AND RESEARCH ARE DOWN. RESIDENCE AND DETENTION ARE FAILING!
BELLWETHER DELGADO'S "NEGOTIATIONS" WERE ONE SIDED--JOIN US OR DIE.
THE MIDNIGHTER TOOK OFFENSE.
LET US HOPE HE HAS NOT IRRETRIEVABLY STEPPED BEYOND REASON...

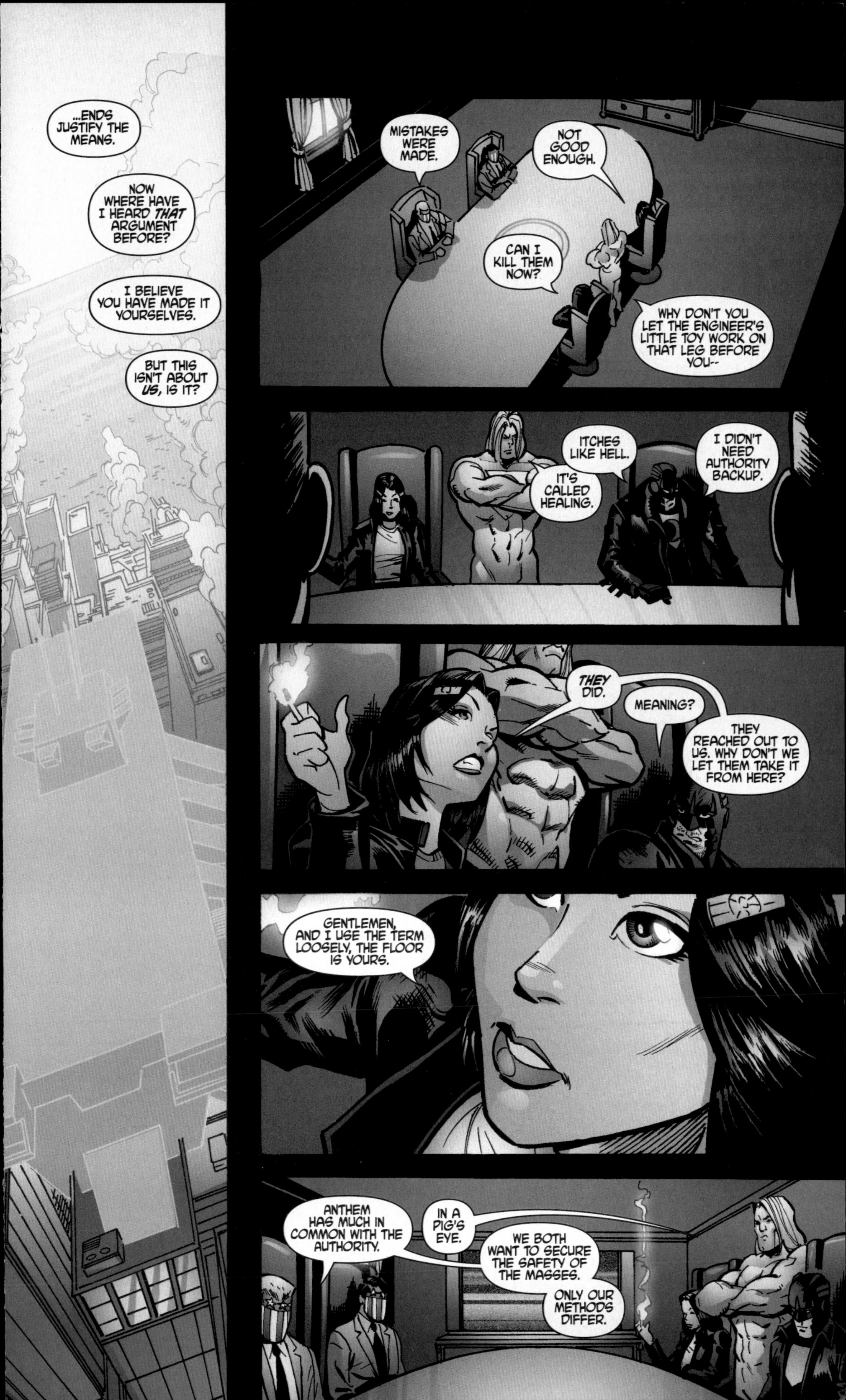
...ENDS JUSTIFY THE MEANS.
NOW WHERE HAVE I HEARD *THAT* ARGUMENT BEFORE?
I BELIEVE YOU HAVE MADE IT YOURSELVES.
BUT THIS ISN'T ABOUT *US*, IS IT?
MISTAKES WERE MADE.
NOT GOOD ENOUGH.
CAN I KILL THEM NOW?
WHY DON'T YOU LET THE ENGINEER'S LITTLE TOY WORK ON THAT LEG BEFORE YOU--
ITCHES LIKE HELL.
IT'S CALLED HEALING.
I DIDN'T NEED AUTHORITY BACKUP.
THEY DID.
MEANING?
THEY REACHED OUT TO US. WHY DON'T WE LET THEM TAKE IT FROM HERE?
GENTLEMEN, AND I USE THE TERM LOOSELY, THE FLOOR IS YOURS.
ANTHEM HAS MUCH IN COMMON WITH THE AUTHORITY.
IN A PIG'S EYE.
WE BOTH WANT TO SECURE THE SAFETY OF THE MASSES.
ONLY OUR METHODS DIFFER.

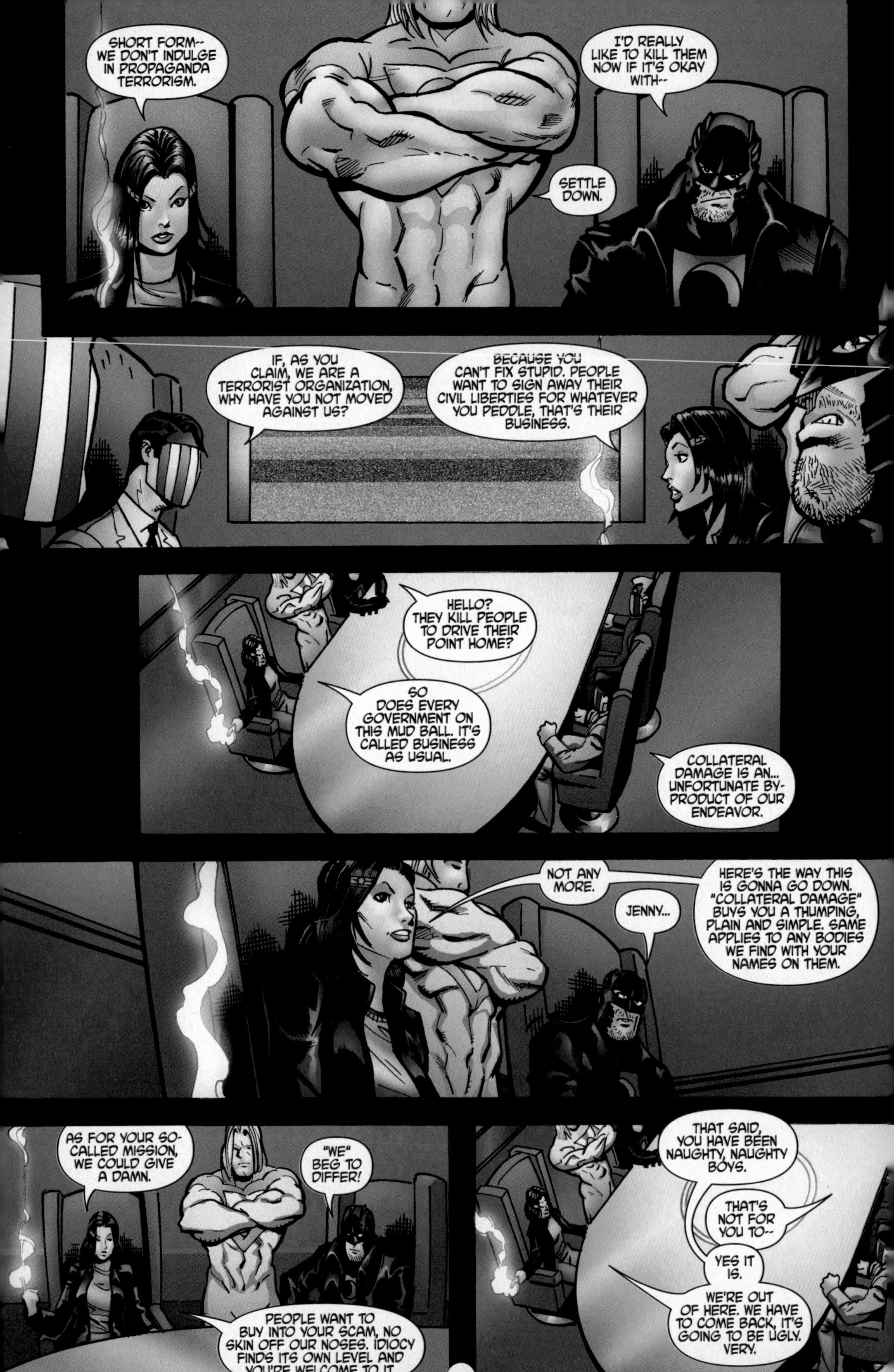
SHORT FORM-- WE DON'T INDULGE IN PROPAGANDA TERRORISM.
I'D REALLY LIKE TO KILL THEM NOW IF IT'S OKAY WITH--
SETTLE DOWN.
IF, AS YOU CLAIM, WE ARE A TERRORIST ORGANIZATION, WHY HAVE YOU NOT MOVED AGAINST US?
BECAUSE YOU CAN'T FIX STUPID. PEOPLE WANT TO SIGN AWAY THEIR CIVIL LIBERTIES FOR WHATEVER YOU PEDDLE, THAT'S THEIR BUSINESS.
HELLO? THEY KILL PEOPLE TO DRIVE THEIR POINT HOME?
SO DOES EVERY GOVERNMENT ON THIS MUD BALL. IT'S CALLED BUSINESS AS USUAL.
COLLATERAL DAMAGE IS AN... UNFORTUNATE BY-PRODUCT OF OUR ENDEAVOR.
NOT ANY MORE.
JENNY...
HERE'S THE WAY THIS IS GONNA GO DOWN. "COLLATERAL DAMAGE" BUYS YOU A THUMPING, PLAIN AND SIMPLE. SAME APPLIES TO ANY BODIES WE FIND WITH YOUR NAMES ON THEM.
AS FOR YOUR SO-CALLED MISSION, WE COULD GIVE A DAMN.
"WE" BEG TO DIFFER!
PEOPLE WANT TO BUY INTO YOUR SCAM, NO SKIN OFF OUR NOSES. IDIOCY FINDS ITS OWN LEVEL AND YOU'RE WELCOME TO IT.
THAT SAID, YOU HAVE BEEN NAUGHTY, NAUGHTY BOYS.
THAT'S NOT FOR YOU TO--
YES IT IS.
WE'RE OUT OF HERE. WE HAVE TO COME BACK, IT'S GOING TO BE UGLY. VERY.

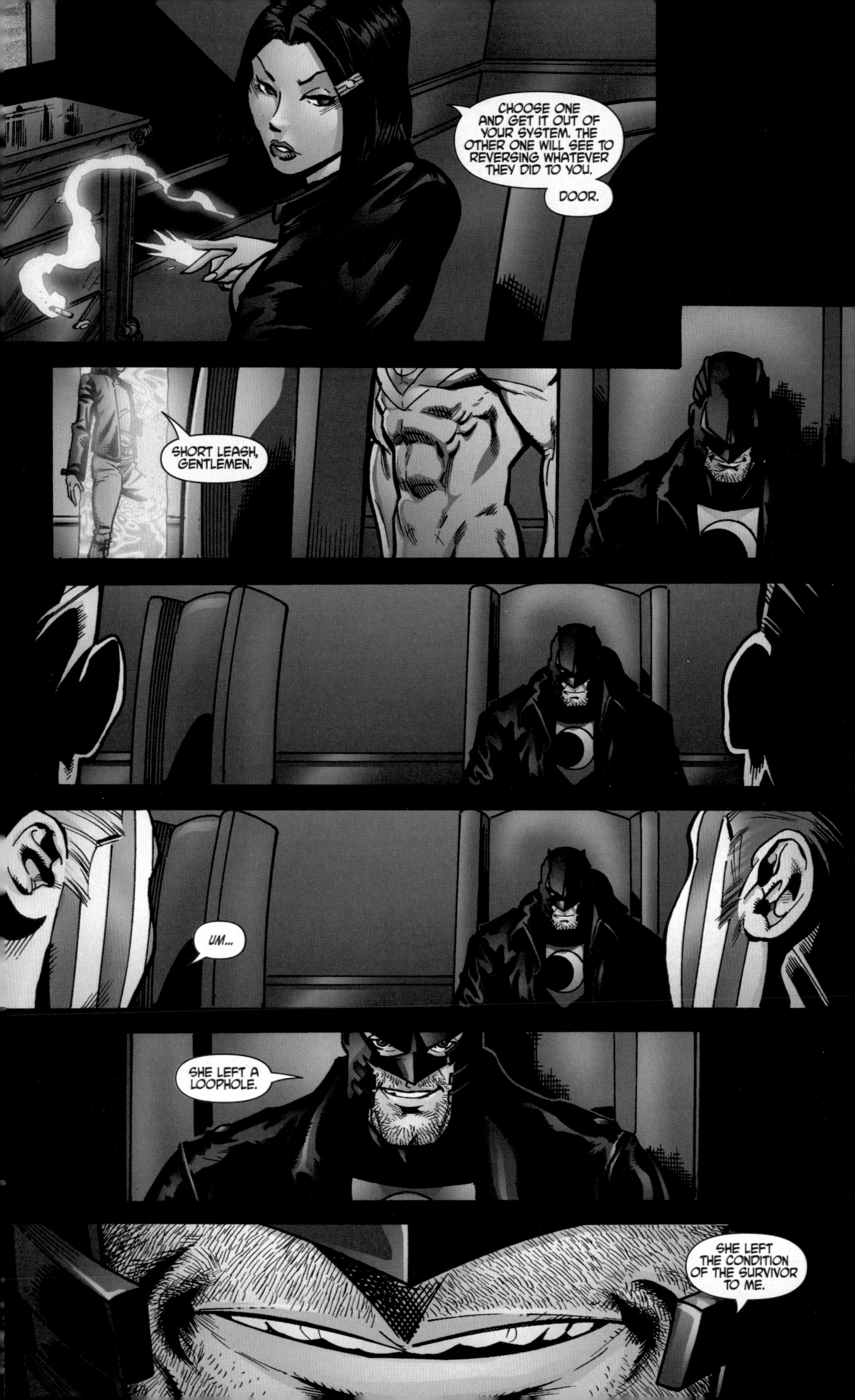
CHOOSE ONE AND GET IT OUT OF YOUR SYSTEM. THE OTHER ONE WILL SEE TO REVERSING WHATEVER THEY DID TO YOU.
DOOR.
SHORT LEASH, GENTLEMEN.
UM...
SHE LEFT A LOOPHOLE.
SHE LEFT THE CONDITION OF THE SURVIVOR TO ME.

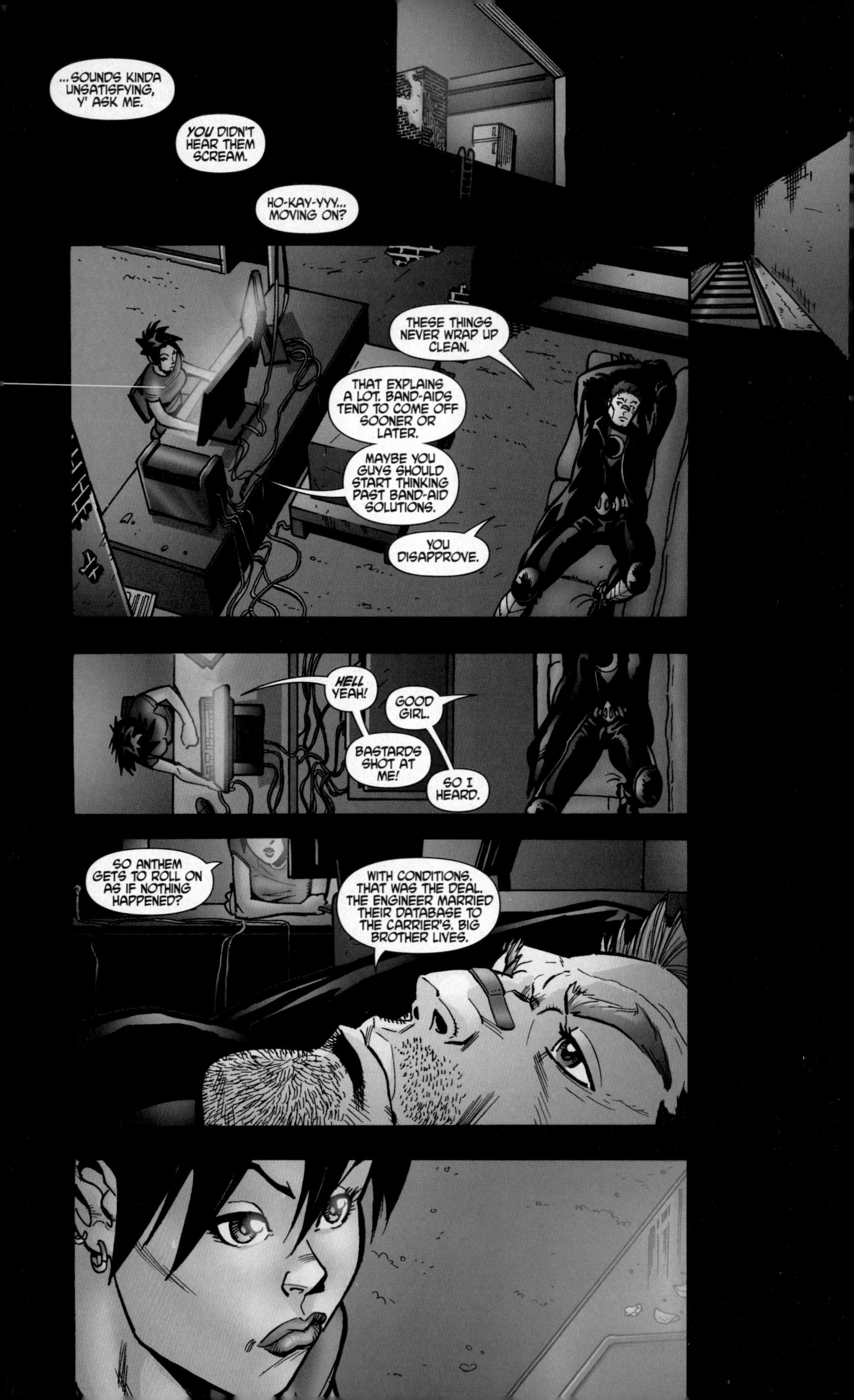
...SOUNDS KINDA UNSATISFYING, Y' ASK ME.
YOU DIDN'T HEAR THEM SCREAM.
HO-KAY-YYY... MOVING ON?
THESE THINGS NEVER WRAP UP CLEAN.
THAT EXPLAINS A LOT. BAND-AIDS TEND TO COME OFF SOONER OR LATER.
MAYBE YOU GUYS SHOULD START THINKING PAST BAND-AID SOLUTIONS.
YOU DISAPPROVE.
HELL YEAH!
BASTARDS SHOT AT ME!
GOOD GIRL.
SO I HEARD.
SO ANTHEM GETS TO ROLL ON AS IF NOTHING HAPPENED?
WITH CONDITIONS. THAT WAS THE DEAL. THE ENGINEER MARRIED THEIR DATABASE TO THE CARRIER'S. BIG BROTHER LIVES.

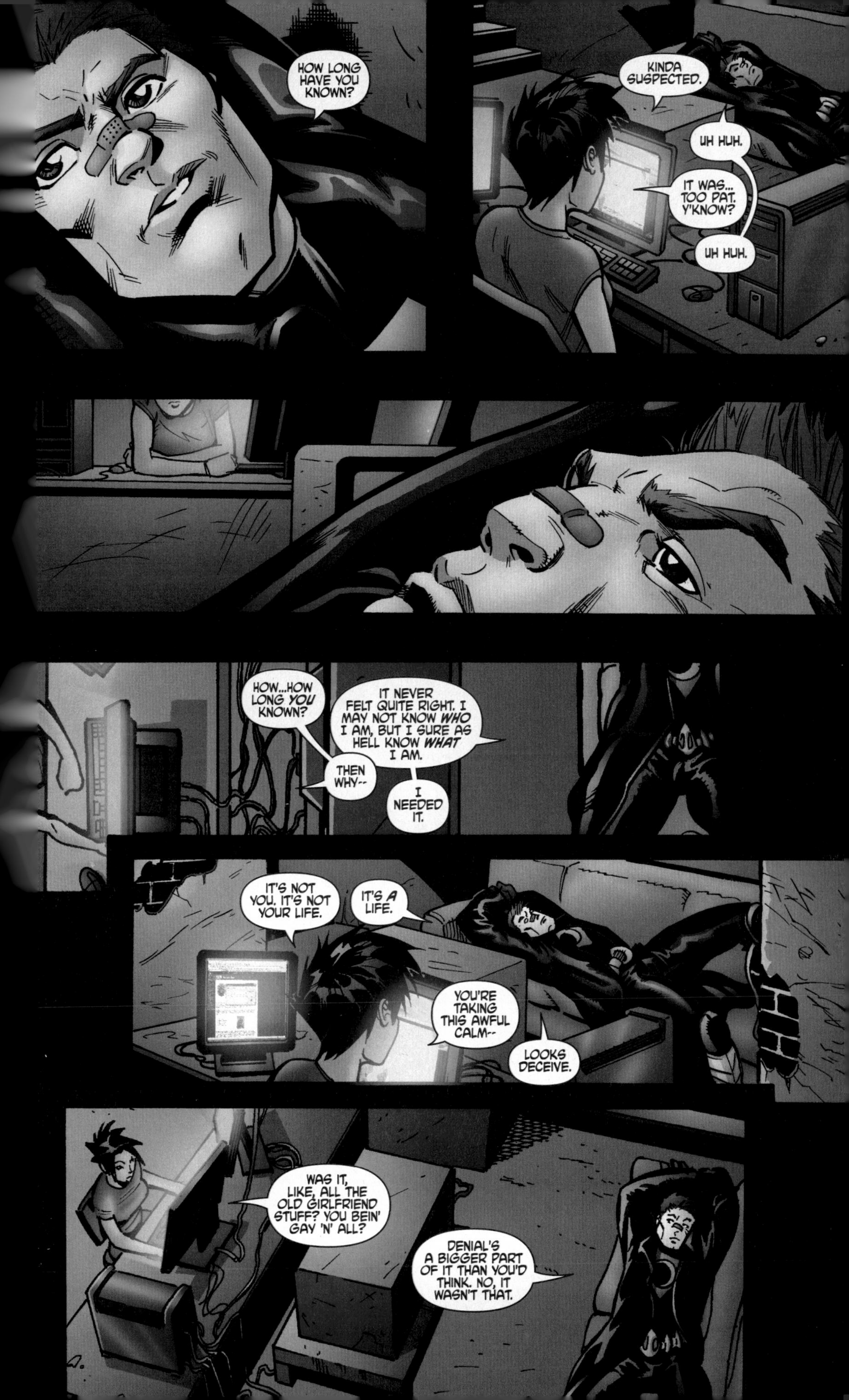
HOW LONG HAVE YOU KNOWN?
KINDA SUSPECTED.
UH HUH.
IT WAS... TOO PAT. Y'KNOW?
UH HUH.
HOW...HOW LONG YOU KNOWN?
IT NEVER FELT QUITE RIGHT. I MAY NOT KNOW WHO I AM, BUT I SURE AS HELL KNOW WHAT I AM.
THEN WHY--
I NEEDED IT.
IT'S NOT YOU. IT'S NOT YOUR LIFE.
IT'S A LIFE.
YOU'RE TAKING THIS AWFUL CALM--
LOOKS DECEIVE.
WAS IT, LIKE, ALL THE OLD GIRLFRIEND STUFF? YOU BEIN' GAY 'N' ALL?
DENIAL'S A BIGGER PART OF IT THAN YOU'D THINK. NO, IT WASN'T THAT.

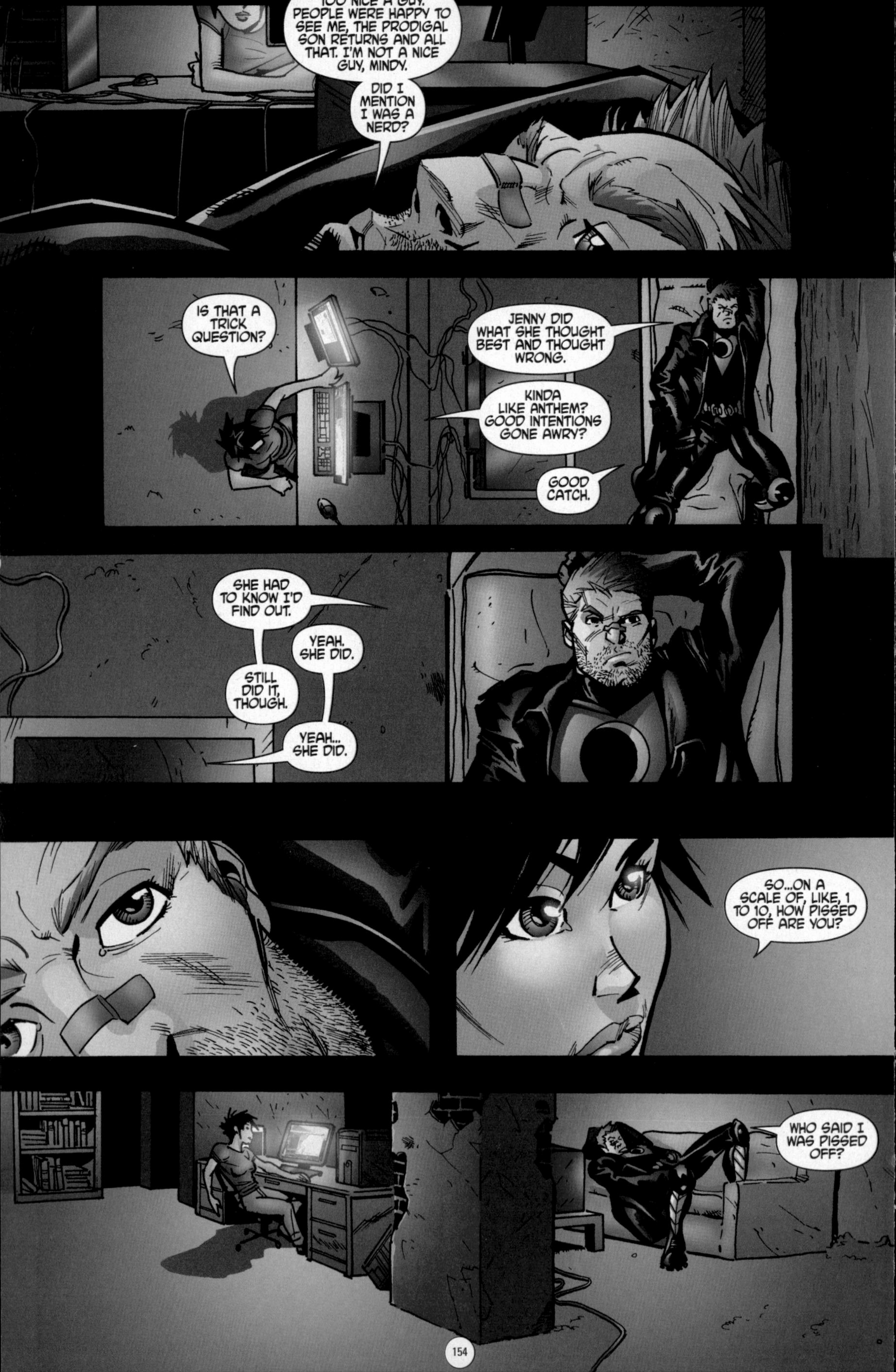
I WAS... TOO NICE A GUY. PEOPLE WERE HAPPY TO SEE ME, THE PRODIGAL SON RETURNS AND ALL THAT. I'M NOT A NICE GUY, MINDY.
DID I MENTION I WAS A NERD?
IS THAT A TRICK QUESTION?
JENNY DID WHAT SHE THOUGHT BEST AND THOUGHT WRONG.
KINDA LIKE ANTHEM? GOOD INTENTIONS GONE AWRY?
GOOD CATCH.
SHE HAD TO KNOW I'D FIND OUT.
YEAH. SHE DID.
STILL DID IT, THOUGH.
YEAH... SHE DID.
SO...ON A SCALE OF, LIKE, 1 TO 10, HOW PISSED OFF ARE YOU?
WHO SAID I WAS PISSED OFF?

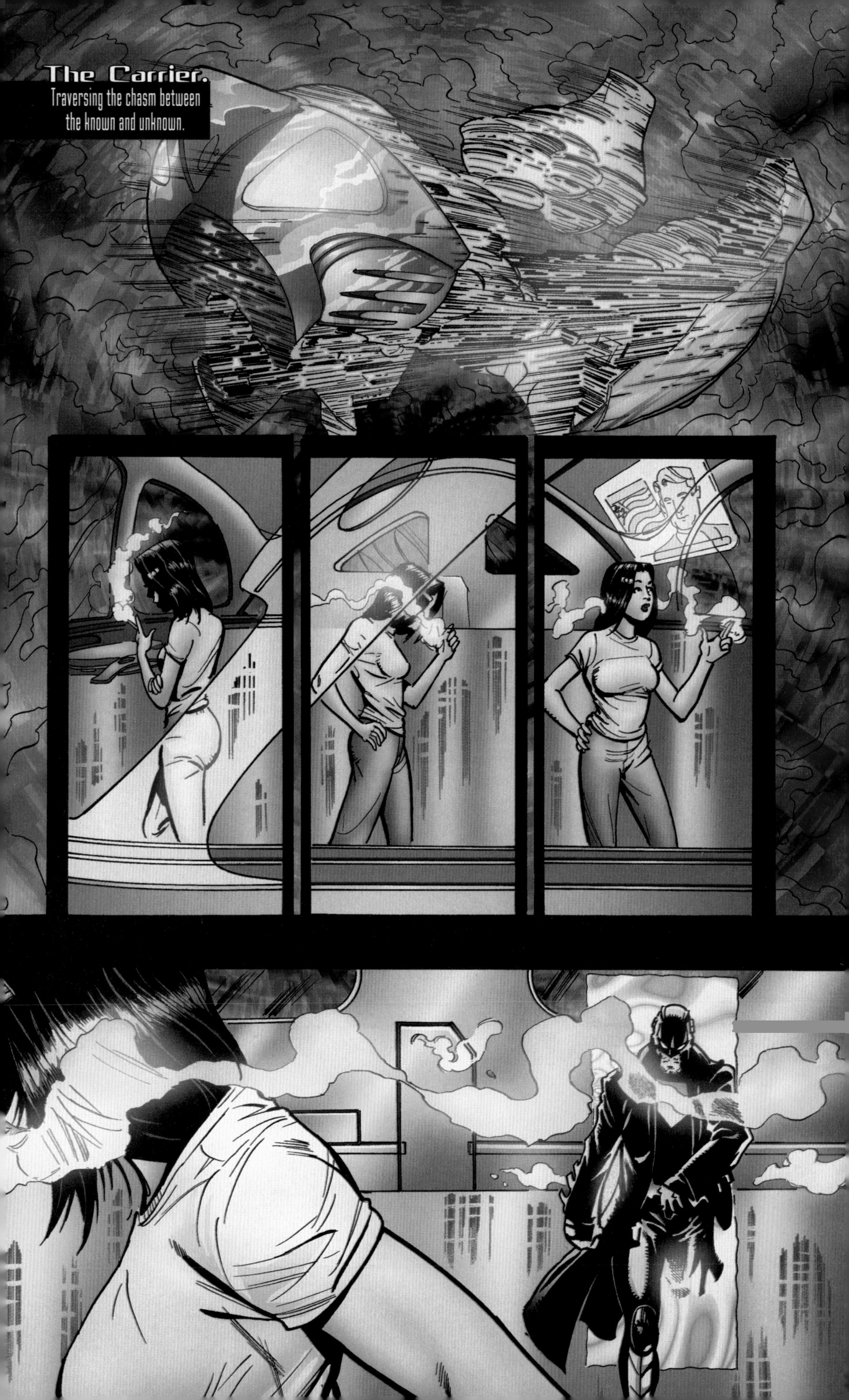
The Carrier.
Traversing the chasm between the known and unknown.

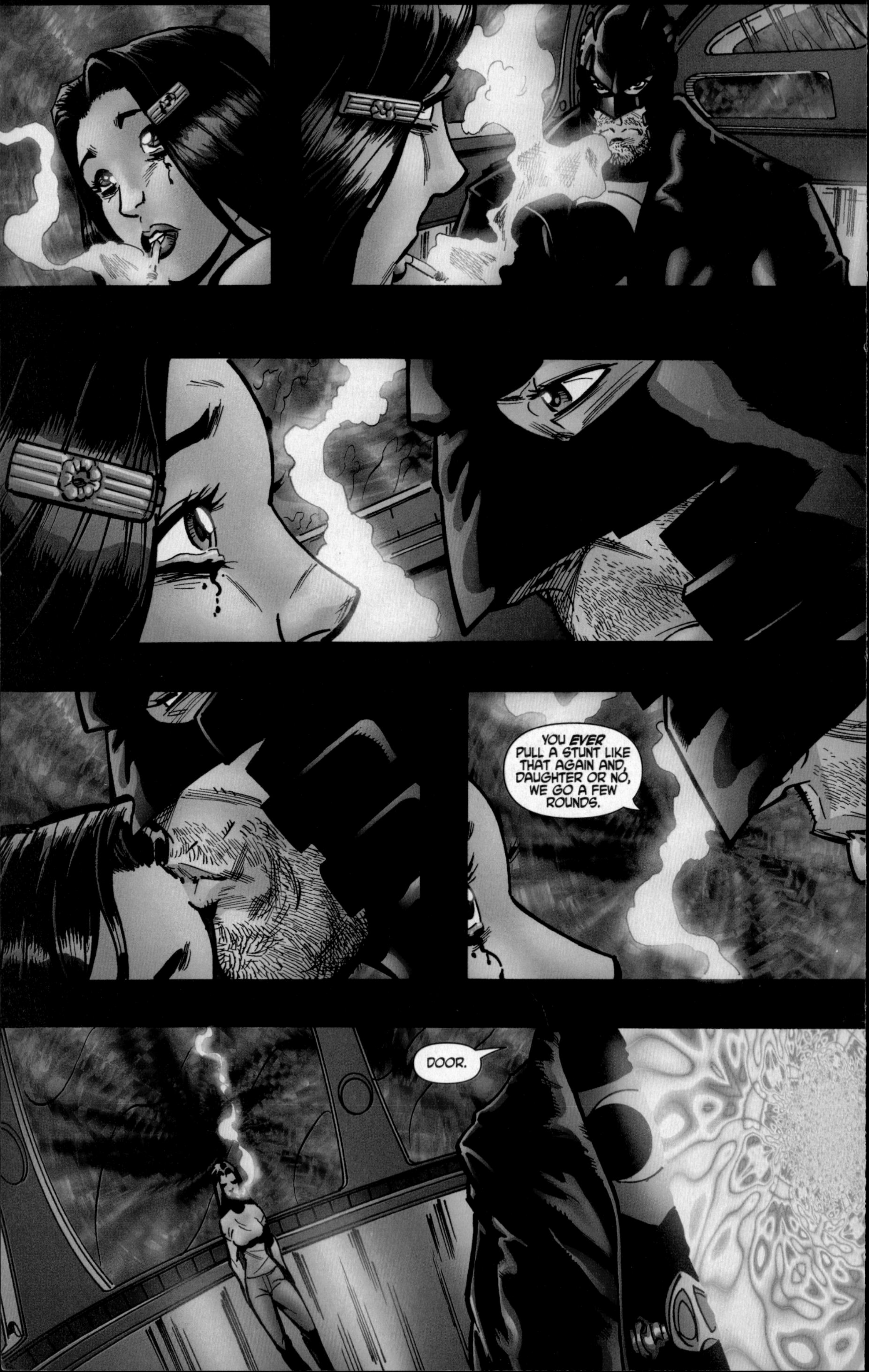
YOU EVER PULL A STUNT LIKE THAT AGAIN AND, DAUGHTER OR NO, WE GO A FEW ROUNDS.
DOOR.

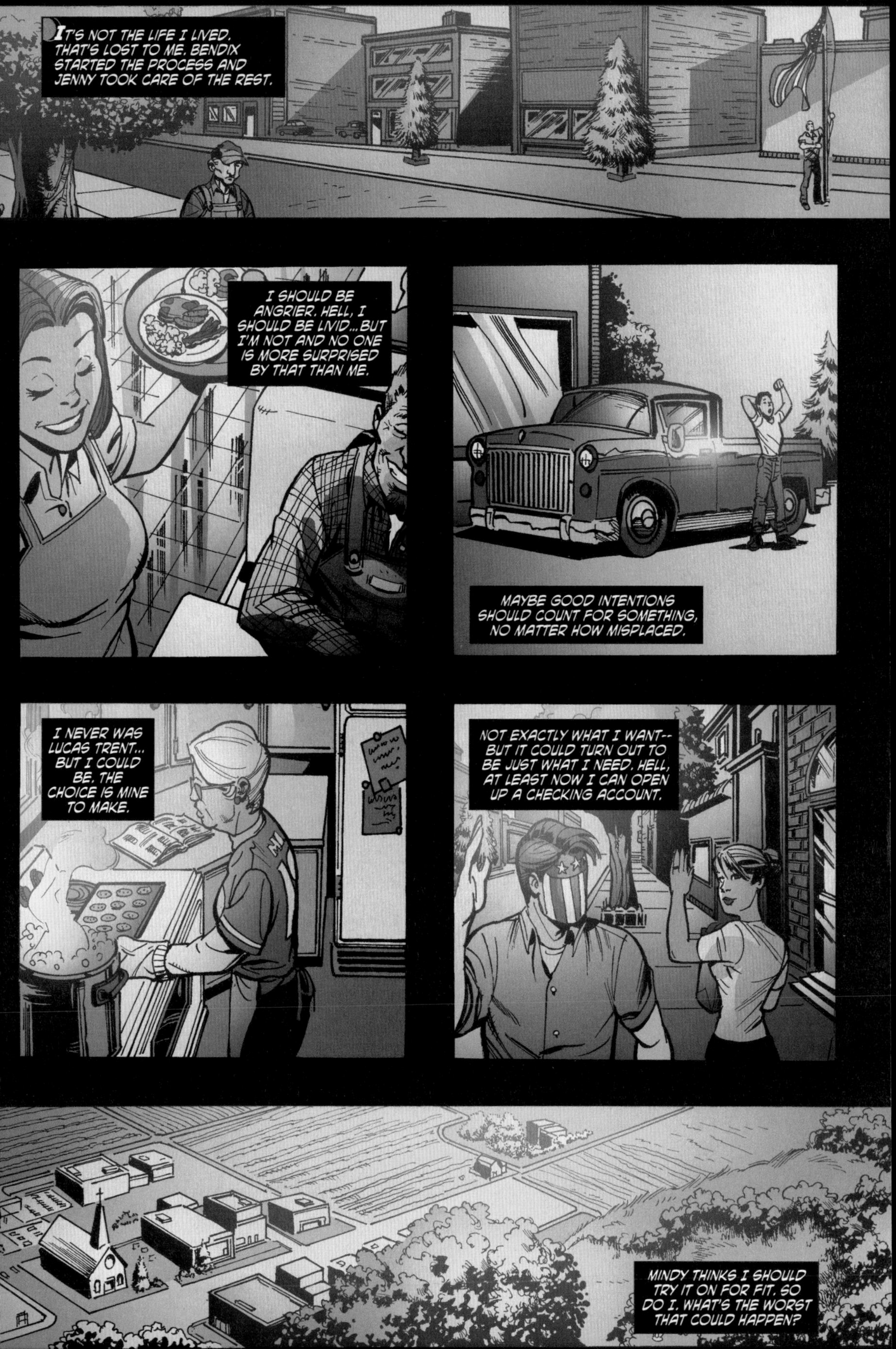
IT'S NOT THE LIFE I LIVED. THAT'S LOST TO ME. BENDIX STARTED THE PROCESS AND JENNY TOOK CARE OF THE REST.
I SHOULD BE ANGRIER. HELL, I SHOULD BE LIVID...BUT I'M NOT AND NO ONE IS MORE SURPRISED BY THAT THAN ME.
MAYBE GOOD INTENTIONS SHOULD COUNT FOR SOMETHING, NO MATTER HOW MISPLACED.
I NEVER WAS LUCAS TRENT... BUT I COULD BE. THE CHOICE IS MINE TO MAKE.
NOT EXACTLY WHAT I WANT-- BUT IT COULD TURN OUT TO BE JUST WHAT I NEED. HELL, AT LEAST NOW I CAN OPEN UP A CHECKING ACCOUNT.
MINDY THINKS I SHOULD TRY IT ON FOR FIT. SO DO I. WHAT'S THE WORST THAT COULD HAPPEN?

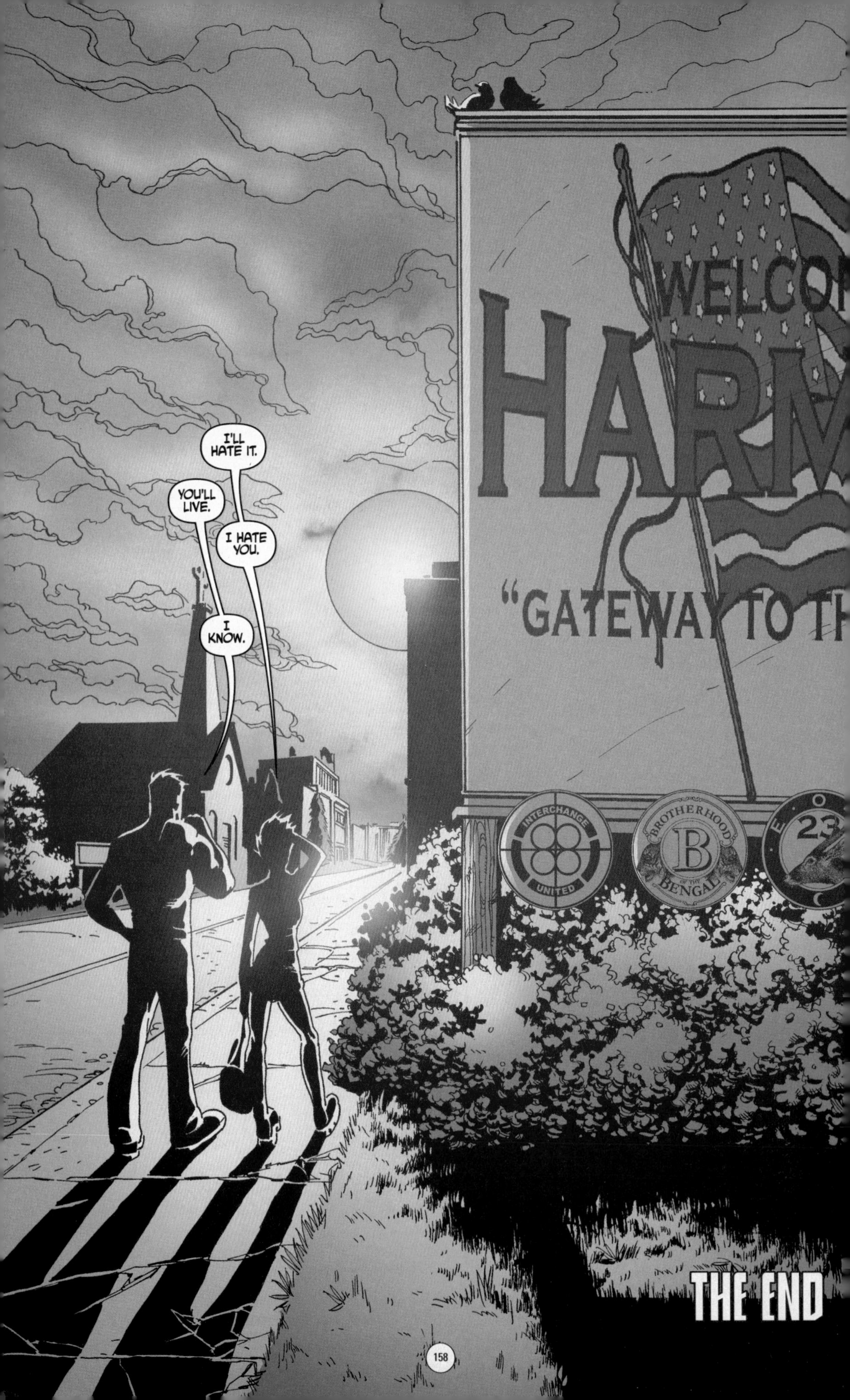
WELCO
HARM
"GATEWAY TO TH
I'LL HATE IT.
YOU'LL LIVE.
I HATE YOU.
I KNOW.
INTERCHANGE UNITED
BROTHERHOOD B OF THE BENGAL
23
THE END

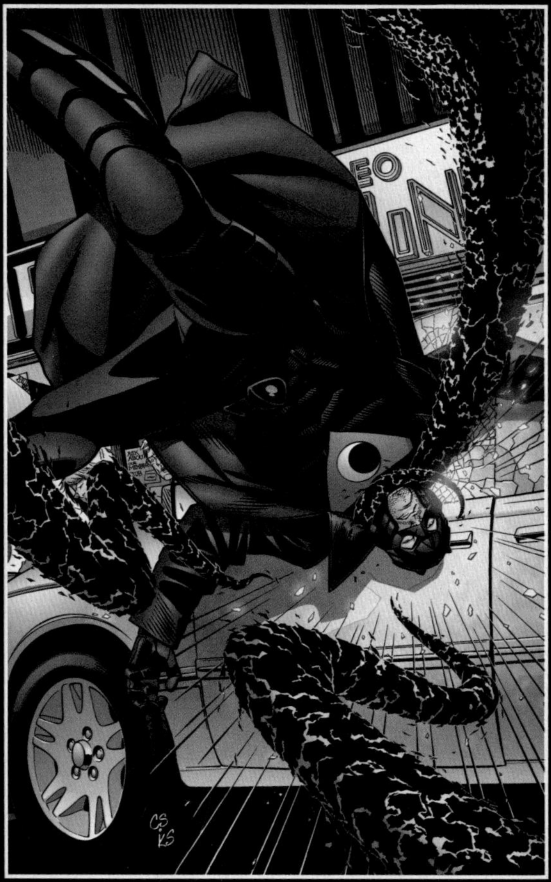

COVER 12

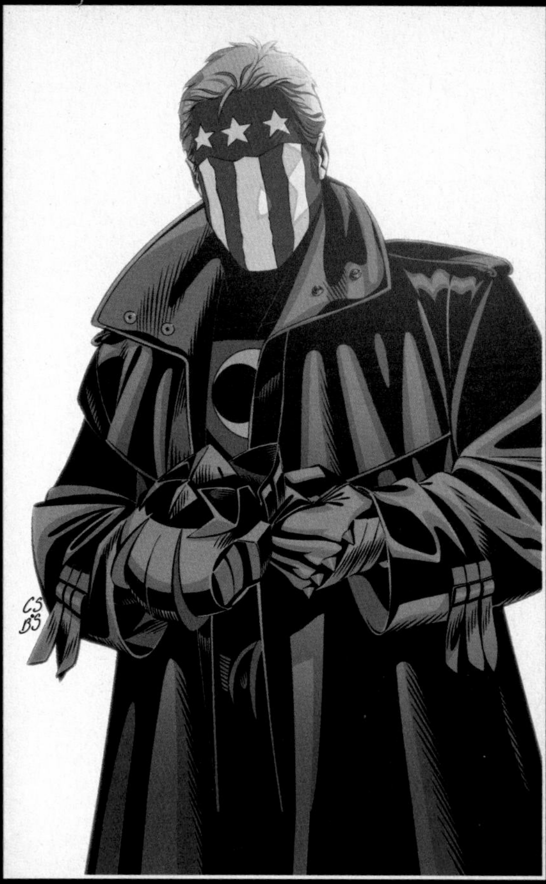

COVER 13

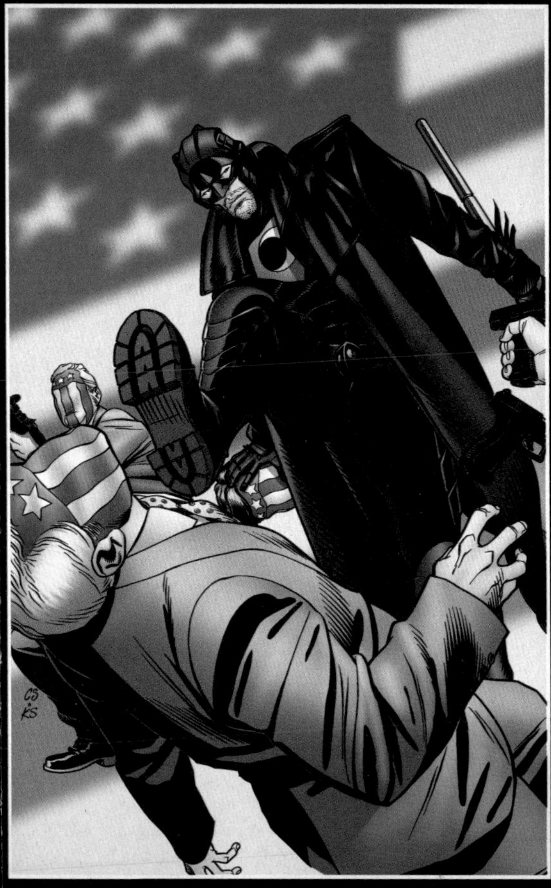

COVER 14

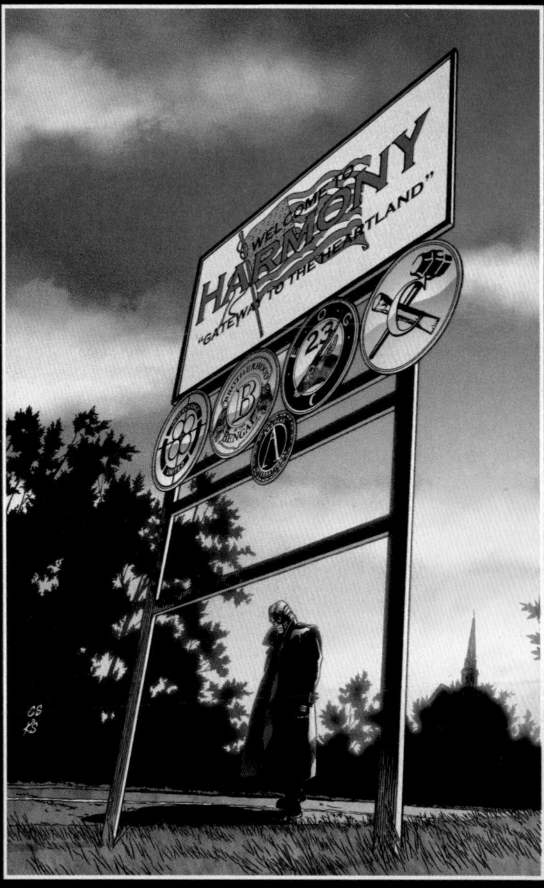
WELCOME TO
HARMONY
"GATEWAY TO THE HEARTLAND"
23

COVER 15

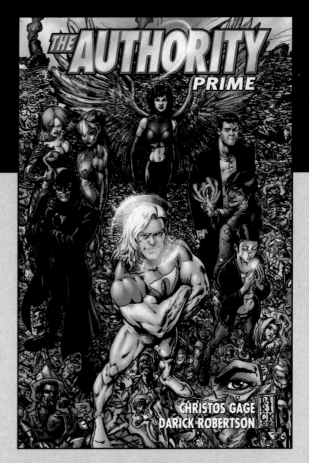